Praise

for *Successful Business Planning in 30 Days*

"The Ultimate Desk Reference: Whether you're looking for investment dollars or creating a three-year plan, this book is a must! Patsula has taken the daunting task of planning a business and turned it into a simple, yet effective formula that works! Besides all the facts this book provides, it did one more thing for me that no other book has—it helped me gage my entrepreneurial skills and guided me towards a more solid approach to running my business. If you're developing a business plan, or just interested in finding out what it takes to be successful in an increasingly challenging market, I encourage you to pick up this book."
— Daniel De Freitas, Vice President of Operations, RDI Consulting, Ltd., May 2004.

"Work of Art: I enjoy reading books based upon business like themes, and I must say that this is one that has completely stood out from the rest that I have read. I recently started my own business after 20 years of experience, and I must say that this book covers not only all the basic methods to start a business, but also to make it shine amongst the rest. It is practical and brilliant at the same time, and very easy to follow for anyone who has the motivation to start their own business. Pave your way to success and climb to the top, using this book as an essential tool."
— Michael K. Johnson, Amazon Review, Dec 2003

"Highly Recommended: Now in a newly updated and expanded second edition by Peter J. Patsula is concise, 'reader friendly,' and contains all the information needed to create a comprehensive business plan for any type of entrepreneurial activity with a 30 day time frame. There is even a section showing how to create a mini-business 'one day' plan in a single afternoon. *Successful Business Planning in 30 Days* offers more than 200 educational and motivational quotations and 33 specific tips for making a profit. Enhanced with time-saving worksheets and checklists, and a sample business plan prototype, *Successful Business Planning in 30 Days* is highly recommended to anyone charged with developing a company mission statement, marketing strategy, or financial breakdown."
— James A. Cox, Editor, *Wisconsin Bookwatch*, Feb 2003

"Jam-packed with information: Brimful with data and stacks of worksheets, this is a good buy for anyone in need of a business security blanket. For those who want the full on approach, this is it!"
— Phil Woolrich, Head of Business, United World College South East Asia, Singapore, April, 2004

"Helpful Examples: I am currently writing our business plan and am using your book. I have several other books, but wasted my money on them. I find the examples helpful and the worksheets easy to use."
— Donna Whyte-English, English Building Systems, Sunderland, MA, May, 2004

"Essential Guide for Business Planning: If you are one of the millions, who has contemplated starting your own business or just curious: Do I really have a valid business idea and will this idea fly? You at least owe it to yourself to find out. By reading and following the outlines provided in this guide, you will finally be able to answer that question and many more. This is a must read for anyone before starting your own business. *Successful Business Planning in 30 Days: A Step-by-Step Guide for Writing a Business Plan and Starting Your Own Business*—the title says it all. Now, ask yourself. Can I really afford not to read this Guide? Worst case scenario, you'll have gained knowledge of what it takes to be successful in business and redirect your efforts."
— Mike Milliken, Barnes & Noble Review, Oct 2001

"Business for Beginners: Some years ago my husband and I started a small consumer electronics export business in San Jose, California, "Silicon Valley". If this book had existed at the time, it would have saved us weeks, maybe even months, of time that we spent gathering basic information from a variety of sources. This book has all the basics, all in one place, with real-life examples and suggestions in a usable and practical workbook format. This may not be the only book you need to get started in business, but it certainly should be the first book you get."
— Farzana Hyland, San Jose, Amazon Review, Sept 2000

Successful
BUSINESS PLANNING
in
30 DAYS™

A STEP-BY-STEP GUIDE FOR WRITING A BUSINESS PLAN AND STARTING YOUR OWN BUSINESS

Third Edition

Peter J. Patsula

PATSULA ● MEDIA

Successful Business Planning in 30 Days™
A Step-by-Step Guide for Writing a Business Plan and Starting Your Own Business

Printed and bound in Singapore by: C.O.S. Printers Pte. Ltd., 9 Kian Teck Crescent, Jurong, Singapore, 628875

First published in 2000, Second Edition 2002, Third Edition 2004, Reprint 2006.

Publisher's – Cataloging In Publication

Patsula, Peter Joseph, 1962–
      Successful business planning in 30 days : a step-by-step guide for writing a business plan and starting your own business / Peter J. Patsula.—3rd ed.
      p. cm.
      Includes index.
      LCCN: 2004094964
      ISBN-13: 978-0-9678-4023-9; ISBN-10: 0-9678-4023-6 (paperback)
      1. Business planning–Handbooks, manuals, etc. 2. Business–Handbooks, manuals, etc. 3. New business enterprises–Planning. I. Title.
  HD30.28.P38   658.4'012   2004

Ordering Information (North America)

Patsula Media offers quantity discounts for colleges, universities, and business schools. Please contact books@patsula.com or visit: **www.bp30.com**

Published by: Patsula Media

Email: books@patsula.com
URL: www.patsulamedia.com

Asia Orders

For orders within Asia, please contact:

Pearson Education South Asia
23/25 First Lok Yang Road
Singapore 629733
Tel: (65) 63199388
Fax: (65) 63199170
Email: higher.education@pearsoned.com.sg
URL: www.pearsoned-asia.com

Published by: Pearson Education South Asia, publishing as Prentice Hall

Contents

■■■

Action Plan

The 30 Day Business Plan™

DAY 11

Outline planned purchases. Computerize operations. Set up business communications. Develop an Internet plan.

DAY 12

Choose an inventory and order entry system. Determine your reorder point.

DAY 13

Make an operations schedule. Outline your quality control plan. Research licenses required and legal considerations. Register your business.

DAY 14

Determine your organizational, management, and personnel needs. Find and select professional advisors.

DAY 15

Research market and industry trends. Detail *needs* you plan to meet.

DAY 16

Describe and analyze your target market. Project market share. Outline how you plan to build repeat business.

DAY 17

Research competitors. Compare strengths and weaknesses. Write your competitive advantage.

DAY 18

Design a business card. Write a slogan.

DAY 19

Outline your customer service and credit extension plan. Write a customer service maxim.

DAY 20

Determine how you will distribute your products or services. Determine how you will test the market.

DAY 21

Set a pricing structure.

DAY 22

Develop a promotion plan. Create a promotion budget. Write a news release.

DAY 23

Develop a packaging concept. Write your warranty. Summarize your marketing approach.

DAY 24

Calculate startup costs. Summarize sources of capital, loans required, and uses of funds.

DAY 25

Prepare a 12-month and three-year income projection. Prepare a cash flow statement. State assumptions made.

DAY 26

Prepare a breakeven analysis and a pro forma balance sheet.

DAY 27

Prepare a current income statement, balance sheet, and asset sheet. Calculate financial ratios.

DAY 28

Describe how you will maximize profits and cut costs. Outline your exit, investment, retirement, and tax plans.

DAY 29

Anticipate the reactions of your competitors. Develop an insurance and risk management plan.

DAY 30

List documents needed to support research.

Cartoons

at a Glance

TEGuS Cartoons by Peter J. Patsula

"After a careful analysis of all the possibilities, I've come up with the perfect business for us!"

page 1

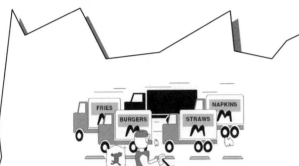

page 9

"So what kind of business are you planning to start?"

page 51

"Something tells me we've finally pinpointed our TARGET MARKET!"

page 161

"You worry too much Harry. Signing bank documents in your own blood is not the least bit unusual."

page 251

"I'm afraid you have the wrong number . . . But wait just a moment! Would you mind if I asked you a few survey questions?"

page 333

World Wide Web:
www.smallbusinesscartoons.com

page 343

91 Guidebooks from *The Entrepreneur's Guidebook Series*™

PERSONAL PLAN

1) Discovering if *YOU* Have Entrepreneurial Talent
2) Developing *MOTIVATIONAL* Skills
3) Developing *TIME MANAGEMENT* Skills
4) *STUDYING* the Lives of Successful People
5) Fine-tuning Leadership and *MANAGERIAL* Skills
6) Sharpening *SELLING* and Negotiating Skills
7) Creating a *RESOURCE* Reading Library
8) Designing a Customized Business *PLANNER*
9) Supercharging Promising Projects with a Plan of *ACTION*
10) Setting-up a Home *OFFICE*
11) Writing a *BUSINESS* Plan

COMPANY PLAN

12) Learning Why Companies *SUCCEED* and Why They Fail
13) Exploring *TOP* Businesses of the Future
14) Selecting *PROFITABLE* Small Business Products and Services
15) Researching *HOT NEW IDEAS* for Products and Services
16) *EVALUATING* Business Opportunities
17) Finding the Best Business *LOCATION*
18) Choosing the Right *LEGAL FORMATION*
19) *NAMING* Your Company and Products
20) Designing *LOGOS*, Business Cards, and Business Stationery
21) Writing a Company *SLOGAN* and *MISSION* Statement
22) Opening *COMMUNICATION* Channels
23) Selecting Computer *SOFTWARE*
24) Buying Computer *HARDWARE*
25) Getting *CONNECTED*
26) Getting *PRINTED*
27) Avoiding the *COMPUTER BLUES*
28) Adopting an Easy-to-Use *ACCOUNTING* System
29) Managing *INVENTORY*
30) Setting-up an Efficient *ORDER ENTRY* System
31) Getting *INSURANCE*
32) Protecting Your Intellectual Property with *COPYRIGHTS*, *PATENTS*, and *TRADEMARKS*
33) Understanding Business *LAWS*, Regulations, and Ethical Codes
34) *LICENSING* Your Operations
35) Opening a Business Bank *ACCOUNT*
36) Finding and Hiring Qualified *PERSONNEL*
37) Using *TEMP* Services and Contract Labor
38) Weighing the Pros and Cons of *EXPANSION*
39) Establishing a Long-term *STRATEGIC* Plan
40) Starting and Operating a *MANUFACTURING* Business
41) Starting and Operating a *WHOLESALE* Business
42) Starting and Operating a *RETAIL* Business
43) Starting and Operating a *SERVICE* Business
44) Starting and Operating a *MAIL ORDER* Business
45) Starting and Operating an *IMPORT/EXPORT* Business

MARKETING PLAN

46) Understanding *WHY* People Buy
47) Spying on the *COMPETITION*
48) Pinpointing Target *MARKETS* with Unmet Needs
49) Uncovering New Consumer *TRENDS* and Demands
50) Building a *LIST* of Potential Customers
51) Developing a Customer *SERVICE* Plan
52) Establishing a *PRICING* Policy
53) Establishing a *CREDIT* Policy
54) Creating a Winning *PROMOTIONAL* Plan
55) Choosing an Advertising Design *THEME*
56) Selecting Advertising *MEDIA*
57) *WRITING* and Editing Like a Pro
58) Creating "Eye Catching" *GRAPHICS*
59) Using *WORDS* That Sell
60) Mastering *AD DESIGN* and Layout Techniques
61) *COLLECTING* Product Info to Help Write and Design Ads
62) Using *ODAC* - The "Advertiser's Soul-mate"
63) Creating *CLASSIFIED* Ads, Space Ads, Brochures and Catalogs
64) Creating *NEWSLETTER*, and Direct Mail Promotions
65) Creating Award-Winning *RADIO*, and *TV* Ads
66) Getting Free *PUBLICITY*
67) Designing *PACKAGING*
68) Preparing Advertising *RECORDS*
69) *TESTING* Promotions and Analyzing Results
70) Conducting *SURVEYS* to Improve Your Marketing Efforts
71) Opening *DISTRIBUTION* Channels
72) Fostering *REPEAT* Business
73) Creating *NEW MARKET OPPORTUNITIES*
74) *INNOVATING* Your Promotional Plan
75) *LICENSING* Successful Products and Services
76) *FRANCHISING* Your Operations
77) *NETWORKING* Your Markets

FINANCIAL PLAN

78) Estimating *START-UP COSTS*
79) Evaluating Renting, *LEASING*, Buying, and Financing Options
80) Preparing a Breakeven Analysis, *CASH FLOW* Statement, and Income Projection
81) *CAPITALIZING* Your Operations
82) *REDUCING* Business and Living Operating Expenses
83) Starting a *RETIREMENT* Plan
84) Building an *INVESTMENT* Portfolio
85) Investing in *REAL ESTATE*
86) Reducing Your *TAXES*
87) *SELLING* Your Company

SUPPORT PLAN

88) Getting *HELP* from the Government and Other Entrepreneurial Organizations
89) Finding a Good *ACCOUNTANT*, Banker, Insurance Agent, and Lawyer
90) *ARMING* yourself with "Kamikaze Survival Techniques"
91) Consolidating Your Future with Thirty *GOLDEN* Rules

Online Guidebooks Available at:
www.BusinessPlanGuides.com

Preface

■■■■■■■■■■■■■■■■■■■■■■■■■■■■■■■■■■ ■

to the Third Edition

The most expedient way to write a business plan is to find one as close as possible to the type of business you want to start and then copy it. But this is certainly not the best way. And it most certainly is not successful business planning, because business planning is more than just a task that needs to be completed. It is a journey to discover your strengths and weaknesses as a marketer, financial planner, and business leader. It is also a search for success and innovation factors that will make your business unique and enduring. Peter Drucker, author of 31 business books and proclaimed by *BusinessWeek* to be "the most enduring management thinker of our time" has emphatically stated: "Business has only two functions—marketing and innovation." Besides being a planning tool, a business plan is a determined bid for distinction, a passionate search for excellence, and a relentless quest for quality in all aspects of production, service, and operations.

In my research, I have also discovered that successful entrepreneurs tend to share three common qualities: (1) they are able to recognize good business opportunities and take action; (2) they know how to *sell* product and service ideas to others; and (3) they aren't afraid of the numbers. All in all, they have become experts at company, market, and financial planning: the pillars of entrepreneurship. *Successful Business Planning in 30 Days*™ is firmly rooted on clarifying these three pillars to help readers succeed.

For this third edition, I have also tried to make the planning worksheets even more usable than previous editions. World-renowned theorists on human decision-making, Tversky and Kahneman, have shown that "the ease with which instances or associations [can] be brought to mind" strongly influences our actions and thinking processes. In other words, information and examples that are made easily available can help you complete your goals faster and with greater precision. Therefore, as much as possible, I've tried to make information, examples, and ideas for inspiration easily available in the worksheets to allow readers to focus their efforts on innovation, rather than articulation. Furthermore, with the 21st century strongly entrenched in the vision of a global community, I've also endeavored to make this third edition more international in scope. There is still a focus on the U.S. (the world's leading economy) and my home country of Canada, but I've also featured international success stories, as well as European Union and Asia Pacific research resources.

To sum up, it is difficult for me to imagine that the original conception of this guide was a much humbler version. It took 14 years of determined effort, exhaustive research, and countless revisions before the original conception grew and blossomed into what you have now and 91 online guides from *The Entrepreneur's Guidebook Series*™. Now in its third edition, *Successful Business Planning in 30 Days*™ has been further revised to refine what I hope to be one of the most usable, educational, and inspirational business planning guides ever published—the guide I truly wanted to have when I first became interested in starting my own business.

Use this guide to plan your business and write a business plan. Use my FREE online guidebooks if you need more helpful tips and information (go to Businessplanguides.com for a complete list of all 91 guidebooks, GB📖). In addition, visit Smallbusinesstown.com—home of the smbtn.com network of small business sites—for access to hundreds of helpful business resources and links. Also visit Bplan-templates.com for links to some sample business plans and Bp30.com for the latest teaching and self-help resources.

With that said, I wish you the best in your entrepreneurial journey, and sincerely hope that *Successful Business Planning in 30 Days*™ takes you where you want to go.

Peter J. Patsula has been a successful educator for over 16 years in Asia, Africa, and North America. Creator of The Entrepreneur's Guidebook Series™ *and Smallbusinesstown.com, he is currently residing and lecturing in Singapore. If you have any feedback, suggestions, or business plan success stories, please send email to: books@patsula.com.*

— Peter J. Patsula

INTRODUCTION

TEGuS Cartoons   *Peter J. Patsula*

"After a careful analysis of all the possibilities, I've come up with the perfect business for us!"

> It's not the plan that is important, it's the planning.
>
> ∞ **Dr. Graeme Edwards**

In this section . . .

- 📄 What is a Business Plan?
- 📄 Why Write a Business Plan?
- 📄 Essential Elements of a Business Plan
- 📄 The 30 Day Business Plan™
- 📄 How to Use this Guide
- 📄 Passion: The Final Ingredient

Introduction

STARTING and running a successful business in today's rapidly changing world is a considerable challenge. If adequate planning and control measures are not established early, a new business can quickly find itself raging out of control. To prevent this, it is necessary to put together a well-thought-out business plan—your blueprint for survival.

Writing a business plan is THE fundamental starting point for ALL entrepreneurial efforts. Time and time again, it has proven itself the single most controllable factor relevant to the success of any business.

What is a Business Plan?

A *Business Plan* is primarily an organizing tool used to simplify and clarify business goals and strategies, which might otherwise appear complex and intimidating. A business plan is also a sales tool. If it cannot convince at least one other person of the value of your idea, then either your idea is not worth pursuing, or your plan needs rethinking. In addition to being clear and straightforward, a business plan is persuasive.

A business plan is also factual, concise, well written, and arranged in a logical sequence. It contains all the pertinent information regarding your business and uses simple uncomplicated language that will not tax your readers. It does not contain unsupported statements, nor information that is ambiguous or poorly explained. The mood of a business plan is calm and clear, with just the right amount of excitement. It is inspirational and positive, but never full of empty promises.

Why Write a Business Plan?

A business plan consolidates your research, acts as a guide during the lifetime of your business, and makes sure you take an objective unemotional look at your business. It also provides potential investors and lenders with detailed information about your company's past, current, and future operations. Furthermore, a good business plan:

- gives you a list of goals and steps to follow.
- helps uncover obstacles you might have otherwise overlooked.

The beginning is the most important part of the work.
PLATO

∗

The harder you work, the luckier you get.
GARY PLAYER
Pro Golfer

A good business plan transforms you into a respected professional.

*To **START** a business, you need an idea! To **STAY** in business, you need a **PLAN**!*

∗

Just as one would not think of sending a man to the moon without a flight plan, one should not think of launching a new business without a business plan.

∗

Planning without action is futile; action without planning is fatal.
ANON

- improves your management capabilities by giving you practice in anticipating situations both good and bad for your business.

- trains you to analyze, organize, and make better decisions.

- transforms you into a respected professional.

You can also use your plan to communicate more effectively with lawyers, suppliers, advertisers, accountants, auditors, business consultants, and any other professionals or laypersons who need to understand the exact nature of your business.

Essential Elements of a Business Plan

THERE are five essential elements every business plan should have:

    I.   Business Overview (Introductory Section)

    II.   Company Plan

    III.   Marketing Plan

    IV.   Financial Plan

    V.   Supporting Documents (Appendix)

These five essential elements are guided by the following rule:

> **WHAT you put in your business plan, HOW you organize it, and WHAT you focus on, depends on WHY you need it, WHO it is for, and which areas of planning will most help you SUCCEED!**

This guide is based on a business plan format used by the U.S. Small Business Administration (SBA). It has been greatly refined and improved by researching the works of hundreds of experts and adding their insights and recommendations. Simple in structure, yet comprehensive in detail, this guide is also packed full of information and strategies to help you make better decisions once your business is under way. It is inspired under the belief that potential entrepreneurs must first **saturate** their brain with business facts and concepts before taking the entrepreneurial plunge. Its goal is to immerse you in the language of business and train you to think and act like an entrepreneur.

The 30 Day Business Plan™

Each planning day in this guide covers one or more *Key Areas* of a business plan. A daily "to do list" along with appropriate worksheets is also provided to keep you on task. Although some days are more demanding than others, if you work on your plan full-time, you should be able to complete it within a month. However, if you find the workload too much, it is better to pace yourself rather than do a rush job. It is also a good idea to set aside some time beforehand to reflect upon your personal strengths and weaknesses, as well as conduct preliminary research. Do some soul-searching. Assess possible product and service solutions. Conduct an informal market survey. And most importantly, start paying close attention to what people *really* want and need, and *why* they buy. Consider starting a daily or weekly journal for business-related observations.

The first thing to do is to start and the second is to continue.
CHINESE PROVERB

After completing the worksheets, use the information and data collected to prepare a formal business plan. Follow the writing strategies on pages 345 to 348 to make sure your final version is well designed—with the right content for your target reader. Review *The 30 Day Business Plan™ Checklist* on the back inside cover to make sure you have not left anything out and to assess the quality and completeness of your information. Evaluate your ideas from the standpoint of a prospective investor, lending agency, or management team, and ask yourself how satisfactory your responses are. Finally, find an expert or colleague who is willing to review your plan and offer constructive criticism. Your business plan is not finished until at least one other knowledgeable person carefully examines it.

The One Day Business Plan™ – At the end of Day 1 are 12 worksheets to help you capture the essence of your business (see pages 18 to 29). These worksheets have been designed to be used for one-day seminars on business planning. In less than a day, you can create a one-page mini-business plan to present your vision and ideas concisely to partners, bankers, employees, management, or even a board of directors. This one-page business overview also makes a perfect summary document for your formal business plan, and can be inserted right after your cover page and *Executive Summary*.

Business Planning in 16 Weeks – The outline on the following page has been provided as an alternative approach to planning your business. There is no reason not to follow our 30-day step-by-step approach, but it is worth keeping in mind that business planning, like entrepreneurship, is flexible, and can be adapted to suit your needs.

Research Goals:

- ❑ assess your strengths and weaknesses
- ❑ conduct an informal market survey
- ❑ find a competitive edge
- ❑ get some idea feedback
- ❑ observe "how" and "what" people buy
- ❑ reflect on potential obstacles
- ❑ search for an unmet need
- ❑ talk to successful business owners
- ❑ visit businesses similar to the type you might start
- ❑ wander around business areas and observe

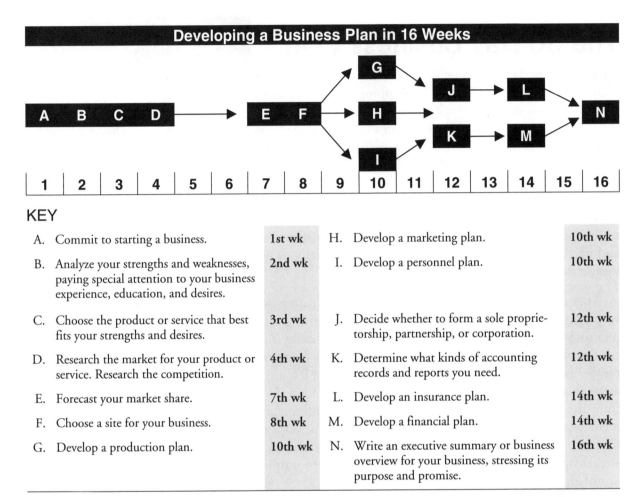

KEY

A. Commit to starting a business.	1st wk	
B. Analyze your strengths and weaknesses, paying special attention to your business experience, education, and desires.	2nd wk	
C. Choose the product or service that best fits your strengths and desires.	3rd wk	
D. Research the market for your product or service. Research the competition.	4th wk	
E. Forecast your market share.	7th wk	
F. Choose a site for your business.	8th wk	
G. Develop a production plan.	10th wk	

H. Develop a marketing plan.	10th wk	
I. Develop a personnel plan.	10th wk	
J. Decide whether to form a sole proprietorship, partnership, or corporation.	12th wk	
K. Determine what kinds of accounting records and reports you need.	12th wk	
L. Develop an insurance plan.	14th wk	
M. Develop a financial plan.	14th wk	
N. Write an executive summary or business overview for your business, stressing its purpose and promise.	16th wk	

The above outline is modeled after an approach suggested by Nicholas C. Siropolis in his text, *Small Business Management: A Guide to Entrepreneurship*, 2nd ed. (Boston: Houghton Mifflin Co., 1982, pp. 138–141).

How to Use this Guide

Successful Business Planning in 30 Days provides a comprehensive outline of section titles and headings that can be used to help organize and write a business plan. It examines all the key areas bankers and investors are most interested in, as well as other areas that are important to proper planning. This outline is also flexible. Change it, expand it, or rearrange it as you see fit, as long as your new outline is logical and better meets your needs and goals. Keep in mind that you do not have to research and explain every *Key Area* outlined in this guide. Use common sense. This business plan guide is meant to help you, not frustrate you.

There is no advancement to him who stands trembling because he cannot see the end from the beginning.

E. J. KLEMME

Start by reading cover to cover. Use a marker to highlight *Key Areas* and ideas applicable to your business and those that need more research. To save time, circle information and descriptive statements to be added to the final typed-out version of your proposal—do not waste time writing down what has already been written for you. Next, study trends, scout locations, visit your library for reference material, and review some of our free 91 online guidebooks (e.g., GB📖 #2 "Developing Motivational Skills"), available at:

Businessplanguides.com

After closely reading this planning guide, spend at least four weeks reflecting on your business goals, obstacles you might encounter, and the nature of your potential customers—their needs and wants. As soon as you know the type of business you want to launch, start with the DAY 1 Worksheets: *Name your company. Write a mission. Develop a One Day Business Plan.* As you write, use keywords, stick to the facts, and scrawl into the margins if necessary (you don't have to write between the lines). Next, commit to completing your plan on schedule. Take your guide wherever you go. Don't leave home without it!

NOTE The worksheets provided in this guide are intended to help create a rough draft of your business plan. Once completed, use your data and responses to prepare a formal, *typewritten* business plan (see page 345 for more "Business Plan Writing Strategies" and pages 351 to 366 for our "Sample Business Plan").

A Few Planning Tools – The "Daily Planner" on page 368 can be used to help you organize your time. Photocopy at about 115% for 8.5 × 11 or A4 paper size. The "Idea Sheet" shown on the right and on page 367 can be used to supplement entries into this guide. You might also consider making a dozen or so copies to fold up and carry with you in your wallet or pocket, so you can jot down ideas whenever inspiration strikes.

Bplan30.com provides extra resources, links, polls, and articles for each of the 30 business planning days. Bforms.com provides extra planning forms and key forms used in this guide.

A "good business plan" is "good business."

A lost "idea" is a lost "treasure."

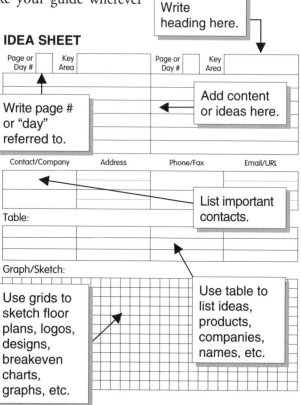

Passion is the single most powerful competitive advantage an organization can claim in building its success.

RICHARD CHANG
The Passion Plan at Work

✱

Passion does not trickle down but rather surges forth from leaders.

RICHARD CHANG
The Passion Plan at Work

✱

Your true passion should be like breathing, it's that natural.

OPRAH WINFREY

Your PASSION is part of your life's purpose.

HAPPINESS in life starts when you pursue it.

EVERYONE has a passion.

ALL passions have value.

ANY passion can be turned into profit.

WALT GOODRIDGE
Turn Your Passion into Profit

NOTE Don't be afraid to adapt this guide to suit your needs. Although this guide has been designed to be self-contained, you may wish to use a notebook to supplement entries, or perhaps additional planning forms from other sources. It is strongly encouraged that you make OUR *Business Planning Guide* … YOUR *Business Planning Guide*.

Passion: The Final Ingredient

There is a very important ingredient necessary for starting a business that is often overlooked. All the planning in the world may fail if "passion" is missing. You must be excited about at least one central aspect of your business. Be passionate about marketing a new feature for an old product, offering the best sushi in town, helping customers lose weight, or building dream homes for retired executives. Without passion, you are more likely to succumb to the pressures and obstacles of building a business. Passion not only inspires innovation, determination, and boundless energy, but it is also contagious. Sharing your passion also helps others tap into their own. Walt Goodridge, author of *Turn Your Passion into Profit*, sums it up well:

> **Value No Competitor Can Match:** "If you create and market a product or service through a business that is in alignment with your personality, capitalizes on your history, incorporates your experiences, harnesses your talents, optimizes your strengths, complements your weaknesses, honors your life's purpose, and moves you towards the conquest of your own fears, there is ABSOLUTELY NO WAY that anyone in this or any other universe can offer the same value that you do!"

If you don't already have passion, find it by listening to your innate sense of who you are and what you've always wanted to be or do. Next, attach a purpose to these desires and dreams. To give this purpose a framework, outline clear expectations further objectified by defined actions and profit goals. And if all this sounds like a bunch of passion-guru self-help mumbo jumbo, just find a business you think you will like doing with workers and customers you like being around.

Of course, bear in mind that passion without planning (i.e., direction) is a sure-fire way to get nowhere quick. Undirected passion will not grow a business. You must also be realistic in what passion can do for you. It won't help you pay your taxes.

Part I

BUSINESS OVERVIEW

TEGuS Cartoons   *Peter J. Patsula*

> When it is obvious that the goals cannot be reached, don't adjust the goals, adjust the action steps.
>
> ❧ **Confucius**

In this section . . .

- 🗎 Cover Sheet
- 🗎 Table of Contents
- 🗎 Executive Summary
- 🗎 Fact Sheet

DAY 1

Name your company. Write a mission. Develop a One Day Business Plan™.

BUSINESS OVERVIEW

YOUR *Business Overview* tells people:

☑ who you are ☑ what you are ☑ what you want

Use this section to grab attention, impress upon others that you have what it takes to be successful, and skillfully cater to the whims of potential investors by implying or stating what's in it for them.

NOTE Business plans are often used as sales tools to sell ideas. But be careful your business plan doesn't read like a company brochure. Don't use fancy words, technical jargon, or advertising puffery to sell your proposal. Let your ideas and research do the persuading. Make your reader see the value of your plan without overarticulating unimportant details or exaggerating sales and profits.

To Do List

I. **Business Overview**
   Cover Sheet
   ✓ Company Name
   ✓ Company Mission Statement
   ✓ The One Day Business Plan™

A business plan forces you to think through every aspect of your business and helps you recognize opportunities for growth and profit.

Cover Sheet

A cover sheet should encourage readership and attract the attention of the desired reader. It should also be kept simple, yet informative. Descriptive elements can be added as long as the end result looks professional and is easy to read (see sample on the right and worksheet on page 38).

Company Name

On your *Cover Sheet*, state the name of your company and have the words "Business Plan" written on it. Include your company's address, telephone number, fax number (with area codes), email address, URL address, and the names, addresses, and numbers of the people who can be contacted if further questions need to be answered.

Holistic Pet Supplies Ltd.
Unit 401 Paramount Building
12 Ka Yip Street Chaiwan, Hong Kong
(Phone/Fax) 852-2555-1HPS

BUSINESS PLAN

HOLISTIC
PET SUPPLIES

Harold W. Lee, *President*
Sally Schmidt, *Vice President*
(EMAIL) hps@holistic-petsupplies.com
(URL) www.holistic-petsupplies.com

Plan prepared January 2004
by Harold Lee and Sally Schmidt ©

copy 1 of 3

In the U.S., many states prohibit using the words "Corporation," "Incorporated," "Inc.," "Company," or "Co." unless your business is indeed such an entity.

A great company name is . . .
easy to remember, easy to pronounce, easy to spell, easy to reproduce on stationery, informative, targeted, unregistered, unique, associated with favorable images, bigger than life, and short (especially if you plan to run classified ads).

A great company name suggests . . .
quality, inspires confidence, sounds good, looks good, rolls off the tongue like fine wine, and builds company character.

Naming Your Company

Find a pen, a blank sheet of paper, and a quiet place to reflect. Jot down as many names as you can—the more the better. From these, select ten or more for closer analysis, criticism, and evaluation from friends, colleagues, and if possible, prospective customers. Try to author a name that is exclusive yet inclusive, compact yet complete, simple yet informative, and can be picked up as a dot.com—e.g., mycompanyname.com. Search all final choices using a search engine like Google.com and a domain registration service such as Buydomains.com. You should also conduct a trademark search, just to be safe (see page 90 for "Trademark Protection").

To help generate ideas, use the following strategies:

Associate your company with . . .

A favorite street, town, city, state, country, or other geographical reference. E.g.: *Bourbon Street* Bakery, *Paris* Furs, *Swiss* International Air, *Asian* Custom Engravers, *Pacific* Interiors, *Far East* Importers, *Amazon*.

Animals. E.g.: *Raven* Truck Box Liners & Woodcrafts, *Lion* Business Machines, *Shepherd* Security Systems, *Cardinal* Building Maintenance, *Shark* Club, *Hawk* Rent a Car, *Baby Bear* Children's Clinic, *Puma*.

Established companies. E.g.: *Xerox* Service Centre, *Oxford* Graphics, *Ford* Auto Repair, *Christian Dior* Singapore. Use the reputation of a larger company or institution to add credibility to yours (seek permission first).

Mythical figures. E.g.: *Unicorn* Driving School, *Atlas* Muffler & Brake, *Midas* Mufflers, *Libra* Connection, *Odyssey* Outerwear, *Neptune* Fashions, *Dragon* Construction, *Hanuman* Imports, *Sita's* Café.

Quality and high standards of production. E.g.: Muffler *Pro*, *Award* Building Maintenance, *Professional* Carpet Cleaning, Golf *Plus*, *Quality* Brake.

Royalty, upper class social structures. E.g.: *Lady* Ming, *Crown*tek, *King's* Crane Service, *Royal* Bank of Canada, *Master*clean, *Grand* Copthorne, *Princess* Flower Shop, *Fairlady* Jewelers, *Paramount* Astrology.

Well-known historical figures, precious metals, gems, natural phenomena, or famous objects. E.g.: *Lincoln* Insurance, *King Sejong* Hotel, *Sun Tzu* Gaming, *Golden* Flooring Accessories, *Raffles* Bus Services, *Sunrise* Doors.

Combine everyday words related to your business into one. E.g.: *Fabriozone* Cleaning Systems, *Weldangrind* Construction, *Heatilator* Fireplaces, *Safeway*, *U-Pak* Shipping, *Execucare* Services, *AsiaMedic* Supplies.

Combine the letters of owners. E.g.: *Alco* Roofing, owners are Allan and Collin; *Backice* Balloon Express, owners are Bobbi, Jacklyn, and Alicia; *Kilee's* Interior Decorating, owners are Monika Kim and Oksun Lee.

Create a fictional person. E.g.: *Ducky's* Office Supplies, *Jack the Stripper* Restoration Services, *Mr. Sweep* Chimney Cleaning, *Soulman* Productions, *PestBusters*, *Auntie Jina's* Furniture Clearance Center.

Create a fictional place. E.g.: Tuxedo Junction, Sherwood Forest, Puppy Island, Dragon City Restaurants, Jack's Place Steakhouse, Pet's Zone.

Imply or state a major benefit of your product or service. E.g.: *Sunshade* Aluminum Products, Balloon *Express*, *Fresh* Food Experience, Club *Fit*, *Breath Easy* Furnace Cleaning, *Vision* Window Cleaning, *Speedy* Instant Printers, *Budget* Bakers, *Comfort* Transportation, *20/20* Optical.

Inspire confidence and trust. E.g.: *Honest Abe's* Shoe Store, *Reliable* Electrical, *Dependable* Courier Service, *Trust*co Insurance.

Keep your name short. Short names are easier to remember than long names. They also lend themselves better to logo design. E.g.: Sony, Nike, Ford, Dell, Ikea, Avis, Fuji, AOL, Best, Intel, Adobe, Acer, NEC.

Look through directories, magazines, and the Yellow Pages. Locate listings of the types of businesses you are interested in. Write down which names inspire you. Ask yourself why they stand out and then use their format as a guide to develop your own names.

Make your name sound bigger than you really are. No one needs to know you're working out of your garage or basement. E.g.: *Millennium* Promotions, *Mega* Gas, *Century* Advertising, *Jumbo* Seafood Restaurants.

Make your name easy to remember. A company name is easy to remember if it is easy to pronounce, relate to, and spell, and has a nice ring to it, rolls easily off the tongue, and is short. E.g.: *Builders First*, *Wired* for *Sound*, *Furry Affairs*.

Personalize your name, then describe it. E.g.: *Salmon Arms* Fish & Tackle House, *Picasso* Graphics Inc., *Beaver* Lumber, *Newman* Plumbing, *Supang* Fashion House, *Indah Rasa* Catering.

Qualify the type of business you are in with a descriptive noun. E.g.: Jim Burge & *Associates*, The Wig *Boutique*, Home Building *Centre*, Billingsgate Fish *Company*, Bali *Construction* (see page 16 for more descriptors).

A good **product** *name associates well with the official company name, that is, both sound good together. For example, "Ford Taurus" is more memorable than "Ford Pisces" as "Taurus" has the same vowel sound as "Ford."*

A man without a smiling face must not open a shop.
CHINESE PROVERB

✳

Good symbols can be powerful, but they aren't always necessary. Microsoft, Ben & Jerry's and Google have created memorable, effective logos using just colors and typefaces. A well-designed wordmark, if it's presented consistently, can be just as effective at showing a company's personality as a symbol.
BOB KADRIE
President, Point of Vision Design Group

TYPES OF MISSION STATEMENTS

*A **COMPANY** mission
statement is useful
for communicating
to customers,
employees,
suppliers, and
investors what
you're all about. A
CONSUMER mission
statement places
more emphasis on
the benefits of your
product or service
to consumers. It
can provide the
backbone of a
strong marketing
plan and is usually
much shorter than a
company mission.
OTHER types of
mission statements
might target staff,
department, or
personal goals.*

Target your name to the people you want to sell to. E.g.: Weight Watchers, Bow Wow Dog Grooming, Lo-cost Furniture Warehouse.

Tell customers your business location. E.g.: *Campus* Eye Center, *River Valley* Equipment Sales, *Boyle Street* Clinic, *Bukit Timah* Refrigeration Service, *Orchard* Bar & Grill, *Singapura* Finance, *Roxas Boulevard* Hotel.

Use alliteration. E.g.: **D**rayden **D**evelopments, **I**carus **I**ndustries, **H**amilton **H**ouse, **S**unshine **S**ecretary **S**ervices, **B**ishan **B**aby & **C**hild **C**are.

Use attractive letters. A well-chosen company name represents itself well graphically. It is also easy to reproduce on signs and letterhead as a logo.

Use made-up words. Add original words to your company name. E.g.: *Atco* Red-Hat Valves, *Nutron* Manufacturing Ltd., *Fesco* India.

Use your own name. This can help avoid costly and time-consuming trademark searches. E.g.: *Al Bundy's* Shoes, *Angela's* Hairstyling, *Kumar* Insurance, *Kumho* Tires, *Petrov* Umbrellas Factory, *Rivera* Inc., *Satou* Food Manufacturing, *Tai Wah* Distributors (Pte) Ltd., *Virginia Lee* Florists.

Write a name with catchy initials. Three initials works best. E.g.: *IBM*, Integrated Business Machines; *JAL*, Japan Air Lines.

Company Mission Statement

A *Company Mission Statement* is an attempt to transform your goals and dreams into a single vision. It is aimed at getting all members of your organization pulling in the same direction and sharing the same view of your company goals, philosophy, and vision for the future. If given the consideration it deserves, it will reward you repeatedly by enhancing your identity and position in the marketplace. A company mission statement is not a few loosely jotted down ideas, a long list of tasks to be completed, or something that pops into your head while watching a soccer game. It is a simple, clear, introspective yet practical statement of purpose that focuses your entire business and helps you recognize *exactly* what business you are in.

Every organization needs a company mission statement and many require individual mission statements for key consumer markets and/or business units. Some experts go as far to say that all business decisions should be, in one manner or another, based on a mission statement. To more effectively position your company in the minds of your targeted readers, you might consider putting your company mission statement on your cover page.

How Long Should Your Company Mission Statement Be?

While a plan of action or customer service policy might be many pages, a company mission statement should be no more than 25 to 80 words and usually no more than one or two sentences. However, although short, keep in mind that a company mission statement is a highly crafted work of ART that will demand a considerable amount of time and energy to refine and transform into the masterpiece it needs to be. A consumer mission statement, which targets benefits to customers, should be shorter than 20 words.

Writing a Company Mission Statement in "Four Steps"

To write a company mission statement brainstorm for ideas on: *who* you are, *where* you want to go, *how* you plan to get there, and *why* you need to do it. More specifically, state what business you plan to go in, who you plan to sell to, and what it is you plan to sell. Summarize by linking these intentions to a compelling reason (see example on the right).

STEP 1 – State WHO you are. *What business do you plan to start?* Write: ❏ your company name ❏ industry area ❏ partnerships with other companies.

STEP 2 – State WHERE you want to go. *Who do you plan to sell to?* Clarify: ❏ markets you wish to target; your market niche ❏ clientele, individuals, or businesses you hope to serve ❏ where markets are located; geography ❏ long-term goals; where you want your company to be in five or ten years.

STEP 3 – State HOW you plan to get there. *What do you plan to sell?* Specify: ❏ products and services you will offer ❏ key benefits of your products and services; company keys to success ❏ what you are really selling; customer needs you will meet ❏ skills and talents you have to crush the competition.

STEP 4 – State WHY you need to do it. *Link your intentions to a compelling reason.* There is an old saying: "If the *why* is important enough, no *how* is too difficult." Consider the following: few of us would parachute off the Empire State Building only for money, but if it meant saving our loved ones, somehow we would find the courage. What turns a mediocre mission statement into one that makes you misty eyed every time you think of it is not a well-thought-out company policy, goal, or target market, but rather a *why* that makes it all worthwhile, a little piece of magic that comes to you in the middle of the night—a seed for great inspiration. Generalize: ❏ values or beliefs ❏ customer service maxims ❏ daily decision guidelines. Answer the question: ❏ "Why should your business exist?" (see pages 17, 20, and 21).

PURE PASSION MISSION STATEMENT

We at Pure Passion Pasta will prepare and provide the finest quality all natural pasta products, made without additives or preservatives, to individuals, restaurants, and organizations that choose to serve nutritious, delicious fresh pasta.

TO WRITE A MISSION STATEMENT STATE:

WHO YOU ARE

Pure Passion Pasta Shop

MARKETS YOU WILL SERVE

individuals, organizations, and restaurants looking for fresh, superior pasta products

PRODUCTS YOU WILL SELL

additive and preservative-free pasta products

REASON WHY

to serve more nutritious pasta

Successful BUSINESS PLANNING 30 DAYS

DAY 1 Worksheets ⏱

Name your company. Write a mission. Develop a One Day Business Plan™.

Company Name

Brainstorm – List important considerations and strategic objectives in naming your company:

STRATEGY: Add a "descriptive noun" (e.g., Tom's "Deli").			
Agency	Deli	Institute	Sales
Asia	Developments	International	Services
Associates	Diner	Limited	Shop
Boutique	Distributors	Lounge	Square
Café	Emporium	Ltd.	Store
Canada	Enterprises	Management	Supplies
Center	Equipment	Manufacturing	Systems
Company	Establishment	Market	Traders
Construction	Global	Marketing	United
Consulting	Group	Mart	Universal
Contracting	House	Place	Unlimited
Corp.	Importers	Products	USA
Corporation	Incorporated	Promotions	Wholesale
Creations	Industries	Restaurant	World

Brainstorm – Use some of the following strategies to create names (refer back to pages 12–14):

- ❏ Associate company with royalty.
- ❏ Combine everyday words.
- ❏ Combine letters of owners.
- ❏ Create a fictional place or person.
- ❏ Imply or state a major benefit.
- ❏ Inspire confidence.

- ❏ Keep name short.
- ❏ Look through directories.
- ❏ Make name sound credible.
- ❏ Make name easy to remember.
- ❏ Personalize, then describe.
- ❏ Target name with customers.

- ❏ Tell customers your location.
- ❏ Use alliteration.
- ❏ Use attractive letters.
- ❏ Use catchy initials.
- ❏ Use made-up words.
- ❏ Use your own name.

Write ten company names. Get objective feedback from friends and experts. Select the best one:

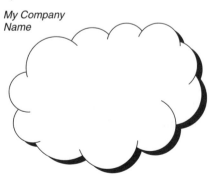

My Company Name

Company Mission Statement

✎ *Draft your company mission using keywords:*

Who are you?

_____
(*XYZ company ...*)

Where do you want to go?

_____
Industry goals you aspire to?
Markets of types of customers/clients you will serve?
(**will become** *the largest air-con manuf. in* [market area])

How do you plan to get there?

_____
What will you do? Products and services? Needs met?
Benefits offered? Competitive advantage?
(**by** *producing superior noiseless, fuel-efficient units*)

Why do you need to do it?

_____
Why should your company exist? Personal goals? Beliefs?
(**We are committed to** *building our business because* ...)

Rewrite in your own words (be creative, shorten, focus on consumers or company):

Sample Mission Statements

Company Directed	Consumer Directed
Asia Travel: "Asia Travel provides economical vacation travel and related services to customers in the Hong Kong area, who expect efficient, problem-free travel arrangements at a low cost."	*AVIS Rent-a-Car*: "Our business is renting cars. Our mission is total customer satisfaction."
IBM: "Our goal is simply stated. We want to be the best service organization in the world."	*LensCrafters*: "Helping people see better, one hour at a time."
McDonald's: "To offer the fast food customer food prepared in the same high-quality manner world-wide, tasty and reasonably priced, delivered in a consistent, low-key, and friendly atmosphere."	*Microsoft*: "To enable people and businesses throughout the world to realize their full potential."
	UPS: "We move at the speed of business."
	Wal-Mart: "To give ordinary folk the chance to buy the same thing as rich people."

The One Day Business Plan™ provided on pages 18 to 29 is a supplement to the worksheets provided in Day 1. Keep in mind that vision, mission, goals, strategies, objectives, plans, and brand promise are all types of goals. However, each provides a different focus for a different purpose. If you read the descriptions closely and consult the examples provided, the functions of each type of goal will become clearer. Corporations invest considerable resources brainstorming on goal-related issues. If goals come too easily, then they probably will not be very useful.

The One Day Business Plan™ Worksheets Successful **BUSINESS PLANNING** **30**DAYS

Vision, mission, goals, strategies, objectives, and action plans are interrelated "company navigators" carefully derived to direct and define your business.

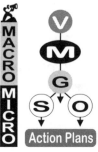

MACRO MICRO

Action Plans

Part I – Business Vision **How** do you visualize your company in the future?
Why is now the right time to start your company?

Business Vision: A vision statement paints an optimistic picture of your business. It is full of passion. It is neither dull nor analytical. Behind every vision also lies a *trend* or *want* in the marketplace that supports the *need* for that vision.

Brainstorm – *Answer the following questions using keywords and short phrases:*

clients employees	benefits company culture	facilities headquarters	exit strategy investment climate	market trends personal beliefs	startup funds strategic alliances
WHO	**WHAT**	**WHERE**	**WHEN**	**WHY**	**HOW**
Who do you WANT to sell to? DON'T want to sell to?	What do you WANT to sell? DON'T want to sell?	Where is the ideal place to locate your business?	When will your business become operational?	Why will customers buy your products or services?	How do you see your company five years from now?
Who do you hope to partner with?	What market need will you meet?	Where are your target markets?	When will you expand?	Why risk starting this business?	How do you wish to grow your business?
Who can help build your business?	Which companies do you wish to emulate?	Where lies the most opportunity?	When will you sell your business?	Why will you be successful?	How much capital can you raise?

Draft – Write keywords and phrases in the blanks below. Rewrite on page 29 using your own words: (see pages 28 and 354 for sample vision statements)

_____ **will grow into a** _____
        company name   adjective (*thriving, profitable, world class*)

❑ local ❑ regional ❑ national ❑ international _____
                                                                        type or description of business

within _____ **years. It will provide** _____
                                                                describe products and services

_____ **to** _____.
        (continued)   describe your customers or clients

_____ **will be successful because** _____
        company name   provide reasons ("*why now*", *trends, skills, talents*)

_____.
        (continued)

After _____ **years** _____ **will** _____
                                          company name   describe what will happen (*expansion, financing, stock offering*)

_____.
        (continued)

Sample Vision Statement

Usable Web Design Consulting will grow into a $1 million national consulting firm within five years. It will provide usable web design solutions to content providers, educational institutions, and corporations. UWDC will be successful because, with Internet traffic projected to double every six months, usability middleman are needed to bridge a widening gap between content and code specialists. After five years, UWDC will more aggressively market to North American Fortune 1000 companies and seek further expansion opportunities in Singapore, Europe, South Korea, and India.

Part II – Company Goals ⊛

How will you achieve your vision? **What** do you promise your customers? **What** is the central purpose or mission of your company?

Company Goals: A company goal features an important *activity* or *benefit* that supports your vision statement. Goals may be further qualified by *strategies*, *reasons*, or *time frames*. Benefit statements are usually directed towards meeting the needs of customers, but can also focus on meeting the needs of your company and other stakeholders such as employees and investors. A *mission statement* is your most important goal. It can focus on your company, your customer needs, or both. A *brand promise* is your next most important goal. It attempts to strategize "the nature of your *relationship* with customers, both tangible and intangible *needs* your brand intends to meet, and *feelings* you want your brand to evoke" (M. Pucci).

Brainstorm – Check four or more goal areas important to the success of your company:

Personal	Operations	Marketing	Financial	R&D	Other
❑ available startup $	❑ customer service	❑ advertising	❑ A/R collection	❑ design function	❑ charity donations
❑ beliefs	❑ labor efficiency	❑ company image	❑ accounting records	❑ idea protection	❑ community
❑ desired profit	❑ quality plans	❑ competition	❑ capital funding	❑ innovations	❑ contract work
❑ personal growth	❑ same day shipping	❑ employee sales	❑ cash flow	❑ laboratory tests	❑ down time
❑ responsibilities	❑ store hours	❑ ideal customer	❑ inventory levels	❑ marketing surveys	❑ golf luncheons
❑ retirement	❑ suppliers	❑ incentive programs	❑ loan terms	❑ new products	❑ government
❑ skill development	❑ turn around time	❑ new accounts	❑ overhead	❑ product testing	❑ joint ventures
❑ vacation time	❑ work team size	❑ publicity tactics	❑ sales	❑ prototypes	❑ manufacturing
❑ work week length	❑ worldwide offices	❑ website traffic	❑ tax liability	❑ usability	❑ public speaking
❑ _____	❑ _____	❑ _____	❑ _____	❑ _____	❑ _____

Skill Development: Read one business development or marketing strategy book per month.	**Turn Around Time**: Personalized 24-hour email response using ACT! Contact Management software.	**New Accounts**: Five "cold calls" a day using lists compiled by income level from Dun & Bradstreet.	**Overhead**: Reduce cost of goods by bulk purchasing and paying before terms are due.	**Prototypes**: Develop prototypes for three innovative bicycle parts for 6/12/03.	**Joint Ventures**: Partner with Oracle to develop AI software training programs for Nortel.

Draft – Write company goal statements using components A, AB, AC, or ABC. *Rewrite* on page 29:

(refer to pages 54 to 58 for more ideas on writing goals; see pages 28 and 354 for more sample goal statements)

A – activity or benefit	B – strategy, reason, how	C – time frame
Goal 1:		
Goal 2:		

A – activity or benefit	B – strategy, reason, how	C – time frame
Goal 3:		
Goal 4:		
Goal 5:		

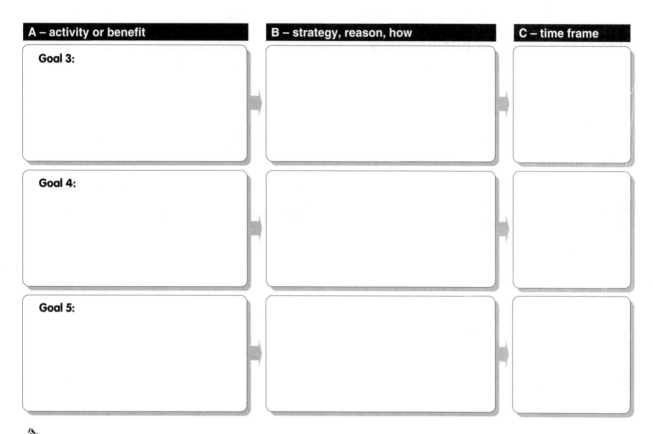 *Draft – Write keywords and phrases in the blanks below. Focus on benefits to **customers**:*
(see pages 28 and 354 for sample mission statements and pages 28 and 360 for sample brand promise statements)

At _____ **, our mission is to** _____

company name   verb (*provide, produce, become, supply*)

_____   _____

benefits (*high quality, luxury, the 1st choice, the fastest*)   product, service, industry (*china, sedans, printing service, delivery*)

for/in _____ .

market (*newlyweds, business women, Florida, Asian tourists, Australian Outback campers*)

Brand Promise: The _____ **brand** _____ .

company, trademark , brand name   verb (*promises to be, will be perceived as, will communicate, will evoke feelings of*)

_____ . ❑ affordable ❑ cutting edge ❑ efficient

benefits (*reliable, flexible, responsive* **or** *reliability, flexibility, responsiveness*)   ❑ fresh ❑ light ❑ rustproof ❑ safe

Part III – Marketing Strategies

How will you grow your business? **What** works in the industry?
How will you reach customers? **What** opportunities exist?

Marketing Strategies: A strategy centers on an important *issue, root cause,* or *symptom* of a *problem* qualified by a *method, way of doing things, innovative approach,* or *solution.* Marketing strategies set the direction, philosophy, values, standards, and methods for building sales and sustaining growth. They help define ways of "solving" or "approaching" marketing problems by summarizing lessons learned and insights gained. They answer questions like: "What key success factors to date have made your business successful?" "What's working and what isn't within your industry?" "What will make your business successful in the future?" More specifically, strategies address *internal* **S**trengths and **W**eaknesses, as well as *external* **O**pportunities and **T**hreats (a SWOT analysis). The main purpose for a marketing strategy is to gain a competitive advantage.

Brainstorm – Select marketing and SWOT issues that would make goal-relevant strategy statements:

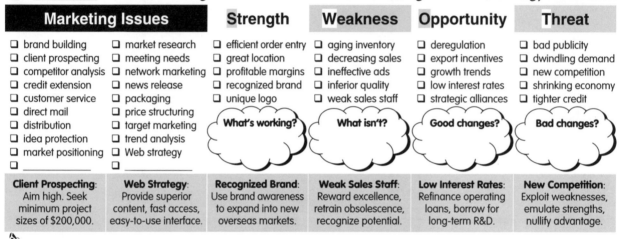

Marketing Issues		Strength	Weakness	Opportunity	Threat
❑ brand building ❑ client prospecting ❑ competitor analysis ❑ credit extension ❑ customer service ❑ direct mail ❑ distribution ❑ idea protection ❑ market positioning ❑ _____	❑ market research ❑ meeting needs ❑ network marketing ❑ news release ❑ packaging ❑ price structuring ❑ target marketing ❑ trend analysis ❑ Web strategy ❑ _____	❑ efficient order entry ❑ great location ❑ profitable margins ❑ recognized brand ❑ unique logo *What's working?*	❑ aging inventory ❑ decreasing sales ❑ ineffective ads ❑ inferior quality ❑ weak sales staff *What isn't?*	❑ deregulation ❑ export incentives ❑ growth trends ❑ low interest rates ❑ strategic alliances *Good changes?*	❑ bad publicity ❑ dwindling demand ❑ new competition ❑ shrinking economy ❑ tighter credit *Bad changes?*
Client Prospecting: Aim high. Seek minimum project sizes of $200,000.	**Web Strategy:** Provide superior content, fast access, easy-to-use interface.	**Recognized Brand:** Use brand awareness to expand into new overseas markets.	**Weak Sales Staff:** Reward excellence, retrain obsolescence, recognize potential.	**Low Interest Rates:** Refinance operating loans, borrow for long-term R&D.	**New Competition:** Exploit weaknesses, emulate strengths, nullify advantage.

Draft – Write marketing strategy statements using components B or AB. *Rewrite* on page 29:

(refer to page 57 for more ideas on writing strategy statements; see page 28 for sample strategy statements)

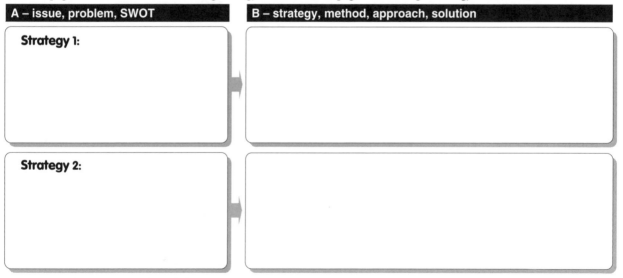

A – issue, problem, SWOT	B – strategy, method, approach, solution
Strategy 1:	
Strategy 2:	

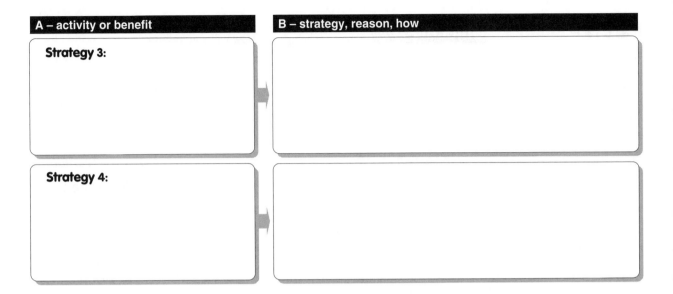

A – activity or benefit	B – strategy, reason, how
Strategy 3:	
Strategy 4:	

✍ *Draft* – *To complete strategy statements, write keywords and phrases in the blanks below:*

We will satisfy customers by _____ .
marketing approach   describe how you will meet customer needs (e.g., *providing speedy turn around time*)

We will build profits by _____ .
                      list strategies for building profits (e.g., *reducing costs* and *developing repeat business*)

We will overcome the threat of _____
SWOT analysis   describe threat (e.g., *new competition*)

by _____ .
                                          describe solution (e.g., *offering a better warranty*)

We will take advantage of _____
                                              describe opportunity (e.g., *deregulation*)

by _____ .
                                          describe solution (e.g., *updating price structures*)

Part IV – Financial Objectives 🧮

What must you accomplish after one year? *How* will you know
goals are being met? *How* will you measure your success?

Financial Objectives: Financial objectives clarify important company *goals*, *activities*, or *strategies* by quantifying them in
terms of *financial results*, *projections*, or *target values*, and *time frames*. They are needed to provide benchmarks to evaluate
progress, and are closely tied in with your vision, mission, goals, and strategy statements. Financial objectives answer questions
like: "What would you like to celebrate at the end of the year?" "How will you evaluate whether strategies are working and
goals are being met?" Goals and marketing strategies can be transformed into financial objectives by adding phrases such as
"generating a [XX]% increase in sales by fiscal year's end" **or** "resulting in a [XX]% decrease in costs by 6/04."

🧠 *Brainstorm* – Check four or more financial activity areas important to the success or your company:

Building Profits		Reducing Costs		Managing Finances	
❑ bulk discounts	❑ product returns	❑ advertising	❑ office supplies	❑ accounting system	❑ financial ratios
❑ cash investments	❑ profit sharing	❑ auto, travel	❑ overhead	❑ advertising budget	❑ income statement
❑ interest charges	❑ repeat business	❑ bad debts	❑ pension plan	❑ balance sheet	❑ operational budget
❑ IRA, RRSP plans	❑ sales growth	❑ employee benefits	❑ phone, utilities	❑ bank loan	❑ pricing policies
❑ Keogh, SEP plans	❑ size of market	❑ entertainment	❑ purchasing, equip.	❑ breakeven analysis	❑ startup costs
❑ mutual funds	❑ stock offering (IPO)	❑ insurance, legal	❑ renting, leasing	❑ cash flow	❑ stock purchases
❑ new accounts	❑ stocks and bonds	❑ interest charges	❑ repairs	❑ depreciation	❑ tax deductions
❑ new market	❑ trade credit	❑ inventory levels	❑ salaries , wages	❑ equity analysis	❑ tax incentives
❑ new products	❑ vertical expansion	❑ maintenance	❑ taxes , licenses	❑ finance accounting	❑ venture capital
❑ _____	❑ _____	❑ _____	❑ _____	❑ _____	❑ _____

New Products:	**Sales Growth**:	**Insurance**:	**Purchasing**:	**Cash Flow**:	**Pricing Policies**:
Introduce a CD by 9/22 and newsletter by 10/19, resulting in 2003 sales of $9,000.	Increase sales 20% to $5 million in 2003; $6 million in 2004, and $7.2 million in 2005.	Raise insurance deductible to $1,000 to reduce insurance premiums by 30%.	Finance purchase of delivery van instead of leasing to save $2,000 on interest charges.	Reduce leasing costs to obtain a positive cash flow of $2,000 per month by 3/8/03.	Achieve billable time of 65%. Restructure charges to recoup lost fees of $8,000.

✍️ *Draft* – Write financial objectives using components AB or ABC. <u>Rewrite</u> on page 29:
(refer to page 54 for more ideas on writing goal statements; see pages 28 and 354 for more sample objectives)

A – objective type (What will happen?)	B – financial result, target, projection	C – time frame
Objective 1:		
Objective 2:		

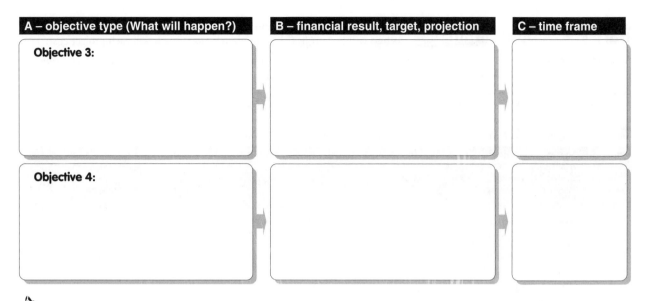

A – objective type (What will happen?)	B – financial result, target, projection	C – time frame
Objective 3:		
Objective 4:		

✍ *Draft* – *To complete financial objectives, write keywords and phrases in the blanks below:*

Sales revenues of $ _____ are projected for _____ , $ _____
                                                              date

for _____ and $ _____ for _____ .
      date   date

Profits of _____ are projected for _____ and _____ for _____
              % or $ date   % or $ date

from our _____ .
                      area (e.g. *retail outlets*)

We will gain a _____ share of the _____ market by _____ and _____ by _____ .
market share   %   type of market   date   %   date
                          (e.g., *home computer*)

Key PI's have the following targets: _____
performance Indicators
                                    List PI target values and date
                                    (e.g., *sales: $2 million by 12/06; Current Ratio 1.8; 12/06*)

_____ .

(continued)

Part V – Support Plans 📇

What specific actions are you taking to achieve your vision?
When will key projects be completed? **How** much will each project cost?

Support Plans: Support plans are specific *actions* or *projects* derived from your vision, mission, goals, strategies, and objectives, and quantified by *completion date*, *cost*, and *person(s) responsible*. Plans are *results-oriented*. They yield specific tangible results, such as products developed, convention attended, or cost reducing strategy implemented. Action plan statements answer the question, "What have you not been doing that you know will make a significant contribution to your business?"

🧠 *Brainstorm* – Carefully **select** six vision, goal, strategy, or objective statements from parts I–IV:

Which goals, etc., are easy to break down into projects?	Which projects are critical to the success of your company?	Which projects have results that are easy to measure?	Which projects give the most results at the cheapest cost?	Which projects are easy to delegate and break up into tasks?	Which projects need to be started right away?
Increase Sales 20%: Develop new nutrition shake for Nov. '02 trade show. Team leader: Ross Sanders.	**Skill Development**: Read *Swim with the Shark*s by 9/31/02 and *One Minute Manager* by 10/20/02.	**Web Strategy**: Speed up site access, shrink all graphics files by 10/4/02. G. Brown responsible.	**Insurance Cost Cut**: Raise deductible to reduce monthly insurance premiums. Deadline: 9/28/02.	**New Competition**: Update warranty in product brochures by end of 3rd quarter. Greene to lead team.	**Joint Ventures**: Head sales rep will email then call Oracle, Genuity, and Nortel by October 10th.
A1	A2	A3	A4	A5	A6

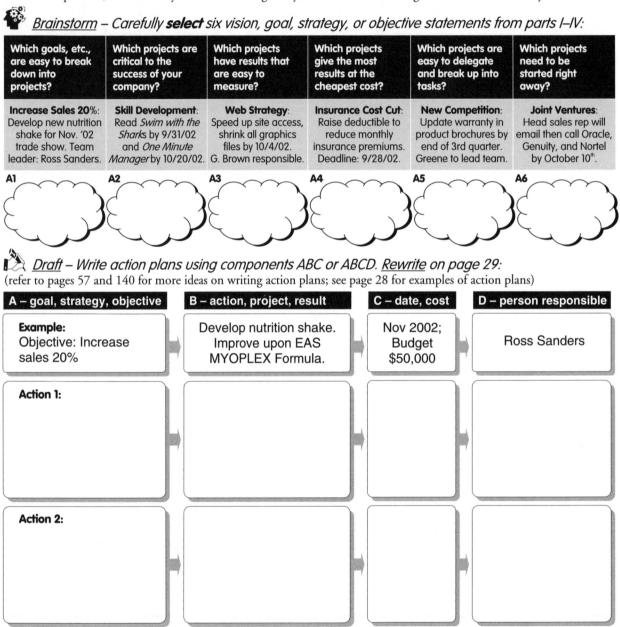

✍️ *Draft* – Write action plans using components ABC or ABCD. <u>Rewrite</u> on page 29:
(refer to pages 57 and 140 for more ideas on writing action plans; see page 28 for examples of action plans)

A – goal, strategy, objective	B – action, project, result	C – date, cost	D – person responsible
Example: Objective: Increase sales 20%	Develop nutrition shake. Improve upon EAS MYOPLEX Formula.	Nov 2002; Budget $50,000	Ross Sanders
Action 1:			
Action 2:			

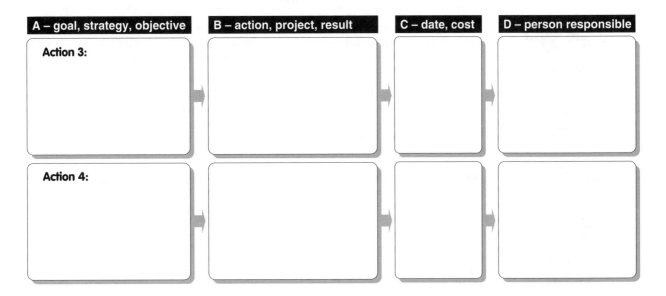

Draft – To complete action plans, write keywords and phrases in the blanks below:

Our main project, _____
primary project   describe main project (e.g., *the development of a company brochure*)

will be completed _____ **by** _____ .
         date (2/04)   person(s) responsible (e.g., *ad team*)

The projected cost of this project is _____ .
         cost and time (e.g., *$2,000 at 50 man hours*)

To complete this project, _____
main tasks   describe task 1 (e.g., *the new logo*)

will be completed by _____
         person(s) + date (e.g., *Fred 8/03*)

and _____
         describe task 2 (e.g., *the taking of photos of company and staff*)

will be completed by _____ .
         person(s) + date (e.g., *Anna 9/03*)

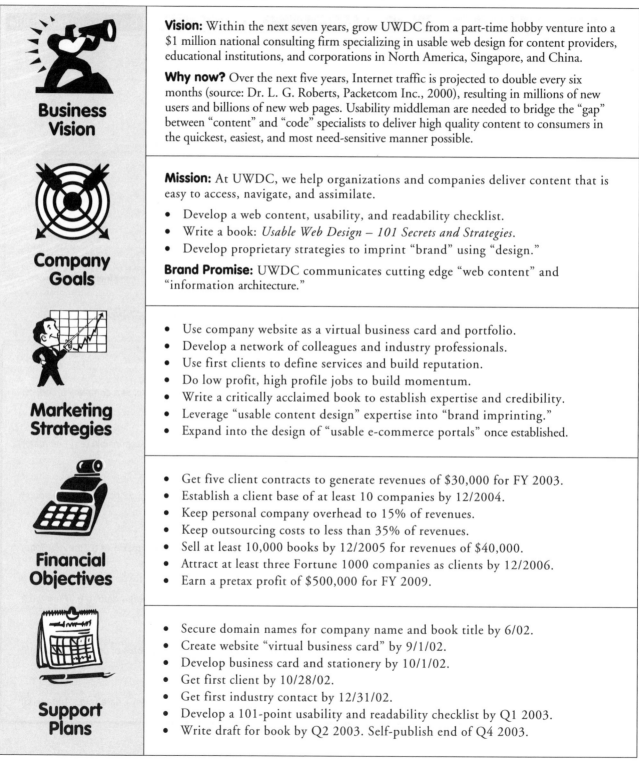

Business Vision

Vision: Within the next seven years, grow UWDC from a part-time hobby venture into a $1 million national consulting firm specializing in usable web design for content providers, educational institutions, and corporations in North America, Singapore, and China.

Why now? Over the next five years, Internet traffic is projected to double every six months (source: Dr. L. G. Roberts, Packetcom Inc., 2000), resulting in millions of new users and billions of new web pages. Usability middleman are needed to bridge the "gap" between "content" and "code" specialists to deliver high quality content to consumers in the quickest, easiest, and most need-sensitive manner possible.

Company Goals

Mission: At UWDC, we help organizations and companies deliver content that is easy to access, navigate, and assimilate.

- Develop a web content, usability, and readability checklist.
- Write a book: *Usable Web Design – 101 Secrets and Strategies*.
- Develop proprietary strategies to imprint "brand" using "design."

Brand Promise: UWDC communicates cutting edge "web content" and "information architecture."

Marketing Strategies

- Use company website as a virtual business card and portfolio.
- Develop a network of colleagues and industry professionals.
- Use first clients to define services and build reputation.
- Do low profit, high profile jobs to build momentum.
- Write a critically acclaimed book to establish expertise and credibility.
- Leverage "usable content design" expertise into "brand imprinting."
- Expand into the design of "usable e-commerce portals" once established.

Financial Objectives

- Get five client contracts to generate revenues of $30,000 for FY 2003.
- Establish a client base of at least 10 companies by 12/2004.
- Keep personal company overhead to 15% of revenues.
- Keep outsourcing costs to less than 35% of revenues.
- Sell at least 10,000 books by 12/2005 for revenues of $40,000.
- Attract at least three Fortune 1000 companies as clients by 12/2006.
- Earn a pretax profit of $500,000 for FY 2009.

Support Plans

- Secure domain names for company name and book title by 6/02.
- Create website "virtual business card" by 9/1/02.
- Develop business card and stationery by 10/1/02.
- Get first client by 10/28/02.
- Get first industry contact by 12/31/02.
- Develop a 101-point usability and readability checklist by Q1 2003.
- Write draft for book by Q2 2003. Self-publish end of Q4 2003.

The One Day Business Plan™ Worksheet – *Summarize your business vision, company goals, marketing strategies, financial objectives, and support plans:*

Business
VISION

What do you want your company to be?

Why is "now" the "right time" to start your company?

Vision	
Why now?	

Company
GOALS

How will you achieve your vision?

What is your central *purpose* or *mission*?

What do you *promise* your customers?

G1	
G2	
G3	
G4	
Mission Statement	
Brand Promise	

Marketing
STRATEGIES

How will you grow your business? What works in the industry?

How will you reach customers?

What opportunities exist?

S1	
S2	
S3	
S4	
Marketing Approach	
SWOT Analysis	

Financial
OBJECTIVES

What must you accomplish after one year of operation?

How will you know goals are being met?

How will you measure your success?

O1	
O2	
O3	
O4	
Sales Revenue	$
Profitability	$
Market Share	
Key PI's	

Support
ACTION PLANS

What specific *actions* are you taking to achieve your vision?

When will key projects be completed?

How much will each project cost?

A1	
A2	
A3	
A4	
Primary Project	
Main Tasks	

To Do List

I. **Business Overview**

Cover Sheet

✓ Company Logo
✓ Confidentiality Agreement
✓ Preparation and Copyright Notice
✓ Principal Business Definition
✓ Summary of Business Proposition
✓ Targeted Reader Statement

A company without a LOGO is like a country without a FLAG.

KEY CHEMICALS

GIRL SCOUTS

Design a logo. Write a principal business definition. Complete cover sheet.

Company Logo

Every company needs a logo. Place your logo on your cover page in a suitable eye-catching spot. Be conservative and limit its size. Also, resist the urge to use too many colors.

Why Every Company Needs a Logo

Five reasons why every company needs a logo:

- **A logo gives your promotions continuity.** Using a logo exclusive to your firm consistently on all printed material unifies your marketing efforts and gives the impression that you know exactly who you are, and perhaps are a little bigger and better than you really are.

- **A logo gives you a company identity.** Developing an easily recognized logo gives you an identification advantage over your competition.

- **A logo is a tangible asset with a cash value.** Consumer trust is hard to come by. When gained, it is extremely valuable. This trust is often attached to a company's logo (or trademark) because people like symbols—e.g., they wear rings on their fingers and drive expensive cars.

- **A logo is visible evidence that you have made an investment in your organization.** A well-designed logo shows that management has a strong self-image, a definite direction for the future, and a commitment to the highest standards of quality and professionalism. A carelessly designed logo or no logo at all is often associated with organizations that are under-capitalized, poorly organized, and of uncertain longevity.

- **A logo makes your ads, letterheads, and envelopes stand out from the crowd.** People DO judge books by their covers. The billions of dollars spent every year on advertising and packaging prove this. A well-conceived logo makes it more difficult for customers to forget you. In the long run, it will generate better returns for your advertising dollars.

Designing a Company Logo in "Eight Steps"

STEP 1 – **Gather information and materials that will help inspire your design.** This includes: ◆ your mission statement, action plan, marketing plan, and expansion plan ◆ company goals and philosophies ◆ a directory of trademarks and logos ◆ as many competitive company logos as you can get your hands on (find these in the Yellow Pages or magazine related to your area) ◆ graphics, photos, and any kind of physical object you feel symbolizes your company name.

STEP 2 – **Determine how your logo will be used.** Logos are meant to be versatile. Their design should lend themselves to any use imaginable. Imagine your logo being used in each of the following media: ◆ magazine and newspaper advertising ◆ billboards ◆ discount coupons ◆ brochures ◆ letterhead ◆ badges or buttons ◆ ball-point pens or pencils ◆ greeting cards ◆ postcards ◆ TV spots ◆ calendars or date books ◆ contests and other specialized promotions ◆ patches or decals ◆ actual products themselves ◆ giant 3-d sculptures outside your office.

EQUAL HOUSING
OPPORTUNITY

STEP 3 – **Decide what purpose your logo will have**. Ask yourself: ◆ What kind of image do you want to create? ◆ Do you want your logo to be formal or informal? ◆ Will it be targeted towards consumers or business people? ◆ Do you want it to symbolize a company that stands for one thing or many things? ◆ Do you want it to jump out at people or slowly slip into their subconscious?

STEP 4 – **Write the name of your company in the center of a sheet of paper.** Keep in mind that logo design is an attempt to complement your company name, not overpower it. Words and meaning come first; graphics second.

STEP 5 – **Sketch ten unique logo designs around your name.** If, after experimenting with the techniques listed below, you cannot come up with a unique design, copy the logo design of competitors and other companies, substituting your company name for theirs. If you like the result, to avoid infringing upon copyright and trademark laws, make enough changes to your final design so your logo could not possibly be mistaken for the one you copied. Experiment with:

❑ length of name
❑ abbreviations
❑ initials
❑ size of letters
❑ lettering style
❑ intertwined images

❑ circular shapes
❑ square shapes
❑ triangular shapes
❑ irregular shapes
❑ shaded areas
❑ different colored areas

❑ upside down views
❑ sideways views
❑ 3-d effects
❑ heavy borders
❑ light borders
❑ doodles

STEP 6 – Scrap or modify your sketched designs based on the following logo design strategies:

Scrap or modify all logo designs that do not have presence. Logos that have presence can be placed on letterhead or in ads in a variety of positions and still look great—e.g., top, bottom, left, right, centered.

Scrap or modify all logo designs cluttered with detail. It is essential that your logo be easy to reproduce. Details can easily be lost in reproduction processes. Too much detail can also detract from your logo's message.

Scrap or modify all logo designs that do not seem versatile. An effective logo can be easily adapted to different media, with the addition or subtraction of a few lines, shapes, and letters, without destroying its basic appeal.

Scrap or modify all logo designs that use letters that are difficult to work with. B, d, f, h, k, l, and t have ascenders that look good on paper. Words that have descenders like g, j, p, q, and y can cause problems graphically.

Scrap or modify all logo designs that do not have unity between graphics and lettering. When lettering and graphics are placed together, disharmonious interaction is possible. A highly stylized letter will almost always distract from the symbol rather than complement it. Your design will then look muddled and disorganized, implying your business is the same.

Scrap or modify all logo designs that cannot be easily rendered in three dimensions. When embossed on letterhead, a logo should make people want to touch it. If turned into a charm, it should make people want to play with it in their hands. If turned into a sculpture, it should make people want to hug it or have their photo taken with it.

Scrap or modify all logo designs with lettering style that does not complement your desired image. Typestyles, like people, have individual characters. Some styles appear feminine, others masculine.

Scrap or modify all logo designs that do not look good in black and white. If your logo only looks good when reproduced in full color and embossed in gold, then you have a serious design problem.

Scrap or modify all logo designs with lines, shapes, patterns, and letters that do not significantly add to its meaning. In logo design, LESS is MORE.

Scrap or modify all logo designs that do not run letters into each other. Letters combined together, so they touch each other, legally become graphic symbols and can be granted better protection under trademark laws.

Scrap or modify all logo designs that are too complex. Keep your logo simple. The best logos leave a strong visual impression after being seen once!

STEP 7 – Select three promising logo designs and prepare finished copies using transfer letter sheets and graphic artist techniques or, better yet, a computer drawing program. *Transfer Letter Sheets* can be found at stores that handle artist's materials and at most office supply stores. They come in various typestyles and sizes. Using transfer sheets, your chosen letters or graphics are applied to a poster board (or piece of high quality paper). Other details can be added in with special black graphic markers and pens. To get the best, cleanest reproduction of your logo, draw it much larger than it will eventually appear on your stationery or other printed matter. Minor imperfections will disappear once it is reduced in size. A photographic negative can then be made of the final design (or use a copy machine to shrink it, then cut and paste it to media of your choice).

STEP 8 – Get critical feedback before selecting your final logo. Don't leave the image of your company in the hands of a few. Survey reactions from as many people as possible, preferably potential customers. Find out if they respond in the way you intended. Do they find your logo appealing, informative, and memorable? If they don't know your business, can they guess it?

Using Clip Art to Create Logos in a Hurry

If you plan to operate a small consulting or contracting business, or perhaps even a corner grocery store, establishing a strong corporate identity may not be high on your list of the most important things to spend startup capital on. Fortunately, by selecting the right typeface for your company name, as well as high quality royalty-free clip art, a cost-effective solution is possible. By experimenting with multiple vector graphics (i.e., clip art that can shrink and expand without loss of detail), and combining various parts of each image to your design, you can create a unique logo. Keep in mind that even a drastically altered clip art image may be impossible to trademark. However, you might consider using your clip art design "as is" until your company gets underway and then later, when cash flow is stronger, replace it with something similar, yet completely original. The design shown below took about an hour to create using MS Word and Photoshop.

In logo design, **LESS** *is* **MORE**.

✳

Which logo design leaves the most lasting impression?

Nike (symbol)   53%
McDonald's (letter) 32%
Coca Cola (word)   15%
SOURCE:
Smallbusinesspolls.com

Logo Design Tips

Cut distracting lines.
In the example shown, the "lion" and "hill" were simplified. If you wish to show a complex image like a bowl filled with salad, simplify it to the point that it has as few lines as possible, but is still easily recognizable.

Change typography.
The example shown uses the "Architect" typeface. However, the "L" has been rotated slightly using MS Word Art. Typography manipulation is a strategy also used by *Dell* with its twisted "E" and *Microsoft* with its chipped "O".

Avoid vertical logos.
A high and narrow logo requires more ad space to get a legible size.

Keep colors simple.
If you do use color, make sure it also looks good in B/W. A B/W logo is easier and cheaper to print. Also, stick to CMYK-colors that exist within the wider RGB color range. This will keep screen colors closer to printed colors.

Confidentiality Agreement

A *Confidential Notice* can be used to discourage unintended readers from reading your business plan. It is also a great way to generate curiosity—e.g.: "(Private and Confidential)". For business plans outlining proprietary information, such as inventions, trade secrets, or even pricing structures, a *Confidentiality* or *Nondisclosure Agreement* (NDA) may be necessary. However, keep in mind that many professional investors, who see hundreds of plans a year, might have a potential conflict and thus will not sign an NDA. To protect yourself, research who you are giving your plan to, and then, give it only to those who are fair and reputable. Use NDAs with private investors, potential partners, and employees.

Preparation and Copyright Notice

Your business plan should state who prepared the plan, along with the month and year it was prepared or updated, to give readers an idea of how current and reliable the information is. You may also wish to describe the preparation process in detail to add credibility to your figures, especially if outside help such as an accountant or business consultant was contracted to review your projections and strategies. A copyright notice can also be included to help protect your ideas and discourage readers from copying your business plan and distributing it without your knowledge—e.g.: "Plan Prepared by Josephine Ma © 2005. All rights reserved." To better keep track of copies, it is also a good idea to include the total number of copies made along with the individual number of each copy—e.g.: "Copy 1 of 5."

Principal Business Definition

A *Principal Business Definition* (or *Business Definition*) is like a *Mission Statement* except that it defines more specifically the exact nature of your business—what it *is* and what it *does*. It does not focus on goals nor plans for the future. It focuses on facts. It can also be used to sum up your company products or services, desired image, legal form, major financial objectives, and/or targeted markets (see page 36 for sample).

Summary of Business Proposition

A *Business Proposition Summary*, unlike a *Company Mission Statement* or *Principal Business Definition*, is most often used to summarize the *purpose* of your business plan (e.g., a loan, venture capital, or joint venture request). It answers: "What's in it for **you** if they like your proposal?" It also targets the needs and interests of your targeted reader—e.g., profit share, stock offering, i.e.: "What's in it for **them**?"

Targeted Reader Statement

In special circumstances, you may want to state the name of a banker, investor, or other specific person on the cover sheet of your business plan to attract their attention—e.g.: "for Farah Hisham CEO of XYZ Inc."

$ucce$$ Story ➜ The "Tiger Balm" King Au Boon Haw

Au Boon Haw was an outrageously wealthy Chinese tycoon of the prewar era who manufactured and marketed little jars of first aid ointment called "Tiger Balm." Millions of jars are still sold each year throughout the world. Tiger Balm® is made from natural ingredients, such as camphor and menthol. Sam King, author of, *Tiger Balm King: The Life and Times of Au Boon Haw*, makes the following remarks about Boon Haw's flair for promotion: "It was likely that the Aw family fortune would have remained a dream if not for his talent. Every customer who came to seek a herbal cure was persuaded to buy a jar of his golden oil. If the customer resisted because of doubt or lack of money, a jar would be pressed on him as a token of goodwill. In return, would the valued customer be kind enough to recommend the ointment to his friends."

In a business plan, clear and informative content is your primary concern. However, considering that venture companies receive several thousand business plans a year, an attention-grabbing cover sheet is worth developing. To grab attention with your cover sheet, be conservative, respectable, and clear.
BUSINESS PLAN WRITING TIP

✱

For purposes of action, nothing is more useful than narrowness of thought combined with energy of will.
HENRI FREDERIC AMIEL

DAY 2 Worksheets ⏱

Write a principal business definition.
Design a logo. Complete cover sheet.

Principal Business Definition

Draft – Write keywords and phrases in the blanks below:

Sample Business Definition – XYZ Inc. is a startup dot.com business venture that provides state-of-the-art exercising equipment to young professionals and athletes in the Los Angeles area. Located in the CBD, we hope to be recognized as the most knowledgeable, highest quality e-retailer in CA.

_____ **is a** _____ _____ **that provides/sells**
company name   ☐ startup ☐ established   ☐ proprietorship ☐ partnership ☐ corp. ☐ dot.com

_____ **to/in the** _____ **. Located in/at**
describe products and services   describe customers and target market area

_____ **, we hope to be recognized as** _____ .
area
(*the XYZ shopping mall*)   desired image and type of business
(e.g., *the leading retailer ...*)

Summary of Business Proposition

Brainstorm – Write keywords and phrases to summarize your business proposition:

_____ _____ _____ _____ _____	**Sample:** XYZ Inc. is seeking $10 million in equity capital for 40% ownership in the manufacture and sale of a newly developed high-speed RAM chip—Xiron. Market testing indicates Xiron will outsell competitors 2 to 1 due to its 50% lower production cost and 210% performance boost. Conservative net profits, after two years, are estimated at $42 million yielding a 168% ROI ($16.8 million).

What's in it for you?

Product information

What's in it for them? (ROI)

Targeted Reader Statement

List targeted reader(s): ☐ bankers ☐ lawyers ☐ management
☐ investors ☐ accountants ☐ owners

Company Logo

Sketch logo designs for others to examine. Select and draw your final choice in the grids below:

FINAL CHOICE

Cover Sheet

Use the following fill-in-the-blanks sheet to help design your cover page:

Company LOGO

Company Name

Address

Phone/Fax

Email

URL

BUSINESS PLAN

Company Name

❑ *Mission Statement* ❑ *Principal Business Definition*
❑ *Summary of Business Proposition* ❑ *Targeted Reader Statement*

Contact

Job Title

Email

Address

Phone/Fax

Name of Author

Date

Plan Prepared by

Copyright © 20___ by

copy ___ of ___

Company Name or Author

(Private and Confidential)

DAY 3

Determine the content and heading structure of your business plan.

Table of Contents

To Do List

I. **Business Overview**
Table of Contents

✓ Table of Contents

Although your *Table of Contents* should be limited to one page, it is the second most important part of your business plan after your *Executive Summary*. Without a proper focus and heading structure for your plan, your ideas cannot be properly communicated to your targeted reader. When designing your table of contents, pay attention to any "hot buttons" your reader may have. Venture capitalists like to read about your management team, key success factors, marketing strategies, intellectual property, and return on investment potential. Bankers want to know your cash position and monthly cash flow so they can better project whether you can meet your loan obligations. Make it easy for your targeted reader to find the information they want. It bears repeating that what you put into your business plan depends on the nature of your company and who your plan is for. A high-tech startup with intangible assets, such as software programming or patents pending, will definitely need to emphasize the commitment and expertise of its business team (see sample outlines 1–6 on pages 39 to 41).

There are many ways to organize and format a successful business plan ... writers must use their judgment about what to include, what to exclude, and what to add.

STEPHEN R. LAWRENCE
College of Business and Administration, University of Colorado

General Business Plan: *Sample Outline #1*

Business Plan Based on U.S. Small Business Administration Guidelines: *Sample Outline #2*

Product or Service Business Plan: *Sample Outline #3*

Determine the content and heading structure of your business plan.

Table of Contents

Review the business plan structures shown below. Search the Web for other business plan outlines and templates related to the type of business you want to start (visit www.bplan-templates.com):

Internet Business Plan:
Sample Outline #4

Manufacturing Business Plan:
Sample Outline #5

Consulting Business Plan:
Sample Outline #6

Table of Contents – *Select <u>C</u>ontent (✓) and structure <u>H</u>eadings (e.g., 1.0, 2.1, 2.1.1). Prioritize components:*

H	C		Not as Important ◄- - - - -► Priority
		BUSINESS OVERVIEW	
	✓	**Cover Sheet**	1 – 2 – 3 – 4 – ⑤
	✓	Company Name	1 – 2 – 3 – 4 – ⑤
	✓	Company Mission Statement	1 – 2 – 3 – 4 – ⑤
	✓	The One Day Business Plan™	1 – 2 – 3 – 4 – ⑤
	✓	Company Logo	1 – 2 – 3 – 4 – ⑤
	❑	Confidentiality Agreement	1 – 2 – 3 – 4 – 5
	❑	Preparation and Copyright Notice	1 – 2 – 3 – 4 – 5
	❑	Principal Business Definition	1 – 2 – 3 – 4 – 5
	❑	Summary of Business Proposition	1 – 2 – 3 – 4 – 5
	❑	Targeted Reader Statement	1 – 2 – 3 – 4 – 5
	✓	**Table of Contents**	1 – 2 – 3 – 4 – ⑤
1.0		**Executive Summary** (Business Overview)	1 – 2 – 3 – 4 – ⑤
	❑	Statement of Purpose	1 – 2 – 3 – 4 – 5
	❑	**Fact Sheet**	1 – 2 – 3 – 4 – 5
2.0		**COMPANY PLAN**	1 – 2 – 3 – 4 – ⑤
2.1	✓	**Company Description**	1 – 2 – 3 – 4 – ⑤
	❑	Accomplishments to Date (Contracts in Force)	1 – 2 – 3 – 4 – 5
	❑	Buildings and Equipment Owned	1 – 2 – 3 – 4 – 5
	❑	Company History (Background)	1 – 2 – 3 – 4 – 5
	❑	Company Philosophy (Values Statement)	1 – 2 – 3 – 4 – 5
	✓	Goals and Objectives (SWOT Analysis)	1 – 2 – 3 – 4 – ⑤
	✓	Keys to Success (Strategy Analysis)	1 – 2 – 3 – 4 – ⑤
	✓	Legal Structure	1 – 2 – 3 – 4 – ⑤
	❑	Location Analysis (Facilities)	1 – 2 – 3 – 4 – 5
	❑	Planned Expansion (Development Plan)	1 – 2 – 3 – 4 – 5
	❑	R&D (New Technology)	1 – 2 – 3 – 4 – 5
	✓	**Merchandising Plan** (Sales Plan)	1 – 2 – 3 – 4 – ⑤
	✓	Description of Principal Products and Services	1 – 2 – 3 – 4 – ⑤
	❑	Feasibility Study (Idea Analysis)	1 – 2 – 3 – 4 – 5
	❑	Future Products and Services	1 – 2 – 3 – 4 – 5
	❑	Purchasing Plan (Suppliers)	1 – 2 – 3 – 4 – 5
	❑	Proprietary and Exclusive Rights Obtained	1 – 2 – 3 – 4 – 5
	✓	**Operating Plan** (Implementation Strategy)	1 – 2 – 3 – 4 – ⑤
	✓	Accounting System	1 – 2 – 3 – 4 – ⑤
	❑	Banking Plan	1 – 2 – 3 – 4 – 5
	❑	Buildings, Equipment, and Other Purchases	1 – 2 – 3 – 4 – 5
	✓	Computerization Plan ⟵ (Technology	1 – 2 – 3 – 4 – ⑤
	✓	Communications Plan Plan)	1 – 2 – 3 – 4 – ⑤
	✓	Internet Plan (Web Strategy)	1 – 2 – 3 – 4 – ⑤
	❑	Inventory Control	1 – 2 – 3 – 4 – 5
	❑	Order Entry and Fulfillment	1 – 2 – 3 – 4 – 5
	✓	Operations Schedule (Milestones/Action Plans)	1 – 2 – 3 – 4 – ⑤
	❑	Production Plan (Service Plan)	1 – 2 – 3 – 4 – 5
	❑	Quality Control	1 – 2 – 3 – 4 – 5
	❑	Required Licenses and Legal Considerations	1 – 2 – 3 – 4 – 5
	❑	Social Responsibility and Community	1 – 2 – 3 – 4 – 5
	✓	**Organizational Plan**	1 – 2 – 3 – 4 – ⑤
	❑	Board of Directors	1 – 2 – 3 – 4 – 5
	❑	Contract and Temporary Help	1 – 2 – 3 – 4 – 5
	✓	Management Team and Key Employees	1 – 2 – 3 – 4 – ⑤
	❑	Manpower/Personnel Required (Team Gaps)	1 – 2 – 3 – 4 – 5
	❑	Organizational Chart	1 – 2 – 3 – 4 – 5
	❑	Ownership Structure	1 – 2 – 3 – 4 – 5
	❑	Professional Advisors	1 – 2 – 3 – 4 – 5
3.0		**MARKETING PLAN**	1 – 2 – 3 – 4 – ⑤
3.1	✓	**Market Description and Analysis**	1 – 2 – 3 – 4 – ⑤
	✓	Industry Environment and Market Trends	1 – 2 – 3 – 4 – ⑤
	✓	Market Needs (Needs We Will Meet)	1 – 2 – 3 – 4 – ⑤
	✓	Target Market Description	1 – 2 – 3 – 4 – ⑤
	❑	Market Analysis and Sales Forecast	1 – 2 – 3 – 4 – 5
	❑	Market Entry Strategy	1 – 2 – 3 – 4 – 5
	❑	Market Share (Growth) and Distribution	1 – 2 – 3 – 4 – 5

H	C		Not as Important ◄- - - - -► Priority
	✓	**Competition Analysis**	1 – 2 – 3 – 4 – ⑤
	✓	Competitor Descriptions	1 – 2 – 3 – 4 – ⑤
	✓	Competitive Advantage (Competitive Edge)	1 – 2 – 3 – 4 – ⑤
	❑	Competitive Position (Strategic Position)	1 – 2 – 3 – 4 – 5
	✓	**Selling Strategies**	1 – 2 – 3 – 4 – ⑤
	✓	Business Cards (Business Card Strategy)	1 – 2 – 3 – 4 – ⑤
	❑	Company Slogans	1 – 2 – 3 – 4 – ⑤
	❑	Customer Service Plan	1 – 2 – 3 – 4 – 5
	❑	Credit Extension Plan	1 – 2 – 3 – 4 – 5
	❑	Distribution Plan	1 – 2 – 3 – 4 – 5
	❑	Market Testing Plan	1 – 2 – 3 – 4 – 5
	❑	Pricing Policies	1 – 2 – 3 – 4 – ⑤
	✓	Promotion Plan (Sales Force Development)	1 – 2 – 3 – 4 – ⑤
	✓	Publicity Plan (Word-of-Mouth Marketing)	1 – 2 – 3 – 4 – ⑤
	❑	Packaging Concept (Product Design Strategy)	1 – 2 – 3 – 4 – 5
	❑	Strategic Alliances (Networking)	1 – 2 – 3 – 4 – 5
	❑	Service and Product Mix Strategy	1 – 2 – 3 – 4 – 5
	❑	Timing of Market Entry	1 – 2 – 3 – 4 – 5
	❑	Warranty Policies	1 – 2 – 3 – 4 – 5
	✓	**Marketing Approach** (Brand Promise)	1 – 2 – 3 – 4 – ⑤
4.0		**FINANCIAL PLAN**	1 – 2 – 3 – 4 – ⑤
	✓	**Capitalization Plan**	1 – 2 – 3 – 4 – ⑤
	❑	Summary of Financial Needs	1 – 2 – 3 – 4 – 5
	✓	Capital Required (Startup Costs)	1 – 2 – 3 – 4 – 5
	✓	Present Financial Structure (Capital Sources)	1 – 2 – 3 – 4 – ⑤
	✓	Funding Required (Loans Required)	1 – 2 – 3 – 4 – ⑤
	❑	**Uses of Funds Statement**	1 – 2 – 3 – 4 – 5
	✓	**Pro Forma Financial Statements**	1 – 2 – 3 – 4 – ⑤
	✓	Assumptions Made	1 – 2 – 3 – 4 – ⑤
	✓	12-month Income Projection	1 – 2 – 3 – 4 – ⑤
	✓	Three-year Income Projection	1 – 2 – 3 – 4 – ⑤
	✓	Cash Flow Statement	1 – 2 – 3 – 4 – ⑤
	✓	Breakeven Analysis	1 – 2 – 3 – 4 – ⑤
	✓	Pro Forma Balance Sheet	1 – 2 – 3 – 4 – ⑤
	❑	**Current Financial Statements**	1 – 2 – 3 – 4 – 5
	❑	Current Income Statement	1 – 2 – 3 – 4 – 5
	❑	Current Balance Sheet	1 – 2 – 3 – 4 – 5
	❑	Current Asset Sheet	1 – 2 – 3 – 4 – 5
	❑	Other Financial Statements	1 – 2 – 3 – 4 – 5
	❑	**Business Financial History**	1 – 2 – 3 – 4 – 5
	❑	Financial and Operating Ratios (Business Ratios)	1 – 2 – 3 – 4 – 5
	✓	Performance Indicators (Benchmarks)	1 – 2 – 3 – 4 – ⑤
	✓	**Profit Plan**	1 – 2 – 3 – 4 – ⑤
	❑	Cost Reducing Measures	1 – 2 – 3 – 4 – 5
	❑	Exit Strategy (Selling the Business)	1 – 2 – 3 – 4 – 5
	❑	Investment and Retirement Plans	1 – 2 – 3 – 4 – 5
	❑	Tax Plan (Tax Strategies)	1 – 2 – 3 – 4 – 5
	✓	**Risk Assessment** (Risks and Assumptions)	1 – 2 – 3 – 4 – ⑤
	❑	Analysis of Competitors' Reactions	1 – 2 – 3 – 4 – 5
	❑	Contingency Plans	1 – 2 – 3 – 4 – 5
	❑	Insurance Plan	1 – 2 – 3 – 4 – 5
	❑	Risk Management Plan	1 – 2 – 3 – 4 – 5
	❑	Security Plan	1 – 2 – 3 – 4 – 5
	❑	**Closing Statement**	1 – 2 – 3 – 4 – ⑤
5.0		**SUPPORTING DOCUMENTS**	1 – 2 – 3 – 4 – ⑤
	✓	**Documents Required**	1 – 2 – 3 – 4 – ⑤
	❑	Contracts and Lease Agreements	1 – 2 – 3 – 4 – 5
	❑	Credit Reports and Income Tax Returns	1 – 2 – 3 – 4 – 5
	❑	Legal Documents	1 – 2 – 3 – 4 – 5
	❑	Letters of Reference	1 – 2 – 3 – 4 – 5
	❑	Personal Financial Statements	1 – 2 – 3 – 4 – 5
	✓	Résumés of Management and Key Individuals	1 – 2 – 3 – 4 – ⑤
	❑	**Other Documents and Support Plans**	1 – 2 – 3 – 4 – 5

Summarize your business idea. List key facts.

Executive Summary

The purpose of an *Executive Summary* is to pique investor interest and to include the main highlights of your business plan. It is the heart of your business proposal and the first part that gets read. It is a mini-introduction to your company in which you try to capture the essence of your business in one or two pages (maximum three) using all the persuasion and excitement you can. If this part of your plan can't garner sufficient attention, chances are neither will the rest.

Writing an "Executive Summary"

To write an *Executive Summary*, choose from three basic writing styles:

Give it to them straight. Summarize the main points and conclusions of each section of your business plan.

Answer the most important questions and objections. Describe the "Who? What? Where? When? Why? and How?"

Tell a bit of a story. Using narrative writing techniques, grab and hold reader interest, while at the same time injecting important information.

The first writing style is the easiest, but usually comes across dry. The second technique requires you to brainstorm for questions readers might have and then answer them. The third style demands a talented writer and works better for businesses with some history. Using this method, greater emphasis is placed on "the business concept" and "the opportunity" rather than operational details.

Perhaps the best solution is to use a combination of the above techniques by giving readers clear-cut facts, answering any important questions and objections they might have, and all the while spinning a masterful web of narrative prose to lure them in, trap their attention, and quietly imprint a compelling snapshot of your company that they will never forget (use worksheet on pages 47 to 49).

NOTE In an *Executive Summary*, subheadings may be used to emphasize key areas of your plan. Subheadings used should also reflect the plan's structure.

To Do List

I. **Business Overview**

Executive Summary

✓ Executive Summary
✓ Statement of Purpose

Fact Sheet

✓ Fact Sheet

The "Executive Summary" is a synopsis of the most important points of your plan.

It's more than just a simple introduction; it's the whole plan, only shorter.
PAUL TIFFANY
Professor of Management, Haas Business School

There's no one right way to go about writing a plan. One of the most effective approaches I've discovered is to begin by writing an executive summary.
DAVID E. GUMPERT
Inc Magazine

What an Executive Summary is NOT

It is NOT an abstract of the business plan.

It is NOT an introduction to the business plan.

It is NOT a preface.

It is NOT a random collection of highlights.

IT IS the business plan in miniature!

Abstracted from the writings of:
DAVID E. GUMPERT
Inc Magazine

Common Mistakes in Writing an Executive Summary

Fails to demonstrate a special or unique opportunity.

Fails to outline the terms of the investment sought.

Fails to generate enthusiasm in the reader.

Lacks a specific focus.

Too long and wordy.

Tries to include everything.

Abstracted from the writings of:
BIZPLANIT.COM

Sample Paragraphs for an "Executive Summary"

[Company] has been formed as a [proprietorship, partnership, corporation] in [year] in [city, state], by [owners] in response to the following market conditions:

- [Startup, growth] opportunities exist in the [product/service] industry.

- According to [research source], due to [list reasons], there has been an increase in [consumption, purchasing, spending] of [describe quantity, verifiable fact, or demographical data to support growth opportunity].

- [Names of customers or clients] are willing to place large [list orders, contracts] within the next [time period].

- Several other prospective [customers, clients], including [list names of customers or clients], have expressed serious interest in doing business with us within the next [time period].

[Company] markets a complete line of [describe products/services]. This [product/service] line has been designed [in my home office, in partnership with the ABC group] and is manufactured and packaged in [China].

[I/We] previously [owned a company, worked within a company] that was active in the [product/service] industry. Over the past [time period], [I/we] have spent considerable effort researching ways to improve overall performance and increase profits in the [product/service] industry. [I/We] have developed ways to:

- advertise more effectively.

- beat the competition.

- expand the market.

- increase quality.

- lower unit costs.

Financial Goals

	Year 1	Year 2	Year 3
Sales (000's)	650.0	840.0	1,050.0
Gross Margin	410.0	620.0	756.0
Net Income	$11.2	$57.0	$125.0

In order to achieve lower costs than my main competitors [list key competitors], [I/we] plan to [describe]. [Our/My] ultimate goal is to build a line so unique that consumers will be willing to pay a premium.

To launch [company], a total of $[XX] has been raised. [I/We] need an additional [loan, investment from private individuals/companies] of $[XX], which will be used to finance [working capital, equipment, real estate], and [describe how additional funds will be used].

Suggested Executive Summary Topics

The following is a list of possible topics to cover in an *Executive Summary*:

- *Benefits of Your Product or Service* – Describe the main need you want to meet and why you think that need exists.
- *Bottom Line Financial Figures* – Discuss sales, projected sales, earnings, and after tax profits.
- *Calculated Risks Involved* – Discuss the major risks that threaten the success of your business and how you plan to beat those threats.
- *Company Goals and Philosophies* – Elaborate upon your mission.
- *Competitive Pressures* – Describe your competition and how you plan to beat them. What is your competitive advantage?
- *Funds Required* – Outline security offered, loan repayment plan, and use of funds.
- *Highlights of Your Marketing Plan* – Talk about why you have chosen the market you have, what its trends and risks are, where you fit into your particular industry, what will ensure a viable future for your business, what your expected market share is or will be, and who your customers are or will be.

- *Historical Perspectives of Your Business* – Talk about how your business came to be or how long it has lasted and why.
- *Important Facts and Figures* – List key facts that may be of interest to your readers.
- *Key Products or Services* – Summarize what you plan to sell.
- *Key Suppliers* – List who you plan to get your merchandise from and what, if any, arrangements or contracts you have made to secure their services.
- *Location of Business/Zoning Laws*
- *Other Businesses You Own* – Describe all your existing businesses including dates of formation and proposed future operations if any.
- *Significant Trends* – Discuss industry technology, changes, perceptions, and significant buying trends. Make assumptions on where you fit into some of these large-scale trends.
- *What's in it for them* – Investors want to know: "*What's in it for me if I read your plan?*" So, tell them right away in the first paragraph.

Using a Business Overview Instead of an Executive Summary

If your *Executive Summary* is less than a page and concisely written, it might be more appropriate to call it a *Business Overview*. A *Business Overview* summarizes key issues in your business plan—quite often under headings using bullets and in point form—and also states what you want to accomplish by having others read your business plan. Usually, it is shorter, less narrative, and more factual than an *Executive Summary*. Using this heading instead of *Executive Summary* may also be less intimidating and appeal more to employees, management, suppliers, and down-to-earth investors.

If your "Executive Summary" is less than a page, consider calling it a "Business Profile" or "Overview."

✱

Let a draft of your executive summary GUIDE your business plan!
IDEASFOR MARKETING.COM

Statement of Purpose

A *Statement of Purpose* is a less commonly used version of an *Executive Summary* that is usually shorter, more pragmatic, and funding-oriented. Use this heading if your business plan needs are very specific (as in a *Summary of Business Proposition*)—e.g., the purpose of your business plan is to get readers to invest in your company, buy shares, give you a loan, become a partner, or extend you an operating line of credit. To write a *Statement of Purpose*:

- Describe **WHO** you are and what you sell (also describe where you are located and when your company was established).

- Explain **WHAT** your main objectives are (also explain how you plan to meet those objectives).

- Explain how and **WHY** your business will be successful (what is unique about your business and what your market niche is).

- If you need a loan, explain how **MUCH** you need, why you need it, and what specifically you plan to do with it (explain how it will make you successful).

- Detail **HOW** you plan to repay your loan (principal and interest).

Sample Statement of Purpose

[Holistic Pet Supplies], established in [January 2004] as a [sole proprietorship], is a [pet food and supply company] that caters to [pet owners] in the [Asia Pacific and U.S. West Coast] area. The company is seeking [growth] capital in the amount of [$25,000] for the purpose of [purchasing machinery, which will allow the company to begin manufacturing, packaging, and distributing its own brand of puppy chow].

This new product has been tested by current customers of [HPS] and has received exceedingly positive responses. Funding is required by [March of 2005]. Repayment of the loan and interest can begin within [30 days] of receipt. This loan can be secured with company assets valued at [$80,000].

Fact Sheet

A *Fact Sheet* can be added to your business plan to summarize important information about your venture at a glance. It can be included as a separate page after your *Executive Summary* or in your *Supporting Documents*.

DAY 4 **Worksheets**

Summarize your business idea.
List key facts.

Executive Summary

Select a summary method you will use to highlight the main points of your business plan:

Executive Summary ☐   Business Overview ☐   Statement of Purpose ☐

Brainstorm – **What** *is the purpose of your summary?* **What** *are you trying to achieve?*

❑ get funds	❑ impress suppliers
❑ get a partner	❑ satisfy bankers
❑ grab interest	❑ sum up ideas
❑ just the facts	❑ create excitement

Executive Summary Worksheets (Jot down phrases, keywords, ideas, sentences. Sequence parts.)

Company Description – **What** *is your business name, type, and legal form?* **Where** *are you located?*

Development Stage – **When** *was your company founded? Is it a startup or already established?*

Mission and Goals – **What** *are your primary goals? Elaborate upon your mission or keys to success:*

Company Background – **How** *and* **why** *did your company come about?* **What** *is the market opportunity?*

Products and Services – **What** will you sell? **Why** will it sell? **Why** is it unique? **What** are its benefits?

Target Market – **Who** will buy what you sell? **How** do you intend to reach your target market?

Competition – **Who** are they? **How** will you beat them? **Why** can you compete (e.g., patents, lease)?

Accomplishments – **What** have you done to date (contracts, profits)? **How** many products sold?

Management Team – **Who** owns and operates the business? **Why** will you be successful (skills, talents)?

Funds Required – **How** much loans or investment is required? **Why** do you need it? **When** will you pay loans back? **How** will you pay? **What** collateral is provided? **How** will investors earn a return?

Brainstorm – *Check and prioritize other areas you wish to discuss. Jot down key facts and phrases:*

- ❏ business environment
- ❏ calculated risks involved
- ❏ competitive advantage
- ❏ competitive pressures
- ❏ critical facts and figures
- ❏ exit strategy
- ❏ future expansion
- ❏ historical perspectives
- ❏ key suppliers/distributors
- ❏ location advantage
- ❏ major contracts secured
- ❏ management team skills

- ❏ marketing strategy
- ❏ milestones
- ❏ operational features
- ❏ other businesses owned
- ❏ product testing results
- ❏ research conducted
- ❏ stage of product creation
- ❏ values and philosophies
- ❏ What's in it for them?
- ❏ _____
- ❏ _____
- ❏ _____

List financial goals:

	Year 1	Year 2	Year 3
Sales ($000's)			
Net Income			
Profit (Contribution)			

Fact Sheet

Draft – *Fill in as many details as you can. Update when your business plan is nearly finished:*

Company		Address			
Contact		Phone		Fax	Email

Form of business organization (proprietorship, partnership, or corporation)	Type of business and industry	Length of time in business

Number and name of founders/partners/shareholders		

Principal products and services (list and describe)

Current and/or projected revenues	$	Current and/or projected market share	%

Funds invested in the business to date and their source

$		$	
$		$	

Additional financing required	$	Proposed terms and payback period	
Total value or net worth of business	$		

Registered patents or trademarks held

Business Advisors:	Name	Address	Phone
Legal Counsel			
Accountant			
Insurance Agent			
Banker			

Part II

COMPANY PLAN

TEGuS Cartoons   *Peter J. Patsula*

Small Business Registry

© Patsula

"So what kind of business are you planning to start?"

> The companies that survive longest are the ones that work out what they uniquely can give to the world—not just growth or money but their excellence, their respect for others, or their ability to make people happy. Some call those things a soul.
>
> ∽ **Charles Handy**

In this section . . .

- 🖹 Company Description
- 🖹 Merchandising Plan
- 🖹 Operating Plan
- 🖹 Organizational Plan

List goals, objectives, and strategies. Choose a legal structure.

COMPANY PLAN

IN YOUR *Company Plan*, summarize business details. Address as many topics outlined in this section as they relate to your business and in an order that seems logical. Be prepared to back up your statements and justify any projections made with data included in your *Supporting Documents* section.

Company Description

When describing your company, refrain from using excessive language in an attempt make it sound bigger or better than it really is. Stick to the facts.

Sample Company Description Statements

In [month, year], [company name] was formed to [manufacture, distribute, service, retail, etc.] innovative [products/services] to/for [market]. This company is located in [city, state]. [I/We] formed this company as a [proprietorship, partnership, corporation]. Others involved in this business include: [list names].

The main goal of this company is to [explain].

Initial financing was arranged through [a home equity loan, savings, venture capital, friends, family]. [Explain terms, rates, and ability to repay loan].

Our venture has been very successful in generating and increasing sales, as well as effective in achieving profitability. This is due to the following:

- [Reason 1]
- [Reason 2]
- [Reason 3]

OR – [Company name] was recently conceived and is still in the beginning stages. To this point the following has been accomplished:

- A team consisting of [list names and primary responsibility—e.g., Bill Smith, Production] has been formed.

To Do List

II. **Company Plan**

Company Description

✓ Accomplishments to Date
✓ Buildings and Equipment Owned
✓ Company History
✓ Company Philosophy
✓ Goals and Objectives
✓ Keys to Success
✓ Legal Structure

BUSINESS PLAN WRITING TIPS

Begin this section with a half or full-page summary addressing the most important areas of your company.

✳

Don't use your "Company Description" to generate PR. Use it to clarify WHO you are, WHAT you plan to do, and WHAT you've already accomplished.

- A prospective [customer/client] list has been drawn up.

- Strategic Planning meetings are being held every Tuesday evening.

- Market research has been conducted in the following areas: [list].

Accomplishments to Date

Listing your company's accomplishments and developments to date gives lenders and investors tangible results to help assess your business proposition. Be specific regarding sales, promotions, profits, and products developed and sold. Also, list and clarify agreements and **contracts in force** including management contracts, shareholder or partnership agreements, franchiser service agreements, and service contracts. Indicate those included in your *Supporting Documents* section.

Buildings and Equipment Owned

List and describe building(s) owned by your company. Include descriptions, conditions, renovations and remodeling required, interior layouts, and interior designs. List and outline your current company assets, along with inventory details such as size, value, rate of turnover, and marketability.

Company History

Provide a background of past company milestones, as well as details of any **other ventures** individuals on your team or yourself have been involved in.

Company Philosophy

A *Philosophy Statement* elaborates upon your *Mission Statement*. It further defines the nature of your business, underlying company values, desired corporate culture, what exactly it is you wish to do, how you plan to interact with employees and outside communities, and any environmental concerns you might have. It also tries to capture the spirit of your company without becoming overly zealous.

Goals and Objectives

Company goals stem from your mission and philosophy. Long-term goals can be broken down into more definable short-term goals or objectives and quantified by stating time limits, financial results, and/or growth projections. You may also need to provide some proof how goals can be reached.

Establishing Long-term Goals and Objectives

To establish long-term company goals (over a year), take a serious look at all the past, present, and future internal and external factors affecting your company. One way to do this is to prepare a SWOT Analysis. A *SWOT Analysis* examines the internal strengths and weaknesses of your business, as well as the external opportunities and threats facing your business.

Identifying Strengths and Weaknesses

1) *Look at how your company will operate.* Consider factors like your location, equipment, order processing, storage facilities, and other functions that affect sales or efficiency of operations.

2) *Look at your financial position.* Consider factors like your bookkeeping method, cash flow, sales revenues, and profits.

3) *Look at your staff.* Consider factors like staff turnover rate, sales performance, and customer service. Look at where individuals are most effective, whether in marketing, product development, customer relations, or management.

Strengths and Weaknesses of Bonachelli's Bakery – Bonachelli's specializes in providing fresh, whole-wheat baked goods for local retail and wholesale clients.

Strengths – ✦ We have excellent quality control for everything we manufacture because of our personal standards and modern facilities and equipment. ✦ We have an efficient bookkeeping information system that helps us keep track of our performance so we can make better decisions.

Weaknesses – ✦ Some members of our baking staff need more training. ✦ Another salesperson would help increase and improve business. ✦ Sometimes delivery is later than promised. ✦ The market does not always seem to know how much healthier our whole grain products are over enriched white flour products.

Identifying Opportunities and Threats

1) *Look at your competition.* Consider location, market share, facilities, equipment, services, and products. What threats must you confront?

2) *Look at local and national economic conditions.* Consider housing starts, retail auto sales, real disposable personal income, unemployment rates, and any other factors than may signal a change in the future demand for your goods and services. What opportunities can be exploited?

Catch a man a fish, and you can sell it to him. Teach a man to fish, and you ruin a wonderful business opportunity.
KARL MARX
✱
Always have a plan, and believe in it. Nothing happens by accident.
CHUCK KNOX

Microsoft's only factory asset is the human imagination.
FRED MOODY
✱
The common denominator among the studies of leadership is that leadership defines follower-ship. Without willing followers, there is no leader.
DR. SHEW SEOW WAH
Chinese Leadership

3) *Look at emerging trends.* Consider factors like new technology, new markets, and changing spending habits of your customers.

Opportunities and Threats of Bonachelli's Bakery –

Opportunities – ◆ Jasper's Bakery down the street has just moved to a new location. We may be able to win over some of their old customers.

Threats – ◆ The opening of a fast-food restaurant near our location may reduce the amount of doughnuts we sell. ◆ Bad wheat harvests in the last two years, and dangerously low wheat reserves, will likely send flour prices skyrocketing.

Defining Long-term Goals

Now that you have a clearer idea of your company's strengths, weaknesses, opportunities, and threats, you will be able to more effectively define precisely what your organization must achieve results in, to achieve the kind of growth desired. Your long-term goals should be realistic, challenging, and attainable statements of where you want your company to be in three to five years following the direction outlined in your mission statement. Long-term goals function as starting and organizational points, to make it easier to process, prioritize, allocate resources, and coordinate related short-term goals and objectives.

Quantifying Long-term Goals

After long-term goals are agreed upon, the next phase is to quantify those that are too general or vague and make them more meaningful from a practical point of view. This means giving general goals a more specific results-orientated description. Three examples are illustrated below:

Example 1 – The goal of "Foster Repeat Business" could be described more specifically as: "We will foster repeat business by becoming more customer-oriented, making it easier for customers to find what they want, offering more competitive prices, and by training staff to make sure customers leave with the feeling their needs have been satisfied and that they want to come back."

Example 2 – The goal of "Improve Financial Position" could be described more specifically as: "We will improve our company's financial position by finding ways to increase our liquidity, solvency, and profitability to the following target values: By Dec. 31, 2004, we want to achieve a working capital position of $_____, a net worth of $_____, and a pre tax profit margin of $_____."

PROFIT TIP

Whenever you start a new business venture or expand into new territory, ask yourself the following:

1. **Who** is my market?

2. **What** can I sell them?

3. **How** can I make them want to buy?

4. **How** can I start small but think big to minimize my risk and maximize my profit potential?

Example 3 – The goal of "Increase Revenues" could be described more specifically as: "We will increase revenues by generating new customers, expanding sales to existing customers, acquiring other related businesses, opening new branches, marketing new products and services, and investing income to achieve $_____ in revenues by Dec. 31, 2003."

Establishing Short-term Goals, Objectives, and Plans

After long-term goals are prioritized and quantified, you are ready to establish short-term goals and objectives (under a year) to support them. Short-term goals and objectives can be thought of as "action plans" aimed at supporting your long-term goals or objectives by specifying *how*, *when*, and *what* you need to do to achieve those goals. They make your long-term goals more realistic by being more specific, measurable, consistent, and time limited (see page 140, *Operations Schedule*). If your long-term goal is to "increase sales by 50% over the next three years," some short-terms goals you might implement to achieve this include:

❑ Change company logo (remove a legal threat).

❑ Develop and market a new service or product (take advantage of an opportunity).

❑ Emphasize the competitive advantage of products in all promotional materials (correct weakness).

❑ Improve customer relations with major clients through increased personal contact (correct weakness).

❑ Retrain sales staff or replace weak sales staff (correct weakness).

❑ Revise traffic flow of store (correct weakness).

Keys to Success

Keys to Success are clear concise strategy statements closely connected to your goals and mission. They enable you to carve out a distinct identity for your business and help you focus your activities by aligning your strengths and interests with real opportunities in the marketplace. They define what you need to accomplish to succeed in your industry and what your company is good at (see page 355 and *Competitive Positioning Strategies* on page 185).

Sample Goal, Objective, and Strategy Statements

We at [company name] believe very strongly in [financial, marketing, and operational] excellence. To reflect this belief we have set three goals.

1) We want to be considered the market leader. We will seek:

☑ industry awards   ☑ solid financial ratios   ☑ a major market share

---

Luck is what happens when preparation meets opportunity.
ELMER G. LETERMAN

∗

The secret of business is to know something that nobody else knows.
ARISTOTLE ONASSIS

∗

In a start-up company, you basically throw out all assumptions every three weeks.
WILLIAM LYON PHELPS

To be great is to be misunderstood.
EMERSON

∗

Our Keys to Success are four priorities that should guide decision-making: Engage People, Deliver Value, Be Cost Efficient, Resource Effectively.
BAKER HUGHES INC
Oil Industry Supplier

Depending on whether you are a proprietorship, partnership, or corporation, include a copy of your business license, partnership agreement, or incorporation charter, articles, and bylaws, in your "Supporting Documents" section.

BUSINESS PLAN WRITING TIP

2) The present market for [product or service] is estimated at $[XX]. Our goal for market share is $[XX] or [XX]% after [X] years. To achieve this, we have the following market share goals:

    1st Year [XX]%   2nd Year [XX]%   3rd Year [XX]%   4th Year [XX]%

3) To further establish [company name] as a market leader, we also plan to: ❑ aggressively recruit the best technical staff in the industry ❑ budget for computer training for new applications ❑ budget for necessary seminars and continuing job-specific education ❑ [decrease, maintain] costs through acquisition of new plant and equipment ❑ increase productivity by investing in employee training and education ❑ develop visibility to generate new business leads ❑ maintain a state-of-the-art accounting system ❑ [set up, maintain] an employee benefit program for continuing college education ❑ support company involvement in various local and national charity events.

Legal Structure

The legal structure of your company can impact your tax rate, personal liability, and, among other things, the willingness of funding agencies to give you money. If a partnership, make sure to list the names and addresses of owners and what percentage of the business they own. If a corporation, give dates of commencement and state of incorporation. Also, list principal shareholders and share distribution. If you plan to change your legal structure in the future, explain reasons, when the change will take place, and how the change will benefit your company.

Sole Proprietorships

A sole proprietorship is a form of business where one person assumes complete liability for all actions of the business. More than 70% of the well over 20 million businesses in the U.S. are in this category (www.census.gov). In Japan, however, only a little more than 50% of business enterprises are proprietorships or partnerships (www.stat.go.jp).

DID YOU KNOW?

In the U.S., sole proprietorships create less than 6% of all revenue but report more than 20% of all profits.

✱

The U.S. government is planning to reduce tax rates on proprietorships over the next seven years to lower than corporate rates.

PROS   ❑ absolute control over decision-making—no bosses to issue orders, supervise your comings and goings, challenge your decisions, or gawk over your shoulder ❑ ease of formation ❑ easy to terminate ❑ flexibility of management ❑ lower startup costs ❑ possible tax advantages ❑ relative freedom from government control ❑ sole ownership of profits—all profits go straight to you, profits become your personal income and are taxed as such.

CONS ❏ difficulty in obtaining long-term financing or startup capital—banks consider you a higher risk than corporations or partnerships ❏ highly subjective decision-making—limited by your own skills, experience, and management capabilities ❏ less available capital ❏ limited business deductions ❏ personal affairs often get mixed up with businesses affairs ❏ unlimited liability—if your business fails creditors can take away your home, automobile, bank accounts, and any other personal assets until all debts are fully satisfied ❏ unstable business life—What happens if you become seriously ill for an extended period?

Partnerships

A partnership is created when two or more individuals, or other partnerships, decide to combine their financial and intellectual resources to create and run a new company. There is no limit to the type of partners or number of partners. The primary advantage of this business formation is the pooling of talent, experience, and capital. However, dual or multiple ownership structures can lead to serious complications if the relationships between individuals break down. Quite often, the *pool* becomes a *drain*.

PROS ❏ avoids double taxation—unlike corporations, the profits from partnerships are not taxed twice as profits are divided amongst partners and each is taxed individually ❏ broader array of skills and talents are available to solve problems and create new opportunities ❏ direct ownership of profits, no need to pay dividends ❏ easier to obtain investment capital—investors and formal venture capital organizations are more comfortable with teams, rather than individual entrepreneurs ❏ emotional support is available when times are tough ❏ flexibility—a partnership is more flexible than a corporation, but less flexible than a proprietorship.

CONS ❏ complex partnership agreement required—a partnership agreement should specify: objectives of partnership, date of commencement, amount of investment contributed by each partner, how profits and losses will be shared, provisions in the event of death, duties and responsibilities of each partner, how decisions will be made, duration of agreement, transfer of ownership procedures, dissolution of partnership, other special clauses ❏ difficulty in finding a suitable partner ❏ difficulty in obtaining long-term financing—partnerships cannot obtain long-term or short-term financing as readily as a corporation ❏ divided authority—there's nothing worse than three people driving the same car ❏ general partnership interest cannot be sold without consent of the other partners.

Before you run in double harness, look well to the other horse.
OVID
Remedia Amoris

✳

One of the most fruitful sources of ruin to men of the world is the recklessness or want of principle of partners, and it is one of the perils to which every man exposes himself who enters into partnership with another.
SIR R. MALINS

Limited Partnership:
Made up of at least one general partner (GP) and one or more limited partners (LPs). Under this legal form, only GPs make decisions. LPs contribute capital, but cannot make decisions. However, unlike GPs, LPs cannot be sued or be liable for debts of the business. International investors favor limited partnerships.

Corporation. An ingenious device for obtaining individual profit without individual responsibility.
AMBROSE BIERCE
The Devil's Dictionary

A SUBCHAPTER S-CORPORATION
Helps you avoid being taxed twice on business income. Many small businesses in the U.S. prefer this type of legal structure.

Corporations

A corporation—sometimes called a "C-Corporation," "Incorporated Company," or "Limited Company"—is a legal entity that is chartered by and subject to the laws of the state or province in which it is incorporated and is separate and distinct from the person(s) who own(s) it. The owners of the corporation, known as its shareholders or stockholders, are not personally responsible for the losses of the business. A corporation may own property, borrow money, incur debts, enter into contracts, and sue or be sued. Generally speaking, the higher the risk and liability, the more money involved, and the larger the scope of your business, the more you should consider the corporate structure.

PROS ❑ delegated authority of management—a board of directors gives structure to the decision-making process ❑ ease of securing funds—corporations have a much easier time attracting investors or securing capital in large amounts and from many investors including banks and individuals ❑ flexible staffing ❑ founders can semi-retire more easily ❑ larger management base ❑ limited liability—shareholders are generally protected from liability and can lose only the money they have invested in the corporation ❑ ownership is readily transferable ❑ possible tax advantages ❑ stability—a corporation is distinct from the individuals who own it and has a continuous existence despite management or ownership changes, or even the death of key shareholders or founding members.

CONS ❑ complex management structure required—need to elect a board of directors, write a charter and bylaws, file articles of incorporation, hire a CEO, VP, and financial officer ❑ corporate activities limited by numerous laws ❑ danger of double taxation, in which both corporate income and individual income is taxed ❑ more costly to form and maintain ❑ more government reporting and bookkeeping.

Comparison of Legal Entities	Difficulty and cost to form	Difficulty and cost to maintain	Risk of owner liability	Difficulty of tax preparation	Flexibility of ownership	Cost of terminating business
Sole Proprietorship	low	low	high	low	low	low
Partnership	low to moderate	low	high	moderate	moderate	high
Corporation	high	high	low	high	high	high
Subchapter S-Corporation	high	high	low	high	low	high

DAY 5 Worksheets

List goals, objectives, and strategies. Choose a legal structure.

Company Description

Brainstorm – *List five major points you wish to summarize to introduce and describe your company:*

1
2
3
4
5

Accomplishments to Date

List and describe successes your business has achieved to date. Include successful projects, partnerships, promotions, # of products sold, clients obtained, total sales, profits, market research, R&D, etc.:

1
2
3
4
5
6

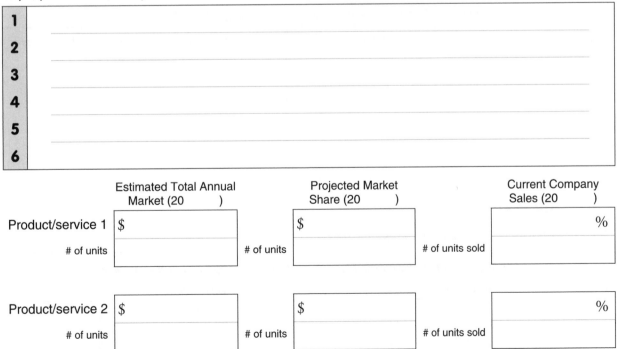

	Estimated Total Annual Market (20)	Projected Market Share (20)	Current Company Sales (20)
Product/service 1	$	$	%
# of units		# of units	# of units sold
Product/service 2	$	$	%
# of units		# of units	# of units sold

<u>*Contracts in Force*</u> *– Describe important details of key contracts and agreements (include in Sup. Docs.):*

	Sample: To ensure a steady supply of [part, item, or materials], we have established a third party supplier relationship with [supplier]. The contract is in force until [date] at a cost of [discuss pricing structure and terms]. We have also negotiated with [names of retailers, clients] to supply [part, item, materials, or product] at a selling cost of [provide details].

Buildings and Equipment Owned

List and describe buildings owned. Describe value, condition, features, and any lease agreements:

Building	Value	Condition/Features	Other Details
	$		

Use keywords to describe your key company assets. Describe value, condition, features, make, and lease or financing arrangements (if applicable). Describe how each asset is beneficial to your business:

Asset	Value	Condition/Features/Make	Financing	Benefits
Packaging Machine	$12,000	New: 1,000 units per hour	Installments	Reduces packaging and fulfillment costs

Company History

State date business was founded or established:

List key dates of past company milestones. Describe what happened or what was produced:

Date	Milestone	Description

Date	Milestone	Description

List founders and key individuals (add résumés to Supporting Documents). Describe other ventures they and yourself have been involved in (refer to "Sample Company Description Statements" on page 53):

Sample: XYZ Inc. was founded by Emilio Sanchez on [date] and shortly thereafter incorporated on [date]. Currently, Emilio is the company CEO. In 1998, Emilio was promoted to general manager for [company] a leader in the field of [your industry]. In 2001, he worked for [name of former employers] where he was responsible for [main accomplishment]. Recently, Emilio has recruited Alicia Park as VP of marketing. Résumés are included in the "Supporting Documents" section.	

Company Philosophy

Brainstorm – Using keywords and phrases, describe your company's philosophy in terms of:

- ❏ Customer Service
- ❏ Environment
- ❏ Growth and Profit
- ❏ Management Style (top-down, bottom-up)

- ❏ New Technology (latest and greatest, time-tested)
- ❏ Personal Goals
- ❏ Price (discounts)
- ❏ Quality

- ❏ Range and Nature of Products and Services
- ❏ Community Relationship
- ❏ Customer Relationship
- ❏ Employee Relationship

- ❏ Industry Relationship
- ❏ Social Goals
- ❏ Value for the Money
- ❏ Work Environment (safety, security)

1	
2	
3	
4	
5	
6	

Elaborate in more detail upon critical points expressed in your company's mission statement:

	Sample: To achieve our mission of providing innovative and top-quality [product, e.g., "blenders"] that [state benefits, e.g., "are easy to use"] and improve the way people [do what, e.g., "prepare food"], we have the following goals: [describe general goals that further expand upon your mission].

Goals and Objectives

<u>SWOT Analysis</u> - *List strengths, weaknesses, opportunities, and threats facing your business:*

Strengths: **W**eaknesses:

A company resource or capacity (e.g., skilled staff, patents, cost advantage, exclusive access to high-grade materials)	*A company limitation, default, or defect* (e.g., poor location, weak brand name, poor access to key distribution channels)

Opportunities: **T**hreats:

Exploit and Search: A favorable situation or trend (e.g., arrival of new technologies, loosening of regulations).	*Confront or Avoid:* An unfavorable situation, trend, or barrier (e.g., emergence of substitute products, new trade barriers)

Turn your SWOT Analysis into three future long-term goals. Quantify these goals (see page 22):

Goal 1:	Goal 2:	Goal 3:

Other Long-term Goals – *Check goals that reflect your long-term plans:*

❏ Achieve a [15%] rate of return on investment.
❏ Achieve a business net worth of [$1m after three years].
❏ Build [new plants, warehouses].
❏ Capitalize on [location, parking, and other facilities].
❏ Enhance insurance coverage.
❏ Enhance the quality of products and services.
❏ Establish a research and development budget.
❏ Foster repeat business.

❏ Improve distributor or supplier relationships.
❏ Improve financial position.
❏ Improve internal communications.
❏ Improve labor relations and personnel training.
❏ Improve the effectiveness of ads and promotions.
❏ Increase market share by [10% in six months].
❏ Increase revenues.
❏ Open new retail locations.

Keys to Success

Describe three key strategies that will make your company successful (also refer to page 22 for ideas):

1		❏ achieving maximum production in one year ❏ brand recognition ❏ convenient parking ❏ competitive pricing ❏ high quality of service	❏ knowledgeable sales people ❏ location ❏ newspaper advertising ❏ repeat customers ❏ responsiveness to clients
2			
3			

Elaborate on your most important "keys to success" strategy:

Sample: For *Taste of Thailand* to succeed in the highly competitive Holland Village district, we need to build name recognition and network within the Singaporean community. Our main chef is well known within the business community, with 15+ years of experience at the Hyatt.

Legal Structure

Describe your current legal form and reasons for choosing it. Will you change it in the future?

❏ Sole Proprietorship   ❏ Limited Partnership   ❏ Subchapter S-Corporation   ❏ Other
❏ Partnership   ❏ C-Corporation   ❏ Limited Liability Company

Sample: LBM Inc. was formed in July of 2004 to manufacture revolutionary long-lasting lithium-ion replacement batteries for IBM, Sony, Toshiba, and Dell notebooks. LBM has been set up as an S-corporation in the state of Delaware, with branch offices in Taiwan and the U.S. The main shareholders are Will Bracken, Leslie Chang, and Selma Rivers.

To Do List

II. **Company Plan**

Company Description

✓ Location Analysis

Location, location, location.

REAL ESTATE MAXIM

✷

A city is like a magnet—the bigger it is, the greater the drawing power.

S. TENENBAUM

More advertising and promotion dollars will be needed to support a poor location.

STARTUP TIP

DAY 6

Find a location and compare it with your competitors'. List pros and cons.

Location Analysis

Finding the right location for your business is a challenging task. A business will often flourish or flounder simply because of a good or bad location. Be prepared, before making any long-term financial commitments, and before investing time and energy developing a site, to roll up your sleeves and conduct thorough research into any factors that might contribute to the success of your location. A little sweat now can prevent a big headache later on.

NOTE Include photos or drawings of your company location, office headquarters, facilities, etc., in your *Supporting Documents* section.

Sample Location Description

[Company name] will operate at [address] in the [describe location—e.g., CBD, XYZ shopping mall]. This location is desirable because: ❑ The area is experiencing rapid growth in our target market. ❑ It is positioned near a major intersection. ❑ Rent is below market. ❑ There is no direct competition in the area. ❑ It is in the heart of the [describe area] where most of the successful baby boomers and seniors live (see page 68 for more reasons). We are renting this building on a [XX] year lease and will be renovating at a cost of $[XX] based upon three estimates. The building is zoned [R-3, for commercial use]. [Satellite locations, office headquarters] are located at [list and describe other locations and reasons for choosing them].

$ucce$$ Story ➡ Founder of Holiday Inns, Charles Wilson

Founding Holiday Inns of America in the early 1950's, Charles Kemmons Wilson built the world's largest motor-hotel chain by manipulating a formula of quality at a reasonable price, customer service, and family accommodations conveniently located near major travel arteries. The Inn's many extras at the time—besides swimming pools and ice machines—included on-call babysitters, clergymen, and even dentists. Wilson was the first to offer standardized hotel rooms across the U.S. Today, there are over 1,900 Holiday Inn Hotels. Wilson's advice on determining what to offer potential customers: "The public will like what I like!" Wilson believes that "mental attitude plays a *far* more important role in a person's success or failure than mental capacity."

Successful
BUSINESS PLANNING
30 DAYS

Find a location and compare it with your competitors'. List pros and cons.

Location Analysis

Brainstorm – Select location type. Highlight the main advantage and disadvantage of this location:

Pros and Cons of Different Locations

❏ **Central Business District (CBD)** – *Pros*: Located in the downtown areas of most cities, usually bustling with people. Located amidst offices, banks, theaters, restaurants, and department stores. *Cons*: Many downtown areas have shifted to a less economically advantaged clientele. Rents are high. Buildings are old.

❏ **Clusters and Freestanding Stores** – *Pros*: Usually positioned at major intersections or located along highways running through cities. Good visibility. *Cons*: Less traffic than shopping centers.

❏ **Community Shopping Center** – *Pros*: With 20 or 30 stores, has parking for hundreds. *Cons*: Less traffic than malls.

❏ **Cooperative Lease** – *Pros*: Great if you can rent with a related business or large firm so you can ride on their coattails. *Cons*: Not easy to find the right match.

❏ **Downtown Location** – *Pros*: Large exposure to a greater number of people. *Cons*: Limited parking facilities, heavy car traffic for customers, higher operating costs, threat of urban decay.

❏ **Executive Suite** – *Pros*: Offers a host of business and support services, including a receptionist and conference room. Prestigious address. *Cons*: Doesn't exactly inspire a sense of stability.

❏ **Home Office** – *Pros*: Lower cost. Easy to set up. *Cons*: Clients may have difficulty getting to you and may feel uncomfortable doing business in your home. In some areas, home offices are illegal.

❏ **Neighborhood Center** – *Pros*: Smaller than community shopping centers, adequate parking spaces, usually consists of a row of stores which complement each other. Frequently, an anchor store, such as a supermarket, is its main attraction. Parking availability is usually good. *Cons*: What if the anchor store fails?

❏ **Neighborhood Shopping Street** – *Pros*: Usually has a well-balanced assortment of chain stores, supermarkets, fast-food outlets, and specialty stores. Rents are usually moderate. Business failures are relatively rare. *Cons*: Empty stores are quickly snapped up.

❏ **Shopping Mall** – *Pros*: Built-in traffic. Great for mass demand. Advertising can be pooled. Lots of parking. *Cons*: Rents are usually high. Not good for narrow product lines or unique services.

❏ **Regional Shopping Center** – *Pros*: Huge, 30 to 50 acres in size. Draws shoppers from villages and towns as far as an hour away by car. Parking facilities can usually handle over 1,000 vehicles. *Cons*: Not convenient for downtown residents. Easy to get lost amidst the competition.

❏ **Rural Location** – *Pros*: Good for warehouses and manufacturing plants. *Cons*: Little traffic. Long commuting times. More difficult getting basic services.

❏ **Secondary Business District** – *Pros*: Found along major arteries leading out of downtown districts. Buildings are newer. Closer to where residents live providing more convenient shopping. *Cons*: Rents are usually high. Compared to neighborhood centers, car traffic is heavier and more frustrating for customers as they come and leave the area.

Check below the most important factors in choosing your location area and site. Describe others:

Choosing the AREA

❑ *Accessibility to Customers* – Is it easy for your target market to drive, bus or walk to your site? If the site is in a remote location, will savings in rent offset the inconvenience?

❑ *Age, Family, and Income Demographics* – Are community demographics agreeable? Is the population growing? Is the area supported by a strong economic base?

❑ *Area Trends* – Is there good potential for economic growth? Is the area new and growing? Are new industries scheduled to open in the next several months?

❑ *Availability of Employee Housing* – If you need to provide employee housing, is it available at a reasonable price?

❑ *Community Services* – Are there good schools, hospitals, and recreation facilities in the area?

❑ *Construction Costs* – If you have to build are construction and labor costs reasonable?

❑ *Distance to Suppliers* – Are raw materials nearby?

❑ *Environmental Restrictions* – Are there noise restrictions?

❑ *Friendliness of Business Climate* – Has the neighborhood or area supported other businesses like yours in the past?

❑ *Insurance Costs* – Are area insurance rates reasonable?

❑ *Labor Pool and Market* – Is there a convenient source of labor from which to hire skilled and unskilled workers?

❑ *Media Channels* – Are advertising and PR opportunities cost-effective? Are there any cooperative ad programs?

❑ *Mortgage Costs* – If you need to build or buy in the area, can you get good terms for a loan or mortgage?

❑ *Municipal Services* – Is there adequate water and sewer services? Is there adequate fire and police protection?

❑ *Residency Quality* – Is there air, noise, or water pollution?

❑ *Support Systems* – Do you have easy access to banking, professional, security, janitorial, and other needed services?

❑ *Tax Advantages* – Are there any incentives for startups?

❑ *Trade Support* – Is there a local Chamber of Commerce, Merchants' Association, or other pertinent trade group?

❑ *Trading Area Size* – Is the "trading area" large enough?

❑ *Transportation Routes* – Is there easy access to highways, buses, taxis, and railways? Is a super highway planned?

Choosing the SITE

❑ *Building Appearance* – Does the building have an attractive exterior, adequate storefront, and highly visible display windows? Are sidewalks in good repair?

❑ *Building Design and Layout* – Does the physical site, fencing, roadways, and the design and layout of the building suit your needs? Does it have special lighting, heating, or ventilation features that you need?

❑ *Building Site Utilities and Communications Access* – Are water, sewer, power, phone, cable, and other utility conditions favorable? Is street lighting good?

❑ *Competitor Saturation* – Are competition levels healthy? Will you have a competitive advantage?

❑ *Convenience to Related Businesses* – Do related businesses nearby encourage greater customer traffic?

❑ *Customer Perceptions* – Does the building and area fit in with the perceptions of your customers?

❑ *Expansion Potential* – Is there expansion potential?

❑ *Future Land Value* – Will the land retain its value and appreciate over the years?

❑ *Leasing Conditions* – Can the site be leased? Under what costs and terms? Is the sq. ft. charge competitive? Does the landlord provide any helpful services?

❑ *Occupancy History* – Were previous stores successful? Is there a low business failure rate on nearby sites?

❑ *Parking* – Is there adequate and convenient parking?

❑ *Renovations* – Are minimal renovations required?

❑ *Site Location* – Is the site on the sunny side of the street? Is the location close to a main artery? How close is the building to bus stops?

❑ *Storage Available* – Is there adequate on-site storage? If not, are affordable warehouse facilities nearby?

❑ *Success Potential* – Are nearby businesses thriving?

❑ *Traffic Flow* – Are there enough pedestrians and cars passing? Does the location look conducive to drop-in customers? Do pedestrians look like prospective customers? Is street traffic fairly heavy all day?

❑ *Zoning Regulations* – Is the site free from local ordinances that would restrict operations?

Using keywords and phrases, summarize attributes of possible site locations (photocopy this work-sheet if necessary to evaluate and compare the pros and cons of multiple locations):

LOCATION ANALYSIS SUMMARY			
Address:		Name of Realtor:	
		Contact person:	
Phone #:		Sq. footage cost/month:	$
History of location			
Location in relation to target market			
Location in comparison to the competition			
Traffic patterns for customers			
Traffic patterns for suppliers			
Availability of parking (draw diagram)			
Notes on walking tour of the area			
Neighboring shops and local business climate			
Availability of raw materials and supplies			
Availability of labor force			
Labor rate of pay for the area			
Housing availability for employees			
Crime rate for area			
Zoning regulations			
Quality of public services, such as police and fire			
Adequacy of utilities (get info from company reps)			
Tax rates (state, county, payroll, special taxes)			

Detailed Location Analysis Worksheets <u>*Best Feature*</u> *– Summarize the main reason(s) for choosing your current or ideal business location (see sample description on page 66):*

- ❏ Convenient for our customers.
- ❏ Convenient for our shippers, suppliers, clients, and employees.
- ❏ Already has the necessary facilities and equipment to operate our type of business.

- ❏ Nearby retail businesses complement our services and attract customers who will likely want our services.
- ❏ Research shows that business failures within this area are rare.

- ❏ There is room for future expansion if needed.
- ❏ Traffic flow has been measured high. Pedestrian traffic is constant.
- ❏ We have negotiated a favorable lease.

_____

_____

_____

Sample: Lim and Ziegler Bolt & Supply will operate at [address] conveniently located in the secondary business district, with access to the growing west end market. We have also negotiated a favorable three-year lease for 3,000 sq. ft. of retail floor space at $.95 per sq. ft. 15% lower than market rates.

Location Cost – Detail the costs of your location and whether it is being rented, leased, or financed:

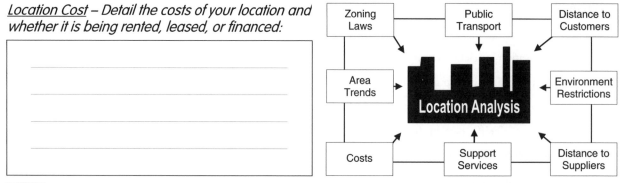

_____

_____

_____

Area – *Describe neighborhood (e.g., quiet, busy, near a college, labor force nearby, low crime rate):*

_____

_____

Describe accessibility to customers (e.g., near subway station, convenient public transportation):

_____

_____

Describe accessibility to suppliers (this is vital for manufacturers):

_____

_____

Describe availability of transport and shipping services (important to manufacturers and wholesalers):

_____

_____

_____

Describe other businesses in the area. Do they look prosperous (e.g., healthy mix of related services)?

_____

_____

_____

Site – *Describe "unique" site features (e.g., on the sunny side of the street, great view for café guests):*

Describe traffic patterns and location visibility (e.g., next to a major intersection, high pedestrian traffic):

Describe parking facilities. Diagram if necessary (e.g., free heated parking available year round):

Facilities – *Describe attributes of sales/office floor space (e.g., 2,000 sq. ft., 11 large display windows):*

Describe shelving, equipment, storage space, etc. (e.g., ovens included, numerous electrical outlets):

Describe condition and renovations required (e.g., carpet five years old, painting required, air con not included, light fixtures need updating, floor tile damaged at entrance, water damage in basement):

Expansion Potential – Describe growth features (e.g., ample storage space, upstairs vacant):

	Sample: Although our consulting firm is currently limited to 900 sq. ft. of office space in a downtown residential area, our site is zoned for commercial use. If we meet our financial goals for the fourth quarter of 2005, we plan to add three additional offices at an expected renovation cost of $32,000. To arrive at this figure, we have averaged estimates from three contractors.

Describe whether relocation will be necessary in the future and if so, its effects on operating costs:

Zoning Laws – Summarize any relevant zoning restrictions on expansion and daily operations:

Competition Comparison *– Compare location to competitors. **What** is your competitive advantage?*

	Sample: Our main competitors are scattered throughout the city in shopping malls and community shopping centers. However, our location is more accessible to college graduates, one of our key target markets. We have also compared pedestrian traffic with [key competitor] and calculated it to be 20% higher on weekends and 35% higher on weekdays.

Describe the main disadvantage of your location and how this might affect operations and profitability:

	Sample: One of the main disadvantages of our location is that our clients may feel uncomfortable visiting our home office. To alleviate this problem, we have added a second entrance for home use. The main entrance is for business use only and is clearly marked with company signage.

DAY 7

Describe growth strategies once initial goals and objectives have been met.

Outline R&D plans.

Planned Expansion

If you plan to expand your business at some point in the future, outline and support how you plan to do this. Keep in mind that market forces should ultimately determine the size of your company. When sales increase, allow your company to expand naturally; don't force it. Likewise when sales decrease, make sure your company can contract so fixed costs don't consume all your profits.

When Should You Actively Pursue Growth?

Before committing to expansion, determine whether you and your business are indeed ready to expand. Consider the following:

Expand if your business is already profitable. Profitability is important to business growth because it makes it easier to obtain financing for expansion. However, this is the opposite of how accounting systems are normally set up for tax purposes. To reduce taxes, accountants and business owners often try to show a loss or as little profit as possible, which allows the business to retain more cash. From this standpoint, if you need financing, your business should be profitable for several years before initiating a growth phase.

Expand if you can project increased profits. Two ways to increase profits are to increase sales volume or increase the profit per sale. If these two can be achieved simultaneously, the resulting growth is that much more profitable.

Expand when you can spot "saturation" or "operational bottlenecks" in your present facility. Determine how many additional customers you could service by building up or out and compare the additional sales to the cost of construction and temporary inconvenience. For example, if you have noticed increasing numbers of abandoned carts in your grocery store, this could mean shoppers are leaving when they realize the checkout line is too long. To solve this problem, increase your number of checkouts.

Expand when you can spread existing fixed costs over a large sales volume. When expansion can result in spreading existing fixed costs over a large sales volume, the decision to increase size is justified. However, whenever

To Do List

II. **Company Plan**

Company Description

✓ Planned Expansion
✓ Research and Development

You make the best products you can, and you grow as fast as you deserve to.
KENNETH OLSEN

✳

During a growth phase, be prepared to experience increased personal commitment, increased pressure, and reductions in cash flow.

✳

Many managers of unprofitable businesses believe to solve their problems they should grow to spread fixed costs over a larger number of units, thereby improving gross margin. This is a mistake. Fix your problem first. Don't make the hole bigger.
PROFIT TIP

you have to increase fixed costs to attain higher sales levels, carefully investigate the proportion of the increase before proceeding with growth plans.

Protecting Your Company from Explosive Growth

Controlled growth is growth that is cautious, carefully charted, and carried along through regular planning sessions, progress reviews, and program modifications. On the other hand, explosive growth is growth that embraces a substantial element of peril that may actually destroy the potential of a new company. When not backed by sales, it scares most bankers and investors and can lead to serious complications (see page 77 for "Symptoms of Dangerous Growth").

Sample Growth Strategy Statements

After having successfully introduced [product name] into the [Canadian] market, we will continue to expand into the following two market areas:

[Market Area #1]	[Market Area #2]

Sample 1 – To increase sales in the [Canadian] market we will increase national advertising and begin targeting smaller accounts and specialty outlets. We also intend to offer our sales reps the opportunity to sell our products exclusively by joining our company, when we reach our first year sales goals. Those who desire to remain independent will be replaced with our own sales staff.

Sample 2 – After having successfully completed our entry phase into the [Vancouver] market, we will expand by: (a) enlarging telemarketing pool from 8 to 15, (b) doubling the number of direct sales reps, and (c) franchising into neighboring cities, including [Seattle, Victoria, and Portland].

Sample Targeting New Market Statements

To foster continued growth, we will use the following methods to expand our customer base and increase sales: ❑ conduct regional market surveys ❑ develop more personal contact with clients to determine new needs ❑ distribute complementary [products, services] to potential customers in the [describe area] ❑ exhibit at local and national trade shows including [list exhibits] ❑ follow up on federal government trade leads ❑ network within [list organizations] ❑ seek new partnerships with the ABC and XYZ corporations ❑ set up a customer referral system ❑ invest $[XX] in R&D.

Research and Development

To stay competitive, you must keep abreast of new technologies and marketing developments that may affect your business and its operations. Research and development is not only for high technology startups and manufacturers. Service operations can also benefit from such efforts.

Sample Research and Development Statements

[Company name] has already spent a considerable amount of time researching and developing [my/our] [product] within a budget of $[XX]. So far [I/we] have been able to discover [describe discovery or development], which has helped [reduce costs, increase sales]. The largest achievement to date is the discovery of ... [describe discovery). However, now that [my/our] research is becoming more [experimental, labor intensive, on the cutting edge], [I/we] anticipate a considerable lag time before results can be realized. [I/We] have budgeted [X% of revenues, $XX] for R&D over the next [X] years.

[My/Our] next research project will center on [describe next project].

[My/Our] present joint research program with [name of university or institution] has proven very beneficial. [I/We] have also been investigating several government funding sources [describe programs].

[Company name] will continue to evaluate new [product, service] opportunities that will foster growth. To facilitate this evaluation, management [has developed, is committed to improving] [describe criteria or standards developed].

> *Excellent firms don't believe in excellence—only in constant improvement and constant change.*
> **TOM PETERS**
>
> ❋
>
> *Capital isn't so important in business. Experience isn't so important. You can get both these things. What is important is ideas. If you have ideas, you have the main asset you need, and there isn't any limit to what you can do with your business and your life.*
> **HARVEY S. FIRESTONE**

$ucce$$ Story ➡ The Wal-Mart Empire of Sam Walton

Every person who dreams of building a great retail business needs to study Sam Walton. Walton took a single dime store in a hard living cotton town and turned it into the Wal-Mart Empire, the largest retailer in the world. An undisputed "Captain of Commerce," he set the standard for listening to his customers and employees. In the words of Jack Welch, past Chairman of the Board for G.E., "Sam Walton understood people the way Thomas Edison understood innovation, and Henry Ford, production. He brought out the very best in his employees, gave his very best to his customers, and taught something of value to everything he touched." Walton was one of the first to implement an employee profit sharing plan that included stock options and store discounts. Sam believed that "individuals don't win; teams do."

DAY 7 **Worksheets**

Describe growth strategies once initial goals and objectives have been met. Outline R&D plans.

Planned Expansion

Brainstorm – Describe how you will expand your business ("Start small, Think BIG!"):

❑ **Downward Vertical Diversification –** If profits depend on the cost of raw materials, a profitable growth strategy may be to buy a farm or mine to produce your own. This strategy also makes sense if product quality is based on a consistent supply of goods at an acceptable quality level.

❑ **Upward Vertical Diversification –** Most manufacturing startups are forced to use existing marketing channels and sell through established manufacturer representatives, independent wholesalers, etc., who have access to the market. However, as you grow, it makes sense to analyze your distribution system to see if you can increase profitability by hiring your own sales team, contracting distributors, buying a truck fleet, opening your own wholesale operation, or adding retail or factory outlet stores.

❑ **Horizontal Diversification –** Horizontal diversification involves adding other similar products or business lines. For example, a soft drink manufacturer sees a new market for bottled water. The bottled water is related to its current activity and uses some of the same equipment, thus reducing overhead costs.

❑ **Relocation –** If it appears unlikely that you can draw more customers to your present location (at a reasonable cost), consider moving closer to your customers. A location on *Main Street*, in a shopping mall, or an industrial park may cost you more in rent, but if you gain exposure to new customers, it may be a sound investment.

Others – ❑ direct marketing ❑ exporting ❑ joint ventures ❑ network marketing ❑ licensing ❑ franchising

Expansion Method #1

	Sample: After having successfully completed our entry phase into the Hong Kong market, we plan to increase our number of direct sales reps in mainland China from three to eight, as well as open a wholesale distribution center in Shanghai. Ella Chan, manager of Kowloon Metal Spring Factory, has expressed interest in managing and funding part of this center.

Expansion Method #2

List and describe other strategies you plan to use to expand your business or increase market share:

Sample: To foster continued growth, we are currently developing a more personal business relationship with Revlon, our top client. We are also working on a joint venture with Calvin Klein to market and distribute personalized sports watches.	

*Write three reasons **why** your company is ready to expand. For startups, write which company goals need to be met or **what** conditions in the marketplace will be necessary to support expansion:*

Sample: If the Canadian government reduces foreign ownership restrictions in the telecommunications industry, opening up the market to U.S. service providers, we are well positioned to expand our phone card service into the Toronto market.

1	
2	
3	

Write down problems you anticipate as your company grows and how you plan to solve them:

Symptoms of Dangerous Growth

- ❑ climbing employee turnover
- ❑ confused lines of authority
- ❑ dissatisfaction and even dissension among customers and employees
- ❑ excessive numbers of employees
- ❑ increased overhead
- ❑ loss of marketing coordination and control
- ❑ proliferation of departments
- ❑ poorly trained department heads and supervisors
- ❑ runaway ad costs
- ❑ slipping profits despite increasing sales

Research and Development

Brainstorm – Describe your research and development strategies:

- ❑ attend industry conferences
- ❑ bigger emphasis on training
- ❑ establish product selection and evaluation criteria
- ❑ improve market research in [list area(s) and describe]

- ❑ increase spending by $[XX]
- ❑ joint venture with [partner]
- ❑ [product] will be upgraded
- ❑ raise quality standards by [describe]
- ❑ read industry publications

- ❑ speed up future R&D by [describe]
- ❑ strengthen development teams
- ❑ test market [describe product]
- ❑ The life cycle of [product] will end in [XX] years. We must [describe].

R&D Strategy #1 – E.g.: ❑ develop a customer satisfaction questionnaire ❑ conduct a website log file analysis

Sample: The *Gartner Group* has reported that, "more than 50% of web sales are lost because visitors can't find content." To keep abreast of customer buying trends and increase visitor retention, we have invested in WebTrends Log Analyzer software to monitor website usage. To facilitate the evaluation of new products to update our website and catalog offerings, we have also developed a 30-point profitability checklist after surveying 20 mail order suppliers.

R&D Strategy #2 – E.g.: ❑ increase R&D staff ❑ reverse engineer company XYZ's thingamabob gadget

What *is your R&D budget?* ***How*** *much are competitors spending on R&D? Do you have any R&D guidelines?* ***What*** *will you do if an existing product or service is threatened by a new competing technology?*

Sample: We have already spent two years researching and developing our U-design bicycle seat within a budget of $85,000. So far we have been able to discover three innovations that have reduced product manufacturing costs and two that have improved seat comfort. For these two latter innovations, we have secured two patents. We have also budgeted $50,000 for R&D in 2005 and for the following three years, 6.8% of gross profits. Currently, we are investigating durability of seat materials.

DAY 8

Describe your principal products and services. Outline future sales plans.

Merchandising Plan

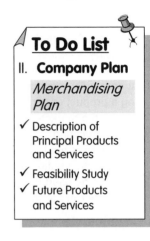

A *Merchandising Plan*, also known as a *Sales Plan*, describes what products or services you will provide or produce. A merchandising plan also makes projections based upon estimated sales to determine the amount of inventory needed. It also details and compares prices, quality, and credit terms of suppliers.

Description of Principal Products and Services

Under this heading, describe your products and services assessing their strengths, weaknesses, and marketability. Explain any regulatory or certification requirements. If you have both products and services that work together—e.g., a warranty service—make sure to mention this. Also, indicate features and benefits that both you and the competition provide, those that some of the competition provide, and those that only you provide. Specific questions you should answer include:

❑ What is special or unique about your product or service that separates it from the competition? Are you the only one who offers it or are there a few others?

❑ Will your product or service be competitive based on its quality, selection, price, value, or location? Will your product or service lead to repeat business?

❑ What are the fixed costs associated with providing your product or service? What raw materials are needed or used?

❑ What are the technologies used and technical advantages of your production techniques over your competitors?

❑ Are any special skills needed to provide the product or service? Do you have these skills?

The information compiled and organized in your "Merchandising Plan" makes great fodder for writing brochures and other promotional items.
MARKETING TIP

Like China, the Internet is a huge new market. It's up to you to figure out what to do with it. Use it as a prospecting tool, make connections with people, add value for your existing customers.
LARRY CHASE
Internet Marketing Consultant

Sample Product and Service Descriptions

[Company name] intends to offer [product, service]. This [product, service]:

Product – ❑ offers the lowest price on the market ❑ is the most technically advanced ❑ offers more useful features than the competition ❑ saves customers time and money ❑ offers our users better value per dollar ❑ provides an alternative way to [describe goal].

Service – ❑ provides a service that is not presently available in this area ❑ is strengthened by a team with combined experience of [XX] years.

We have a [copyright, patent, trademark] and exclusive marketing rights for this [product, service] in the [geographical area]. Our exclusive marketing rights will last until [XX] years at which time they may be extended for [XX] years. Even though the technology used to create [product] is new, we expect that others will be able to reproduce our results within [XX] years. To remain competitive, we will need to devote approximately [XX]% of revenues towards R&D.

Researching Hot New Ideas for Products and Services

To hunt down new products and services, read consumer magazines, trade publications, and competitors' catalogs. Make it a habit of visiting libraries, government research centers, manufacturer representatives, trade fairs, and anywhere particulars about people's buying habits and needs can be observed. Keep your eyes peeled for technological, lifestyle, demographic, and competitive trends. Learn everything you can about your target market.

> **Realize that the key to knowing what can be sold tomorrow is understanding what is being sold today.**

Get every easily available catalog or magazine targeted towards your target market. Interview friends, family, and people on the streets who might be interested in your business. Ask them what products and services they want or need. Visit your local library and make a list of all available resources and which are most useful to you. Check if you library has: ❑ *Thomas Register of American Manufacturers* (identifies suppliers, distributors, customers, and competitors) ❑ *Small Business Sourcebook* (lists trade shows and publications). Also visit the *World Trade Organization* (wto.org), which has extensive resources covering topics such as trade, e-commerce, and IPR.

Feasibility Study

A *Feasibility Study* assesses the viability of a specific business concept, product, or service in terms of: (1) the market, (2) the competition, and (3) the opportunity for sales. It can also be used to identify pitfalls and how you plan to avoid them. Start by identifying products and services you plan to sell, along with the needs they satisfy. Describe whether these needs are presently unfulfilled, whether demand can be easily influenced by advertising, and to what extent the market is saturated. Use the "80 Drill Questions" on pages 84 to 85 to help assess potential.

Future Products and Services

The word "entrepreneur" means *to act*. Entrepreneurs *continuously search* for new areas of opportunity, envisioning what the future will be like, how it will change, and what needs may result. Under this heading, describe growth areas, along with strategies you will use to develop new products and services.

Creating New Market Opportunities

Search for the unmet need. Entrepreneurs are bloodhounds, sniffing out the unmet needs and wants of the target market they wish to serve. To *win* new customers, ask yourself: "What's the unmet need and how can I meet this unmet need before someone else does?" To *keep them for life*, ask: "How can I anticipate their unmet needs before they even know they have them?" Outlined below are two strategies for finding unmet needs:

- *Look for an existing network of distributors or dealers who do not have access to a product.* Sometimes, consumers can't get products because local suppliers don't have them or can't get them due to unforeseen circumstances—e.g., a blizzard closes down city roads and railways, hence essential items have to be flown in by air.

- *Look for pain in people's lives and solve it.* Pain can be found by looking at routine activities and noticing their rhythms. Where does the rhythm fail, where does anxiety build? At that point, an opportunity waits.

Exploit change. There is no doubt that the entrepreneurs who prosper *tomorrow* are the ones who "adapt quickly to change" *today*. However, of more interest is the fact that the overwhelming majority of truly successful entrepreneurs are the ones who actually "seek and exploit change." Spotting change is a manner of having big ears and watchful eyes. It means jotting down notes everywhere you go hoping that one day they may add up to something no one else has yet recognized or taken advantage of. It means going to trade shows and business conferences, and listening in office elevators. It means reading carefully the business pages of newspapers and watching for contracts received and personnel changes. It even means getting invited to your competitors' office parties by hook or by crook.

To exploit change and create new opportunities look for: ✦ changes in perception ✦ changes within industries ✦ changing values between suppliers and customers ✦ complacency ✦ converging technologies ✦ demographic changes ✦ intellectual arrogance ✦ industry regulation or deregulation ✦ lack of change ✦ rapid growth ✦ recession ✦ unexpected success or failure.

A new product is developed and marketed. What is the probability that it will fail in the marketplace? (4 in 5).
A. JAMES FIX
The Odds Almanac

✳

If only we could sell a set of lamps for every Chinese bike.
DANSK INDUSTRI
Denmark, Workshop Tagline

I invent nothing. I rediscover.
AUGUSTE RODIN

✳

A generation ago, there were a thousand men to every opportunity, while today there are a thousand opportunities to every man.
HENRY FORD

✳

When one door of happiness closes, another opens; but often we look so long at the closed door that we do not see the one which has been opened for us.
HELEN KELLER

Foster innovation. Innovation is organized, systematic, and rational work that begins with the analysis of opportunities. These opportunities exist only in the marketplace. Profitable innovation is the result of an *effect* in the economy or society, a change in the *behavior* of customers, or a change in a *process*—i.e., how people work and produce. Profitable innovation is always close to the market, focused on the market, and inspired by the market. It begins by finding practical needs and then meeting those needs.

To foster innovation and create new market opportunities: ◆ allow your workers to develop ideas in small unified teams ◆ avoid tunnel vision ◆ carefully analyze all the necessary factors before you innovate ◆ develop a specialty skill ◆ don't be different for the sake of being different ◆ don't splinter your efforts ◆ don't try and innovate for the future—innovate for the present ◆ don't copy or steal—improve and emulate ◆ encourage free thought during meetings ◆ focus on actual progress, not paperwork ◆ give a little to gain a lot ◆ keep funding low, deadline pressure high ◆ keep your innovations simple ◆ look, ask, and listen ◆ nurture experimentation ◆ put together a "reverse engineering" team ◆ put yourself in the shoes of others to gain objectivity over your new innovation ◆ strive to be the market standard ◆ take advantage of someone else's innovation ◆ try not to be too clever ◆ urge your people to make at least ten mistakes a day ◆ when introducing an innovation, don't be tentative about it.

Enter a new market with an old product or introduce a new product to an old market. Entering a new market with a new product or service is very challenging, especially for a startup business. You can never accurately predict whether the product or service will perform satisfactorily nor may you have the experience to be certain it will meet the needs of your customers. Likely, you will end up with the impossible task of trying to sell something you have never sold before to people who have never bought anything from you. You may even lose old customers who are left wondering where your loyalties went. When entering new markets or introducing new products, be cautious. If entering a *new market*, it is wiser (and more profitable) to sell *old products* with proven sales. On the other hand, if introducing a *new product*, it is wiser to target an *old market*.

Entering New Markets

	Existing Product	Innovative Product	New Product
Existing Market	Women's Shampoo	Alternative Greeting Cards	Solid State Digital Camera
Identifiable Market (targetable)	Clothes for Professional Women	Two Way Cable TV	Specialty Sports Car
Unknown Market	Mobile Pet Grooming Service	Personal Computers	Video Disks

DAY 8 Worksheets 🕐

Describe your principal products and services. Outline future sales plans.

Description of Principal Products and Services

Profitable Products – Check the following factors and characteristics as they apply to your product:

- ❑ better than the competition
- ❑ comes complete with everything you need
- ❑ convenient to use
- ❑ sells 3 to 4 times more than cost
- ❑ does not demand more time than it is worth to develop or market
- ❑ durable, unbreakable
- ❑ easily understood through its advertising
- ❑ easy to ship or mail

- ❑ easy to maintain
- ❑ fully guaranteed
- ❑ hard to find in retail stores
- ❑ has a definite targetable market
- ❑ has no moving parts to break down (and if it does, moving parts are hermetically sealed against the probing fingers of three-year-olds)
- ❑ has sold well previously through mail order and retail
- ❑ has universal appeal

- ❑ made out of quality materials
- ❑ necessary to enjoy sports or other leisure activities
- ❑ novel and unusual
- ❑ recommended by experts or authorities
- ❑ safe to use (will not injure children and cause lawsuits)
- ❑ satisfies a real customer need
- ❑ scientifically constructed
- ❑ will generate repeat orders

Profitable Services – Check the following factors and characteristics as they apply to your service:

- ❑ has a definite targetable market
- ❑ has done well previously as a home or service business
- ❑ has general appeal

- ❑ has not saturated the market
- ❑ keeps customers coming back
- ❑ lends itself to the merchandising of related products

- ❑ produces long-lasting results
- ❑ satisfies a real customer need
- ❑ does not demand more time than it is worth to develop or market

Describe your principal product or service line. **Why** *will it be profitable? (refer back to pages 79–80):*

Sample: [Product line], our principal product line, is [describe]. This line has historically sold very well to the [type of] market. We have also developed our own [product A]. Spin-off accessories have also been designed, though these will not be ready for shipment until [date].	

Conduct a SWOT Analysis of your main product or service (or product or service line):

S	
W	
O	
T	

Using keywords and phrases, provide details and an analysis of other important products and services:

	Product/Service	Description	Unique Features (SWOT Analysis)	Development Stage
1				
2				

Describe customer/client benefits of using your product or service (see GB📖 #59 and GB📖 #62):

Sample Benefit and Feature Statement: "Families will feel safer (*benefit*) when riding on the latest model of our XYZ steel-belted radials due to a new patented interwoven-blankets-of-steel design embedded deep in the tread (*product feature*)."

	BENEFITS of Using Your Product or Service		
	❏ authentic	❏ exclusive, distinctive	❏ nothing artificial
	❏ built to last	❏ innovative, new	❏ one size fits all
	❏ comfortable	❏ laboratory tested	❏ quality controlled
	❏ compact, portable	❏ limited edition	❏ reinforced, rugged
	❏ confidential	❏ long-lasting results	❏ saves time, labor
	❏ convenient	❏ low-cost installation	❏ simple to operate
	❏ custom-designed	❏ minimal timeframe	❏ space-saving
	❏ durable construction	❏ modified, improved	❏ uniform production
	❏ easy to repair	❏ multipurpose	❏ usable, easy to use
	❏ endorsed by …	❏ newly redesigned	❏ wholesome

Feasibility Study

🧠 *Brainstorm – Select and answer from the "80 Drill Questions" on the next page those most applicable to your business idea, product, or service. Answer quickly without second-guessing yourself. Eventually, you should become so familiar with these questions that they become second nature (i.e., drilled into you). Summarize the most important factors that address the feasibility of your business concept.*

Future Products and Services

List strategies you will use to find new products and services (e.g., exploit change; see pages 81–82):

1	
2	
3	

List possible future products or services you plan to provide your target market. Describe reason(s) why:

1

2

3

4

❏ **Idea** ❏ **Product** ❏ **Service**

80 Business "Drill Questions"

MARKET DEMAND
❏ Is there a definite targetable market?
❏ Is the target market responsive?
❏ Is the target market stable?
❏ Is the target market not yet saturated with competitive interests?

❏ Is the target market growing?
❏ Do you have enough experience and training to understand the needs of the target market?
❏ Are the strategies of other companies, who have already successfully catered to the target market, easy to duplicate?

❏ Can advertising easily influence the target market?
❏ Is the target market more than large enough to make the project worthwhile?
❏ Are you genuinely interested in the typical customer representative of the target market?

PRODUCT/SERVICE VALUE
❏ Is it a quality product or service?
❏ Is it unique?
❏ Is it competitive? ❏ Is it innovative?

❏ Does it offer real value to its customers?
❏ Will it be easy to sell?
❏ Does it have one easily desirable benefit of incredible value?

❏ Will you have no fear of financial loss if you give it an ironclad guarantee?
❏ Would you buy it yourself?
❏ Does it truly interest you?

COMPANY EASE OF FORMATION
❏ Is it compatible with your current mission statement and company philosophy?
❏ Does it lend itself easily to a catchy name?

❏ Does it lend itself easily to a catchy slogan?
❏ Can it be trademarked or branded?
❏ Will your logo look impressive attached to it?
❏ Is it photogenic?

❏ Can it be easily packaged?
❏ Is it not too revolutionary?
❏ Will it create customer apprehension?
❏ Does it fit in with your own personal image?

COMPANY SET-UP COSTS
❏ Can a company be set up to sell it with little capital investment?
❏ Will it generate a return on investment fast, so you won't suffer cash flow problems?
❏ Is there little government red tape?

❏ Can a company be set up quickly?
❏ Will you be able to convince a bank to lend you money for it if you need it?
❏ Will you be able to convince friends, family, relatives, and your spouse to support it?
❏ Can you accumulate resource materials on it?

❏ Do you know people who would be willing to help you set up a company to sell it?
❏ Does it allow you to take advantage of advanced technology?
❏ Can you run the business part-time so you won't have to quit your regular job?

ADVERTISING POTENTIAL
❏ Can you use cheap advertising to market it?
❏ Can you take advantage of as many forms of advertising as possible to market it?
❏ Can it be explained easily through words?
❏ Will it live up to its advertising?

❏ Can it be explained easily through pictures in advertising?
❏ Will it give your customer just what they expected, and a little bit more?
❏ Can it be promoted well through direct marketing channels?

❏ Can it be made to appeal to a customer's basic instincts, desires, and drives?
❏ Will it take little advertising before the consumer overcomes reservations about it?
❏ Will you be able to copy your competitors' more successful advertising practices?

MARKET POTENTIAL
❏ Can it be tested without investing a large amount of capital?
❏ Does it lend itself to a variety of market testing strategies?
❏ Will market testing results be accurate?

❏ Can your friends or family test it and give you accurate feedback?
❏ Can recognized institutions test it and give you accurate feedback?
❏ Can you find a good mailing or customer list for it in which to test market response?

❏ Can you promote it at a trade show?
❏ Will you be able to test it within a short period of time?
❏ Is the market timing of it right?
❏ Can strangers test it and give you accurate feedback?

EXPANSION POTENTIAL
❏ Does it fit in with your long-range plans?
❏ If it takes off, do you have the resources to capitalize on it?
❏ Will it be easy to find the right kind of skilled labor if your company needs to hire?

❏ Can you easily train staff to promote it?
❏ Can it be sold through regular distribution channels?
❏ Would the government or large corporations be interested in it?
❏ Can you sell it internationally?

❏ Will it have a long sales life or is it just a fad?
❏ Can you improve upon it at a later date and offer a better version?
❏ Will you be able to sell the idea to other entrepreneurs?

PROFIT POTENTIAL
❏ Does it have a high enough markup that people are willing to pay?
❏ Is it unlikely to be returned?
❏ Does it lend itself to repeat sales?

❏ Will company overhead be low?
❏ Will it be easy to transfer profits to other investments?
❏ If you tire of the business, will it be easy to sell?
❏ Are there tax advantages in selling it?

❏ Will you be able to build owner's equity by buying quality commercial land?
❏ If sales start to lag, will you be able to cut your losses and start another project?
❏ Will it be easy to protect with patents, etc.?

Research Sources – *Check and list research sources for new products and services (see* GB📖 *#15):*

General

- ❏ Business Newspapers (e.g., *Wall Street Journal*, www.wsj.com)
- ❏ Business Periodicals (e.g., *Advertising Age, Forbes*)
- ❏ Corporate Annual Reports
- ❏ Customer Surveys
- ❏ Focus Groups
- ❏ Government Docs. (The U.S. Dept. of Commerce compiles statistical data from the Census Bureau including *The U.S. Industrial Outlook*)
- ❏ Internal Records (previous buying patterns, stock records, complaint analysis)
- ❏ Newspaper Content Analysis (monitor headline frequency for trends)
- ❏ Observations (other businesses, flea markets, gift shows, areas in transition, nearby cities)
- ❏ Trade Associations (usually have trade and industry studies)
- ❏ Trade Shows and Conventions
- ❏ Trash Analysis (knowing what people throw out tells you what they buy and don't want anymore)

Online

- ❏ American Society of Association Executives (www.asaenet.org)
- ❏ Dun Bradstreet (www.dnb.com) for credit reports and financial info
- ❏ Federal Statistics (www.fedstats.gov)
- ❏ Forrester.com (customer trends)
- ❏ Gartner.com (biz and tech research)
- ❏ Google.com (keyword search for products, trade names)
- ❏ Hoovers.com (background information on individual companies)
- ❏ Jupiterresearch.com (Internet data)
- ❏ LexisNexis.com (legal and biz info)
- ❏ National Association of Manufacturers (www.nam.org)
- ❏ SEC Online (www.sec.gov) public information on specific companies
- ❏ Statistics Canada (www.statcan.ca and www.strategis.ic.gc.ca)
- ❏ Statistics.com (data sources directory)
- ❏ U.S. Stats (www.stat-usa.gov)
- ❏ U.S. Census (www.census.gov)
- ❏ U.S. International Programs Center (www.census.gov/ipc/www/)
- ❏ U.S. List of Statistical Websites (www.census.gov/sdc/www/)

Library

- ❏ *Business Periodical Index* (lists articles of major business publications)
- ❏ *Consumer's Index* (lists articles evaluating products and services)
- ❏ *Dialog* (has over five billion pages of info; indexes commercial market research studies; www.dialog.com)
- ❏ *Encyclopedia of Business Information Sources* (lists major sources of statistical info, trade associations)
- ❏ *InfoTrak* Database (magazine and journal articles back to 1980)
- ❏ *Predicasts F&S Forecasts* (index to articles from 700+ business trade magazines, publications, and reports)
- ❏ *Small Business Sourcebook* (lists trade shows, publications, etc.)
- ❏ *Sources & Business Organizations, Agencies, and Publications Directory*
- ❏ *Standard Rate & Data Service (SRDS) Catalogs* (bible of the advertising media trade)
- ❏ *Statistical Reference Index* (SRI indexes studies from organizations and trade associations)
- ❏ *World Chambers of Commerce Directory*

European Union and Asia Pacific Business Research – *Check sources for new product and service ideas:*

Online

- ❏ Asia Pacific Economic Cooperation, APEC (www.apecsec.org.sg)
- ❏ Association of South East Asian nations (www.aseansec.org)

- ❏ Cordis (www.cordis.lu) European Union research and innovation documents and news
- ❏ EUbusiness.com (Europe's leading independent online business information service about the EU)

- ❏ Europa (www.europa.eu.int) portal site of the European Union with free statistical info at Eurostat
- ❏ National Bureau of Statistics of China (www.stats.gov.cn)
- ❏ Taiwan Trade (www.cetra.org.tw)

Find suppliers. Take steps to protect your ideas.

To Do List

II. **Company Plan**

Merchandising Plan

✓ Purchasing Plan
✓ Proprietary and
  Exclusive Rights
  Obtained

Purchasing Plan

In this section of your *Merchandising Plan*, explain when orders will be placed, when delivery will be received, when inventory will peak, when re-orders will no longer be placed, and when certain items will no longer be stocked. Also, describe where you get inventory and raw materials from, buying terms, volume discount policies, and delivery policies. Discuss and list names and addresses of key suppliers. Describe where they are located, why you chose them, and other qualities unique to each supplier. Include cost breakdowns and rate sheets to back up your statements. Outline any policies you might have for dealing with suppliers.

Choosing Suppliers

A reliable supplier is critical to business success. But don't make the mistake of relying only on one. Find at least two or three suppliers for each product you sell. Let them compete against each other for your business.

Getting the Most Out of Your Suppliers

To get the most out of your suppliers, use the following strategies: ◆ ask suppliers if they have a program to contribute to advertising costs ◆ buy from suppliers during their slow periods to get discounts or better terms ◆ buy in volume for discounts ◆ buy only the amount you expect to sell regardless of how favorable the price or credit terms—especially when starting out ◆ develop multiple supply sources and alternative sources for raw materials ◆ don't always pay what suppliers ask—negotiate a favorable supply contract ◆ establish your credit by paying on time ◆ maintain good business relations with all suppliers ◆ offer partial or advance payment in return for discounts ◆ prepare a written policy for dealing with suppliers ◆ take advantage of discounts for early payment ◆ to keep your cash a bit longer, send your payment checks just before they are due.

Developing a Purchasing Budget

In developing a purchasing budget, start by making sales projections as accurate as possible. Also, make sure to leave enough room to maneuver to

When a man is trying to sell you something, don't imagine he is that polite all the time.
EDGAR WATSON HOWE

✳

Nothing astonishes men so much as common sense and plain dealing.
RALPH WALDO EMERSON

Having too many suppliers can lead to wasted time with sales people, costly bookkeeping, duplication of lines, and mixed-up inventory.
PROFIT TIP

take advantage of current deals or discounts by incorporating a *reserve fund* into your budget.

Planning Stock Purchases with Sales – A good purchasing plan maintains inventory levels in close relation to monthly sales to prevent over-or under-buying. For different months of the year, stock levels should adjust. Sales records will show peaks and valleys, and purchases must be precisely timed to move with customer buying. Stock levels must peak just before major customer buying periods and diminish as demand tapers off. Failure to peak or diminish stocks at the right time can seriously affect sales and profits.

Remaining "Open to Buy" – "Open to buy" is a condition whereby the merchant leaves a portion of the purchasing budget to buy additional items as the season progresses. It provides a built-in flexibility to take advantage of special deals.

Calculating a Profitable Reorder Point

A good purchasing plan outlines when stock should be reordered so you don't run out (and lose sales) or carry too much (and increase carrying costs). To determine your *reorder point*, that is the minimum stock level at which additional quantities need to be ordered, calculate your *Economic Order Quantity* (EOQ), and how many days it takes to receive a new order (refer to pages 127–129).

Reorder Point for a Shoe Wholesaler – Sue Smith owns XYZ Shoes Inc. and sells 10,000 pairs of slippers per year. She calculates her EOQ for the slippers to be 3,162 units per order (see page 128 for calculation). According to her EOQ, her inventory of slippers should turnover 3.162 times a year or every 115 days. Since it takes 14 days to receive an order, she needs to reorder 3,162 pairs of slippers 101 days after receiving her last order. To keep from being overstocked, she reorders when her inventory records show that she has 385 pairs of slippers left. She calculates this value by finding the percentage of stock needed to last until a new order is received (total $ value of stock can be used instead of EOQ):

Reorder Point = EOQ × [# of days to receive order ÷ inventory turnover days]
= 3,162 units × [14/115] = **385 units**

Establishing a "Receiving" or "Order Inspection" Policy

The criteria and procedures used to inspect incoming raw materials and inventory should be documented and publicized to all parties involved. An order inspection policy outlines: (1) *What is done at time of delivery*—e.g., each carton is carefully examined for damage and all merchandise is counted; (2) *What is done if damage is discovered*—e.g., damaged materials are held at the point they are received; (3) *What procedures are followed for carrier inspection of damaged items*—e.g., steps are taken to make sure all damaged items are not moved before they are inspected by the carrier; and (4) *What is done after inspection*—e.g., damaged materials are kept until written authorization from the supplier is received to return damaged items. To facilitate this task, the use of a "Receiving Report" is common practice.

Receiving Report				
Report #:		**Date:**	**Our P.O. #:**	

Received From:		**For:**	
Name:		Name:	
Address:		Address:	
Phone/Fax:		Department:	

Shipped VIA	Express	Transport	Mail	**Delivery Charges**	Prepaid	Collect	**C.O.D. Charges**	**Bill of Lading #**	**No. of Packages**	**Total Kg**
					☐	☐				

Quantity	**Item #**	**✓**	**Weight**	Accepted	Rejected	**Description**

Received by	**Inspected by**	**Complete**	**Partial**	**NOTES:**

Establishing an Inventory Discontinuation Policy

The last part of a purchasing plan involves establishing a set of guidelines to help determine when to discontinue stocking an item. These guidelines can be based on criteria such as the following: ✦ a newer model of the product has come out making the older one obsolete ✦ the product failed to meet a pre-calculated sales quota ✦ the product's turnover rate is well below your average turnover rate ✦ the product's profit margin has shrunk well below your average profit margin per inventory item due to reasons such as increased product costs, price wars, surpluses within the industry, or the need for drastic discounting due to what can only be described as lack of consumer interest ✦ the dust on the product's packaging is thick enough to write your name on it.

Marcaria.com
Offers trademark registration and protection services in America, Europe, and Asia.

Proprietary and Exclusive Rights Obtained

If you have a great idea with huge profit potential, you can bet once it goes public, others will find ways to copy or steal it. After all, being innovative—the most important skill any business person can have—is based upon taking an existing idea and changing it a lot or a little to benefit yourself and others. Thus, it can be argued that protecting a new idea is almost as important as coming up with it. However, acquiring intellectual property rights (IPR) protection can be costly and cumbersome. Types of protection in the U.S. are outlined in the chart below. For Asia, consult Arthur Wineburg's *Intellectual Property Protection in Asia, 2003 Edition*. For Canada, visit www.cipo.gc.ca. For Europe, visit europa.eu.int/business/en/topics/ipr/.

Protecting Ideas, Products, Services

Copyright Protection © – Protects a work created by an author, artist, or composer such as a novel, screenplay, computer program, painting, photograph, choreographic work, sculpture, musical composition, ad, or song lyrics. However, copyright law states quite clearly that there is no copyright in facts or ideas, only in the form or expression of the idea. Average copyright protection is the life of the creator plus 50 years. For more information go to the U.S. Copyright Office: www.loc.gov/copyright/.

Patent Protection – Protects a process, way of making things, or invention that is essentially better in some way than what was made or done before. A patent excludes others from making or selling your inventions. "Patent Pending" means your application has been received and a serial number issued for tracking purposes (usually takes six months after filing). Total time for processing an application may take several years. U.S. patent protection is 20 years from date of issue and is non-renewable. For free online patent searches, go to the U.S. Patent and Trademark Office: www.uspto.gov/main/patents.htm.

Business Names and Trade Names – These are not entitled to protection under trademark law, unless a business uses its name to identify its product or service and that name is distinctive enough. Buying a **domain name** does not mean you automatically have trademark protection.

Service Mark Protection ℠ ® – A service mark is pretty much the same as a trademark, except that it protects branded services and events (e.g., Wendy's restaurant services). The SM designation usually appears next to the brand name or logo in advertisements for the services.

Trademark Protection ™ ® – Protects a distinctive word, brand name, symbol, design, or device, or combination thereof such as a logo, used or intended to be used, in commerce to differentiate one company's products or services from another. A TM symbol is used to indicate a claim of ownership. To use it properly, identify your marks with the symbol on products, packaging, and ads, and notice your claim by adding statements where the mark appears such as, "Mytradmark™ is a trademark of Mycompany." It is not necessary to have a federal registration or even a pending application to use TM. An ® indicates that the trademark is registered with the U.S. Patent and Trademark Office. To be granted protection, trademarks must be "fanciful," "arbitrary," or "suggestive." A "fanciful word" is an invented word that does not have any meaning associated with it (e.g., XEROX). An "arbitrary word" has an ordinary meaning; however, this meaning is entirely unconnected to its use as a trademark (e.g., Apple). A "suggestive mark" indirectly describes or refers to the product (e.g., Nike logo). Trademarks can't be descriptive, deceptive, generic, surnames, scandalous, or immoral. U.S. trademark protection is 10 to 20 years from date registered and is renewable. For free online trademark searches go to the U.S. Patent and Trademark Office: www.uspto.gov/main/trademarks.htm.

Certification Mark – A type of trademark used by a respected entity to certify origin, material, mode of manufacture, quality, accuracy, region, or other characteristics of the goods (e.g., "ISO 9002" rating).

Trade Dress – In some cases, distinctive packaging, décor, or architecture used to distinguish goods and services in the marketplace can be protected under trademark laws (e.g., Kodak's yellow and black film box).

Successful
BUSINESS
PLANNING
30 DAYS

Find suppliers.
Take steps to protect your ideas.

Purchasing Plan

Summarize key points in your purchasing plan:

Sample: To meet our product needs, we have compared the offerings of four suppliers: [list names]. Having reviewed our credit rating, [Supplier A] is willing to offer us 60 days credit at a purchase limit of $[XX]. They charge [X]% for overdue accounts. [Supplier B] is willing to offer 30 days credit with no purchase limit. They charge [X]% for overdue accounts. We have also prepared a policy statement for suppliers outlining our delivery requirements and returns procedure for damaged goods.

List and compare suppliers:

Comparing Suppliers	Name of Item(s):						
Name of Supplier	Address of Supplier	Phone/Fax Number	Cost	Discounts Offered	Delivery Time	Shipping & Del. Costs	Reorder Policies

Cost of Goods and Discounts – How competitive are the prices of the supplier? What quantity discounts are offered?

Delivery Time – How many days or weeks does it take the supplier to deliver the merchandise to your store? How long does it take to reorder?

Shipping and Delivery Costs – Who pays for freight, you or supplier (these costs are a big expense item)? Where is the F.O.B. point?

Reorder Policies – What is the supplier's policy on reorders? Do you have to buy by the hundreds or by the dozens, or can you buy only two or three items?

Floor Stock – *Where* do you plan to buy floor stock for resale (product and service firms)? *Where* do you plan to buy your raw materials and component parts (manufacturing firms)? List details of key inventory items, raw materials, and parts ordered from suppliers. If you have only one supplier, list alternate sources. Explain **how** you will handle the loss of a supplier or sudden increases in orders:

> **Sample:** Our key suppliers are [list names and locations and products supplied]. With [Supplier A] we have negotiated a one year contract for them to supply [item name] at a cost of $[XX]. This contract is renewable for three additional years at an increase of [X]% per year. [Supplier B] has also agreed to offer volume discounts at a rate of [X]% for orders over 100 and [X]% for orders over 1,000. If [Supplier A and B] cannot meet our needs due to an unexpected increase in product demand, [name of other suppliers] are available to meet our supply needs.

Name of Item/ Raw Material/ Component	Name of Supplier	Price	Order Policy	Discounts Offered	Delivery Time	Freight Costs	Back Order Policy
XYZ Widget	Big Widget Idaho	$3.22	minimum order size 100	2/10 net 30	2 weeks	$ Free	7 weeks if out of stock

Operating Supplies – *Where* do you plan to buy **operating supplies and materials** (product and service firms)? *Where* do you plan to buy your consumable tools and shop supplies (manufacturing firms)? List details of key operating supplies and materials you will order from suppliers:

Name of Item/ Tool or Supplies	Name of Supplier	Price	Order Policy	Discounts Offered	Delivery Time	Freight Costs	Back Order Policy
		$				$	

Purchasing Budget – *Outline your purchasing budget based on sales projections. List % of total sales each month. Detail any assumptions made or special trends. Do you have a purchasing reserve fund?*

Sample: With projected sales of $[XX], our budget for purchasing is $[XX]. However, if seasonal demand is greater than expected, we have also allocated $[XX] to our purchasing reserve fund. We have also established a revolving line of credit with [Bank] for $[XX] at [X]%.

	Actual Sales Last Year			Planned Sales This Year				Actual Sales Last Year			Planned Sales This Year		
	COST	SALES	% of Total	*COST*	SALES	% of Total		*COST*	SALES	% of Total	*COST*	SALES	% of Total
Jan							Jul						
Feb							Aug						
Mar							Sep						
Apr							Oct						
May							Nov						
Jun							Dec						
Purchasing Budget							Total			100			100

Calculate reorder points for key inventory items: *Describe additional reorder policies:*

Item(s)	Total Sales Year	EOQ* or $Value**	Turnover Days	# of Days to Receive Order	**Reorder Point**	
XYZ Widget	$16,100	$3,220	73 Days	14 Days	$617.50	

Reorder Point $= EOQ \times [\dfrac{\text{\# of days to receive order}}{\text{inventory turnover days}}]$

* **EOQ** $= [(2 \times F \times S)/(P \times C)]^{-1/2}$
F = cost of placing an order **S** = annual sales # of units
C = carrying costs expressed as % of inventory value
P = cost per unit of inventory (see page 128)

** ***Note*** Total $ Value of an item you plan to stock can be substituted for EOQ (# of units). Reorder Point is then expressed in $ Value

Highlight the main points of your order inspection or receiving policy:
❑ we use a receiving report ❑ we have clearly laid out policies and procedures for processing supply orders

	Sample: Each carton must be clearly marked with [e.g., item number, purchase order number]. A packing slip must be legible and contain [list requirements]. Shipments of more than six cartons must be palletized on standard 40 × 48 pallets with only one item number per pallet. We reserve the right to refuse shipments which do not conform to our receiving policy or to charge $[XX]/hour for materials and labor to bring the shipment into compliance. All shipments shipped freight collect will be refused.

Highlight the main points of your inventory discontinuation policy:
❑ If [product] fails to meet a sales quota of $[XX], we [describe]. ❑ Obsolete inventory is discounted by [X]%.

	Sample: If a product's turnover rate is [X]% higher than the average inventory rate, or if manufacturers discontinue an item, the item will be discounted by [X]% for the first month, [X]% for the second month, and sold at cost after four months. According to industry historical data, [X]% of inventory will need to be discounted each year.

Proprietary and Exclusive Rights Obtained

Discuss and list any company, product, or service proprietary and exclusive rights obtained, such as:
❑ copyrights ❑ patents ❑ trademarks ❑ service marks ❑ licensing agreements ❑ domain names
❑ industrial designs owned or currently under application ❑ franchise territories ❑ distribution rights
(Note: it might be more appropriate for your business plan to include this section after your *Description of Principal Products and Services*)

	Sample: [Product] is protected by [list trademarks, patents, copyrights, etc.]. We also have a [licensing/royalty] agreement with [company] for our [describe] technology [or service]. The general terms of this agreement are [explain]. Further proprietary information not disclosed in this business plan is available to investors upon signing a Nondisclosure Agreement.

DAY 10

Choose a single-entry or double-entry accounting system.

Open a business checking account.

Operating Plan

Begin this section with a summary covering accounting procedures, legal considerations, inventory control, computer systems, and other concerns important to the operation of your business. Summarize production and operating processes, but avoid getting too technical. List key dates in your *Operations Schedule* (see pages 140 and 143).

Accounting System

Accounting is essentially the "counting" and "keeping track of" money. Adopting the best system for your needs can spell the difference between knowing what's really going on and ending up profitless and clueless about where revenues actually went and disappeared to. It is important that banks and investors trust your competence, not only so you can pay your taxes, but also be in a better position to monitor cash flow, estimate profits, and pay off loans. Prospective investors and lenders also like to see your books being audited by a reputable outside source, just to make sure all your numbers are upfront.

What Makes a Good Accounting System?

A good accounting system is simple to use, easy to learn, accurate, and flexible to change. It also: (a) protects your business from fraud and error; (b) takes into consideration the size, nature, and extent of your business, as well as your accounting abilities; (c) provides accurate information for every business transaction in a manner that allows no needless overlapping or repetition of procedures; (d) gives information on a timely basis; (e) is within budget to implement and maintain; and most importantly, (f) consumes as little time as possible. Furthermore, a good accounting system recognizes the following two important needs:

1) **Management Needs** – A good accounting system compiles and organizes information to help improve management's decision-making process.

2) **Government Needs** – A good accounting system meets the minimum record keeping requirements of government income tax laws.

Canceled checks are one of the best source documents along with receipts and sales slips to prove a business expense deduction.
PROFIT TIP

Nowadays, you hear a lot about fancy accounting methods, like LIFO and FIFO, but back then we were using the ESP method, which really sped things along when it came time to close books. It's a pretty basic method: if you can't make your books balance you take however much they're off by and enter it under the heading ESP, which stands for Error Some Place.
SAM WALTON

What Kinds of Accounting Records Should You Keep?

As a general rule, tax departments do not specify the exact type of records you should keep, other than they be permanent, contain a systematic account of all income and expenses to determine taxes payable, and be supported by vouchers or other source documents. To meet these basic requirements, your accounting system should keep track of: ❑ A/P's and A/R's ❑ assets, equipment, and inventory ❑ business expenses ❑ capital gains and losses ❑ cash disbursements and cash receipts ❑ employment taxes including income tax withholdings, social security, Medicare, and federal unemployment taxes ❑ employee expenses ❑ medical and dental expenses ❑ gross sales (and other sources of business related income) ❑ travel, transportation, entertainment, and gift expenses.

Setting up an Accounting System

There is no single accounting method required of all taxpayers, other than you clearly show all income and expenses, maintain adequate records so you can file a correct return, support your entries with receipts, invoices, etc., and use the same method from year to year. Your accounting system could range from a simple single-entry journal system to a more sophisticated double-entry computerized system supplemented with monthly consulting services by a financial accountant.

In a traditional accounting system:

ENTER all transactions as they occur into a *General Journal.* File any related documents to prove these transactions. Protect this *Journal* at all costs, whether it's a computer file or a book purchased at a stationery store. It is the soul of your accounting system. If disaster strikes and your records and calculations are completely wiped out, as long as you've kept your journal in a safe place, you can always rebuild your system.

POST journal entries to an appropriate account in your *General Ledger.* A *Ledger* is usually a hardcover book in which each individual type or group of transactions are maintained separately on different pages. These groups of related transactions are called ledger accounts. The chief function of a ledger is to record and keep track of the balances of individual accounts. It will typically contain anywhere from a dozen to a hundred or more asset, liability, equity, revenue, or expense accounts, depending upon management needs and the size of your business. To set up your ledger, assign each account: (1) an account title, (2) an account number, and (3) a ledger page or pages. Next, create a Chart of Accounts. A *Chart of Accounts* is like a table of contents at the beginning of a book. It is a list of all the account titles and numbers used in your accounting system. Account numbers are listed between 10 and 59, 100 and 599, 1000 and 5999, or even 1000 to 9999 (see page 109 for a list of possible accounts).

SUM UP and analyze account balances periodically.

These three basic accounting procedures can be further broken down into eight sub-processes, commonly referred to as the **ACCOUNTING CYCLE**:

A. Transaction Occurs

B. Transaction Entered in General Journal

C. Journal Entry Posted to General Ledger

D. Trial Balance Prepared

E. Trial Balance Adjustments Made

F. Financial Statements Prepared

G. Financial Statements Posted to Ledger

H. Books Closed and Prepared for Next Cycle

NOTE Consult your telephone directory for listings of accountants who can help you choose and set up an accounting system for your business (refer to GB📖 #28 for more detailed information on accounting systems).

Support Vouchers

To prove business transactions and verify income and expenses, file away canceled checks, account statements, cash register tapes, and all vouchers such as receipts, sales slips, deposit slips, paid bills, and invoices. A check register, or even a checkbook with enough space to clearly identify sources of disbursements, can be used as a basic record for deductible expenses. To verify **expenses** file: ✦ canceled checks ✦ cash register tapes ✦ account statements ✦ credit card sales slips ✦ invoices ✦ petty cash record system. To verify **purchases** file: ✦ canceled checks ✦ cash register tape receipts ✦ credit card sales slips ✦ invoices. To verify **gross sales** file: ✦ cash register tapes ✦ bank deposit slips ✦ receipt books ✦ invoices ✦ credit card charge slips.

Making Journal Entries

All transactions are entered into the General Journal the order in which they occur. Each entry requires that you:

1) Date the entry on the left edge.

2) Write the debit account title(s) as far to the left as you can, along with its corresponding dollar amount in the left-hand money column (to ease posting to the General Ledger, also write the corresponding account number).

3) Write the credit account title(s)—indented a half-inch or so—and its corresponding dollar amount in the right-hand money column (a debit can be entered in red ink and a credit in black ink—don't reverse).

4) Write a brief note of explanation regarding the transaction (see example shown on the next page).

NOTE All journal entries require at least three lines on a page: ✦ a line for a debit entry ✦ a line for a credit entry ✦ a line for an explanation (quite often a single transaction can impact more than two accounts and thus take up more than three lines).

When preparing a trial balance, the total debits must equal the total credits. Don't be discouraged if they don't. Bookkeeping errors happen. Just think of the trial balance as a tool to find the errors.
BUSINESS OWNERS TOOLKIT
www.toolkit.cch.com

Not using checks makes it difficult to monitor expenses, increases the time spent on book-keeping, increases the probability of double payments, and communicates to suppliers that your business is a marginal operation.
SBA
✳
In 25 years experience with the [accounting] profession, I have never seen an auditor go soft on a client because other work was at stake.
JOHN HARVEY
Former Australian Pricewaterhouse Coopers chief executive

The accounting forms you use should allow easy routine processing. They should flow automatically to bookkeepers, computer staff, or other individuals who process them and enter them into your records, without increasing the likelihood of errors or misplacement.

Making Ledger Entries

When making a General Ledger entry:

1) Write down an explanation.

2) List a posting reference (P/R), referring back to the original entry in your journal (usually listed as a page number).

3) *Debit* or *credit* the accounts in question. Posting a transaction to the ledger is never a one shot deal. Each transaction represents both at least one debit and credit account.

4) After the transaction has been fully posted to all its appropriate accounts, make a check mark beside the column total in the journal to show that it has been posted.

NOTES (a) All entries are in ink except for the balance column. The balance entry may be kept in pencil in case an error is made. (b) Each account appears on a separate page and is numbered in accordance with your Chart of Accounts. (c) If you are using a computer program, most programs automatically post the journal entry to the appropriate ledger account thus saving time. (d) Post journal entries at a minimum four times a year when you make your quarterly tax installments.

General Journal

	p.1		*Holistic Pet Supplies*		DEBIT ACCOUNT	CREDIT ACCOUNT	P✓	
	DATE		DESCRIPTIONS	AC#				
1	Jan	12	Merchandise	130	1 2 0 0 0 00		1/12/05	1
2			Accounts Payable	210		1 2 0 0 0 00		2
3			*Purchase of Bulk*					3
4			*Puppy Chow*					4

General Ledger

	DATE		Account Name and No. Merchandise AC#130 DESCRIPTIONS	P/R	DEBIT (IN)	CREDIT (OUT)	BAL	
1	Jan	12	Purchase of Merch. on account	p. 1	1 2 0 0 0 00		1 2 0 0 0 00	1
2	Feb	12	Purchase of Merch. on account	p. 2	5 0 0 0 00		5 0 0 0 00	2
3	Feb	13	Return of Merch. on account	p. 2		1 0 0 0 00	1 6 0 0 0 00	3
4	Feb	26	Purchase of Merch. on account	p. 3	6 0 0 00		1 6 6 0 0 00	4

Single-entry Cash Based Systems

For a small home, service, or contracting business, which uses part-time help and has no inventory for sale, the single-entry *cash method* of accounting is a good choice. This system consists of little more than a carefully annotated checkbook in which all receipts and expenditures are recorded, supported by forms of original entry, such as invoices, receipts, and cash tickets. Sales are recorded when cash is actually received and expenses are recorded when they are actually paid. A single-entry cash based accounting system as illustrated in IRS publication 583 "Starting a Business and Keeping Records," suggests using: ✦ Daily Summary of Cash Receipts ✦ Monthly Summary of Cash Receipts ✦ Check Disbursement Journal ✦ Employee Compensation Record ✦ Annual Summary ✦ Depreciation Worksheet ✦ Bank Reconciliation (see GB📖 #28 for a sample of this system).

Double-entry Accrual Based Systems

As your business grows, switch to the *accrual method*. Under this method, record sales and expenses when they are incurred rather than when they are collected or paid. You should also switch to the double-entry accounting method, whereby ALL transactions are entered first in your *General Journal*, and then posted to at least two balancing *debit* and *credit* accounts in your *General Ledger*. This system should be used by businesses that have daily cash sales, credit customers, inventory items, and employees. One such system, as illustrated in an Alberta government publication, "Bookkeeping for a Small Business," suggests using: ✦ Daily Cash Sheet ✦ Synoptic Ledger ✦ Accounts Receivable Ledger ✦ Accounts Payable Ledger ✦ Weekly Summary Payroll ✦ Bank Reconciliation ✦ Asset Depreciation Records ✦ GST (Federal Tax) Records (see GB📖 #28 for a sample of this system).

Condensed Single-entry Accounting Systems

Special condensed single-entry journals, available at stationery stores for a variety of businesses, can be used to group common types of transactions and simplify bookkeeping. These journals are single-purpose versions of the *General Journal* in which the explanation line is omitted and only one line is used to enter debit and credit accounts (see Form 15 "Weekly Sales and Cash Report" available at bforms.com).

Envelope Journal Systems – If you own a small part-time business and have only a few transactions per day, week, or month, consider photocopying and stapling on to a 9 by 12 envelope a single-entry journal page. Every time a transaction occurs put the receipt into the envelope, then make an entry on the journal page. When the page is full, or at the end of a specified period (a week or month), file the envelope and start a new one. Receipts from transactions can be stored in a safe place, like a cash box, and then re-

*Using the **accrual method** can give you a better idea of long-term profitability, but can be misleading if you need to know how much cash is on hand. Your income ledger may show thousands in sales, but in reality, your bank account is empty because no one has paid you yet.*

*Using the **cash method**, one month may show huge sales, when actually sales were slow and many credit customers just happened to pay their bills that month.*

corded and put inside the envelope when convenient. All expenses are paid by check. At the end of the year, total the envelope summaries and prepare financial summary statements.

NOTE Although condensed single-entry journals can simplify bookkeeping, they lack room to record vital pieces of information particular to individual transactions. This can become a serious problem if you need to verify a transaction. To prevent this, file all support documents according to dates. If you then need to verify an expense of $37.50 paid on Monday, April 12th, all you need to do is look in your file cabinet and pull out the file that contains receipts for that date.

Single-entry Income and Expense Journal Systems

Instead of using a *Daily Cash Sheet* and *Synoptic Ledger*, record your income and expenses using an *Income Journal* and an *Expense Journal* (also called a *Sales* or *Cash Receipts Journal* and a *Cash Payments* or *Disbursements Journal*). It is quite common for businesses to base their entire accounting system around these two journals. Both can be purchased at stationery stores.

Using an Income Journal

The *Income Journal* is used for recording all incoming revenue, whether cash or check. In the example, shown on page 102, Harold W. Lee of Holistic Pet Supplies has entered sales income and other particulars over a three-day period. Explanations for these entries are provided below:

Columns 1–4 – On May 1, by examining sales invoices and cash register tapes, Harry found he had cash sales of $430.00 and sales of $120.00 on account (these amounts include sales taxes collected). In his Income Journal, he recorded the *cash sales* in column 1 and the *credit sales* in column 2. In column 3, he shows $30 worth of returned merchandise. Column 4 then shows the total sales for the day, cash sales plus credit sales minus merchandise returned.

Column 5 – In column 5, Harry recorded cash received on previous credit sales. He did not include this amount in his total daily sales figure, as he would have included it in the total sales figure for the day the goods were actually sold on account. On May 1st, he had received $240 from A/R customers.

Column 6 – In column 6, Harry recorded any cash or other income he received during the day. On May 1st, he received $10 in interest from an overdue A/R. On May 2nd, he received a $25 deposit refund from a gas company that earlier had been recorded as a business expense. On May 3rd, he received $625 for selling his old company truck.

Column 7 – In column 7, Harry calculated how much he received during the day. On May 1st, he recorded: $430 - $30 + $240 + $10 = $650. As his daily sales figure may not be equal to the cash he received, this column ensures he ends up with the correct figure at the day's end.

Column 8 – In column 8, Harry recorded his actual cash count. On May 1st, he was $2.00 short.

Column 9 – In column 9, Harry recorded how much money he was short or over.

Column 10 – In column 10, Harry recorded how much he deposited into his bank account by subtracting from column 7 all his cash disbursements as noted in his Expense Journal (make a point of depositing the exact amount of cash received, as noted in column 7, minus any cash expenses, for then your Income Journal will provide an accurate record of funds you have deposited and their sources).

Other Procedures – Once Harry made the appropriate daily entries in his Income Journal:

a) he added the sales on account (accounts receivables) for the day to the individual account cards of the people to whom he made the sales;

b) he credited the cash received on account to the individual account cards of the people from whom he received it; and then

c) he filed away cash register tapes, canceled checks, and copies of his sales invoices (and all other vouchers that document his sources of income, such as bank statements and deposit slips), so that he could easily review them at a later date. At the end of each month, Harry then totals each column and starts a new sheet for the next month.

NOTE You can alter the format of your Income Journal to suit your business. If you operate a farm, for example, you may have 20 large sales in a year, instead of many small sales each day. In this case, you may wish to record your income as you make each sale, instead of recording daily totals.

Using an Expense Journal

The *Expense Journal* is used for recording business expenses. The simplest method of recording these expenses is a basic columnar sheet (see page 102). Keep in mind that a sales invoice, agreement of purchase, receipt, or some other voucher must be filed away to support each business expense. A paper trail must also be provided for all sources of reported income.

Column 1 – In column 1, Harry recorded the numbers of the checks used to pay for expenses as written in the *Particulars* column. If cash was used, or if the purchase was on account, a note to this affect was also made. On May 1st, he took the $300 ABC Radio bill he received and made a note on it that it was paid by check number 0407 on May 1st. He then filed this bill away in an appropriately titled expense file. This file was a simple folder that would hold all his advertising bills for the year.

NOTE Retain all canceled checks received from the bank. This is part of your proof that the bill was paid or the asset purchased. As with the sale invoices and the bills, keep the canceled checks in an orderly manner so that any one of them can be easily reviewed at a later date.

Column 2 – In column 2, Harry recorded the purchase of $1,729.14 worth of inventory. When using credit, he also makes sure to make a corresponding entry in his Accounts Payable record.

Columns 3–8 – In columns 3 to 8, Harry recorded the amount of his expenses (you can modify these headings to suit the type of business you have).

Column 9 – In column 9, Harry recorded all his miscellaneous expenses. On May 3rd, he put $1.85 back into his balance (change) fund to make up for money lost or stolen ($2.00 – $0.15).

Column 10 – Harry recorded the amount paid for the capital purchase of a used half-ton truck. At the end of each month, Harry totals each column and starts a new sheet for the next month.

My money goes to my agent, then to my accountant and from him to the tax man.
GLENDA JACKSON
Movie Actress

✳

The graduate with a Science degree asks, "Why does it work?"

The graduate with an Engineering degree asks, "How does it work?"

The graduate with an Accounting degree asks, "How much will it cost?"

The graduate with a Liberal Arts degree asks, "Do you want fries with that?"

ANON

Put all of your small business purchases on a corporate charge card that provides you with regular reports. This will save you time and money during tax preparation time.
PROFIT TIP

Income Journal

Date	Particulars	1 Cash Sales	2 Credit Sales	3 Merch. Returned	4 Total Sales 1 + 2 – 3	5 Cash Rec. on Credit Sales	6 Other Cash Received	7 Total Cash Received 1 – 3 + 5 + 6	8 Actual Cash Count	9 Cash Short or Over	10 Bank Deposit 7 – Exp.'s
May 1	Daily Sales	430.00	120.00	30.00	520.00	240.00		650.00	648.00	(2.00)	505.00
May 1	A/R Interest						10.00				
May 2	Daily Sales	565.25	99.00		664.25	110.00		700.25	700.40	.15	700.25
May 2	Deposit Refund (Gas)						25.00				
May 3	Daily Sales	540.00			540.00	55.68		1,220.68	1,220.68		1,218.83
May 3	Auto Wreckers						625.00				

Expense Journal

Date	Particulars	1 Check Number	2 Inventory Purchases	3 Accounting and Legal	4 Advertising	5 Insurance	6 Phone	7 Utilities	8 Salaries	9 Misc. Expenses	10 Capital Items
May 1	ABC Radio	0407			300.00						
May 1	Salary for Sally	0408							565.00		
May 1	Window Decorations	(cash)								130.00	
May 1	Petty Cash Slips	(cash)								15.00	
May 2	Ottawa Insurance	0409				250.00					
May 3	Jim's Accounting	(credit)		140.00							
May 3	Wholesale Supply	0411	1,729.14								
May 3	Ed's Used Cars	0412									1,800.00
May 3	Bal. Fund Restored	(cash)								1.85	

Commercial Accounting Systems

Numerous commercial copyrighted accounting systems are available for small business owners to simplify bookkeeping. These systems are usually based on easy-to-use single-entry journals and come complete with instructions. You can examine many of them at office supply stores or send away for free catalogs. Companies that sell such systems include: ✦ McBee Systems (offers a simplified business checkbook and journal system) ✦ Pegboard Accounting Systems ✦ Safeguard Business Systems ✦ The Johnson Systems (offers simplified bookkeeping systems for many businesses including grocers, manufacturers, and pubs).

Computerized Accounting Systems

Accounting software can be purchased from retail and online software houses, as well as numerous book and stationery stores. Three of the most popular over-the-counter accounting packages for small businesses are *QuickBooks Pro*, *MYOB*, and *Peachtree*. All packages claim to be relatively easy to use, but this is something you must find out for yourself (see page 121 for more software packages). Business editions of personal finance software like *Quicken* and *Microsoft Money* may also be sufficient for a small service or contracting business.

NOTE To keep federal tax authorities happy, at a minimum, your accounting system must produce legible records and provide the necessary information needed to determine your correct tax liability. You must also keep a complete description of the computerized portion of your accounting system. This description should outline applications being performed, procedures used in each application, controls used to ensure accurate and reliable processing, and controls used to prevent the unauthorized addition, alteration, or deletion of retained records.

Banking Plan

One of the first things to do when starting a business is open a business checking account. Good business practice dictates that you keep your personal financial affairs separate from your business financial affairs. In fact, it is just as important for a home-based business to open a business banking account as it is for any small business.

Setting up a Business Checking Account

To open a business checking account, you will need to bring with you a copy of your business registration to verify your business name (in the U.S. this registration statement is called a DBA or "Doing Business As" statement). You will also need to do some research to find the *right* bank to meet your needs. Besides considering location and convenience, especially for retail business owners who need to make nightly cash deposits, the following steps should be taken when selecting a business checking account:

STEP 1 – **Avoid banks with unreasonable and expensive checking account policies.** Good business practice dictates that every disbursement be made by a pre-numbered check. This will assure you of a formal record of all payments and expenses. Avoid banks that charge excessive checking fees. Try to stay away from commercial banks unwilling to offer interest on balances in business accounts. Consider dealing instead with a trust company or Credit Union. These institutions are often willing to give you a daily-interest checking account with statement privileges. To attract depositors, they are also more likely to experiment with no-fee or low-fee accounts that further minimize extra charges.

The more daily transactions your business has, the more you need a computerized accounting system, or a specialized system setup or designed specifically for your business by a professional.

PROFIT TIP
✳

Excelco.com compares major brands of accounting software including Business Management software and Enterprise Resource Planning (ERP) software. Also try:

2020software.com
ctsguides.com
taxsites.com

*Gomez.com rated Citibank.com, Firstib.com, and Wellsfargo.com as the top U.S. online banks in 2002. American Express Bank, Net Bank and E*TRADE Bank have also received positive reviews from customers.*

STEP 2 – Choose a bank that offers "overdraft" protection. Considering the number of checks you will write as a business owner, and the resulting wildly fluctuating balances, you may inadvertently bounce a check. It is paramount that you protect yourself in such cases to avoid extra fees and embarrassment to suppliers and creditors. Talk to your bank or trust company branch manager about overdraft protection. Ask for an automatic overdraft protection of $1,000 on your account, secured by your name only, that is without collateral. Most managers have the authority to do this, if you ask.

STEP 3 – Choose a bank that offers telephone banking. Many banks now offer services that allow you to transfer money between accounts, make credit card inquiries, pay bills, and check account balances using a push button phone to enter account numbers and other pertinent information. These services can also be accessed using a cellular phone.

STEP 4 – Choose a bank that offers online banking. The ability to make financial transactions over the Web is destined to speed up cash flow more than any other current technology. Businesses are already using computerized order entry systems, which enable customers to reorder merchandise and check shipping dates directly. The next step will be the invoicing of customers via computer, and then receipt of payment electronically by wire transfer from the customer's bank to yours. As encryption software and sophistication improves, Internet banking will gain a larger share of the banking industry and even influence the way business is conducted. To its advantage, online banking takes less paper and less transit time, reducing the work and cost of paper invoices, payroll, and bills and thus solving two of the biggest problems bothering commercial depositors. It also makes long-distance transactions as convenient as dealing with a neighborhood bank, opening up the entire world to financial interfacing. Already, more and more banks are offering online banking privileges to small businesses, enabling them to have the convenience and cash management control enjoyed by larger corporations. Using these services, you can use your PC to check balances, transfer funds, consolidate cash between accounts, and pay bills. You can even use accounting software such as QuickBooks®, Quicken®, and Microsoft® Money to access and manage your online accounts.

STEP 5 – Also consider the following: ❑ *Availability of FDIC Deposit Insurance* – Covers up to $100,000 of an account. ❑ *Banks' Riskiness* – Smaller banks in smaller communities tend to be more conservative in their lending. ❑ *Interest Rates* – Review the interest rate paid on deposits and rate charged on loans. ❑ *Loyalty to Customer* – Will the bank pressure you to liquidate a loan during an economic downturn? ❑ *Maximum Loan* – Usually limited to 10% of the bank's capital account. ❑ *Minimum Balance* – Do you have to maintain a minimum amount? ❑ *Revolving Line of Credit* – What is the interest rate? ❑ *Specialization* – Larger banks can offer separate departments specializing in a variety of banking services. ❑ *Other Services* – Does the bank offer electronic bill payment, foreign currency accounts, lockbox services, low-interest credit cards, merchant accounts, or wire transfers?

Checking Account Strategies

To get the most out of your checking account, use the following strategies: ❑ Always make payments by check to document business expenses. ❑ Use a checkbook with enough room to write details of the payment and type of expense. ❑ Write checks payable to yourself only when making withdrawals from your business for personal use. ❑ Avoid writing checks payable to cash. If you must write a check for cash to pay an expense, include the receipt for the cash payment in your records. If you cannot get a receipt for cash payment, make an adequate explanation in your records. ❑ Never bounce a check without telling your bank first and giving them a chance to fix it.

Factors That Affect Your Credit Rating

A good credit rating is vital in determining whether you can obtain a credit card, line of credit, mortgage, or business loan, and what price you pay. In Canada and the U.S., factors considered in assessing your credit score (also known as your FICO, Beacon, or Emperica score), include: ✦ What is your payment history? Do you pay on time and in full? (35%) ✦ How much do you owe? (30%) ✦ How established is your credit? (15%) ✦ How many credit accounts or applications do you have and what is your mix of credit cards and loans? (20%). Length of time at the same residence, education attained, age, income, marital status, dependants, and credit references, can also help you obtain credit. To improve your credit rating score, make sure you have or seek to acquire the following eight elements:

Eight Elements of a Positive Credit Profile

1. A positive up-to-date credit report
2. A home with a mortgage
3. An American Express card and/or Diner's Club card
4. A job you've held for a year or more
5. A current or paid-off bank loan or car loan
6. A MasterCard or VISA
7. A department store credit card
8. A telephone in your name

In 2001, 20% of U.S. households performed banking transactions online, up from 15% the year before. By 2006, it is estimated that half of all banking households will bank online.
JUPITER MEDIA METRIX

A credit repair company cannot remove negative, but accurate, information on your credit report. It will be removed only after the required amount of time as stated in the Fair Credit Reporting Act. For example, records of bankruptcy can remain on a your credit report for 10 years and foreclosures are reported for seven years.
BETTER BUSINESS BUREAU

DAY 10 Worksheets ⏱

Choose a single-entry or double-entry accounting system. Open a business checking account.

Operating Plan

Summarize key points of your operating plan: ❑ accounting ❑ banking ❑ purchasing ❑ technology
❑ Internet plan ❑ inventory ❑ order entry ❑ operations schedule ❑ quality control ❑ licenses

1	
2	
3	
4	
5	

Accounting System

Describe your accounting system or method of record keeping: ❑ Peachtree ❑ MYOB ❑ QuickBooks Pro
❑ One-write System ❑ Income and Expense Journal ❑ Double-entry Accrual Based ❑ Single-entry Cash Based

	Sample: [Company] uses a double-entry accrual based accounting system. We are currently using *QuickBooks Pro* with plans to upgrade to iCode's all-in-one *Everest* small business management software. Financial statements are prepared and reviewed quarterly by management. Our accounting system and chart of accounts was set up with the help of [accounting firm].

Who *handles bookkeeping? Will you use an outside accountant? If so, state their name, company, and address.* ***When*** *did they last audit your books? Also, state who within your company is experienced at reading and analyzing financial statements and thus able to implement changes to maximize profits:*

	Sample: [Staff name] is responsible for daily bookkeeping and preparation of bank reconciliation statements. Quarterly financial statements are prepared by management and reviewed at the end of the fiscal year by [accounting firm]. [Name of accountant] at [firm] is also consulted as needed at a cost of $[X]/hour.

Keeping Records – Check the types of records you will keep and procedures you will implement:

On a DAILY BASIS record:

❑ *cash sales and receipts*

❑ *all funds disbursed* by cash or check

❑ *cash on hand* and *bank balance*

❑ *errors* – discovered in the recording of previous transactions

❑ *miscellaneous sources of income* – including income from professional fees, property, investments, capital gains, estates, trusts, employment, and pensions

On a WEEKLY BASIS record:

❑ *accounts receivable* (A/R's) – so you can take action on slow payers

❑ *accounts payable* (A/P's) – so you can take advantage of discounts

❑ *amount of weekly payroll* – employee name and address, SSN, date ending the pay period, hours worked, pay rate, wages paid, total deductions, net pay, and check #

❑ all *withholdings set aside for State and Federal Governments* – including sales tax, employee income tax withholdings, social security payments, pension plan payments, and unemployment insurance payments

On a MONTHLY BASIS record:

❑ *amount of business done in cash and credit*

❑ *amount of business tied up in A/R's*

❑ *amount of collections and losses from credit sales*

❑ *amount owed to creditors and suppliers*

❑ *total expenses*

❑ *gross profit*

❑ *net profit earned and taxes owed*

❑ *which products and services made a profit and which lost money*

❑ *amount of money invested in stock*

At the END of MONTH, make sure that:

❑ all *journal entries* are classified according to like elements and posted to the Ledger

❑ a *Cash Flow Statement* is prepared

❑ an *Income Statement* and *Balance Sheet* for the month is available within a reasonable time, usually 10 to 15 days following the month's end—for small business semi-annual statements are sufficient

❑ *Petty Cash* account is in balance

❑ *Bank Statement* is reconciled—the owner's books agree with the bank's record of the cash balance

❑ all *Federal Tax*, FICA tax, state tax, and withheld income deposits have been made

❑ *A/R's* are aged 30, 60, 90 days, or past due

❑ *Inventory* is inspected to determine which items need to be reordered and which need to be discounted due to slow turnover

Check strategies and guidelines you will use to streamline your accounting system:

❑ Always use pre-numbered checks instead of paying cash.

❑ Always use pre-numbered cash receipts or invoices.

❑ Always support accounting records with a paper trail (*paper* or *audit trails* consist of sales slips, invoices, receipts, canceled checks, or other paper records of business transactions; each transaction should contain the date of purchase, the name and address of the seller or supplier, the name and address of the purchaser, and a full description of the goods or services).

❑ Avoid setting up too many accounts in your "Chart of Accounts."

❑ Develop profit centers for different products or services.

❑ Don't encourage employee dishonesty with sloppy cash habits.

❑ Establish a filing system for all bills and sales invoices.

❑ Group similar entries (e.g., it is not necessary to enter each individual bill of sale from individual customers, who purchase items from your store).

❑ Keep business financial affairs separate from personal financial affairs.

❑ Keep records of assets bought and sold.

❑ Keep records for at least seven years after you have filed a tax return.

❑ Make detailed deposit slips. Make sure to keep a copy.

❑ Never throw away canceled checks.

❑ Prepare a monthly bank reconciliation (download GB📖 #28 for information on how to prepare a bank reconciliation; bank reconciliation form also available at bforms.com, Form #24).

List any additional strategies and guidelines you will use to streamline your accounting system:

Sample: To simplify the tracking of hotel and air travel costs, supply costs, and other business-related expenses, we are using a business credit card by American Express with a credit limit of $50,000. Expense management reports are available online as needed.	

Give reasons for choosing your accounting system (e.g., low cost, less bookkeeping, allows for growth):

Chart of Accounts – *Describe your "Chart of Accounts." See page 109 and circle accounts you will add:*

NOTE: Account numbers can be changed to suit your system. For example, "Salaries Expense" could be changed from "510" to "560" or even "6100." Discuss this with your accountant.

Time Frame – *Specify your time frame and schedule for the implementation of your accounting system:*

Banking Plan

Give the name and address of your bank. Describe services they offer that can help your operations:

❑ Online Banking ❑ Phone Banking ❑ Business Credit Cards ❑ Short-term Line of Credit ❑ Overdraft Protection

Sample: Our banking needs are handled by [name of bank]. To meet any unexpected increases in working capital needs, we have negotiated $3,000 in overdraft protection and a $50,000 revolving line of credit at 6.7%. This line of credit has been secured by inventory and accounts receivable.

Describe your credit profile. **What** *is your credit rating score? (FICO scores available at www.myfico.com)*

Obtain credit reports at: ❑ Equifax.com ❑ Experion.com ❑ TransUnion.com ❑ Dun & Bradstreet (sbs.dnb.com)

Sample: With a favorable FICO score of 785, I have secured a $50,000 home equity loan .81% lower than average market interest rates and a $10,000 limit business credit card. According to Equifax, the national average FICO credit rating score is 678. A copy of my credit profile is available upon request.

BALANCE SHEET ACCOUNTS

Asset Accounts
100–199

Company assets are anything of value including cash and tangible real goods owned by or owed to your company and contribute to the net worth of your business. In the case of real goods, the full value of the asset is listed regardless of whether it is fully paid for or not (all asset accounts are considered debit accounts unless otherwise noted).

NOTE *Soft assets* include such intangibles as goodwill, patents, formulas, and capitalized research and development. Soft assets are more difficult to keep track of and value. They should be approached with caution when incorporated into an accounting system.

Current Asset Accounts

Current asset accounts are accounts that can be easily turned into cash if necessary within one year. They are listed in order of their liquidity.

100	Cash on Hand (Cash)
105	Petty Cash
110	Cash in Bank
115	Short-term Investments
116	Long-term Investments
120	Accounts Receivable
121	Interest Accrued Receivable
125	Allowance for Bad Debts
130	Merchandise
131	Merchandise Discount
132	Merchandise Returns and Allowances
135	Raw Materials
136	Finished Goods
137	Work in Progress
140	Supplies
145	Prepaid Expenses
146	Prepaid Insurance
147	Prepaid Property Tax
148	Prepaid Rent
149	Prepaid Supplies

Fixed Asset Accounts

Fixed assets (also called real or tangible assets) are difficult to turn into cash. Fixed assets are of a long-term or permanent nature and include assets such as land, buildings, automobiles, and equipment. They are not intended for resale.

150	Land
160	Buildings
165	Leasehold Improvements
170	Equipment
175	Furniture and Fixtures
180	Allowance for Depreciation
181	Allowance for Depreciation of Buildings
182	Allowance for Depreciation of Leasehold Improvements
183	Allowance for Depreciation of Tools and Equipment
184	Allowance for Depreciation of Furniture and Fixtures

Liability Accounts
200–299

Liabilities are legal claims against a business by persons or corporations other than the owners. These claims come before the rights of the owners. They consist of money owed to suppliers or vendors for inventory or supplies; money owed to banks or loan companies for buildings or equipment purchases; money owed for taxes; and anything else bought on credit. Liability accounts normally have credit balances.

Current Liability Accounts

Current liabilities are obligations that must be paid within the year (or one operating cycle).

210	Accounts Payable
220	Salaries Payable
230	Tax Payable
231	Federal Income Tax Payable
232	State Income Tax Payable
233	Self-employment Tax Payable
234	Sales Tax Payable
235	Property Tax Payable
236	Payroll Payable
237	Payroll Taxes Payable
240	Short-term Loans Payable
245	Interest Payable
246	Dividends Payable

Long-term Liability Accounts

Long-term liabilities are funds a company owes (outstanding balances less current portion due) spread out over a period longer than a year.

250	Long-term Loans Payable
260	Mortgages Payable
270	Bonds Payable

Owner's Equity Accounts
300–399

An *equity* is any debt a business owes, whether to outsiders or to its owners. *Owner's Equity* refers specifically to the owner's claim to the net assets of the company (assets minus liabilities). An *Owner's Equity* account is also known as a *Capital* account, *Net Worth*, or simply an *Equity* account. *Owner's Equity* accounts normally have credit balances.

300	Capital Stock
310	John Doe, Capital
315	John Doe, Drawing
320	Retained Earnings
346	Dividends Paid

INCOME STATEMENT ACCOUNTS

Revenue Accounts
400–499

Revenues are the earnings, income, or cash inflow of your business. Revenues can come from the sale of products or the sale of services whether they are in the form of cash or A/R's. Your income records should show date, amount, source, and whether you received as payment cash, property, or services.

410	Sales Revenue
414	Sales Tax Collected
415	Sales Returns and Sales Tax Refunds
416	Sales Discount
420	Service Revenue
430	Other Income
440	Interest Revenue
450	Dividends Revenue
460	Royalties Revenue
465	Rental Income
470	Gain from Sale of Fixed Assets
475	Gain from Sale of Marketable Securities
480	Loss from Sale of Fixed Assets
485	Loss from Sale of Marketable Securities
490	Recaptured Allowance for Depreciation
495	Retirement Loss

Expense Accounts
500–599

Expenses are the day-to-day expenditures arising out of current business activities. It represents an asset that you have for a very short time. Setting up a special expense account is easy. Just give it a title and a name.

510	Salaries Expense
512	Factory Labor Expense
520	Rent Expense
522	Mortgage Expense
525	Bad Debts Expense
530	Income Tax Expense
532	Property Tax Expense
535	Office Supplies Expense
540	Supplies Expense
550	Telephone
560	Utilities
565	Advertising
570	Insurance
575	Interest Expense
580	Depreciation Expense
585	Cost of Goods Sold
586	Freight and Delivery
587	Selling Expense
588	Administrative Expense
590	Miscellaneous Expense

To Do List

II. **Company Plan**

Operating Plan

✓ Buildings, Equipment, and Other Purchases
✓ Computerization Plan
✓ Communications Plan
✓ Internet Plan

Software cannot replace greyware.

ANON

COMPUTER BUYING TIPS

A good rule of thumb is to buy third chip down from the top of the line.

✱

It is generally accepted that 256 colors (VGA) is fine for mainstream business users.

✱

Ink-jet printers may be cheaper upfront, but usage costs are much higher. For a $20 replacement cartridge, expect about 200 pages. On the other hand, a 600 DPI laser printer cartridge will cost about $60 or less for 2,000 pages.

DAY 11

Outline planned purchases. Computerize your operations.
Set up business communications. Develop an Internet plan.

Buildings, Equipment, and Other Purchases

To consider loan requests, banks want detailed information about all major purchases. List buildings, equipment, supplies, inventory, land, raw materials, vehicles, and other purchases required. Give reasons why they are necessary and how they will improve your business. Include costs and whether you will lease or buy.

What to Look for When Signing a Property Lease

Before signing a lease, be sure to check it thoroughly. Have an attorney or realtor familiar with lease agreements go over it. He or she might be helpful in tailoring a fair contract and in making useful suggestions on available options. When signing a lease, pay close attention to the following areas:

❑ Are there any tenant association fees, promotion, or mandatory advertising fees?

❑ Are you able to keep your location if it proves successful?

❑ Are you free to move after a reasonable length of time if the location is not profitable (a short-term lease with an option to renew is desirable)? Can built-in equipment and fixtures be installed and removed?

❑ Can all or any of the property be sublet?

❑ What are the common charges? (e.g., parking, marketing, snow removal).

❑ What is the liability if you default?

❑ Who is responsible for alterations?

❑ Who is responsible for building, property, and liability insurance?

❑ Who is responsible for utilities, maintenance, and supplies?

❑ Who takes care of plumbing, electrical, or air conditioning repairs?

❑ Will you be able to expand?

❑ Will leasing costs increase annually? If so, how? By consumer price index? By higher maintenance fee?

Computerization Plan

In this section, describe what kinds of computer software you will need and what kinds of computer equipment you need to run the software.

Selecting Computer Software

Computerizing your business is usually a software problem first and a hardware problem second. Think of a computer without software, as a hammer without its head. To create the perfect "computer solution," understand what it is you need to accomplish, and then match those needs with what the market has to offer.

Selecting Computer Hardware

If your business is just getting under way, the purchase of a high technology computer system could seriously tax your cash reserves. And perhaps worse, the time and energy required to learn how to use it could be better spent finding customers. However, properly incorporated into your everyday workflow, a computer can greatly improve the efficiency and effectiveness of your business. It is the *wheel* of the modern age. For most entrepreneurs, it is not a question of whether you should computerize, but when and how much you should spend.

Avoiding the Computer Blues

The fundamental rule for avoiding the computer blues is "*plan* for the worst and *prevent* for the best." Avoiding the computer blues starts by selecting the right equipment and applications. It also involves training personnel, establishing security, maintaining equipment, and learning how to protect yourself from all the computer viruses out there just waiting to reformat your hard drive.

Avoiding the Hardware Blues – Computer systems and associated equipment are extremely reliable. If they've been running for ten hours without mishap, they shouldn't need doctoring for a long time. Electronic components seem to either die almost immediately or last until external problems like heat, dust, moisture, power brown outs, and electrical disturbances do them in. To help avoid the *hardware blues*: ✦ don't allow cables to form loops to induce electrical noise and current ✦ don't plug computer equipment into shared wall outlets to avoid IC chip destroying power spikes from equipment containing motors ✦ keep your computer away from dust, cigarette smoke, airborne grease, liquids, food, and moisture ✦ keep your computer cool as excessive heat will kill electronic components faster than dirt and grease ✦ keep your computer safe from static electricity ✦ regularly vacuum, clean, and treat all computer electrical contact points ✦ turn your computer off during thunderstorms ✦ use proper electrical protection.

Avoiding the Software Blues – Waiting for things to go wrong is the best way to give yourself a computer-induced ulcer. Avoiding the *software blues*, like avoiding the hardware blues, centers on careful planning and preven-

DID YOU KNOW?

A "computer virus" is a program that attaches itself to a file and duplicates itself without the user's knowledge. Left unrecognized, viruses have the potential to create a number of costly problems. Anti-virus experts have isolated more than 7,000 different types, most of which infect the Master Boot Record (i.e., they plonk themselves in the computer's memory when a system boots).

NIOSH, the National Institute of Occupational Safety and Health, found that VDT operation in clerical jobs showed the highest levels of stress of any occupation group ever studied by the agency, including air traffic controllers.
COMPUTER MAGAZINE

tion strategies. Plan to: ✦ make regular back-ups of all vital material ✦ choose software carefully ✦ don't place floppies near strong magnetic fields ✦ protect from viruses.

Avoiding the CTS and VDT Blues – Numerous studies have investigated the effects of long-term work with computers on our health. What scientists have found is that like the problems associated with smoking, drinking, and overeating, computer-related problems usually develop slowly over a long period of time, but when they arrive, they arrive with a vengeance. Three of the most common problems are CTS (Carpal Tunnel Syndrome or wrist inflammation), VDT Syndrome (Video Display Terminal Syndrome), and lower back pain. Out of the above three, CTS is the newest and most insidious. CTS is classified as a repetitive strain injury. It is caused by the repetition of nearly identical keystrokes at a high rate of speed, tens of thousand of times per day. Each keystroke causes the muscles to contract and the tendons to move. This in turn irritates the tendons as they slide over the bones in the back of the hand, eventually leading to pain and inflammation. Other problems linked to computer use include fatigue, shoulder and neck pain, nerve damage, angina or chest pain, blurred vision, chronic headaches, dizziness, facial rashes, irritability, nausea, shortened attention span, reduced productivity, sleep disturbances, and sore toes (from having computer components accidentally dropped on them). To help avoid the CTS and VDT blues: ✦ design an ergonomic workstation (*ergonomics* is the part of design that refers to the comfort and safety features of a product) ✦ take planned breaks ✦ limit the time you spend in front of a computer ✦ quit when tired.

Avoiding the Computer Crime Blues – Computer crime can range from vandalism or burglary, to serious damage inflicted by disgruntled employees who use their access to divert money and goods, or destroy records—with surprisingly little chance of being caught. To protect yourself from computer crime: ✦ know the real costs of producing computer records and get coverage to compensate in case of tragedy ✦ assign security passwords to staff to help prevent unauthorized users from stealing, modifying, or destroying data ✦ change passwords frequently and on an irregular basis ✦ do not give too much control over company funds to any single employee without establishing checks and balances ✦ label all disks to identify contents ✦ keep a meticulous computer log and review it to make sure employees not authorized to work in certain areas do not overstep their bounds ✦ keep diskettes, removable hard drives, and other vital data in a safe locked compartment ✦ make back-up copies of all vital material and store them in

CTS FACTS

Since 1985, 200 out of 1,100 reporters and editors working at the "L.A. Times" have sought medical attention for repetitive strain injuries and CTS.

∗

Two million workers' compensation cases were reported in1995. CTS was the most common and costly disorder and accounted for one-third of all the cases.

∗

CTS and lower back pain now account for more lost days of work than any other single cause— almost 30 billion dollars a year in the U.S. alone.

a fireproof, waterproof container, preferably off your business premises ◆ shred sensitive material from computer printouts ◆ spot-check usage of computers to reveal possible abuses of the system ◆ use file encryption software to scramble critical data.

NOTE Increasing reliance on the Web for business-related transactions has created a new source for computer related blues: the threat of cyberwar. In a recent Black Hat Security Conference in Las Vegas, keynote speaker Richard Clarke, presidential advisor on Cybersecurity, stated the following warning to conference attendees: "You all have a responsibility to say we're vulnerable and we need to invest more money in training and technology, so that when a cyberwar comes—and it will—we will win that war."

Communications Plan

Perhaps a telephone, pager, and answering machine are all you need to get a consulting business underway. But, considering that your first communication with a potential customer will likely be through the phone, fax, or e-mail, and since first impressions create lasting impressions, make smart choices. Imagine what could happen to your professional image, if a client calls your home office and gets your four-year-old son. *Good* communications is *good* business.

Answering Machines

One of the most useful functions of an answering machine it to provide clients with additional information about company hours, beeper numbers, fax numbers, or where key personnel can be reached during non-business hours. When recording your announcement, speak in a clear positive voice, giving the name of your company, and exactly what it is you want potential customers or clients to do. Customers like to know right away they have reached the right number and then specifically what is required of them.

Answering Services

Leaving a message with a person—especially during emergencies—is far more reassuring to nervous clients than voice mail or answering machines. A professional answering service will answer your phone with the name of your company, followed by *Message Center*. Clients get the idea that there are several receptionists madly taking down messages, creating the impression that your business is larger than it really is. High-end outfits will also answer the phone exactly the way you ask them to, page you, or forward all

---

Security is considered "sexy" in the software arena. But no one thought firewalls were sexy until Check Point Software went public and started growing with 50 percent pretax margins. Then, all of a sudden, security was hot.
MARC A. FRIEND
General partner, Summit Accelerator Fund

OFFICE TIPS

Answering machines will never replace human beings. People dislike leaving messages on machines especially if they have an urgent problem.

✳

An answering service or machine playing the old standard "you have reached Jones and associates … we're either with a client or on another call, so leave a message and we'll get back to you" is the oldest trick in the book. It doesn't fool anyone.

Some experts predict that worldwide cell phone usage will reach 1.2 billion people by 2005.

NWFUSION.COM

❋

The average cost per cell phone user in August 2001 was $37.25.

TELDOTCOM.COM

If you travel frequently, consider signing up for a nationwide pager service such as SkyPager or MobileMail from SkyTel. Usage costs average $15 to $50 a month.

❋

URL's of some of the best-known cellular, pager and PDA Mobile service providers are:

❑ Arch.com
❑ ATT.com (AT&T)
❑ BellMobility.ca
❑ Sprint.com
❑ Skytel.com
❑ VerizonWireless.com
❑ VoiceStream.com

your messages or only certain messages, or even hunt you down in an emergency. Before signing up with an answering service, talk to other entrepreneurs in your area who use the service. In many cases, you get what you pay for. Prices range from $40 to $100+ a month.

Cellular Phones, Pagers, and PDA's

Communication gadgets have become an essential part of both our business and personal lives. Though some people hate them, many of us love them. Your competition will certainly be looking for ways to go digital and gain an edge.

Cellular Phones – Cellular phones are the ultimate communication tools of the 21st century. They are addictive; almost too convenient. However, even though the cost of operation has been cut in half since the 90's, they're still more expensive than regular phones. Airtime costs vary from city to city. You can reduce charges by shopping around for promotional discounts, and packaged service plans, and using additional services such as call display, voice mail, and call forwarding. You should also be wary of cellular phone crime. Clone phones that steal code numbers from telephone users, account for hundreds of millions of dollars a year in losses. Another word of warning: studies have linked brain tumors to cell phone usage. Better to be safe than sorry, and use an earpiece.

Pagers – Before cell phones came along, pagers were the fastest way to contact people on the go. Pagers can receive words, numbers, email, and voice. They're still going strong because they are smaller, simpler, and less expensive to operate, costing as little as $15 a month. Studies also indicate that having a pager increases the probability of call completion to 90%. And some of today's pagers are so light and compact, you won't even know they're there—until you have to.

PDA Wireless – Forget cell phones and pagers. The PDA Mobile Internet/email phone has arrived. It may take a few years to iron out all the kinks and bring usage and purchases prices down to reasonable levels, but it will happen. You can use them to call anyone (wherever, whenever), access POP3 email accounts, purchase pizza on the Internet, sync with MS Outlook for your calendar and contacts, store valuable computer data, and organize your life, all while listening to the Eagles or Chopin MP3 files. You may not have to jump on the bandwagon right away, but you will. Prices start at $400 and are dropping. Packages can be found for $35 for 200 minutes per month; 40 cents each additional minute.

Fax Machines

The fax revolution spelled the death of telex transmissions, and in its hey-day, increased telephone revenues by $2.5 billion a year. Still going strong, fax machines can be used to send and take orders, as well as distribute product information, news, ads, and illustrations anywhere in the world, as long as recipients also have a fax. Fax machines are not exactly high technology anymore, but they are still quite user friendly when compared to other forms of electronic gadgetry. Most people prefer paper to electronic text.

Telephone: Installing a Home Business Line

The telephone is often the first and only means of contact you have with clients. Use it to make a favorable impression. If you work at home, install a separate business line. You can't afford to lose business when your phone is tied up with personal calls, but you will, if callers hear a busy signal every time you're online. The same is true if potential clients want to send a fax when you're not home but can only reach your answering machine. A business line also allows you to have a business listing in the Yellow Pages and, if you pay for it, a space ad.

Installation Procedures – Check whether your house or apartment is wired for an extra line by calling your phone company. If not, arrange for installation. Prices vary depending on where you live. The alternative to a residential line is a business line, which offers a free listing in the Yellow Pages. The downside is that you pay for every call you make including local calls. One way to save money is to install a business line for incoming calls and use your personal, residential line (which offers unlimited local calling for a low flat fee) to make outgoing calls.

Internet Plan

Every business needs a business card. Every business should have a brochure. And now at the turn of the millennium, pretty much every business needs a website. At the minimum, a company website can function as an online brochure or portfolio, providing information about your company, your products, and your services. All you have to do is hand out your business card with your URL and you never again need to carry around boxes of promotional materials. The structure of your *Internet Plan* (a.k.a. Web *Strategy* or *Web Development Plan*) should contain the standard parts as outlined on the next page. Of course, the exact nature of your plan will depend upon your unique marketing and company needs.

I'm no better at clairvoyance than most industry forecasters, but I would advise IT budget overseers to take their cues from some of the world's most established corporations, which are investing significantly in Web services.
MARK W. VIGOROSO
EcommerceTimes Columnist

Internet traffic is as vital to a website as circulation to a publication, or as audience is to a broadcasting channel. You can't develop an Internet Web plan without projecting Internet traffic.
BPLANS.COM
∗

A good web site is not about technology. It is about communication and reaching your customers.
JAKOB NIELSEN
Norman Nielsen Group, Silicon Valley

Structure of an Internet Plan

Standard Format

❑ **Website Strategy Summary –** Open with a statement that describes the key issues of your Internet Plan.

❑ **Business Model –** Your "Business Model" describes how your website will make money. In traditional business, you simply "sell something for a profit." But the Internet is a new creature of commerce, still evolving and mutating. There are infinite possibilities to get your site to "payoff" and an equal number that just won't work.

❑ **Site Positioning –** Relate benefits offered to your target users. Position towards strengths and away from weaknesses (see competitive positioning, page 185).

❑ **Traffic Forecast –** A traffic forecast provides monthly and yearly projections connecting site traffic with online sales. It also describes how you will build traffic and get visitors to come back. Monthly projections are needed if your traffic is seasonal. Make sure to track site activity that truly measures whether you are achieving your objectives. Page views and unique visitors are easy to track, but they don't mean much until you compare them with sales-related measurements.

❑ **Front-end Development –** *Front-end* development deals with what the user experiences and interacts with. Such issues and requirements include user interface design, menu navigation, usability concerns, site maps, search tools, customization, merchandising strategies, and strategies for keeping users on site rather than clicking off.

❑ **Back-end Development –** *Back-end* development deals with technology needs such as hardware and software, web hosting service, site design, technical expertise, and site maintenance. It also looks at your fulfillment services such as: order entry, inventory warehousing, and shipping.

Web Hosting Service – The majority of business websites are hosted by host server providers, such as Hostway.com, ipowerweb.com, and Verio.net (visit Hostindex.com for more top providers). Each host offers a wide range of options specifying things like how many MBs you can store, number of free email accounts, and GBs of data transfer allowed. Prices range from $5 to $100 per month. Also try geocities.com.

offer free hosting with the inconvenience of pop-up ads (try www.thefreesite.com or www.100best-free-web-space.com for more free hosting solutions). Others can cost thousands of dollars a month. Some businesses choose to host their website by plugging their own server directly into the Internet.

❑ **Resources Needed (Budget Concerns) –** Project site expenses. What will you do if online sales pick up? What will you do if sales shrink or fail to meet projections? A site can range from a simple one-page design created by yourself to a multi-million-dollar website requiring a team of developers, technicians, and content providers. It is important to match your website needs with your business plan objectives—i.e., don't spend money if it won't significantly generate, lead to, or support sales.

❑ **Future Development –** Outline how your site will grow and develop. What improvements are planned? How might changes in technology and online support structures affect your site?

❑ **Milestones –** If your *Web Strategy* is critical to the success of your business, it might be appropriate to list key activities, goals, objectives, and milestones to document the course of its proposed development—e.g.: interface designed 3/12/03, content added 4/31/03, site tested and launched 5/22/03, support form added 7/19/03.

Other Website Concerns
(issues affecting other sections of your business plan)

❑ **Website Marketing Strategy –** Depending upon the importance of your website to your overall business strategy, you may need to clarify your *Online Sales Strategy* and *Sales Forecast* either in this section or in your marketing plan.

❑ **Market Analysis –** A *Website Demographics Summary* might be needed to clarify who you think will be visiting your site and what their needs, buying patterns, and spending habits might be.

❑ **Advertising and Marketing Partnerships –** With popular search engines starting to charge $300+ per year for directory listings, and others instituting cost per click charges, it's a good idea to build strategic relationships with other sites to help build traffic.

Successful
**BUSINESS
PLANNING
30** in **DAYS**

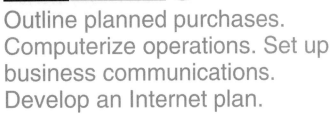

DAY 11 **Worksheets** ⏱

Outline planned purchases.
Computerize operations. Set up
business communications.
Develop an Internet plan.

Buildings, Equipment, and Other Purchases

Buildings Required – *List and describe any buildings that need to be built, purchased, or leased:*

Sample: One of the major startup costs required to launch our business will be the purchase of a storage warehouse located at [address]. The sellers are currently asking $350,000. However, because the warehouse has been on the market for two years, the sellers are willing to carry the mortgage at 7%, providing we can make a 15% down payment.

Describe physical needs and improvements: ❑ floor space ❑ office space ❑ utilities ❑ leasehold renovations

Sample: We have estimated that the warehouse facility will require an additional $75,000 in renovations and repairs to meet our shipping needs. We have included quotations from three contractors in our appendix for updating electrical wiring, adding a receiving office, and repairing the loading dock.

Indicate the space required or allocated to each of the following activities:

Manufacturing Activity	Sq. ft.	Other Activity	Sq. ft.
Fabrication		Storage	
Machining		Shipping and Receiving	
Assembly		Office Areas	
Finishing		Display Areas	
Inspection		Restroom and Employee Facilities	
Other		Other	
		Total Space Required or Allocated (sq. ft.)	

Develop a scale drawing or floor plan of the physical layout of your store, warehouse, plant, or facility:

<u>*Property Leases*</u> *– Describe costs and terms of any leases signed.* **Who** *handles repairs?* **What** *happens if you need to break the lease? (see page 110 for property leasing tips)*

	Sample: Office space is available in the downtown area ranging from $2.12 to $2.76 per square foot. One of the locations we are favoring requires a five-year lease with an option to renew. Escalation of the lease payment is tied into the Consumer Price Index and local property tax increases.

<u>*Equipment and Supplies*</u> *– Describe machinery, fixtures, and supply needs (see page 254 for equipment leasing tips). Provide rough illustrations of equipment layout and production flow in your appendix:*

	Sample: Our current production capacity for [product A] is [XX] units per week. However, new technology is available to increase production to [XX] units per week. To secure a competitive edge, we need to purchase [describe equipment]. It is estimated that this equipment will increase profits by [X]%.

List fixtures and equipment required. List machinery needed to perform any manufacturing. Indicate costs and installation charges, and from who and where purchases are to be made:

Type of Fixture, Machinery, or Equipment	Buy or Lease from	Installation Charge	+ Number Required	x Unit Cost	= Total Cost
		$		$	$

Total Cost $

Inventory, Supplies, and Raw Materials – *Summarize inventory needed. Specify total cost, depth, quality level, and any specific details worth mentioning. List cost and quantity of key inventory and consumable supplies and tools. Summarize raw materials needed and whether they are readily available:*

Sample: To produce [product A], we need the following supplies and raw materials [describe]. However, to keep shipping and raw materials carrying costs to a minimum, we have located our manufacturing plant within a 20-km radius of our major suppliers. Using just-in-time inventory management software, we are able to reduce our production cycle from two weeks to six days.	

❑ Product Items ❑ Raw Materials ❑ Component Parts	Quantity	x Cost / Unit	= Total Cost
		$	$

A) Total Cost $

Consumable Supplies and Tools	Quantity	x	Cost Per Unit	=	Total Cost
			$		$

B) Total Cost	$
C) Total Opening Inventory Requirements (C = A + B)	$

Land Required – *Provide details of site plan, and costs of land, including installation of services:*

Vehicles Required – *List the makes, models, and costs of any cars, vans, or trucks required:*

Other Purchases Required – *Detail other important purchases. Describe these costs:*

Computerization Plan

Brainstorm – *Describe how computerization can help your business. Check objectives that apply:*

- ❏ analyze market trends
- ❏ control and track inventory
- ❏ design and lay out ads
- ❏ handle mass correspondence
- ❏ keep track of product costs

- ❏ keep transaction records for tax purposes
- ❏ manage sales contacts
- ❏ manage client lists
- ❏ manage A/R's and A/P's

- ❏ organize payroll
- ❏ place and receive orders from other businesses
- ❏ schedule and track projects
- ❏ store and retrieve customer data

<u>*Software Needs*</u> – *Specify costs, special features that improve efficiency, and special hardware needed to run required software, such as RAM, CPU, hard disk space, and video memory:*

PROGRAM	Special Features	Hardware Needed	Purchase Cost	Updates	Tech Support
			$	$	$
		TOTAL	$	$	$

Check applications you wish to purchase. Visit Amazon.com or Buy.com for the latest prices and info:

Buyer's Guide for Business Software

OPERATING SYSTEMS 🖫

❏ **Windows98** – *Launches* 36% faster than Win95. Allows you to store 28% more on your hard drive, but crashes a lot. Requires at least a 486–66 MHz, 16 MB of RAM, preferably 32MB, and 150–200 MB on HD.

❏ **Windows XP-Home Edition** – Win XP is more stable than Win98 or WinME. Many software installations will not require reboots. It also protects applications and the operating system from crashes caused by other applications to help reduce data loss and lower software maintenance costs. Requires at least a Pentium 233 Mhz, 256 MB of RAM, and 1.5 GB free on HD. Win XP Pro is a better solution for businesses that need greater security.

❏ **LINUX** – LINUX is a free version of the UNIX operating system. CD-ROM starter kits, with manuals, are available for under $20. This is a serious operating system with a bright future. Microsoft considers LINUX a serious threat. Runs on a 386, 486, or Pentium. Requires 32 MB of RAM and over 300 MB on HD.

❏ **Mac OS X (Panther)** – Apple claims that OS X has "the power of UNIX with the simplicity of Macintosh." With good looks and "cutting edge" graphics, the Mac OS is still popular with DTP and graphic software users. Its disadvantage, compared to Windows, is less available software. General business users should avoid it.

BUSINESS SOFTWARE 🖫

❏ **Accounting Packages** – Leading Brands:
Entry Level Packages
MS Money Small Business .... $50–$75
Quicken Premier Home & Business . $50–$70
Home Office or Small Businesses
MYOB Plus................................... $200–$250
Peachtree Accounting................... $140–$350
QuickBooks Pro .... $100–$280
Simply Accounting Pro .... $80–$100
Medium to Large Businesses
ACCPAC (modules)......................... $1,000+

Money and *Quicken* are the easiest to use, but limited. *QB Pro* is a popular solution, as are *MYOB* and *Peachtree* (watch for rebates). *SA Pro* is the top selling program in Canada. Visit findaccountingsoftware.com for more help.

❏ **Contact Management** – Leading Brands: *ACT!* and *Telemagic* by Interact Commerce (Interact.com), *Maximizer* by Multiactive.

❏ **Database** – Leading Brands: *Access, File-Maker Pro, dBASE, Lotus Approach, Oracle, SyBase.*

❏ **DTP** – Leading Brands: *Ventura, Microsoft Publisher, PageMaker, QuarkXPress.* QuarkX-Press is the #1 choice for printers and DTP.

❏ **E-mail** – Leading Brands: IE and Netscape have adequate email features. However, for serious users, either *Eudora PRO* (free) or MS *Outlook* is a better solution.

❏ **Graphics** – Leading Brands:; Adobe *Illustrator, Canvas* (Mac), *CorelDraw* (PC), Macromedia's *FreeHand. Illustrator* is the industry standard.

❏ **Integrated Packages** – Leading Brands: Microsoft *Works* and *AppleWorks.* These all-in-one packages include spreadsheet, database, and word processing. Limited but cheap.

❏ **Office Suites** – Leading Brands: *WordPerfect Office* by Corel, *Lotus SmartSuite* by IBM, *Office* by Microsoft, and *StarOffice. Office* has 90% of the market (Office 97 can be found for under $100). *StarOffice* is open source (free); runs on Linux and Windows (Sun sells for $75 MSRP).

❏ **Photo** – Leading Brand: Adobe *Photoshop* is the industry standard. Includes *ImageReady* to optimize Jpegs and Gifs to speed up your site.

❏ **Presentation** – Leading Brands: *Freelance Graphics* by IBM, *PowerPoint* by Microsoft. *PowerPoint* is easily the industry leader.

❏ **Spreadsheet** – Leading Brands: *Excel* by Microsoft, *Lotus 123* by IBM.

❏ **Virus Protection** – Leading Brands: *Norton AntiVirus* by Symantec and *VirusScan* by McAfee. A must buy, if you use the Internet!

❏ **Word Processor** – Leading Brands: *Lotus WordPro, WordPerfect, MS Word. Word* is #1.

❏ **Web Browsers** – Leading Brands: *Netscape Communicator, Internet Explorer* by Microsoft, and *Opera.* If you plan to develop a website, you need to have all browsers to preview your site to ensure compatibility.

❏ **Web Page Design** – Leading Brands: *FrontPage, Dreamweaver,* and *HomeSite.* Many website designers prefer *Dreamweaver.* At $99, *HomeSite* is considered the best HTML code editor and is now included in *Dreamweaver MX 2004.*

Indicate what steps you will take to protect your computer system and data:

❑ regular back ups ❑ virus protection with monthly updates ❑ user login ❑ power backup ❑ security password

<u>Hardware Needs</u> – Detail your computer budget and purchasing criteria. Describe your current system:

❑ desktop ❑ notebook ❑ storage devices ❑ backup ❑ PDA ❑ wireless ❑ value for the money ❑ cutting edge

Recommended PC Configurations						
USAGE	**COST**	**CPU/RAM**	**Storage**	**Video**	**Peripherals**	**Software**
❑ *Home Business* (economy)	$500–$1,000	P4, Anthalon 256MB	40 GB	15" 32MB 800 × 600	CD-RW, Ink Jet, 56K Fax/Modem	Win2000, Office 2000, Quicken or MS Money
❑ *Small Business* (middle-end)	$1,000–$1,500	P4, 2.4 GHz 512MB	80 GB	17" 64MB 1024 × 768	CD-RW, 600 DPI Laser, Broadband Cable Modem	Win XP Pro, Office XP, QuickBooks Pro
❑ *Power User* (graphics)	$1,500–$2,500	P4, 3.0 GHz 1GB	160 GB	19" 128MB 1600 × 1200	DVD-RW, 1200 DPI Color Ink Jet, Broadband	Win XP Pro, CAD, Photoshop, Office XP
❑ *Client-server / Web-server*	$1,000–$2,500+	1-2 Xeon 2.6 GHz, 1–8GB	4x80 GB SSCI	15" 8MB 1024 × 768	48X CD-DVD, Ethernet, 1200 DPI Laser, T1	Novell, Linux, Sun Solaris, Win NT Server

To make the right purchasing decision read through the following suggestions and component considerations (visit computers.com, cdw.com, or pcconnection.com for the latest prices):

❑ *CPU* – Never buy the latest chip unless you really need it. For value for the money, buy three chips down from the top. Keep in mind that an old Pentium I or II running Windows 98 can still meet most business needs, as long as you don't need the latest software.

❑ *RAM Memory* – Shoot for 256 MB of system memory, with 64 MB as a bare minimum if using Win98. Extra RAM will give better performance than a faster CPU.

❑ *Hard Drive* – Get at least a 20 to 40 GB hard drive. Choose the more expensive SCSI storage system if you need to use imaging peripherals such as scanners and handle large video, graphics, or sound files.

❑ *Video Card* – To display true color (16.7 million colors) on a 15-inch or smaller display in 800 × 600 mode, your video card needs at least 2MB of video memory. On a larger monitor (17-inches and above), you need a minimum of 4MB of video memory.

❑ *Monitor* – Get a 15-inch if you're content to work at 800 × 600 resolution. A 17-inch screen will give you more room to display more applications at 1024 × 768. Dot pitch should be 0.28 mm or less and support a refresh rate of 75Hz to 100 Hz (higher is easier on your eyes). Bright flat panels are also easier on the eyes.

❑ *CD-ROM, DVD-ROM* – A 20X or 32X CD-ROM is sufficient. Recordable CD-RW drives are highly recommended if you need to archive data.

❑ *Sound Card and Speakers* – Look for sound cards with wave synthesis and full-duplex features. These produce real instrument sounds and can play and record simultaneously for real-time long-distance computer conferencing. To complete your multimedia system, you'll need powered, magnetically shielded speakers. Add a sub-woofer for deep bass to make your PowerPoint presentations rumble.

CPU (MHz)	RAM (MB)	Hard Disk Storage (GB)	Video Memory	Sound Card	CD-RW, DVD-ROM

Monitor	Fax/ Modem	LAN Card	Printer/ Scanner	Other Devices	**TOTAL Estimated Cost**
					$

Communications Plan

Describe how you will communicate with customers, suppliers, and business associates:

❑ Answering Service ❑ 800 Number ❑ Cellular ❑ Email ❑ Fax ❑ Pager ❑ Voice Mail ❑ Online Forums

PHONE and EMAIL COMMUNICATION STRATEGIES			
❑ 27/7 1-800 support ❑ always be brief: the attention span of a sales rep is 10 secs. for unexpected calls ❑ clear messages imply success	❑ email response within 24 hours ❑ for important ideas, your target reader is a forth grader ❑ limit the number of concepts expressed	❑ there should always be an "executive summary" in every phone conversation or email (anything over three lines is not a summary)	

What communication equipment do you need to purchase or lease? List monthly maintenance costs:

❑ Answering Machine ❑ Cellular Phone ❑ Computer for Voice Mail ❑ Fax Machine ❑ Pager ❑ PDA Mobile

Equipment	Purpose (used for)	Purchase Price	Monthly Costs
		$	$

If you need Internet access, give monthly fees, per hour charges, bandwidth, and connection speed:

Internet Plan

Website Strategy – **What** *is the purpose of your site?* ❑ content ❑ community building (to create loyalty)
❑ e-commerce (transactional) ❑ promotional/portfolio (to make buying decisions easier) ❑ combination

Business Model – **How** *will your site make or save money?* **How** *will it support sales at retail locations?*
What *percentage of total sales will each business model contribute? Which areas are most profitable?*

	BUSINESS MODELS		
	❑ advertising (banner, click-on-link) ❑ downloading of software, audio, PDF reports ❑ improve customer satisfaction ❑ make buying decisions easier	❑ members only (users pay to access restricted areas) ❑ online application services (software is used from your main server) ❑ per-use (audio, video, articles)	❑ reduce costs (save on marketing) ❑ sponsorship and partnerships ❑ subscriptions (e.g., paid newsletters) ❑ substitute for phone communication ❑ support services

Site Positioning – **Who** *is the product or service designed for? Describe it.* **What** *is its most important benefit?* **Who** *are your main competitors?* **How** *are you different?* **What** *is the benefit of that difference?*

Traffic Forecast – *Describe how you will build traffic.* **How** *will customers find you?* **Why** *will they return?*

	STRATEGIES for BUILDING SITE TRAFFIC		
	❑ always include your URL in ads and company literature ❑ build community by offering forums ❑ form partnerships with other sites ❑ get listed in Yahoo, Google, and MSN	❑ get ranked high in search engines ❑ get reviewed by popular media ❑ offer free site memberships ❑ provide high quality content (the strategy that built Amazon)	❑ provide free use of application software from your server ❑ provide free information ❑ swap links or banner ads with other sites ❑ start a newsletter

List website activity and sales ratios you will track. **What** *will happen if you don't meet your projections?*

TRAFFIC PROJECTIONS	Monthly	20___	20___	20___	Sample
Unique Visitors					9,000
Page Views					30,000
Online Purchases					312
Sales per Visitor					3.5%

<u>*Resources Needed*</u> *– Describe your "Internet Plan" budget for the next three years (explain costs if appropriate). If online sales projections are too high or too low, how will this affect your budget?*

WEB BUDGET	Monthly	20___	20___	20___
Hardware Required				
Software Required				
Design Costs				
Web Hosting Service				
Site Maintenance				
TOTALS				

<u>*Front-end Development*</u> *–* **What** *features do you want your site interface to have?* **How** *will you make your site usable and appealing? Check strategy statements below and elaborate upon if necessary:*

- ❑ A sitemap and search function has been included in the navigation bar.
- ❑ Each page is under 50K to minimize download times.
- ❑ It only takes users a maximum of three clicks to find anything they want from our home page.
- ❑ Site directory structure has been simplified to three levels.

- ❑ Site design has been tested and is compatible with Mac and PC IE 4.0+, Netscape 4.0+, Opera 5.0+.
- ❑ Usability testing indicates that our target market will react quite well to the site design [provide details].
- ❑ Buying decisions have been made easier through [one-click shopping, secure credit card processing, 24/7 toll-free telephone support].

Our site has the following features:
- ❑ customer product ratings
- ❑ customer reviews and opinions
- ❑ easy six-step membership form
- ❑ industry leading privacy policy
- ❑ real-time inventory information
- ❑ secure customer support forms
- ❑ secure shopping carts
- ❑ storage of customer preferences
- ❑ storage of payment information

Sample: Since the majority of the site will consist of PHP running on an Apache server, only three templates will be required for front-end development. The content of the top header and top menu will remain static, while the left menu and main body column will be dynamically updated using content management technology. The Webmaster is responsible for creating and updating all site content. Our Marketing Manager, in collaboration with a Graphics Designer, is responsible for creating a Flash product/feature tour.

Back-end Development – *Describe technology needs.* **Who** *will host your site?* **Who** *will design it?* **What** *software will be used?* **Who** *has technical expertise?* **Who** *will maintain and update?* **How** *will inventory, order fulfillment, and delivery be handled? Check relevant statements and elaborate where necessary:*

❑ We will be using a [Linux, Solaris, Win 2000] based server platform with [Firewall, SSL (https) security].

❑ Our site will be hosted by [web hosting service] at a cost of $[XX] per month. This service provides [150 MB storage, unlimited traffic].

❑ Tech support staff will be [in-house, out-sourced].

❑ To design our site we will be using [FrontPage 2003, Dreamweaver MX 2004, HomeSite 5.5, ImageReady], and [describe additional software].

❑ [Java-script, CGI, PHP, ASP] coding will be [developed in-house, open source, licensed from XYZ Company, purchased off-the shelf and customized by UWDC Inc.].

❑ Online purchases will be integrated with our current database to facilitate just-in-time inventory control.

❑ Our inventory will come from [suppliers XYZ and ABC] and be warehoused at [location]. Delivery will be provided by [UPS, FedEx].

❑ Site maintenance and updates will be handled by [person/team].

Future Development – *Describe future changes and improvements to content or design. Will any new technologies be used? Do you anticipate new buying trends?* **How** *will you react to future competition?*

Sample: In the future, we hope to reorganize our website around an ASP.NET architecture instead of our current PHP platform. We are also planning to launch an XML-based Web service to meet our competition's current JAVA-based service. Our research indicates that although in the short term an investment in XML technology will have a low ROI, in the long term, it will outperform existing solutions.

Milestones – *List three key dates of your website development.* **What** *will happen?* **Who** *is responsible?*

20		20		20	

DAY 12

Choose an inventory and order entry system. Determine your reorder point.

To Do List

II. **Company Plan**
   Operating Plan

✓ Inventory Control
✓ Order Entry and
  Fulfillment

Inventory Control

Consider inventory carefully. Buying too little or too much, the wrong type or size, can quickly lead to financial problems. It doesn't take long for excess inventory to become dated and hard to clear, nor does it take long for customers to become dissatisfied with your selection, or rather lack of selection, and take their business elsewhere. To help prevent these problems and maximize profits, set up an inventory control and management system following these four steps:

STEP 1 – Determine your ideal inventory level. ❑ Find the average inventory turnover rate for your industry (see trade journals). ❑ Determine ideal inventory level based on factors such as capital available, consumer demand, historical sales patterns, quantity discounts, storage space, and supply levels. ❑ Calculate carrying costs. ❑ Calculate EOQ and inventory turnover rate.

STEP 2 – Establish a purchasing plan. ❑ Establish guidelines for buying and selling inventory items. ❑ Find suppliers. ❑ Establish an incoming order inspection policy. ❑ Calculate reorder points for each item in your inventory. ❑ Establish a discontinuation policy (see page 89).

STEP 3 – Set up an inventory record keeping system. ❑ Select a "periodic" or "perpetual" record keeping method. ❑ Develop a "Period Ending Inventory Record." ❑ Develop an "Inventory In-stock Record."

STEP 4 – Evaluate other concerns. ❑ Establish a markdown policy for products that don't move quickly enough at normal price levels. ❑ Establish a policy for valuating inventory to determine your cost of goods sold (COGS) for income tax purposes (select the FIFO, LIFO, Specific Identification, or Average Cost method).

Determining Your Ideal Inventory Level

In a manufacturing or service business, inventory levels must be kept up to maintain production efficiencies. In a retail or wholesale firm, inventory must be kept up to prevent loss of sales. To find the right inventory level, strike a *balance* between: ❑ maintaining a wide assortment of stock, but not spreading popular goods too thin ❑ increasing inventory turnover, but not sacrificing service ❑ keeping stocks low, but not sacrificing production effi-

Information technology and business are becoming inextricably interwoven. I don't think anybody can talk meaningfully about one without the talking about the other.
BILL GATES

WHAT DOES INVENTORY MEAN?

The term "inventory" includes retail and wholesale merchandise or stock, raw materials, work in process, finished products, and supplies that physically become a part of the item intended for sale.

ciency ❑ buying in volume to get lower prices, but not ending up with slow-moving inventory ❑ having adequate inventory on hand, but not getting caught with obsolete items.

Calculating a Profitable Inventory Turnover Rate

Since the goal of inventory management is to provide a sufficient amount of inventory to meet sales demand and maximize profitability, you need to develop an effective method for determining: ✦ the minimum annual cost of ordering and stocking each item in your inventory ✦ the average minimum cost of ordering and stocking all the items in your inventory ✦ the average number of times your inventory is sold within a specific period of time (your inventory turnover rate) ✦ how much money should be invested in inventory at any one time.

Using the EOQ Formula – If you are in the business of buying and reselling goods, a handy tool to help reduce inventory costs is the "Economic Order Quantity" (EOQ) formula. This formula calculates the minimum annual cost for ordering and stocking an inventory item (or group of items) by considering the total units sold per year, the cost of placing and receiving orders, and inventory carrying costs for each item. By knowing your optimal order size for ALL inventory items, you can average these to calculate your average turnover rate.

Calculating your EOQ – The EOQ model states that given certain assumptions, the order quantity that minimizes inventory cost can be found using:

$$\boxed{\textbf{EOQ}} = \sqrt{\left(\frac{2 \times F \times S}{P \times C} \right)}$$

P is the purchase price the firm must pay per unit of inventory.

F is the cost of placing and receiving an order (e.g., labor, inspection, transport, handling).

S is the annual or projected sales in units.

C is carrying or holding costs expressed as a % of inventory value (e.g., storage, insurance, theft, interest charges, rent, depreciation, stock deterioration).

EXAMPLE If you own a shoe wholesaling company and sell 10,000 pairs of slippers per year, where your average purchase cost is $5 per pair, your fixed cost per order is $500, and carrying costs are 20% of the inventory value, then according to the EOQ model, the quantity of slippers you should order each time is:

$$[(2 \times \$500 \times 10,000) \, / \, (\$5 \times 20\%)]^{1/2} = [(\$10,000,000)/ \, (\$1)]^{1/2}$$
$$= \textbf{3,162 pairs}$$

Using a variation of the inventory turnover ratio (where units are substituted for dollar value), this gives you an inventory turnover rate of:

10,000 units per year / 3,162 units
= **3.162 times per year**

With an average turnover rate of 3.162 times a year, you should reorder new stock every 115 days (365 days per year divided by 3.162).

Using the "Total Sales Divided by Six" Rule: For most businesses, total inventory should turnover at least six times per year. Using this rule of thumb, to figure out how much capital you should invest in inventory, divide your yearly cost of goods sold by six. For example, if you project annual sales of $400,000 at a cost of $240,000, then you should carry on average $40,000 worth of inventory.

NOTE If your plan to retail high-ticket items (which tend to have a slower turnover), a more realistic rule would be: total sales divided by *four* or *four and a half*.

Calculating a Profitable Turnover Rate for a Manufacturing Business – For a manufacturing business, rather than figuring the amount of inventory it should carry in *dollars*, it's easier to figure it in terms of *days of sales*. Consider the following example: a shoe manufacturer plans to stock a minimum inventory of sandals equivalent to three weeks (15 working days) of the projected sales rate to ensure having enough to satisfy demand (the maximum inventory might be six weeks of the projected sales rate to limit the investment in raw materials). If the sales rate of sandals were 150 pairs per day, then the inventory days for the minimum inventory planned would be 2,250 pairs of sandals. If the sandals cost $10 a pair to manufacture then the minimum inventory planned would be $22,500 (2,250 units × $10 per unit) and the daily cost would be $1,500 per day.

Developing an Inventory Records System

An *inventory record keeping system* is primarily used to determine your company's *Cost of Goods Sold (COGS)*, as well as provide information for financial statements. It helps you provide better service to your customers by helping you dispose of unwanted items, keep "hot" items in stock, and see that parts and materials are not lost through theft, shrinkage, error, or waste. To meet these objectives, your records system needs to tell you the following three things:

Displaying older inventory prominently and monitoring its turnover daily, can help prevent losses due to obsolete inventory.
PROFIT TIP

There is a trend towards carrying smaller inventories due to faster and more efficient shipping and ordering processes. More companies are aiming to achieve a rapid turnover on all inventories, believing that the fewer dollars they tie up the better. This strategy allows them to quickly reinvest capital to meet new consumer needs.
PROFIT TIP

1) **Approximately or exactly how much of an item you have in stock at any particular moment in time.** You need this information to maintain sufficient stock of hot-selling items to meet customer demand (see the "Inventory In-stock Record" shown below).

2) **Exactly how much inventory you "have in stock" and "have sold" at the end of the month, quarter, and year.** You need to keep track of this information for accounting and sales information purposes by selecting either a "periodic" or "perpetual" inventory system (see examples below): (a) In a *periodic* system, inventory value is determined only at particular times, such as at the end of an accounting period or the end of the year. (b) In a *perpetual* system, inventory value is monitored on a regular basis (e.g., daily, monthly), and if using a computerized system, in real-time.

3) **How much stock is on order.** So you don't order the same item twice.

As your company grows, you should also: ❑ integrate your inventory record keeping system with other company systems that track sales, production, and purchasing activities ❑ regularly compare projections with actual results and analyze differences ❑ develop procedures to correct problems once spotted to improve business performance.

Perpetual Inventory Method

Activity (manufacturer)	Value in Units
Beginning inventory (*last year's*)	100
Sales (*from records*)	(75)
Production (*actual units made*)	95
Ending inventory* (*estimated*)	**120**

*100 – 75 + 95 = 120

Periodic Inventory Method

Activity (retailer)	Value in Units
Beginning inventory (*counted*)	1,500
Sales* (*estimated units sold*)	(800)
Purchases made (*from PO's*)	900
Ending inventory (*counted*)	**1,600**

*1,500 + 900 – 1,600 = 800

Inventory "In-stock" Record

INVENTORY CARD for *Holistic Pet Supplies*		Item: *Dog Collar* Model: *deluxe leather*			
	Received		Withdrawn		Balance
Date	Quantity	Value	Quantity	Value	Quantity	Value
12/31/04					20	$140.00
1/1/05	80	560.00			100	700.00
1/1/05			10	70.00	90	630.00

Period Ending Inventory Record

PERIODIC INVENTORY RECORD for *Holistic Pet Supplies*		DATE: *1/1/05*	
Item	Description	Quantity	Value
Stock #101	*Deluxe Leather Dog Collars*	90	$630.00
Serial # 871	*Enamel Bird Cage*	1	1,000.00
Stock #511	*HPS Brand Canned Dog Food*	350	402.50
	Other misc. items	23	1,145.00
	Total Physical Inventory	464	3,177.50

Establishing an Inventory Valuation Policy

At the end of each fiscal year, you must determine your income to calculate taxes owed. An essential step in completing this is to carry out an annual inventory to determine your cost of goods sold. An *annual inventory* is a list of goods held for sale at the end of the year (see "Period Ending Inventory Record" on page 130). When picking your inventory valuation method, keep in mind that the value of your inventory is a major factor in determining your taxable income. Furthermore, once you pick a method, you must generally stick to it for the life of your business. Although the methods allowed vary internationally, there are four generally recognized methods for valuing inventory for tax purposes, as commonly used in the U.S. and Japan.

Specific Identification Method – When the individual units in inventory are unique and there are a small number of items in inventory, e.g., "big-ticket items" like jewelry or cars, use the "specific identification" or "cost" method.

1. *Cost Method* – Using this method, you determine the value of your entire inventory at the cost (or "market value") of each inventory item (see LCM, page 136). (i) For retailers and wholesalers, the value of your inventory generally includes all the direct and indirect costs of acquiring it, such as the cost of goods purchased, *less* discounts, spoilage, and returns, *plus* transportation and other charges incurred in acquiring the goods. (ii) For manufacturers, the value of your inventory includes raw materials on hand, labor costs and plant overhead used in production, work-in-progress, and finished products.

FIFO, LIFO, and Average Cost Methods – Use these methods if you cannot identify specific items with their costs or if items are intermingled in your inventory and cannot be identified with specific invoices. These methods are used for companies with large, quick-moving inventory of smaller items.

2. *FIFO Method* – The FIFO method (first in, first out) assumes any inventory you sold was from the first inventory you purchased. Using this method, the items in inventory at the end of the tax year are matched with the costs of items of the same type that you most recently purchased or produced. In the U.S., the IRS prefers this method. It is easy to apply, systematic, objective, and not subject to manipulation. It also coincides with the business practice of trying to sell older items first, before they become obsolete.

3. *LIFO Method* – The LIFO method (last in, first out) assumes any inventory you sold was from the last inventory you purchased. Using this method, the items in inventory at the end of the tax year are matched with the costs of items at the beginning of the year. Although firms prefer the LIFO approach during periods of high inflation, the IRS does not favor it. The rules are more complex and require additional reporting. For example, firms that choose LIFO have to specify in a footnote the difference in inventory valuation between FIFO and LIFO. This difference is called the "LIFO reserve."

4. *Average Cost Method* – Using this method, both the cost of goods sold and inventory are based upon the average cost of all items purchased during your fiscal year. For periodic inventory systems, the "weighted average cost" method is used.

One consequence of using FIFO is that if prices are generally going up over time, your gross income will be matched against the lowest-priced items in your inventory, resulting in higher net profits. In contrast, LIFO would match your gross income against the most expensive items in your inventory, resulting in lower net profits and, consequently, a lower tax bill. If your business and inventory are constantly growing over time, LIFO will generally be preferable.

PROFIT TIP
Source:
Completetax.com
CCH Incorporated

The IRS is more concerned with you being consistent from year to year, than the nuances of the specific inventory procedures you use.

JOHN Q. SMITH
CPA

Problems You Are Likely to Encounter When Valuing Your Inventory – Although counting in-stock quantities is straightforward, difficulties can present themselves when determining its exact value. One problem you might face is the evaluation of work-in-progress. This is because you have substantial leeway in valuation, derived from the variety of choices available to you as to the manner in which goods flow through your establishment. The best advice here is to come up with as simple a method as possible and stick to it. Another problem created is when you have similar items of different costs as a result of being purchased at different times of the year or from different suppliers. Both of these problems are further aggravated, since the values at which your inventories of merchandise, materials, work in process, and finished goods are recorded, have a dual significance: *first*, the amount shown in your balance sheet as a current asset is likely to be a significant working-capital component—shareholders and investors like to see a company with lots of working capital. And *second*, the accounting valuation which you place on your inventories directly affects your net income for the period and hence your taxes (for more information on inventory valuation, consult with your tax advisor or accountant).

Order Entry and Fulfillment

The purpose of setting up an order entry and fulfillment control system is to help you process and keep track of customer orders. A good system also simplifies the buying process for customers, based on an analysis of their buying habits and practices as they deal with the idiosyncrasies of your business. More specifically, it recognizes areas in the ordering process that hinder buying decisions and then offers solutions to remove these obstacles permanently. Order entry and fulfillment systems are usually sales receipt based, cash register based, coupon based, form based, or computer based (see page 137 for more details on each).

Improving Your Order Handling Efficiency

It is difficult for a small product or service business to compete with big firms on areas like assortment, price, and promotion. However, *selling effort* and *customer service* are two places where the small product or service business can compete with larger competitors—and win. To improve order handling efficiency: (1) design a great order entry form; (2) train sales staff to handle orders better; (3) remove ordering "bottlenecks"; and (4) if your inventory is large enough, computerize your order entry system. Each of these strategies are discussed in greater detail.

Designing a Great Order Entry Form – If you plan to use forms in your order entry system, and most likely you will, heed the following advice: poorly designed forms cost time, money, and customers. According to a report published by a business communication newsletter, more than five billion forms are thrown away each year. This happens when people try to fill out forms, make mistakes, and have to start over again. Likewise, in a survey of 3,800 *Modern Maturity* readers, it was found that 58% of people who try to fill out forms give up after their first attempt. To design a great order form:

- *Simplify entry points for customer information.* Consider using narrative fill-in-the-blanks points of entry, especially when targeting kids, such as: My name is *Jack Benign*. I live in *New York*. My street address is . . . etc.

- *Use words readers will understand.* Avoid phrases like, "payment recovery is voided" when you mean, "you can't get your money back." Also, cut unnecessary jargon. Don't say, "charge for excess drip" when you mean, "charge for extending wire more than 500 feet from the premises."

Training Sales Staff to Take and Handle Orders More Efficiently – There are three types of sales personnel who handle orders and who need to be trained properly to perform at peak efficiency. These personnel are the "order handler," the "order taker," and the "order getter." The characteristics of each of these types of sales personnel, along with strategies you can use to get them to operate smarter and better, are described on page 138.

Removing Ordering "Bottlenecks" – The ordering process can be broken down into five distinct areas: order writing, forwarding orders, receiving orders, processing orders, and filling orders. Each of these processes harbors potential "bottlenecks." Worksheet C on page 139 outlines procedures and strategies for overcoming or preventing potential bottlenecks in the order fulfillment process.

Computerizing Your Operations – Not that ago, computers revolutionized the "back end" of business operations with the spreadsheet program. Now, with falling prices in hard drives, faster processors, and the growth of the Internet, computers are learning how to handle information extracted from super-databases with ease, thus encroaching ever more into the order entry area as well. Soon they will completely revolutionize the "front end" of business operations as well. Computerized order entry systems have the potential to prevent errors, improve quality of service, and reduce costs by providing feedback and suggestions to sales staff as each order is entered (see page 137 for more information on computer based order entry systems).

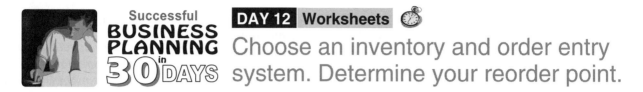

Choose an inventory and order entry system. Determine your reorder point.

Inventory Control

Summarize your inventory management system. Estimate turnover rates:

Sample: In the retail sports clothing industry, a key success factor is to maintain sufficient inventory to meet seasonal sales demand without overestimating need and ending up with a large quantity of leftover stock that requires heavy discounting. To address this problem, we have researched turnover rates from [list sources] and have calculated that we need to hold $[XX] in inventory to generate maximum sales revenues of $[XX] with a minimum loss. To dynamically track inventory, we are also using point-of-sale software from [software company] at a cost of $[XX].

Inventory Level – Check factors that bear the most importance in determining your ideal inventory level:

❑ **Amount of Capital or Financing Available –** How much capital is available to purchase inventory? How will financing charges affect your cash flow? Do you have a special reserve fund to meet sudden high demand for a particular product?

❑ **Consumer Demand and Projected Sales –** How much and what kind of consumer demand exists in the marketplace and how will this affect sales projections? Keep in mind that holding inventory levels at less than what is needed to support sales will cost your firm business, while holding more inventory than present demand will generate excessive inventory holding costs.

❑ **Historical Sales Patterns –** How much inventory have you sold in the past? Which key items will you need to order more frequently and when will you need to stock up to meet seasonal demands?

❑ **Industry Averages –** What are the average inventory level and corresponding stock turnover rates for your industry? Consult trade journals.

❑ **Inventory Carrying Costs –** What and how much are your inventory carrying costs and how do they increase as your inventory levels increase? Consider theft, deterioration, physical damage, and obsolescence costs, as well as tax expenses and the costs of keeping stock control records, ordering stock, and tracking, shipping, and receiving stock (be as precise as possible in calculating these costs).

❑ **Quantity Discounts –** Can quantity discounts actually save you money in the long run? Will discounts received, for large single orders of goods or raw materials rather than numerous smaller ones, more than compensate you for the resulting increased carrying costs and increased probability of spoilage and damage?

❑ **Storage Space –** How much space do you have to store and display inventory?

❑ **Supply Levels –** How much inventory do your suppliers have available to sell to you? It is important when launching a large promotion to make sure your suppliers have enough merchandise to meet your needs.

Outline key inventory control procedures, such as balance between "popular stock" and "variety of stock" that may also affect inventory levels (see page 127). **What** *is your markdown policy (see page 227, "Establish a markdown policy")?* **How** *will you prevent theft?*

Sample: To help maintain a balance between popular sales items, such as [describe], and holding a variety of stock items, we have developed several eye-catching displays that can be used to help promote slow-selling items. To reduce theft, we are implementing electro-magnetic (EM) or Radio Frequency Identification (RFID) technology at a cost of $[XX].	

Describe any additional factors, such as seasonal fluctuations, to determine your ideal inventory level:

Sample: Consulting trade journals in our industry, we have determined that sales are slowest in the summer months of June, July, and August at 19% of total annual revenues and peak during the Christmas season months of October, November, and December at 36% of total annual revenues.	

EOQ – Calculate your EOQ and turnover rate (annual unit sales/EOQ) for key inventory items. Also, calculate annual turnover rate for your entire inventory by projecting sales and dividing this by the current or projected value of inventory that you will be carrying at any one time. Compare with standard industry turnover ratios:

F = cost of placing and receiving an order
S = annual sales (# of units)
P = purchase price the firm must pay per unit of inventory
C = carrying costs expressed as a % of inventory value

Item(s) **EOQ** $= [(2 \times F \times S)/(P \times C)]^{-1/2}$	F ($)	S (# of units)	P ($/unit)	C (%)	EOQ (units)	Turnover (S/EOQ)	Turnover Days (365/T)
XYZ Widget	$97	5,000	$3.22	30%	1,002	5.0	73 Days

	EOQ	Turnover Days
Average Turnover Rate and Days (Average of S/EOQ Turnover Rates)		
Projected (or Actual) Turnover Rate and Days (Sales/Inventory)		
Industry Standard Turnover Rate and Days)		

Detail inventory carrying costs and other EOQ considerations. Comment on any differences between your turnover rate and industry standards. **What** *is your minimum level of inventory to be maintained?*

> **Sample:** Because our industry is new and little data is available for ratio analysis, to maximize sales and reduce carrying costs, we have researched turnover ratios of similar retailers selling large-ticket items and have determined that for [product A], we need to hold $[XX] of inventory, while for [product B] we need to hold $[XX]. For $[XX] of inventory, our carrying costs are $[XX].

<u>*Record Keeping*</u> *– Summarize your inventory record keeping system.* **What** *kinds of forms will you use? Will you computerize?* **How** *will inventory control be connected to order entry and fulfillment?*

We will use a ❑ periodic ❑ perpetual inventory system and [count, monitor] inventory every [time period].

> **Sample:** Even though inventory turnover is high, because we stock less than 15 items, we have decided that a paper-based record keeping system is currently more cost-effective than other solutions. Our system includes: (1) a Period Ending Inventory Record to count inventory levels at the end of each fiscal year; and (2) an Inventory "In-stock" Record updated every month from sales receipts. We will use this record to list inventory purchase orders, as well as number of units received and sold.

<u>*Inventory Valuation Method*</u> *– State method you will use. Explain reasons for doing so:*

Sample: For income tax purposes, we will be using the FIFO (first in, first out) method of inventory valuation.

❑ **FIFO** – highest value of ending inventory; lowest CGS; highest Gross Profit; higher taxes during periods of inflation.

❑ **LIFO** – lowest value of ending inventory; highest CGS; lowest Gross Profit; cost of record keeping higher than FIFO.

❑ **Average Cost Method** – The "periodic" system uses "weighted-average" cost (total cost of units divided by total units available for sale).

❑ **Cost Method** – specific cost of items must be known; easy to understand; opportunity to manipulate income (see "LCM" below).

Lower of Cost or Market Method (LCM) - The "lower of cost or market method" is the same as the "cost" method except when using this method you compare the "market value" of each inventory item with its cost and use the lower value. If at the end of the year you have the following items on hand, as shown in the chart on the right, using LCM, the value of your closing inventory would be $800. If you use this method, you must value each item in the inventory as such. You may not value the entire inventory at cost ($1,200) and at market ($850) and then use the lower figure of ($850).

Items	Cost	Market	Whichever is Lower
A	$300	$350	$300
B	$400	$250	$250
C	$500	$250	$250
Totals	$1,200	$850	$800

Order Entry and Fulfillment

Summarize your order entry and fulfillment control system. Do you have any special strategies?

❑ Sales Receipt   ❑ Cash Register   ❑ Coupon   ❑ Order Form   ❑ Computer
   Based System   Based System   Based System   Based System   Based System

Sample: To ensure quality, customer satisfaction, and repeat sales, we monitor and manage the delivery, billing, warranty service, and repair of our products. Sales are processed and tracked using [software]. To avoid hiring new employees and increase operating efficiency, by [date] we plan to outsource [product division] fulfillment to [name of fulfillment company]. Their customer service record is outstanding and their facility is "state of the art."

Types of Order Entry Systems

❑ **Sales Receipt Based Systems –** A sales receipt based order entry system is usually seen in a small service firm in which services rendered and occasional purchases are always written on a receipt. The receipt becomes the order entry form and the record for accounting and tax purposes. The receipts are usually stored in a cash box along with the change fund and sales revenues. This type of system is very cheap to set up and simple to operate, but very limited as a management tool.

❑ **Cash Register Based Systems –** In this type of system, the cash register is the initial point of entry and is used to keep track of total sales, and within limits, individual items sold to aid in inventory control. However, this system, originating in the 19th century, is not much use to a large retail chain and should only be considered if you operate a small restaurant, corner grocery store, or small independently run retail outlet. It offers little help in controlling a large inventory. To its advantage, it is relatively easy to set up and operate.

❑ **Coupon Based Systems –** A coupon based order entry system is often used by mail order operations, where newspapers and magazines are the chief promotional media. A coupon based system uses coupons that can be mailed in as the initial point of entry. The coupon functions as a simplified order form.

❑ **Order Form Based Systems –** Before computers came along, businesses used invoices, sales orders, and purchase orders (many businesses still do) to organize their orders and purchases, and keep track of their inventory for management and accounting purposes. Of special interest to mail order operators is a "Daily Record of Responses" (a copy of this form can be printed from bforms.com, Form #30). This form allows you to keep track of individual orders or inquiries, how much cash is received, and which advertising pulled in that order. This form can be used as your initial order entry point.

❑ **Computer Based Systems –** A computer based order entry system is potentially the most cost-efficient order entry platform available to small business owners. Such systems range from simple order and receipt entry systems to highly complex point-of-sale systems that keep track of inventory and other factors needed by management—all automatically. The latter systems do not come cheap. Not only is costly software required, but you may also require specialized electronic peripherals to scan in sales, in addition to a secure, reliable computer network. To find a suitable solution for your business, start by researching what the competition is using. QuickBooks, Peachtree, MAS90, Great Plains, ACT!, Goldmine, ACCPAC, and MYOB offer order entry features, but integration and usability is limited. Try the award-winning *Everest* small business management system at www.iCode.com starting at $1,500 or search www.findaccountingsoftware.com for other solutions.

A. Order Entry Forms – *Describe order entry processing and how it works with inventory control:*

Types of Retail Sales Personnel

(classified by level of creative effort)

Routine Effort				Creative Effort
	Order Handler	Order Taker	Order Getter	

B. Order Fulfillment – *How long does it take to get, process, and ship orders? Describe how orders are:* ❏ acquired ❏ received ❏ forwarded ❏ filled ❏ shipped

	Order Handlers – Order handlers perform such tasks as taking tickets at a concert or checking out food at a grocery store. Typically, they are the first to receive your customer's money and the last to say goodbye. They work in a routine selling environment. Due to the nature of their jobs, they will be asked numerous questions and be the first to hear complaints about prices and services. It is thus important to encourage them to be pleasant at all times and help keep them abreast of important facts within the industry. Make it easy for them to communicate to you, so you can quickly recognize problems.
	Order Takers – Order takers receive, handle, and fill orders. They can also be trained to generate additional sales through *suggestion selling*. In suggestion selling, a counter attendant at a fast food restaurant might ask a customer if he or she would be interested in a hot apple pie, milk shake, or perhaps larger order of fries, after the initial order has been taken.
	Order Getters – Order getters operate at their wits' end. They handle order transactions just like other staff, but more importantly are expected to go out and GET orders. For many clothing, furniture, and appliance stores, their success rests solely on the creative efforts of their order getters. However, to make order getters truly effective is no simple task. Educating them on store policies and acceptable selling techniques in an attempt to standardize your service is critical, but more than that, order getters must be encouraged to become "super sales staff." This can only be accomplished by setting up reward structures that foster creativity, courtesy, and exceptional customer service with bonuses, promotions, extra training, and peer recognition.

C. Ordering Bottlenecks – *Describe steps you will to take to remove ordering "bottlenecks":*

Sample: To increase order processing efficiency, we have taken steps to improve order flow by [describe method]. We are the first in the [business type] industry to employ this strategy and have projected an overall cost savings of $[XX]. We have also increased processing capacity by [X]% by implementing [explain method]. To lower startup costs and preserve working capital, we are outsourcing shipping and delivery to [e.g., UPS, FedEx, DHL].

❑ **Order Writing** – All sales reps should be thoroughly trained to complete the order form properly. This applies not only to any field sales staff you may have but also to inside sales staff. Terms, discounts, names, addresses, delivery information, and all special instructions must be written legibly. Poorly written-out order forms, or forms with mistakes should be acted on immediately (time can be saved and careless omission or errors avoided when order forms are carefully tailored to the needs of your business).

❑ **Forwarding Orders** – It's essential that orders gathered by sales staff be transmitted as quickly as possible to order processing. A delay of even a day or two can result in customer dissatisfaction. If a sales rep's territory is within an hour's drive of your office, a good procedure is to have the salesperson deliver the day's orders in person, either immediately after completing rounds, or early the next morning. Of course, if your sales force operates at substantial distances from your home office, orders should be emailed or faxed.

❑ **Receiving Orders** – Regardless of the method employed in getting orders to your office (in-person, fax, or telephone) there should be a central clerk to receive all orders. It is this person's responsibility to check orders for accuracy, clarity, and conformance with company policy. Those that contain mistakes or omissions should be put aside for rechecking later. This clerk should be instructed to record every order on a printable order sheet. Each day's sheet should have columns for writing in the order number, the time received, the customer's name, and the salesperson's signature or stamp.

Give prompt attention and quick dependable service to incoming orders. Ideally, every incoming order should be filled and the merchandise sent on its way within 48 hours. Strategies should also be in place, when orders come in heavy quantities (as happens before a holiday season or specific holidays), or when there isn't enough labor available to fill them, or when transportation facilities are overburdened.

❑ **Processing Orders** – If additional copies of an order are needed, avoid transcribing the information. Use an office copier. Send copies first to the internal sales department where prices are checked, then to the credit desk for an okay. After approval, they're sent on to the warehouse for filling.

❑ **Filling Orders** – On receiving an order, a warehouse or order supervisor should register it in a logbook and check over details. At this point, priorities and shipping considerations can be taken into account. With respect to shipping, transportation runs to different areas can be scheduled for different days of the week or month. Orders destined for those areas can be stacked in difference boxes or trays. As order pickers become available, orders can be distributed. Various types of handling equipment—dollies, carts, and conveyor belts—can facilitate movement of merchandise from the warehouse to the loading area (good warehouse layout and proper utilization of space is important).

Establish procedures for double-checking orders. All outgoing orders should be double-checked before shipping to prevent wasted time and money handling returns or reshipping missed items.

DECISION POINTS

A "decision point" is a checkpoint for measuring your results. Significant dates, sales levels, and production levels can be listed as decision points.

No one knows what he can do till he tries.
PUBLILIUS SYRUS
✳
Management by objectives works if you know the objectives. Ninety percent of the time you don't.
PETER F. DRUCKER

Make an operations schedule. Outline your quality control plan.

Research licenses required and legal considerations. Register your business.

Operations Schedule (Milestones)

An *Operations Schedule*—which can also be referred to as *Company Milestones* or *Work Schedule*—outlines dates assigned and expected dates of completion for key activities, objectives, and *decision points* (i.e., *checkpoints*, such as the completion of a budget). It also describes steps that will be taken to meet goals related to management, public relations policies, guarantees, and personal objectives. Month by month or quarterly flow charts can be used to outline specific actions to be taken and by whom.

Setting Tasks and Monitoring Progress

Once you have established short-term and long-term goals and objectives (see pages 54–57), you will need to break down these goals into more specific tasks and action plans. Next, you will need to prioritize which of these are most important, assign responsibility, establish target dates, and create decision points to monitor progress. When planning, consider: (1) how each task will affect revenues and expenses, particularly monthly cash flow and profitability; and (2) how long employees estimate a task will take to complete.

NOTE Action plans of great importance—but equally great cost—may have to be implemented gradually as your budget allows or perhaps put on hold indefinitely. Don't get overly ambitious when assigning target dates. Allow the recipient of the delegated responsibility to tell the group how long it will take, and then within reason, accept that as the target date. Remember, in most cases, your employees will already have a full day's schedule and little spare time. If they are not given sufficient time to achieve what they have been assigned, your plans may quickly be viewed as impossible to accomplish and will become next to useless.

Production Plan (Service Plan)

Outline how you will make your product. Include a description of your production or manufacturing process (but don't get too technical). If you offer a service, title this section *Service Plan* and comment on how you will deliver your service.

Sample Production Plan Description

We will be using a [method of assembly or construction] for our [product]. Our main supplier of component parts will be [primary supplier, location]. In the event that they are not able to ship according to our specifications, our secondary supplier will be [secondary supplier, location]. Parts will be shipped to us by [method of transport].

The actual machinery used in the production line will be manufactured by [name of company, location]. They will also be doing all scheduled maintenance under a service contract. This machine will allow us to [describe how the equipment will improve operational efficiency].

With [equipment name] our labor and production costs will be reduced by [XX]%. We anticipate the following outlay for this capital equipment:

A&M Machines $[XX]	Service Contract $[XX]

Quality Control

Assuring continued quality of your products and services is critical for business survival. Quality control starts with a **T**otal **Q**uality **M**anagement policy. At some future point, you might also seek ISO 9000 certification. Certification in accordance with ISO standards recognizes the efficiency of your organization and helps build customer confidence. A TQM policy addresses issues such as: (1) customer satisfaction, (2) leadership roles, (3) employee motivation, (4) resource management, (5) integration of company processes, (6) continual improvement, (7) factual approach to decision-making, and (8) mutually beneficial supplier relationships (for details see www.iso.ch).

Required Licenses and Legal Considerations

Laws and regulations pertaining to small businesses can be quite extensive and thus have a major impact on how business is conducted. Under this heading, discuss licenses and permits required, important legal issues, and inspections needed (search Google.com for "Doing business in [country]."]

Registering Your Business

To register your business, contact your local small business center or tax assessment office. Find these numbers in your phone book under city, state/province, and federal government listings (in the U.S., phone 1-800-U-ASK-SBA). Ask what city, county, state/province, and federal forms, licenses, and permits are required—be specific about what kind of business you are starting (a *license* is a privilege granted by a legislative body; a *permit* is a right that anyone can obtain if the requirements of the granting agency

---

If self-regulation worked, Moses would have come down from Mount Sinai with the ten guidelines.
ANON

✳

The great object of the law is to encourage commerce.
JUDGE CHAMBRE

✳

Don't just stand there—undo something.
MURRAY WEIDENBAUM
Economist on Government Regulation

There is too much waste in our work environment. While we talk constantly about the difficulties in making money, we tend to ignore the waste that surrounds us and to overlook opportunities for improvement.
KIYOSHI SUZAKI
The New Manufacturing Challenge

are met). In addition, although you are not expected to be a lawyer, you need a basic knowledge of the laws and legal matters affecting your business. Become aware of: ❑ Occupational Safety and Health (OSHA) requirements ❑ regulations covering hazardous material ❑ local ordinances covering signs and snow removal ❑ federal small business tax code provisions ❑ federal regulations on withholding taxes and social security ❑ state workers' compensation laws ❑ special laws affecting your industry.

Social Responsibility and Community

Beyond all the laws and regulations that govern the legal actions of a business, is where a great company makes its mark. It takes responsibility for the community it serves. *Social responsibility* is a true measure of a company's dedication to its target market and its commitment to bringing "value" to the lives of real people. It unmasks the true nature of the owners and more than anything else, develops a productive corporate culture. Being a "good company" is also a wondrous marketing tool.

Community Involvement – Being a good "corporate citizen" can boost employee morale. It also helps you network with other companies, gives you increased visibility, and can even be used to attract top personnel who respect your ideals and commitment.

Developing a Business Code of Ethics – A *Business Code of Ethics* governs how you handle the "gray areas" of the law. It also attempts to reinforce your company's philosophy by establishing concrete guidelines and value statements for company management and staff.

$ucce$$ Story ➡ Bunsha: "Small is Better" Management

Kuniyasu Sakai and Hiroshi Sekiyama are legendary post World War II founders and managers of a leading high-tech manufacturing group of over forty thriving and profitable individual companies now better known as the Bunsha group of companies. Rather than building an industrial giant like Mitsubishi or Sony, Sakai and Sekiyama believe that as a company grows, the number of employees who feel responsible for its success becomes smaller. Thus, it is better to divide a company once it becomes profitable and stable, to keep employee ambitions high and avoid complacency. Sakai explains that Bunsha "offers a vision for improving the lives of each and every employee increasing both worker and management motivation, as well as a viable plan for rapid revitalization of any company" (quoted from *Divide and Prosper: An Asian Model for Successful Business Growth*, 2003).

DAY 13 **Worksheets** ⏱

Make an operations schedule. Outline your quality control plan. Research licenses required and legal considerations. Register your business.

Operations Schedule

*Summarize your most important goal or objective in your "Operations Schedule." **Who** is responsible for completing this task? **What** impact will its completion have on your business?*

Company Milestones – *Provide a detailed work schedule with tasks or action plans, starting dates, and deadlines by week and month for your first year of operation. Use the "Current Status" box to indicate how near the task is to completion (25%, 50%, 75%) or whether it is already finished (100%):*

OPERATIONS SCHEDULE									
Starting Date	Action Plan, Task, or Project to Be Completed			Target Date	Task Assigned to	Current STATUS			Priority
Notes									
Notes									
Notes									
Notes									
Notes									
Notes									

Key Decision Points – *Summarize your most important checkpoint for measuring your success:* ❏ sales goal reached ❏ contract won ❏ new product launched. *Include dates.* **What** *will happen afterwards?*

	Sample: If sales volume does not reach $[XX] by [date], we will [describe strategy]. If we have not reached our breakeven point by [date], the following strategies will also be implemented: (1) pricing will be modified to become more competitive; and (2) a radio advertising campaign will be launched.

List other key decision points and action plans:

Key Decision Point (and Related Goal)	Decision Date	What Will Happen If Goal Is Met	What Will Happen If Goal Is Not Met
Website gains 100,000 active members.	June 1 2003	We will add a paid membership login. Old members will have free access for three years. New members will pay $19.95/year.	We will seek out a strategic alliance with [ABC and XYZ] to build more site traffic. We will also add new content and MP3 downloads.

Production Plan (Service Plan)

List the basic procedures and key issues in the manufacture or delivery of your product or service:
❏ methods of construction ❏ breakdown of service process ❏ production stages ❏ new technologies utilized
❏ out-sourced parts/services ❏ labor needs ❏ methods to increase productivity ❏ plant capacity

1		**Sample:** Our production process uses a new patented technology that reduces per unit costs by $[XX]. To further lower costs, we have reduced labor hours required to manufacture each unit by improving workflow from each production station. Machinery used in the production of [product A] will be leased from [company A] at a cost of $[XX] per year. As part of the leasing agreement, [company A] will also be handling all scheduled maintenance.
2		
3		
4		
5		
6		

Quality Control

How *will you maintain quality and efficiency in the production of your products or delivery of services?*
Product Quality – ❑ appearance (finish unscratched) ❑ consistency (units identical) ❑ reliability (runs 1,000 hrs)
Service Quality – Staff are: ❑ adaptable ❑ dependable ❑ informed ❑ responsive to needs ❑ well-trained

PRODUCTION and QUALITY CONTROL STRATEGIES			
❑ A comprehensive production manual has been written. ❑ [Company ABC], with greater experience in developing the [XYZ component] will be subcontracted.	❑ Client comments are surveyed quarterly to ensure consistency in service delivery. ❑ Every [100th] product off the assembly line is tested for performance.	❑ [Supplier] is willing to underwrite our R&D for [product]. ❑ We will work with suppliers to keep raw materials at adequate levels. ❑ We have ISO 9000 certification.	

Required Licenses and Legal Considerations

Summarize legal, licensing, inspection, or certification obstacles. Can you foresee any difficulties that will postpone or prevent startup? ❑ FDA Approval ❑ ISO 9000 Certification, www.iso.ch (Quality Management) ❑ ISO 14000 (Environment Management) ❑ OSHA Approval ❑ Underwriter's Laboratories (UL) Testing

Sample: To open a karaoke restaurant nightclub in Hong Kong that serves clay-oven baked pizza, we need the following licenses: general restaurant license, liquor license, branch registration certificate, mobile radio system license, bakery license, import license, and a karaoke establishment permit.	

List licenses, permits, etc., obtained and those yet to be obtained (refer to lists on pages 146–148):

License, Permit, Registration or Necessary Inspection	Date Obtained or Completed	Date Planned to Obtain or Complete

Review the following basic procedures. **Check** *licenses, permits, tax ID numbers, etc., obtained.* **Circle** *those required, but not yet obtained. Summarize the most important of these on page 145:*

Tax ID Numbers	Basic Procedures for Registering and Licensing a Business

Tax ID Numbers

❑ An **SSN** (Social Security Number) is issued by the U.S. Social Security Administration in the following format:

000-00-0000

❑ An **SIN** (Social Insurance Number) is issued in Canada by Social Security Services in the following format:

000-000-000

❑ An **EIN** (Employer Identification Number) is issued by the IRS in the following format:

00-0000000

❑ An **ITIN** (Individual Tax Payer Identification Number) for non-U.S. citizens doing business in the U.S. is issued by the IRS in the following format:

000-00-0000

Basic Procedures for Registering and Licensing a Business

All Countries

❑ Develop a detailed business plan to determine the feasibility of your venture.

❑ Use your plan to shop for equity capital, venture capital, or financing.

❑ Obtain financial commitments before incurring any startup costs.

USA

❑ For individual counseling, contact your local SCORE office.

❑ Obtain proper state and federal licenses. Contact licensing section of local government or Office of the Secretary of State.

❑ If you intend to operate as a proprietorship or partnership under a fictitious name, file a DBA statement with your county office. If you plan to incorporate, contact your state corporate registration center.

❑ Contact your local zoning or licensing authority in your city, town, or municipality to obtain local operating restrictions.

❑ Contact the IRS and file for an Employer ID Number (EIN). To do this you will need to fill out an SS-4 form.

❑ If you hire employees, register with the Workers' Compensation Board.

❑ Obtain any additional special licenses or permits that you may require.

Hong Kong

❑ Register with the Business Registration Office of the Inland Revenue Department within one month of starting business.

❑ Appoint an agent who is a Hong Kong resident to act on your behalf.

❑ Display your Business Registration Certificate in a conspicuous place at your business location.

❑ Visit www.licence.tid.gov.hk for details.

CANADA

❑ For counseling, contact your local Economic Development and Trade office.

❑ Obtain the proper provincial and federal licenses. Contact the licensing section of the Consumer Relations Division of Consumer and Corporate Affairs.

❑ If a proprietorship or partnership, register your business name with Central Registry, Department of the Attorney General. If you plan to incorporate, contact the Corporate Registry, Consumer and Corporate Affairs.

❑ Contact the local zoning or licensing authority in your area to obtain local operating restrictions.

❑ If you hire employees, register with the Workers' Compensation Board.

❑ If you employ five or more people, register with the Health Care Insurance Commission.

❑ Contact Canada Revenue Agency (CRA), to obtain a Business Number (BN) for Unemployment Insurance and Canada Pension Plan Deductions.

❑ Contact your provincial Employment Standards Branch to ensure that you comply with pertinent labor regulations.

❑ Obtain any additional special licenses or permits that you may require.

Doing Business in ...

❑ **China:** Visit www.tdctrade.com or www.HSBC.com.hk

❑ **Japan:** Visit Japan External Trade Organization at www.jetro.go.jp

❑ **Mexico:** Visit www.naftaworks.org

❑ **Singapore:** Visit International Enterprise Singapore at www.iesingapore.com

❑ **UK:** Visit www.companies-house.gov.uk and www.businesslink.gov.uk

Review the following regulations. **Check** *licenses, permits, tax ID numbers, etc., obtained.* **Circle** *those required, but not yet obtained. Summarize the most important of these on page 145:*

❑ BusinessLaw.gov provides legal and regulatory information for small businesses in the U.S.
❑ The National Federation of Independent businesses (www.nfib.com) provides information on legal issues.

Licenses, Regulations, and Legal Requirements

Municipal – Local governments have the authority to issue their own business licenses within their jurisdiction. Since there is no uniformity throughout the state/province regarding municipal licenses, you must consult with the appropriate local officials to determine if your business is affected by local regulations, licenses, or zoning requirements. City business licenses are generally required to control businesses which pose special problems to health, fire, safety, disturbance to the physical and social environment, and so on. Research the following:

❑ Building Codes and Building Permits
❑ Home Owner Regulations
❑ Local Ordinances
❑ Occupant Permit
❑ Zoning Bylaws

Rural – Outside of all cities and towns, business development must confirm with zoning laws administered by the local county concerned, the municipal district, the regional planning commission, or the State Planning Board. Approval from one of these bodies is necessary to construct a commercial building in a rural area.

State/Province – The state or province in which you plan to operate may require you to obtain the following licenses and/or meet the following regulations:

❑ Agricultural Licenses
❑ Consumer Protection Bonds
❑ Environment Restrictions and Regulations
❑ Fictitious Business Name (FBN), also known as a DBA, "Doing Business As" statement (for the U.S.)
❑ Highway Development Permits
❑ Limited Partnership and Trusts
❑ Liquor License
❑ Register for Sales Taxes
❑ State Employers' Registration (U.S.)
❑ State Seller's Permit (U.S.)
❑ Strategic Materials and Equipment Permits
❑ Retail License
❑ Workers' Compensation

Federal – The federal government has wide licensing powers within the fields of agriculture, manufacturing, communications, and both interstate and international transport. The following list contains the more pertinent licenses, permits, regulations, and requirements of the Federal Government:

❑ Agricultural Permits
❑ BN (Business Number) for Canada – The BN is designed to replace the multiple numbers that businesses require to deal with the Canadian government. Each business is assigned a unique registration number. The BN consolidates corporate income tax, import/export, GST, and payroll deductions. Online BN registration is available at www.businessregistration.gc.ca.
❑ Broadcasting Licenses
❑ Employee Forms – In the U.S., new employees will need to fill out Form I-9 and Form W-4. If your employees qualify for advance payment of the earned income credit, they must complete Form W-5. In Canada, your main responsibility involves filling out T4 slips at the end of the tax year for each employee.
❑ EIN (Employer Identification Number) for the U.S.
❑ Export/Import Permits
❑ Hazardous Materials Regulations
❑ Labor Union Regulations
❑ Occupational Safety and Health Requirements (OSHA)
❑ Patents, Trademarks, and Copyright Registration
❑ Payroll Deductions (Form 941 U.S.)
❑ SSN (U.S.) SIN (Canada) ❑ ITIN (non-U.S. citizen)

International Trade Laws

❑ The Hieros Gamos Law and Research Center (www.hg.org) provides information and links on global trade regulations and laws for 230 countries.

❑ The World Trade Organization (www.wto.org) and the United Nations (www.un.org) also provide information on international trade laws.

Review businesses that frequently require licenses and permits. **Check** *areas that may apply to your operation.* **Circle** *areas that require more research. Summarize licensing requirements on page 145:*

Businesses Around the World Frequently Requiring Licenses or Permits

-A-
- ❏ alcohol, retailers and distributors
- ❏ ambulance, emergency first aid services
- ❏ amusement parks and arcades
- ❏ appliance testing labs
- ❏ asbestos abatement
- ❏ auctioneers
- ❏ auto body repair
- ❏ auto rental, U-drive
- ❏ auto sales, new and used

-B-
- ❏ billiards, pool halls, bowling alleys
- ❏ broadcasting stations, TV, radio
- ❏ bulk sales operations

-C-
- ❏ cable TV and Internet service providers
- ❏ carnivals, circuses
- ❏ cemetery operations
- ❏ cigarette sellers
- ❏ coin operated amusement devices, vending machines
- ❏ collection agencies and finance companies
- ❏ commercial trucking and bus operations
- ❏ concrete technicians, testing labs
- ❏ contractors, builders, plumbers, electricians

-D-
- ❏ dairy plants, operators, and distributors
- ❏ dance halls and schools
- ❏ daycare centers
- ❏ detective and security agencies
- ❏ drinking water supply facility operations

-E-
- ❏ elevator and escalator manufacturers
- ❏ employment agencies
- ❏ engine fuel, lubricants
- ❏ engineering firms
- ❏ exporters and importers

-F-
- ❏ farm implement dealers
- ❏ firearms seller
- ❏ firefighting equipment servicing
- ❏ fishing, hunting, and trapping operations
- ❏ fishing vessel operations
- ❏ fish market and processing operations
- ❏ food, beverage seller or preparation service, mobile food units
- ❏ funeral homes

-G-
- ❏ gambling halls, bingo halls
- ❏ game or bird farms
- ❏ garbage removal
- ❏ go-cart track operators

-H-
- ❏ hawkers and peddlers of crafts, balloons, gifts
- ❏ hazardous chemicals or flammable waste disposers
- ❏ horse-drawn vehicle-for-hire operators
- ❏ hotels, guest-houses, inns, motels, bed and breakfasts, apartment houses

-L-
- ❏ land and air transport
- ❏ lotteries, sweepstakes, raffles

-M-
- ❏ manufacturers who dump waste products, dispose of chemicals or effluent, store dangerous goods, produce air pollutants, store pressurized gases, operate boilers
- ❏ massage parlors, body painting studios, public bathhouses
- ❏ mines, oil and gas drilling operations
- ❏ miniature golf course
- ❏ movie theatres, theatres
- ❏ museums
- ❏ music and dance bars

-N-
- ❏ nursing home operators

-O-
- ❏ outdoor advertisers, billposting services

-P-
- ❏ paint spraying services
- ❏ pawnbrokers, junk dealers, secondhand dealers
- ❏ pet shops, riding schools, aquariums, zoos, stables
- ❏ pipeline builders
- ❏ public places of adult entertainment, peep shows, adult cabarets
- ❏ private school operators

-R-
- ❏ radio-controlled device manufacturers
- ❏ restaurants, cafes
- ❏ restricted pesticide dealers and applicators

-S-
- ❏ sanitarium operators
- ❏ sawmills and timber cutting operators
- ❏ school operators: tutorial, flying, driving
- ❏ shooting galleries
- ❏ skating rinks
- ❏ sound trucks

-T-
- ❏ taxicab drivers, for-hire vehicles, limo services, tuk-tuk drivers
- ❏ telecommunications
- ❏ tour operators
- ❏ towing businesses
- ❏ traffic escort services
- ❏ travel agencies

Social Responsibility and Community

Describe key attributes and goals of your social responsibility and community involvement plan:

COMMUNITY INVOLVEMENT IDEAS and STRATEGIES		
❑ budget funds for local charities ❑ donate company facilities for community use ❑ donate old computers to schools ❑ help residents recycle and conserve	❑ offer discounts to economically disadvantaged ❑ participate in and organize community events ❑ purchase environmentally friendly products	**Areas of Concern** ❑ Arts and Music ❑ City Preservation ❑ Conservation ❑ Cultural Tolerance ❑ Gender Equality ❑ Healthy Lifestyles ❑ Racial Harmony ❑ Sports Sponsorship ❑ Technology Ed

Business Code of Ethics – *List important policies and guidelines that will address issues such as:*

❑ expense accounts ❑ favors to clients ❑ gifts from suppliers ❑ staff Web surfing ❑ use of company property

❑ **Demonstrations** – Be truthful at all times when performing demonstrations. There is no point in trying to trick your customer. Short-term trickery will be outweighed by the long-term loss of trust.

❑ **Environmental Concerns** – As a small business owner you should consider the impact your business will have on the local environment. As it is, every year fields and groves are being sprayed with pesticides and dusted with chemicals while poultry, cattle, and other livestock are being raised on chemical fatteners. Lakes, streams, and rivers are quickly being contaminated with industrial waste while at the same time the atmosphere is being polluted with harmful levels of sulfur and carbon compounds from factories and from the millions of vehicles. And if that isn't enough, peoples' ears are assaulted every day by the din of city traffic, roaring machinery, and thundering aircraft overhead. As a business owner, what are you going to do to make your community a healthier place to live in?

❑ **Exploitation of Children** – Promotions directed towards children should not exploit their credulity, lack of experience, or sense of loyalty.

❑ **Extending Goodwill** – Inherent in the concept of a democratic society is the belief that those who are more affluent are responsible for the less able and less fortunate, hence, the social security system, programs for the hard-core unemployed, anti-discrimination laws, and the welfare system. A successful company is ethically responsible for giving something back to the community it has become rich off.

❑ **Honesty** – An entrepreneur who has a respectable function in a community is someone who does not cheat suppliers or customers, advertises and markets without the intention to deceive, and acts with integrity in all dealings, rather than aiming at profits at any cost.

❑ **Indecent Material** – Do not promote or sell material that would cause widespread offense due to the derogatory, vulgar, or indecent nature of the material.

❑ **Social Conflicts** – Modern managers and business owners should be aware of social, racial, and politically charged issues that could have negative affects on their operations if handled poorly. Tact and sensitivity can create an opportunity for good PR.

Determine your organizational, management, and personnel needs.
Find and select professional advisors.

Organizational Plan

An *Organizational Plan* helps you delegate work, responsibility, and authority. It describes who runs your company, controls day-to-day operations, influences decisions, and more specifically, who does all the work (this section could also be titled "Management and Organization Plan" or even "Our Team").

Board of Directors

If your business is incorporated, list members on your board of directors (include address and role in company). Tell when members meet and whether they have a financial interest in your company.

Contract and Temporary Help

List contracted professionals and consultants who provide assistance when needed in specialized or deficient areas such as marketing, sales, or production. Also, list temporary help available to meet fluctuating labor needs.

Using Temp Services and Contract Labor

It is usually recommended for a new or growing business that needs help in the early stages of a project, to initially stay away from hiring permanent staff. This not only protects you from overstaffing and runaway overhead, but also saves paperwork and extra responsibilities. Whenever your future staffing needs are uncertain, it is cheaper, less risky, and ultimately wiser to use a temp agency, employee leasing agency, or private sub-contractor, rather than hire.

Understanding the Hidden Costs of Hiring Employees – On the surface, it may appear that Temp services cost more than hiring additional employees, but there are many costs usually overlooked. Mandatory costs such as social security, unemployment insurance, and workers' compensation amount to over 11% of the basic salary. Payments for time not worked, including vacations, holidays, and sick days, amounts to about 9%. Then there are

The number-one issue for startups used to be access to capital. No more. Now it's recruiting.
ERIC BECKER
✳
In an organization, if the Chief Executive Officer (CEO) is corrupt, this dishonesty will spread throughout the organization such that even the office boy will not think twice about bringing office stationery home.
DR. SHEW SEOW WAH
Chinese Leadership

company benefits such as health insurance, pension plans, and discounts, as well as record keeping, payroll, and paperwork costs, which can easily amount to another 5% to 20%. Total hidden costs are over 40%, meaning a basic $300 weekly salary actually costs your company $420 (and this doesn't include the costs of recruiting and training).

Management Team and Key Employees

Provide brief biographies of management, key personnel, and owners. State ages, educational background, business experience, abilities, related skills, other credentials, and main responsibilities within the company. If needed, include a one-page résumé for each in your *Supporting Documents*. Don't forget to include your own qualifications, and how you plan to get help in areas you are deficient in.

NOTE If incorporated, give detailed information on all corporate officers. Who are they? What are their skills? Why were they chosen? If your business is a partnership, explain why certain partners were chosen, what they add to the company and how their skills and experience are complementary.

Sample Management Team Descriptions/Biographies

President – [Name], Chief Executive Officer since [date]. Director and President since [date]. [Name] is the founder of [your company]. [He/She] has had experience in the [product/service] field with [his/her] own firm, [Johnson Inc., of Stockholm, Sweden], from [date] to [date]. This firm was sold to [company] in [month, year]. Since then [name] has held a [job type] position with [ABC Inc.]. [Name] graduated from the [university] in [date] with a [business degree in economics].
◆ Responsible for entire operation. Oversees management and all other executives. Salary: $50,000.

Chief Financial Officer – [Name], CPA, Chief Financial Officer, Treasurer, and Director. [Name] joined [your company], Inc. on [date] as a financial consultant. [He/She] was named CFO on [date]. [Name] served as corporate controller of [XYZ Shoe Company] from [date] to [date]. [Name] graduated from [Nanyang University in Singapore] in [year] with a [bachelor's degree in accounting]. Since [date], [he/she] has been licensed as a Certified Public Accountant in the [Province of Ontario] and is a member of [the Canadian Association of Certified Public Accountants].
◆ Responsible for financial operations, A/P's, A/R's, interaction with auditors, and investor relations. Salary: $40,000.

Vice President – [Name], Secretary, Executive Vice President, and Director. [Name] supervises company's sales to our largest corporate customers, including [list corporate contracts]. [Name] has served as Secretary and a Director since [date], has been [VP of Operations] from [time period], and Executive VP since [year]. [Name] has been involved since [date] with [your company]. [His/Her] duties included [manag-

A frightened captain makes a frightened crew.
LEWIS SINCLAIR
✳
The new leader is a facilitator not an order giver.
JOHN NAISBITT
✳
For many bankers and investors, the most important part of your plan is who is involved: their, skills, credentials, and experience. Your team will be closely scrutinized to determine if they truly have what it takes to build your proposed business.

If you want one year of prosperity, cultivate grains.

If you want ten years of prosperity, cultivate trees.

If you want one hundred years of prosperity, CULTIVATE PEOPLE.

CHINESE PROVERB

ing the sales department]. From [time period], [he/she] was a [sales rep for XYZ Company, New Delhi, India]. [Name] attended [Cambridge University] from [time period] where [he/she] received a [degree].

◆ Responsible primarily for sales and sales support. Salary: $35,000.

Vice President of Marketing – [Name] Vice President of Marketing. [Name] has been the Company's VP of Marketing since [date]. From [time period], [he/she] was involved in [sales and marketing for Toys "R" Us, New York]. From [time period], [he/she] was self-employed as an [independent sales rep]. [Name] graduated from [Boston University] in [year] with a B.A. in Philosophy. [He/She] is employed by the Company on a part-time basis.

◆ Responsible for marketing, human resources, and training. Salary: $25,000.

Total Executive Compensation: $150,000.

Manpower/Personnel Required

In this section of your *Organizational Plan*, describe all full-time and part-time personnel required. Describe the skills each need and whether they are readily available to work in your location area. Include job descriptions of duties and responsibilities of important personnel, along with salaries and wages. Also, list details of employee compensation, including plans for employee training and fringe benefits. Furthermore, describe what openings are not yet filled, gaps in your management team, and if urgent, how these positions will be filled. End this section by describing how you expect your organization to develop over the next few years and what your future personnel requirements will be.

Writing a Job Description

Writing job descriptions helps you determine more precisely your recruiting needs and set a framework for staff policies. Furthermore, it simplifies the placement and training of employees, improves communication, and establishes a record of job responsibilities in case they come into question in the future. In addition, all the information gathered can be used to create newspaper or bulletin board ads if and when a position needs to be filled.

Parts of a Job Description

A *Job Description* specifies job duties and responsibilities. It may also indicate specialized skills, education, and qualifications required. By laying out these criteria, you give your prospective applicants ample material to help them decide whether they meet the requirements of your job. And your personnel department gets the necessary information to screen applicants (see examples on page 157).

Organizational Chart

An *Organizational Chart* shows at a glance who is responsible for the major activities of your business and who reports to whom. It also summarizes your management structure and helps identify staffing needs (see corporate and sole proprietorship examples below).

NOTE Initially, your organization might be built around yourself acting as the owner/manager, and a few other co-owners or employees, ideally, each with different backgrounds and aptitudes. Hence, your name may occur more than once in your organizational chart, as you will likely have numerous responsibilities (see worksheet on page 159).

> *As a general view, remuneration by fixed salaries does not in any class of functionaries produce the maximum amount of zeal.*
> **JOHN STUART MILL**

Ownership Structure

If your company is a partnership or corporation, you will need to describe the ownership structure of your business. This is especially important if shares have been issued. Information on "Ownership Structure" may also be added to your section on the "Legal Structure" of your company.

Professional Advisors

As a small company, you can function quite well without the full-time services of an accountant, banker, lawyer, or insurance agent. However, once you start to deal with large amounts of money or develop plans for serious expansion, it is wise to seek the guidance and experience of professionals. You might also consider using a consultant who is able to fill the gaps in your management team.

Judging the Personality of a Firm

Companies have personalities that are usually determined by the style and values of upper management. Accounting firms, banks, insurance agencies, and law firms also have personalities. Some are aggressive and risk-takers, others are cautious and conservative; some are people-oriented, others are formal; some are willing to work with new companies, others will consider you a nuisance. To learn the personality of a firm you wish to work with, talk to their present and former clients. Be candid during screening sessions.

Example #1

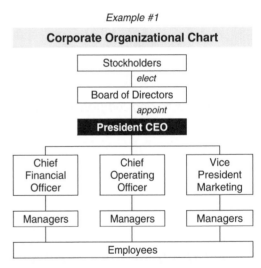

Example #2

DAY 14 **Worksheets** ⏱

Determine your organizational, management, and personnel needs. Find and select professional advisors.

Organizational Plan

Summarize the most important points of your organizational plan. **Why** *will your team be successful?*

	LEADERSHIP SKILLS and STRATEGIES

LEADERSHIP SKILLS and STRATEGIES

❑ able to inspire staff and colleagues
❑ can delegate responsibility effectively
❑ demands account-ability but treats individuals fairly
❑ exudes charisma

❑ erases the "them" vs. "us" feeling
❑ facilitates rather than dictates
❑ has an uncanny knack for finding talented [staff]
❑ knows how to crunch numbers

❑ knows when to get out of the way to let workers achieve
❑ management has [XX] years com-bined experience within the [industry]
❑ takes action
❑ works with passion

Board of Directors

Outline the size and composition of your board of directors. Detail meeting schedule:

Sample: An outside board of directors, in-cluding an oil drilling engineer, Professor of Geology from Indiana University, CPA, and a retired CEO with 20 years of experience in the oil and gas exploration industry, will as-sist our management team in making planning and drilling decisions, as well as helping us develop an IPO exit strategy.

Present a brief résumé of three individuals on your board who are not part of your management team:

Individual Position on Board	Salary Fees or Bonuses	TOTAL Compensation	Qualifications and Experience
	$	$	
	$		
	$	$	
	$		
	$	$	
	$		

Contract and Temporary Help

Describe contract or temporary help needed—e.g.: ❑ "Our [bookkeeper] is available on a PT hourly basis, as needed. The initial agreement calls for services not to exceed _____ hours per month at _____ per hour."

Sample: To bring experience and new ideas to our management team, we have retained the services of [name], a marketing consultant with ten years of experience in our industry. Additionally, our Web team is supported by [name], a freelance programmer who is helping to debug our online catalog PHP scripts.	

Management Team and Key Employees

Who *is on your management team?* ***What*** *is their management style?* ***Why*** *will this team succeed?*

MANAGEMENT STYLE			
❑ a sense of team-work has grown ❑ clear policies between workers and managers ❑ management is open to suggestion (we don't "shoot the messenger")	❑ outstanding em-ployees awarded with stock options ❑ responsibilities allocated by [func-tion, product line] ❑ stand up meetings ❑ team approach used in production	❑ to empower project leaders a "horizon-tal" management structure is used ❑ top-down lines of authority are de-emphasized ❑ work relationships are kept informal	

Present a brief résumé of important team members, featuring key strengths they bring to your team:

❑ President/CEO ❑ Chief Operating Officer ❑ Chief Financial Officer ❑ Vice President ❑ VP of Marketing/Sales
❑ Production Manager ❑ HR Manager ❑ Chief Technology Officer ❑ Purchasing Director ❑ Webmaster

Compensation ❑ Salary ❑ Commissions ❑ Bonuses ❑ Profit Sharing ❑ Company Stock ❑ Stock Options

Key Member		*Job Title*		*Compensation*	$
Experience					
Education					
Responsibilities					
Key Member		*Job Title*		*Compensation*	$
Experience					
Education					
Responsibilities					

Key Member		Job Title		Compensation	$
Experience					
Education					
Responsibilities					

Strengths ❏ analytical ❏ connected ❏ creative ❏ innovative ❏ knows how to sell ❏ objective ❏ resourceful

Manpower/Personnel Required (Gaps in Team)

Personnel Required – *List full-time and part-time staff needs. Summarize plans for employee training:*

	Sample: Presently, our company consists of 21 staff members plus management. To meet projected market demand over the next five years, we will hire 14 additional staff members, including six part-time sales staff. To train new staff, we have developed a customer service training video and manual.

Gaps in Team – *List and discuss gaps in your team.* **How** *and when will vacancies be filled?*

	Sample: Our current management team lacks marketing experience in the wholesale cosmetics industry. We have recently interviewed six prospective candidates, but they do not quite match our needs or budget. Nevertheless, if this vacancy is not filled by the fourth quarter of 2005, we will outsource advertising to [name of advertising firm].

Job Descriptions – *Write job descriptions for key positions not yet filled. Check important criteria:*

Parts of a Job Description

❏ **Name of Company or Organization** – The top of your job description should have your company name or organization.

❏ **Competition Number and Deadline** – The competition deadline, along with the competition number is often located at the top of the job description. Often used by large organizations and governments with large staffing requirements.

❏ **Job Title** – Under your company name, write the title of the job. This is what makes the job different from other jobs.

❏ **Organization Unit** – If your company is large you may need to indicate which division, department, location, or section of your company needs to fill the position (e.g., assistant copywriter, advertising dept.).

❏ **Accountability** – Title of person to which the job reports.

❏ **Supervisor** – Name of person to which the job reports.

❏ **Job Summary** – A job summary may be a short statement outlining the purpose or mission of the job in question, or it may touch upon many aspects of the job ranging from its basic function and work to be performed, to its supervisory, technical, or administrative scope.

❏ **Compensation and Job Benefits** – Describe how employees will be paid—e.g., commissions, pay period, shift bonuses. Also describe company benefits such as: ✦ holidays ✦ groups insurance ✦ hospitalization and surgery ✦ free parking ✦ training programs ✦ Christmas bonus ✦ savings plan ✦ profit sharing plan ✦ suggestion awards ✦ jury duty ✦ military leave ✦ old age benefits ✦ unemployment compensation ✦ equal employment opportunity.

XYZ Inc. – JOB DESCRIPTION

Job Title: Retail Salesperson

Duties: Greets and waits on customers; acquires and communicates product knowledge; records sales, provides change; wraps for shipping; bags items; stocks and organizes shelves; directs deliveries; opens and closes store when manager is away.

Responsible to: Store manager

Requirements: Applicants must be bondable; good mathematical skills; previous sales experience; be available to work nights and weekends; able to operate a cash register.

Personal: People-friendly; appropriate dress; nicely groomed; punctual and reliable; able to withstand long hours on the floor.

XYZ Inc. – JOB COMPETITION # C241

Competition Deadline: 5/12/2005

Job Title: Assistant Manager

Job Summary: Manager, Pet Supply Shop

Primary Duties and Responsibilities: Will be responsible for opening and closing the store on weekends and assisting in all aspects of running the store. Some cleaning up at the end of the day required.

Skills/Qualifications Required: Accepting high school graduates with five years pet industry experience or college graduates with a business degree in marketing.

Terms of Employment: Base salary of $1,200 a month. 5% commissions on sales.

Prepared by: Sally Schmidt **Approved by:** Harry Lee

Date Posted: 1/12/2005

Qualifications	
Duties	
Other _____	
Responsibilities	
Compensation	$ .... Benefits

Qualifications	
Duties	
Other _____	
Responsibilities	
Compensation	$ .... Benefits

Qualifications	
Duties	
Other _____	
Responsibilities	
Compensation	$ .... Benefits

Summarize other positions in your operation. Check if they are filled ✓ or not filled:

Other Jobs	Duties and Responsibilities	Qualifications Required	Full-or Part-time	Salary or Wage	Benefits	✓
				$		
				$		
				$		
				$		
				$		
				$		
				$		

Organizational Chart

*Develop an organization chart indicating **who** is responsible for **what** and to **whom** for each of the major areas of activity in your business.*

Function	Performed by:	Responsible to:
Sales		
Marketing		
Operations Management		
Bookkeeping and Accounting		
Personnel Management		
Technology Management		
Research and Development		

Organizational Chart – *Modify* and fill in as required the following organizational chart (the chart below has been set up for a small manufacturing firm with 50 to 100 employees):

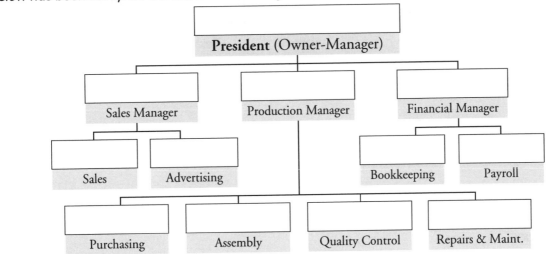

Ownership Structure

Summarize the ownership structure of your business. **How** *much does each partner own? If you are incorporated,* **how** *many shares were authorized at the time of incorporation?* **How** *many shares were issued?* **What** *options are available for your management team or others to acquire additional stock?*

Sample: At the time of incorporation, 10,000 shares of [company name] stock were authorized by [the State of Delaware]. At this time, 3,000 shares have been issued. Of the original stock issue, the company president has been provided with 51%, while the other founding members have been allocated [X]% each.

Major Shareholder	Type of Share Held	% of Total Issued	Number of Shares Held	x	Value of Each Share	=	Total
President (Kelly Berg)	Preferred	51%	1,530		$20.00		$30,600
Others							
Total Shares Authorized		100%			Capitalization		$

Professional Advisors

Provide details about your professional advisors and consultants. How do they add to your company?

❏ Logo Designer ❏ Management Consultant ❏ Marketing Consultant ❏ Quality Advisor ❏ Technical Advisor

Advisor	Name	Address	Telephone	Fees or Retainers Paid
Accountant				
Banker				
Insurance Agent				
Legal Counsel				

LARGEST INTERNATIONAL ACCOUNTING FIRMS (number of countries with international offices) ◆ PricewaterhouseCoopers (150) ◆ Ernst & Young International (133) ◆ KPMG International (157) ◆ Deloitte Touché Tohmatsu (135) ◆ BDO International (86) ◆ Grant Thornton International (91) ◆ Howarth International (86) ◆ RSM International (74) ◆ Moores Roland International (87)
Source: *Accountancy International*, *World Trade Organization*, and *Business Journal* (2004)
Accountingweb.com (try CPAdirectory.com to find a CPA in the U.S.)

LARGEST INTERNATIONAL LAW FIRMS (number of lawyers per firm) ◆ Baker & Mackenzie (2,625) ◆ Clifford Chance/Punder/Rogers & Wells (2,600) ◆ Skadden Arps Slate Meagher & Flom (1,366) ◆ Freshfields (1,327) ◆ Jones Day Reavis & Pogue (1,319) ◆ Allen & Overy (1,285) ◆ Eversheds (1,062) ◆ Linklaters (1,036) ◆ White & Case (1,017) ◆ Latham & Watkins (984)
Source: *International Financial Law Review* (2000)
Lawmoney.com (try Lawquote.com to find a lawyer in the U.S.)

Part III

MARKETING PLAN

TEGuS Cartoons   *Peter J. Patsula*

"Something tells me we've finally pinpointed our
TARGET MARKET!"

> The purpose of business is to create and keep customers.
>
> **∽ Peter F. Drucker**

In this section . . .

- 🗎 Market Description and Analysis
- 🗎 Competition Analysis
- 🗎 Selling Strategies
- 🗎 Marketing Approach

DAY 15

MARKETING PLAN

To Do List

III. **Marketing Plan**

Market Description and Analysis

✓ Industry Environment and Market Trends
✓ Market Needs

IN YOUR *Marketing Plan*, explain and answer the following:

1) **WHO is your target market?** How did you research and determine this? What are their unmet needs? (*market description*)

2) **WHO are your competitors?** What is your advantage? (*competition analysis*)

3) **WHAT steps will you take to open new markets?** How will you gain a market share? Why will consumers ultimately choose your company over both direct and indirect competitors? (*marketing* or *selling strategy*)

4) **HOW do you plan to combine all the above activities?** (*marketing approach*)

Market Description and Analysis

No business plan is complete without a detailed description of target markets followed by an analysis of the trends and conditions of the general marketplace, and how these trends and conditions will affect the outcome and profitability of your business. You don't have to be a trained statistician to analyze the marketplace, nor does your analysis have to be costly. Analyzing the market is simply gathering as many facts as you can about potential customers to determine the demand for your product or service. The more information you gather, the better your chances of meeting their needs and capturing a segment of the market.

Industry Environment and Market Trends

Discuss the business environment, industry outlook, and growth potential, as well as new products or technological developments and influences that will affect your market. State your sources of information and how you plan to keep up with new developments. Discuss population shifts, economic indicators, environmental considerations, political influences, business cycles, consumer demand, cultural and social changes, changing tastes in markets, new research and development, and relevant market demographics such as age trends, spending habits and trends, and income growth trends.

Begin this section with a half or full-page summary addressing all the key areas of your marketing plan.
BUSINESS PLAN WRITING TIP

Finding a need that isn't being met doesn't guarantee success. This need must be tied into a group large enough to generate a profit. If you develop a drug that prevents cancer, then your market would be cancer patients worldwide. However, if the drug is very expensive to manufacture, then your market may be millionaires only.
PROFIT TIP

Uncovering New Consumer Trends and Demands

Forecasting the future is not as difficult as a psychic or fortuneteller would have you believe. Market researchers regularly uncover trends by analyzing patterns in technological advancements and discoveries, market supply and demand fluctuations, government and corporate research policies, and the moods, needs, and spending habits of consumers. These patterns can be uncovered by the analysis of data taken from polls, surveys, news clippings, or any media where information can be accumulated. From these patterns—as well as knowledge of past tendencies, historical cycles, an empirical understanding of human nature, and primitive gut reactions—researchers can derive astoundingly accurate predictions. You can benefit from their hard work by searching for your own patterns in their predictions. In the end, you may never quite piece together exactly what the future will be like, but you can make pretty good guesses.

Market Needs

Under this heading, point out a problem or unfulfilled need in the marketplace. Explain why a solution is needed. Show that you have a bona fide solution and convince readers that you also have the credibility to make the solution work. Use the following strategies:

STRATEGY 1 – Find a need that presently isn't being met. Research the marketplace for a specific need that the competition has ignored, doesn't know about, can't seem to meet, or hasn't bothered to meet. For example, if you find an area with a high crime rate, then it is reasonable to assume that its inhabitants are concerned with safety. The need you can meet is the need for security. Your target market would be people with expensive homes or businesses with large amounts of inventory. Your most likely products or services would be alarms, watchdogs, and security patrol services.

The market is not an invention of capitalism. It has existed for centuries. It is an invention of civilization.

MIKHAIL S. GORBACHEV

✳

There's a tremendous difference between what the public wants and what the critics want.

ALLAN STILLMAN
New York City Restaurateur

✳

Entrepreneurs do one thing and they do it consistently—they add value to peoples' lives.

STRATEGY 2 – Make sure enough people have this need. Find out if the market is big enough to justify the cost of developing a new product or service.

STRATEGY 3 – Pinpoint what you are really selling. Customers don't like buying *things* as much as they like buying what a product or service *stands for*, that is, what it *really means* to them. As an advertiser, this means that if you want people to buy your product or service, pay particular attention to the *real need* it meets. Don't sell "alarms"; sell "security" (refer to chart on the right and chart below).

STRATEGY 4 – Conduct a needs analysis to support "why" your solution is best. Examine more closely, *why people buy* your types of products or services. Detail and break down more specifically individual needs, causes of those needs, buying sensitivities, buying objections, internal and external motivations and influences, and how your company, products, and services aim to satisfy each of these. For example, the need for "security" is motivated by fear and uncertainty. Therefore, in refining your selling approach, you might strategize: Don't sell "security," sell "peace of mind" and a "worry-free lifestyle."

What are you really selling?

NEEDS BEING MET	POTENTIAL MARKETS	SELL THEM
security	people with expensive homes	patrol services, alarms, dogs
stress relief	9–5 workers	weekend getaways
increased harvest efficiency	farmers	new improved combines
increased productivity	service industry workers	computers, faxes, info services

Write Down Here

NEED YOU WILL MEET	MARKET YOU WILL TARGET	PRODUCT YOU WILL SELL

NOTE Don't sell *products*; sell *needs met*. Don't sell clothes; sell style, image, and attractiveness. Don't sell beer; sell sex, fun, and the good life.

Basic Needs ――――――――――――▶ Higher Level Needs

Self Actualization
Esteem
Love & Belonging
Safety & Security
Survival Needs

Abraham Maslow's **Hierarchy of Needs**

Need clean air, water, food, clothes, shelter, transport	**Need** stability, peace of mind	**Need** acceptance, family, passion	**Need** recognition from others, peer respect	**Need** achievement, fulfillment, self-improvement
Sell air purifiers, water filters, grocery stores, houses, tailors, hiking boots, cars, heaters, plumbers, tables	**Sell** gold, bank accounts, life insurance, alarms, guard dogs, reinforced doors, locks, pepper spray, baby alarms, smoke detectors	**Sell** designer label jeans, polo shirts, private clubs, company retreats, salsa dance lessons, romantic dinners for two	**Sell** luxury cars, award plaques, Rolex watches, rare paintings, jewelry, designer furniture, Gucci handbags	**Sell** adventure travel, advanced degrees, music for meditation, yoga, hobby equipment, religious retreats

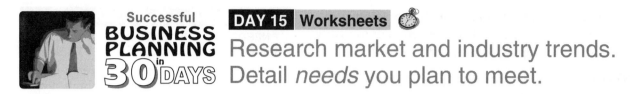

DAY 15 **Worksheets** ⏱

Research market and industry trends.
Detail *needs* you plan to meet.

Market Description and Analysis

Brainstorm – *Using keywords, phrases, and short sentences, summarize your market and industry:*

1	
2	
3	
4	

Industry Environment and Market Trends

Industry Environment – *Describe what's going on in your industry. Is it healthy? Is it shrinking/expanding?*

	Sample: The [product/service] industry has grown from $[XX] million in [year] to $[XX] million in [year], representing a growth of [X]% in [X] years. According to [trade journal, research firm, industry report, trade organization, WTO, the Gartner Group], the market for the [product/service] industry is expected to grow at a rate of [X]% over the next [X] years. By the end of [year], the industry is expected to be valued at $[XX]. The fastest growing area of the [product/service] industry is the [market segment] sector.

Industry Trends – *Describe key industry trends and factors likely to affect them. Indicate sources:*

1	
2	
3	

Consumer Trends – *Outline three important trends that indicate growth potential in your market area:*

1	
2	
3	

<u>*Past and Future Sales Trends*</u> – **What** *were some of the sales trends for your principal products and services over the last five years? Describe what analysts are predicting for the next five years (list research sources). Describe how these trends might affect the performance of your business:*

Sample: Due to the increasing buying power of professional women in the 25- to 40-year-old range, the sale and consumption of [principal product] has increased by [X]% in only [X] years. Presently, competitors, such as [list] are either struggling to reinvent their business model or reacting too slowly to meet demand. This has left the doors wide open for new entries into the marketplace.

List past and present sales figures for your principal products and services. Estimate future sales:

	Product/Service Sales	3 Years Ago	2 Years Ago	Last Year	This Year	Next Year	In 2 Years	In 3 Years
1		$	$	$	$	$	$	$
2								
3								
4								
5								

Market Needs

<u>*Needs Met*</u> – *Describe a market need that presently isn't being met, as well as size of this market:*

Sample: It has been estimated by [research source] that small businesses are losing $[XX] million a year due to inventory mismanagement and inaccurate sales projections. Current accounting software providers are restricted by outdated pricing structures and usability paradigms, and hence have overlooked the need for an all-in-one small business solution for more efficient purchasing, order processing, inventory control, and financial planning. We currently are able to offer retailers, wholesalers, and manufacturers, a cost-effective solution that reduces inventory control losses by 25%, improves online order processing times, and dramatically lowers software training needs.

Show "how" and "why" you can meet this need in terms of your company resources and strengths:

<table>
<tr>
<td>

_____

_____

_____

_____

</td>
<td>

Sample: At [company] we have developed a proprietary Radio Frequency Identification (RFID) technology that eliminates the need for point-of-sale scanning devices and streamlines inventory management. Although there are no guarantees that our competitors will not develop a similar solution, our early entry into the market combined with a strong marketing team gives us a competitive advantage.

</td>
</tr>
</table>

Explain what you are "really" selling based on customer perceptions. **What** *is the "real" need being met?*

<table>
<tr>
<td>

_____

_____

_____

_____

</td>
<td>

Sample: Although our target market is interested in travel tours to exotic locations at a reasonable price, what they really want is freedom and escape from the pressures of work life. To meet this need, we take extra steps to reduce travel document preparation, ensure fast and convenient airport transportation, and only contract air carriers, hotels, and restaurants known for high standards of customer service.

</td>
</tr>
</table>

Buying Motives – Describe "wants" and "desires" that motivate your target market to buy (see GB☐ #46). **What** *are they most sensitive to?*

❑ price ❑ quality ❑ service ❑ warranty ❑ after-sales service ❑ ease of purchasing ❑ quantity discounts

Customer Buying Motives: "Our target market is particularly sensitive to brand, quality, and warranty. They are looking for prestige and a distinctive style of furniture to make them stand out from the crowd. They don't want delivery problems."

<table>
<tr>
<td>

_____

_____

_____

</td>
<td colspan="3">

BUYING REASONS: People are motivated to buy because of ...

</td>
</tr>
<tr>
<td></td>
<td>

❑ advertising
❑ convenience of use
❑ convenient location
❑ desire to make money
❑ ease of purchase
❑ easy credit
❑ efficient service
❑ health benefits
❑ helpful sales staff
❑ increased productivity

</td>
<td>

❑ knowledgeable staff
❑ nature of clientele
❑ packaging
❑ product features
❑ quality workmanship
❑ return policy
❑ savings, good deals
❑ simple instructions
❑ special offers
❑ store décor

</td>
<td>

❑ superior service
❑ up-to-date technology
❑ value for the money
❑ **desire** to emulate those they admire
❑ **need** to feel good about themselves, stay young, sleep better, avoid pain

</td>
</tr>
</table>

DAY 16

Describe and analyze your target market. Project market share.

Outline how you plan to build repeat business.

Target Market Description

As a marketer, you can market to the masses or market to a select group of individuals who have common identifiable needs and desires—a target market. *Mass marketing* is a little like firing a shotgun into a flock of geese. Although having the potential to be extremely profitable, it's often ineffective in today's highly sophisticated and segmented markets, and what's worse, can easily cost you a fortune. Mass marketing is usually reserved for big businesses with big budgets, huge marketing and distribution departments, and production capacity able to keep up with sudden demand. It is for people who want to sell engine oil, shampoo, deodorant, chocolate bars, chewing gum, soda pop, life insurance, and beer.

On the other hand, *target marketing*, your second choice, and the only reasonable choice for startups, is a marketing strategy comparable to using a high-powered rifle to crush the head of a pin. Most startups have limited resources to spend on marketing activities. Concentrating efforts on a few key market segments is more likely to lead to success, allowing you to extract a higher order rate per advertising dollar than the mass marketer. Target marketing means you know your customer like your best friend. Target marketers believe if you think small—and tailor your products, prices, promotions, distribution, sales presentations, and ad copy towards serving a specific group of customers—you can win big, and beat the big guys!

NOTE Going after a target market larger than your ability to serve, can lead to bankruptcy, not fortune—greed is no substitute for good planning. On the other hand, going after a target market too small to support your business is just plain silly. A target market must be big enough to earn a profit.

Sample Target Market Descriptions

Product – The [product] was introduced into the market in [year]. [Product]s remained much the same until [year] when [new technology] allowed some enhancements to be made to the basic design. The market for [product]s has closely followed the population growth. At this time, there are approximately [XX] companies worldwide making [product]s.

INDUSTRIAL MARKETS
⇩
Producers:
Raw Material Extractors
⇩
Manufacturers
⇩
Resellers:
Wholesaler Distributors
⇩
Retailer Distributors
⇩

CONSUMER MARKETS
❑ adventure seekers
❑ Americans
❑ blue-collar workers
❑ Californians
❑ country music lovers
❑ drivers of luxury cars
❑ elderly persons
❑ fitness addicts
❑ government workers
❑ hikers
❑ home owners
❑ housewives
❑ pet owners
❑ retired couples
❑ single white females
❑ teenagers
❑ white-collar workers
❑ yuppies
❑ *any group of people who have needs that are similar*

Service – [Service] companies have enjoyed a period of steady growth over the past [XX] years. This demand is due to many factors, not the least of which is [describe the most important factor]. In our proposed marketing area, there are [XX] [service] services with average estimated sales of $[XX].

Market Analysis and Sales Forecast

A *Market Analysis* breaks down likely purchasers of your product or service into market segments. It also more closely examines their buying patterns especially during holidays such as Christmas, and spring, fall, summer, and winter seasons. A market analysis may be needed for each main product or service offered. In your analysis, you should also include a *Sales Forecast* of major market segments by product or service line over the next 12 months.

NOTE Consider moving your *Sales Forecast* to your *Assumption Made* section. A *Sales Forecast* can also be called a *Summary of Projected Sales*.

Market Entry Strategy

In this section of your *Market Description and Analysis*, summarize how you plan to introduce your product or service to your target market.

Sample Market Entry Strategies

Product – Our [product] has been designed by [name of designer]. We are able to manufacture [product]s using the latest in [new technology] and the [describe production method]. This gives us a tremendous price advantage.

We intend to market our [product] through all the normal distribution channels available to this [product]. These include retail, wholesale, and [describe others]. To penetrate our target market efficiently and swiftly, we intend to initially use commission sales representatives strategically located throughout [geographic area]. We also will start a [local, national] advertising campaign targeting end users who read [names of publications].

Our sales representatives will be chosen based on their own experience in the marketplace. It is our intention to hire the best and the brightest among those available. A list of sales representatives already contacted is included in the *Supporting Documents* section at the end of this business plan.

Service – Over the past few years, we have noticed an increase in demand for [service]. Our computerized office allows us to track our clients' needs and schedule house calls on one hour's notice. We intend to attack this market very aggressively through the use of: ❏ door to door flyers ❏ advertisements in local magazines ❏ house-to-house visits to neighbors of present clients ❏ radio advertisements on weekends ❏ sales calls to [list potential customers or clients].

Market Share and Distribution

Market share projections are not easy to make. In fact, if you can't make them accurately, it is better to "say so" and instead focus on other pertinent issues. When estimating your share, be reasonable; don't exaggerate. Back up findings with research and growth estimates by industry experts. Determine: ❏ What is the total value of the market? ❏ How fast is it growing? ❏ What will its value be in one year? Two years? Five years? ❏ What percentage do you expect to obtain after one year? Two years? Five years? ❏ What percentage do your competitors have?

Sample Target Market Share Statements

The [Asian] market for [product/service] is estimated at $[XX] annual sales based on data furnished by [name of data source]. We estimate that we can achieve [XX]% market share within [XX] years. Marketing data for other markets is in the process of collection (use this same format for additional markets).

Building a List of Potential Customers

To approach the problem of building a growing body of satisfied customers, start by compiling a list of your present customers and then augmenting this list with lists from outside sources. Having a *customer list* (a.k.a. *house list*) will allow you to carry out promotional activities with catalogs and email, inform established clients with a company newsletter about new product innovations and trends, and perform surveys to learn how to serve your customers better.

To build your customer list: ❏ add anybody who buys goods or services from you, makes an inquiry, visits your business and signs in, writes in to request a catalog, or visits your trade show exhibit and leaves a business card ❏ have a contest to collect names ❏ offer free products or promotional items at reduced prices to get names ❏ place inquiry ads in classified sections offering free information ❏ seek out referrals (ask customers you have a good relationship with for any friends or colleagues they have who might be interested in your offerings).

Some business owners feel uncomfortable about the concept of targeting for fear of losing business they could have had if their marketing efforts had been more general. However, it has been consistently shown that for almost all businesses, sales and profits come from a relatively small number of customers.
PROFIT TIP

The destiny of Hong Kong is now the same as the destiny of China. There is no escaping.
T. L. TSIM
∗
Japan is the world's second largest market. With 125 million people, 15% of the world's economy is in Japan. 25% of the world's high-tech products are made in Japan.
Eurotechnology.com

Build Your House List Using Compiled Lists

Compiled lists can be bought, rented, and found for free. Names from compiled lists can be tested, and if responsive, added to your house list. Sources of compiled lists include: ❑ the Yellow Pages ❑ Direct Mail Lists, Rates and Data (a directory that lists companies that offer lists for rent) ❑ Dun & Bradstreet (if you want to find people with certain kinds of credit) ❑ the federal government (the Government Printing Office publishes a free list called *Directories and Lists of Persons and Organizations*) ❑ local governments (public tax records, birth registrations, marriage licenses, and building records can be used to create customer lists) ❑ magazines (almost every magazine is willing to rent you its list of subscribers) ❑ mailing list brokers (can rent to you almost any list imaginable).

Fostering Repeat Business

Not all customers are created equal. Eighty percent of your business will come from 20 percent of your customers—this is called "the 80/20-rule" (one repeat customer is worth four one-timers). It therefore makes sense to focus 4/5th of your time and effort getting to know and serving the 1/5th of your customers who keep coming back and who ultimately will give you most of your profits.

To help build good relationships with your customers and keep them coming back, make it a habit of looking at your business from their point of view. Find as many ways as possible to give them what they really want and need—which is good value, good service and good follow-up—and always be reliable, credible, attractive, responsive, and empathic. It is also important to: ❑ always plan what you are going to sell to your customers next (never send a package to a customer without including an order form for reorders and sales literature on other products you think they might need) ❑ constantly rediscover who your customer is (never forget your customer and they won't forget you) ❑ develop a line of products to complement existing products ❑ give your best customers occasional discounts or freebies, and make sure they know they're getting special treatment ❑ sell consumables—i.e., products that are used up and need to be regularly replaced ❑ take surveys of your customer interests ❑ treat the *second order* as gold.

NOTE Once you have a successful retail outlet with plenty of repeat customers or a successful service with numerous repeat customers, don't be tempted to expand your operations too quickly. Rapid expansion may fragment customer loyalty. Carefully test all new products and services.

DAY 16 **Worksheets** ⏱

Describe and analyze your target market. Project market share. Outline how you plan to build repeat business.

Target Market Description

🧠 *Brainstorm – Check questions you wish to answer in your target market description:*

- ❏ Where do your customers live, work, and shop? Will your business be conveniently located for the people you plan to serve?
- ❏ What are their needs and desires?
- ❏ What common characteristics do customers share? Will these lead to the decision to buy from you?
- ❏ How will they learn about your product or service?
- ❏ What kind of advertising are they responsive to?
- ❏ What do existing customers like best about your company or product?

- ❏ Who else has a need for the product? Where are they?
- ❏ Will you be offering the kind of products or services that they will buy?
- ❏ Are your target markets consumers or businesses (B2B)? If they are other businesses: What do they produce or sell? Who is the contact? How are they being serviced now? What is their history?
- ❏ Is the market close to your location (e.g., if you are in the business of selling and repairing computers, how many computers are owned within a certain radius of your shop)?

Describe and define potential users of your product or service and where they are located:

IMPORTANT FACTORS in Defining Your Target Market		
Target market …	**Consumer**	**B2B**
❏ has characteristics which relate meaningfully to the decision to buy	❏ age range	❏ industry type
	❏ education level	❏ industry sector
	❏ ethnic group	❏ # of employees
	❏ family size	❏ # of retail outlets
	❏ gender	❏ # of branch offices
❏ is affordable to market to	❏ home ownership	❏ legal structure
	❏ income range	❏ years in business
❏ is large enough to turn a profit	❏ lifestyle	❏ annual sales
	❏ occupation	❏ stock value
❏ is reachable through advertising	❏ shared needs	❏ company structure
	❏ purchase behavior	❏ purchasing policies
❏ is expanding at a rate of [XX]%	❏ willingness to spend money	❏ willingness to buy from new suppliers

🧠 *Brainstorm – Using keywords and phrases, describe your target market and prospective customers in terms of geography and other demographics (see "Customer Profile Checklist" on page 177):*

Customer Profile – Write a customer profile (use keywords and phrases from previous page):

Example 1 At *Hot Air Adventure Tours*, our target customers will be consumers comfortable with long-distance shopping and recently retired executives interested in adventure, socializing, good health, and the magazines "Jet Set at 60" and "Hot Air Ballooning." Our target customers want to escape a boring retired life.

Example 2 At *BJ's Pasta Supreme*, we will target 25- to 40-year-old health-conscious male and female vegetarians and athletes. We will also target restaurants, daycare centers, and other businesses that prefer to serve fresh natural pasta products without additives or preservatives. Our target customers desire pasta that tastes homemade.

Customer Profile

Market Analysis and Sales Forecast

Summarize seasonal buying patterns that might affect budgeting, sales, and cash flow (% + or –):
❑ cash flow increases or decrease ❑ increased expenses ❑ inventory surplus ❑ short-term loan required

Spring	Summer	Fall	Winter	Christmas

Purchasing Behaviors – Describe factors potential customers consider when buying a product or service like yours. Outline key benefits they will receive purchasing from you rather than competitors:

Sample: Although our target customers are quite sensitive to brand quality and like to shop in clean facilities, we have observed that they strongly dislike aggressive sales tactics. Unlike [list competitors], our sales staff do not operate on a commission basis and have been recruited based on qualities we believe customers appreciate. To reduce unneeded staff/customer interaction, all prices are clearly marked. We have also designed our displays to sell: "so our staff can serve."

Market Segmentation – *Summarize how your target market is segmented. Outline how these segments have changed over time and how they might be expected to change in the future:*

Sample: The [product/service] segment [is shared by [X] competitors in the [area] region. Based on sales data over the past three years, it is estimated that this market will grow from $[XX] to $[XX] by [year]. With market demand being historically stable in this region, we estimate acquiring a $[XX] share by [date].

Sales Forecast – *Describe any daily, weekly, monthly, seasonal, holiday, or other sales or buying patterns for specific market segments and product/service lines (estimate sales by month in $, % of total sales, or units):*

Market Segment 1

Product/Service Line	1	2	3	4	5	6	7	8	9	10	11	12	TOTAL

TOTAL

Market Segment 2

Product/Service Line	1	2	3	4	5	6	7	8	9	10	11	12	TOTAL

TOTAL

Market Entry Strategy

Summarize your target market entry strategy:

❑ opening day party ❑ introductory pricing ❑ promotional blitz ❑ open quietly to avoid arousing competitors

	Sample: To penetrate our target market efficiently and swiftly, we intend to launch a promotional blitz three weeks before opening our doors to the public. This includes a direct mail campaign to local college student associations, offering heavily discounted fitness club package rates for groups of three or more students, as well as free monthly passes to be raffled. Our public relations spokesperson is also scheduled for three radio interviews and a cable TV talk show and will be providing exercise and nutrition tips for young adults.

Market Share and Distribution

Estimate the present market share for your product or service in total units or dollars. Include your present or projected share (make a pie chart of your market share compared with competitors). **How** *do you expect your market share will grow over the next few years? (see page 171 for sample statements)*

	Market Size (in $ or units)	Main Competitors	Projected Sales (in $ or units)	Percentage of Market Share
		A		%
		B		%
		C		%
		D		%
		Others		%
		Your Share		%

Repeat Business – Outline strategies you will use to build repeat business (see page 172 for more ideas):

	BUILDING REPEAT BUSINESS		
	❑ develop complimentary product and service lines ❑ offer special deals for good customers ❑ provide attractive surroundings ❑ know the customer inside and out	❑ reward staff who treat customers well ❑ sell consumables ❑ train sales staff how to be responsive, courteous, and empathetic ❑ treat customers with fairness and dignity	**We provide:** ❑ free balloons to kids ❑ fresh, free coffee ❑ great service ❑ reliable service ❑ speedy follow-up ❑ truthful advice ❑ value for the money

CUSTOMER PROFILE Checklist

1. Type of *shopper*
   - ☐ retail
   - ☐ long-distance
2. Type of *market*
   - ☐ industrial
   - ☐ consumer
3. Size of *market*
   - ☐ < $1 Million
   - ☐ $10 Million+
   - ☐ $1–10 Million
   - ☐ _____
4. Rate of *growth*
   - ☐ decreasing
   - ☐ 10–15%
   - ☐ steady
   - ☐ 15–20%
   - ☐ 0–5%
   - ☐ 25%+
   - ☐ 5–10%
   - ☐ _____
5. Projected market *responsiveness*
   - ☐ moderate demand
   - ☐ high demand
6. Planned marketing *strategy*
   - ☐ mass marketing
   - ☐ target marketing

INDUSTRIAL SEGMENTATION
(for B2B Markets Only)

7. Type of *industry market*
   - ☐ producer
   - ☐ service supplier
   - ☐ manufacturer
   - ☐ retailer
   - ☐ reseller
   - ☐ government
   - ☐ wholesaler
   - ☐ raw materials
   - ☐ distributor
   - ☐ _____
8. Type of *business formation*
   - ☐ proprietorship
   - ☐ corporation
   - ☐ partnership
   - ☐ _____
9. Number of *employees*
   - ☐ 1–5
   - ☐ 20–100
   - ☐ 6–19
   - ☐ 251+
10. Annual *sales volumes*
    - ☐ < $1 Million
    - ☐ $10 Million+
    - ☐ $1–10 Million
    - ☐ _____

GEOGRAPHICAL SEGMENTATION

11. Market *climate*
    - ☐ hot
    - ☐ dry
    - ☐ cold
    - ☐ windy
    - ☐ warm
    - ☐ rainy
    - ☐ cool
    - ☐ snowy
    - ☐ humid
    - ☐ _____
12. Market *geographical terrain*
    - ☐ desert
    - ☐ farming land
    - ☐ mountains
    - ☐ ocean
    - ☐ valley
    - ☐ _____
13. Market *location*
    - ☐ town
    - ☐ city
    - ☐ suburbs
    - ☐ downtown
    - ☐ rural area
    - ☐ county
    - ☐ state / province
    - ☐ national
    - ☐ global
    - ☐ _____

DEMOGRAPHICAL SEGMENTATION

14. Customer *age*
    - ☐ child (0–12)
    - ☐ middle (35–59)
    - ☐ teen (13–19)
    - ☐ mature (60+)
    - ☐ young (20–35)
    - ☐ _____
15. Customer *sex*
    - ☐ male
    - ☐ female
16. Customer *marital status*
    - ☐ single
    - ☐ divorced
    - ☐ married
    - ☐ _____
17. Customer *life cycle*
    - ☐ newly married
    - ☐ married 20 yrs.
    - ☐ married 10 yrs.
    - ☐ _____
18. Customer *number of children*
    - ☐ one
    - ☐ two
    - ☐ three+
    - ☐ _____
19. Customer *ethnic background*
    - ☐ African American
    - ☐ Native American
    - ☐ Asian
    - ☐ _____
    - ☐ Caucasian
    - ☐ _____
20. Customer *education level*
    - ☐ high school
    - ☐ university
    - ☐ trade school
    - ☐ _____
21. Customer *income level*
    - ☐ $15–25,000
    - ☐ $40,000+
    - ☐ $25–$40,000
    - ☐ _____
22. Customer *location*
    - ☐ in same building
    - ☐ out of area
    - ☐ walking distance
    - ☐ out of town
    - ☐ 5 minutes by car
    - ☐ _____
23. Customer *occupation*
    - ☐ white collar
    - ☐ retired
    - ☐ blue collar
    - ☐ entrepreneurs
    - ☐ professional
    - ☐ _____
24. Customer preferred *payment* method
    - ☐ cash
    - ☐ purchase order
    - ☐ check
    - ☐ financing
    - ☐ credit card
    - ☐ _____

PSYCHOGRAPHICAL SEGMENTATION

25. Customer *lifestyle*
    - ☐ conservative
    - ☐ trendy
    - ☐ exciting
    - ☐ thrifty
    - ☐ family oriented
    - ☐ _____
26. Customer *attitudes*
    - ☐ environmentalists
    - ☐ security-conscious
    - ☐ religious
    - ☐ _____

27. Customer *interests and activities*
    - ☐ sports
    - ☐ physical fitness
    - ☐ reading / books
    - ☐ weekend athletes
    - ☐ shopping
    - ☐ vegetarians
    - ☐ walkman users
    - ☐ computer users
    - ☐ movie goers
    - ☐ _____
28. Customer *social class*
    - ☐ lower
    - ☐ middle
    - ☐ upper
    - ☐ _____
29. Customer *opinions*
    - ☐ easily led
    - ☐ opinionated
30. Customer *level of desire*
    Do your target customers actually want your product or service or will they need a great deal of persuasion?
    - ☐ high
    - ☐ low
    - ☐ medium
    - ☐ _____
31. Customer *advertising responsiveness*
    Are your target customers easily influenced by advertising or rebellious towards it? How do they handle direct mail? Classified ads? Phone sales?
    - ☐ easily influenced
    - ☐ neutral
    - ☐ indifferent
    - ☐ rebellious
32. Customer *needs*
    Are the needs of your customers new needs created by change or old needs presently being neglected? Are customers stable or fickle?
    - ☐ new
    - ☐ neglected
    - ☐ fickle
    - ☐ stable
33. Customer *benefits desired*
    - ☐ economy
    - ☐ luxury
    - ☐ convenience
    - ☐ high quality
    - ☐ reliability
    - ☐ performance
    - ☐ easy access
    - ☐ fast delivery
    - ☐ _____
    - ☐ _____
34. Customer *buying preferences*
    - ☐ single orders
    - ☐ bulk orders
    - ☐ several orders
    - ☐ _____
35. Customer *seasonal buying patterns*
    - ☐ spring
    - ☐ winter
    - ☐ summer
    - ☐ Christmas
    - ☐ fall
    - ☐ _____
36. Customer *reasons to buy from you*
    - ☐ you're the best
    - ☐ friendly staff
    - ☐ you're the cheapest
    - ☐ reliable service
    - ☐ you're the fastest
    - ☐ no competition
    - ☐ you're an expert
    - ☐ _____
37. Customer *usage patterns*
    - ☐ light users
    - ☐ repeat users
    - ☐ medium users
    - ☐ non-users
    - ☐ heavy users
    - ☐ _____

To Do List

III. **Marketing Plan**

Competition Analysis

✓ Competitor Descriptions

✓ Competitive Advantage

✓ Competitive Position

Love your enemies, for they will tell you your faults.

BEN FRANKLIN

❋

I don't meet competition; I crush it.

CHARLES REVSON
Founder of Revlon

Competitor Assessment

EXAMPLE

Betty's Bakery has both direct and indirect competitors for her Whole Wheat Bread Products

Direct Competitors

• Local fresh bread producers

• Brand name bread manufacturers

Indirect Direct Competitors

• Rice, potatoes, fries, and pasta

• Vegetarian food producers

DAY 17

Research competitors. Compare strengths and weaknesses. Write your competitive advantage.

Competition Analysis

No marketing plan is complete without a description of your competitors and how they affect your marketing strategy. *First*, find out who they are. *Second*, describe them. *Third*, show how you plan to beat them.

Competitor Descriptions

List who your major competition is (if there is any), including estimates of their market share and profit levels if possible (report who is doing well and who isn't). Include descriptions of their location, products and services they offer, computerization and technology used, equipment assets, promotional methods, personnel, reputation in the minds of customers, and anything else that may give them a competitive advantage or disadvantage.

Sample Competitor Descriptions

[Name] located at [address] is our main competitor. Its strengths include:

❑ *Effective Location* – located on a major artery; next door to supplier ❑ *Competitive Pricing* – known for aggressive pricing policy; low-cost producer ❑ *Fast Delivery* – ships overnight to most major cities anywhere in the world ❑ *Respected Management* – everyone in upper management has an MBA.

To its disadvantage, [competitor] has: ❑ *Poor Service* – takes more than three months to receive spare parts ❑ *Questionable Dedication* – If sunny outside, management is playing golf or hitting the ski slopes ❑ *Obsolete Machinery* – Unless replaced within six months ❑ *High Overhead* – Spend lavishly on company cars.

Studying the Competition

Never underestimate your competitors *before*, *during*, and *after* startup. Those who fail to do so risk losing their market share, in some cases overnight. To stay ahead of the competition, develop strategies enabling you to react quickly and effectively to whatever your competition tries next, keep track of their selling activities and movements in the marketplace so you are constantly aware of the threat they pose to your business, and stay teachable—read, observe, and listen.

Start by recognizing *exactly* who your competition is, both directly and indirectly. Next, identify the most successful of them and learn as much as possible about *why* they are succeeding. To do this: ✦ check the Yellow Pages ✦ conduct informational interviews with present and former clients ✦ conduct a survey of people on the street ✦ get hold of their products (analyze, dissect, evaluate, find weak points and strong points) ✦ get hold of their advertising and promotional material ✦ keep a file on each competitor containing their ads, articles, brochures, newsletters, etc. ✦ recruit a researcher/spy ✦ seek help from people who are running the same kind of business as you outside your city (people in other regions will probably consider you a colleague rather than a competitor).

Evaluating the Competition

Take a good look at competitors who are superior due to better service, quality, promotion, location, pricing strategies, displays, packaging, and market timing. Also look at additional benefits competitors offer consumers specific to your industry. Pay attention to that nebulous, sometimes indefinable ingredient called "brand image." In short, learn everything you can. In business, what you don't know *can* hurt you. Evaluating the competition can also help you gain insights into the spending habits of consumers (use the *Competitor Profile Worksheet* provided on page 186).

Competitive Advantage

Show how you plan to beat the competition by making a comparison of strengths and weaknesses and how in the end, you come out on top. Provide study or survey results that support your conclusions—it is not good enough to say you have a competitive edge; you must convince yourself and readers of your superiority with proof. If you can't come out on top, which is often the case since your company is new and unproven, then at least make a fair assessment of where you rank. Also, describe major opportunities for growth and major threats, and indicate any special market appeal of your products or services that may put you on top in the future.

Sample Competitive Advantage Descriptions

The competitive advantages which [company] brings to the market are:

> [I/We] will be able to reduce overhead as a percentage of sales thereby increasing the amount of profit retained. With [my/our] aggressive pricing policy, more people will purchase our merchandise thus increasing [my/our] market share.

Don't forget to research "indirect" competition. For example, an arcade may find competition from a bowling alley or pool hall.
MARKETING TIP

In new business, if you engage in anything short of a direct assault on the jugular vein, you're in the Mickey Mouse League.
WILLIAM HOLDEN

✷

Nothing focuses the mind better than the constant sight of a competitor who wants to wipe you off the map.
WAYNE CALLOWAY
CEO of PepsiCo

✷

In business, the competition will bite you if you keep running; if you stand still, they will swallow you.
WILLIAM S. KNUDSEN

[I/We] at [company] propose to use [my/our] good solid business sense, economies of scale, and efficient financial techniques. This will allow [me/us] the following options: ✦ increase advertising ✦ increase customer service ✦ increase profits ✦ increase selection offered ✦ reduce prices.

This plan will give us tremendous flexibility to use any of these options or a mix of them to effectively attack our target markets and meet our long-term goals. [My/Our] combination of experience, sophistication, capitalization, and innovation will assist [me/us] as [I/we] strive to reach [my/our] sales and profit objectives.

Competitive Position

If a prospective customer cannot tell the difference between you and your competition, then you have a problem. Nothing is preventing them from seeing your promotion, loving it, and then going out and buying someone else's products or services. To overcome this problem, prove to them that your offerings are distinct from the competition's by finding and promoting something that gives you a competitive advantage OR in the least makes you *appear* more competitive. Even when dealing in basic commodities like batteries or aspirin, marketing execs have gone to all sorts of extremes to create brand awareness and product differentiation—e.g., the *Eveready Bunny*? "It keeps going and going ..."

How Positioning Works in the Marketplace

Once customers have tried your products or services, they have a perception of your company. However, they will only become loyal customers once they fully believe that what you are selling is more beneficial than competitor products. Knowing this, the most successful businesses strive to determine exactly how products and services are being perceived by customers, and then take steps to position their brand more strongly in the marketplace, in comparison to competing brands. They do this by strategically targeting their promotions to key aspects of their product. For example, a bakery that offers fresh, better tasting, high quality whole wheat bread made without preservatives and additives will try to position itself in the marketplace as "a consistently good-tasting, healthy, whole wheat product." It is interesting to note that brand positioning is in effect an attempt to "brainwash" consumers to choose one brand over another. But today brand choices are so numerous and differentiation so negligible in terms of product functionality that consumers are being "whitewashed" instead—that is, they don't know what to buy. Proper positioning enables prospective buyers to identify your unique benefits providing a clear focus to ease decision-making (see page 185 for ten different approaches to positioning your brand).

Successful
**BUSINESS
PLANNING
30 in DAYS**

Research competitors. Compare
strengths and weaknesses.
Write your competitive advantage.

Competitor Descriptions

Describe who your main competition is (use "Competitor Profile Worksheet" on page 186):

Sample: Our main competitors in the [product/service] market are [competitor A, B, and C]. [Competitor A] is known for aggressive pricing, while [competitor B] has a first-rate customer service plan. [Competitor C] has been in the market since [year] and has the largest market share. However, in the last [X] years they have become complacent.	

Summarize their product and service offerings compared to yours:

Summarize their main competitive advantage and disadvantage (use worksheet on page 182):

Briefly describe OTHER major industry participants:

Name and Location of Competitor	Estimated Sales	Estimated Market Share (%)	Principal Strengths and Weaknesses
	$		
	$		

Competitive Advantage

Brainstorm – Compare the advantages and disadvantages of your business with two competitors:

Factor	Your Company	Competitor A	Competitor B
Price			
Convenience of location			
Availability of parking			
Image			
Breadth of product/service line			
Depth of product/service line			
Credit policy			
Display and fixtures			
Sales training and effectiveness			
Sales support			
Availability of delivery			
Breadth of product line			
Depth of product line			
Performance (for manufacturers):			
speed and accuracy			
durability			
versatility			
ease of operation or use			
ease of maintenance or repair			
ease or cost of installation			
size or weight			
design or appearance			

Brainstorm – **How** will you beat the competition? **What** is your main competitive advantage? Indicate what, if anything, is unique about your offerings. Check **competitive advantage** statements shown below that apply to your company. **Write** your own competitive advantage statement:

❑ A high level of capitalization allows [me/us] to fully address our target market with a comprehensive marketing and customer service plan.

❑ A newsletter directed at both current customers and prospective customers is published quarterly.

❑ A toll-free national 800 number is available for customers to make orders and inquiries.

❑ As a unique [product/service] company, we will be able to keep our margins high, allowing us to provide internal financing for expansion.

❑ At [company name] our pricing structure carefully factors in our costs and what the market will pay.

❑ By purchasing in large amounts, [my/our] per unit costs and shipping costs are lower than competitors'. Through these economies of scale, we can also offer lower prices.

❑ Companies with which [I/we] have established contracts with are known to be financially secure.

❑ [I/We] and [team members] have over [XX] years of combined hands-on experience in this industry.

❑ [I/We] have secured a six-year lease at below market rates.

❑ [I/We] have secured a prime location.

❑ [I/We] will print complete four-color catalogs on a yearly basis. Price lists will be updated as needed.

❑ [I/We] have a history of innovative ideas [list your most meaningful ideas and any future ideas].

❑ Lower than average overhead will allow [me/us] to funnel profits back into operations thus avoiding high debt ratios or lost sales opportunities.

❑ [Product/Service] pricing will include a range of quantity discounts, as well as early payment discounts.

❑ Rather than being strictly local, [I/we] will expand into the national market.

❑ Sophistication in management, finance, and distribution allows [me/us] to run an efficient and lean structure, yet still provide quality service to our clients and customers. This also results in [me/us] being the low-cost supplier in a price-sensitive market.

❑ To control foreign exchange risks, [I/we] will monitor the markets and hedge accordingly. [I/We] will also use overseas bank accounts.

❑ With [my/our] level of capitalization, should an unexpected downturn occur, [I/we] will be able to continue operations on a positive scale.

Competitive Edge – *Summarize other advantages of your operation compared with competitors:*

Sample: Although our firm is new and unproven, we have two additional advantages over our competitors: (1) Dr. Thomas Shumba, head of our marketing team, is a leading expert in Africa's medical infrastructure with invaluable industry contacts. (2) We have also obtained exclusive distribution rights to XYZ Inc.'s top-selling [product] line.

Competitive Position (Strategic Position)

*Competitive Position Statement – Summarize your positioning strategy (refer to the next page for "Ten Tactical Positioning Strategies"). In your positioning strategy, answer the following: (a) **What** is your product or service and who is it for? (b) **What** is its single most important benefit? (c) **Who** is your main competition and how are you different? (d) **How** are your products or services different or unique?*

Sample Statement – For anybody who is thinking about starting and running a new company, or seeking outside funding and interest for their business idea, *Successful Business Planning in 30 Days* helps produce a professional business plan quickly and easily. Unlike competitive products, SBP30 is supported by over 4,000 pages of online content at bp30.com.

WHO and WHAT	
Main Benefit	
Main Competitor	
Main Difference	

Rewrite the above answers into a coherent positioning strategy statement:

Describe how your positioning strategy will give you an advantage in the marketplace:

Sample: We have positioned Homeowner Solutions Inc. in the [location] area as a convenient, less expensive and threatening alternative to larger contracting companies with reputations of shoddy workmanship and hidden materials and labor costs. We charge a set fee at the beginning of each contract and guarantee our workmanship until clients are satisfied. Although we have lost money on some jobs, this strategy has allowed us to increase our client base by [X]% in one year through positive word-of-mouth referrals to achieve a net profit of $[XX] for fiscal year 2004.

Ten Tactical Competitive Positioning Strategies – *Select strategies that best fit your marketing goals:*

❑ **Compare your product or service favorably to a competitor's.** This type of positioning involves implicit or explicit comparisons. Implicit comparisons never mention a competitor's name though the inference is obvious. Often the unmentioned competitor is made fun of or looked down upon. Explicit comparisons make a comparison with a direct competitor (usually the market leader), with the goal of attracting their customers (e.g., the Pepsi Challenge); or it can use the compared product as a reference point with no attempt to attract the customers of the compared product (e.g., the Volkswagen Dasher: "Picks up speed faster than a Mercedes and has a bigger trunk than a Rolls").

❑ **Disassociate yourself completely from the product class.** This type of positioning is particularly effective when introducing new products amongst heavy competition. For example, Intel with its Pentium Chip attempted to disassociate itself from its 8086, 286, 386, and 486 lineage in an effort to lessen the gains made by other chip manufacturers such as AMD and Cyrix. The name change also helped ward off the threat of the PowerPC chip being perceived as new 90's technology and Intel as old outdated 70's technology.

❑ **Offer a range of packages for the same product or service.** This type of positioning involves selling the same product in a range of packages of different sizes, design, or even label, as well as using different distribution channels to reach the various segments that each packaging variation targets. Beer, for example, can be sold in kegs, cases, twelve-packs, six-packs, twelve-ounce cans and bottles, on tap, and by the pitcher. The beer in each container is exactly the same but appeals to separate market segments with different needs. Services can also be packaged in a variety of ways. For example, skis can be rented in novice, intermediate, or expert packages, and vacations can be sold in economy, family, honeymoon, or deluxe packages.

❑ **Position against older products.** This type of positioning is particularly effective when used to introduce new products that differ from traditional products. Lead-free gasoline was at one time positioned against leaded gasoline as being cleaner burning and friendlier to the environment.

❑ **Promote a specific use for your product.** This type of positioning works best when you can easily teach your customers how to use your product via a promotional medium that allows a demonstration. For example, to promote egg consumption using TV advertising, show how many ways to cook an egg (scrambled, poached, boiled).

❑ **Promote a unique product or service benefit.** This type of positioning is generally more effective then positioning by features because it's easier to sell customers on what a product or service can do for them rather than explain how it does it.

❑ **Promote a unique product or service feature.** This type of positioning is very common whether you're selling services or manufactured goods, as long as your product or service has some unique features of real value to your customers. Even if your product or service does not have a unique feature, you may be able to gain an edge over your competitors, by studying and mapping the *perceptions* of consumers concerning your products or services in relation to those of your major competitors. Any perceptions you discover to be in your favor should be exploited.

❑ **Satisfy a specific need.** This type of positioning is built around satisfying a special customer need in an innovative manner. Some experts say that this is the only reason for starting a business and about the only way to stay in business.

❑ **Target the user.** This type of positioning directs its efforts to using people in its advertising that the target customers can identify with. Models aren't necessarily gorgeous or handsome. They are more like everyday folk with everyday problems, and are always shown in a positive light after using a product or service.

❑ **Use a combination of strategies.** Incorporate elements from several of the above types of positioning. Most small business owners should use this approach especially if operating in a small trade area where there isn't a large enough customer base to justify the expense of separate marketing approaches.

Competitor Profile Worksheet – *Create a profile for each main competitor (photocopy if needed):*

Name of COMPETITOR:	Owner:
Location:	URL:

Item	Comments
PRODUCTS and SERVICES OFFERED	
Size, Weight	
Durability, Versatility, Ease of Use	
Uniqueness and Perceived Value of	
Pricing Structure	
METHODS of DISTRIBUTION	
Wholesale, Retail, Reps	
Web, Mail Order, Personal Selling	
MARKET SHARE	
Growing, Stable, or Declining	
Number of Customers	
Estimated Sales	
% Share of Market	
Location of Customers	
COMPANY IMAGE	
Packaging	
Promotional Materials	
Methods of Advertising	
COMPANY PERFORMANCE	
Competitive Advantages	
Location Advantages	
Profitability	
Do they have a Market Niche?	
STRENGTHS	
WEAKNESSES	

DAY 18

Design a business card. Write a slogan.

Selling Strategies

Lack of a selling or marketing strategy is a serious weakness in many plans. You must prove that you have given the marketing of your product or service a lot of thought by describing: ✦ how you expect to get customers to buy your product or service ✦ how you plan to gain a market share if the competition is tough ✦ what business are you *really* in (i.e., what will your customers *really* be buying) ✦ what do you do best (strengths) ✦ what do you need to work on (weaknesses).

Business Cards

A *Business Card* sums up *who* you are and *how* you wish to be perceived. It is the first and most important step in the marketing of your business.

Business Card Design in "Five Steps"

STEP 1 – Brainstorm for content. On a piece of paper, write down everything you might want on your business card.

STEP 2 – Separate optional and essential information. Now that everything is on paper, determine what's absolutely necessary and what's not.

STEP 3 – Experiment with design using essential information. Using only information that is absolutely essential, experiment with layout, logo, and lettering size to create your basic business card design.

STEP 4 – Incorporate optional information into your basic design. Using your optional information, determine whether its incorporation into your basic business card design complements it enough to warrant inclusion.

STEP 5 – Produce final design. Printing shops, and outlets like *Office Depot* and *Staples*, can help you select a final design. Browse through cards they have made for other clients, pick one you like, and have them substitute your information.

NOTE Use the back of your business card to summarize principal products or services or provide other detailed information. However, print only what is

To Do List

III. **Marketing Plan**

Selling Strategies

✓ Business Cards
✓ Company Slogans

Include useful information on your business card, not directly related to your business, like a calendar or a metric-imperial conversion chart. This way, your card has a better chance of becoming a permanent part of someone's wallet or purse.
MARKETING TIP

✳

POLL

What is the most effective promotional tool for a small business startup?

Brochures	50%
Business Cards	**27%**
Classified Ads	9%
Display Ads	8%
Stationery	3%

SOURCE:
Smallbusinesspolls.com

Business Card Folding Designs

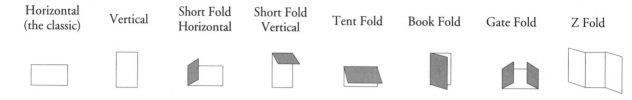

| Horizontal (the classic) | Vertical | Short Fold Horizontal | Short Fold Vertical | Tent Fold | Book Fold | Gate Fold | Z Fold |

necessary and useful to your client or customer. Don't get carried away. If you need more space than the standard business card size permits, experiment with folding techniques (see examples above). With proper design, you can turn an ordinary business card into a great mini-brochure.

Company Slogans

One of the first steps in building a magnetic company identity is to come up with some memorable company slogans. Slogans are words or phrases used to sum up and express the spirit or aim of your company, and unlike a company name, logo, or trademark, can easily be changed to reflect new marketing strategies. This is their greatest strength. More specifically, slogans can be used to: ✦ liven up letterhead ✦ add pizzazz to logos ✦ consolidate company philosophies ✦ supplement lackluster company names ✦ give details about what a company actually sells ✦ motivate customers to buy ✦ zero-in on target markets ✦ help position your company and product or service in the minds of consumers ✦ inspire entire promotions ✦ add punch to order forms ✦ single-handedly change the public's perception of a company from being "boring" and just like everybody else to that of being "cool" and finely tuned to their needs.

Common Denominators of Great Slogans

Great Slogans are difficult to forget after being heard once. They are not artificial nor contrived, and are neither general enough that they don't mean anything nor specific enough that they pigeonhole your business. Great slogans also: ✦ beg to be chanted or sung ✦ create vivid pictures in the consumer's mind ✦ get advertised free by word of mouth ✦ summarize completely your field yet also provide identity through uniqueness ✦ follow your mission statement ✦ tie in well with your company name and logo ✦ use as few words as possible.

A proverb [slogan] is a short sentence based on long experience.
MIGUEL DE CERVANTES

POLL

Which slogan leaves the most lasting impression?

Don't leave home without it! (American Express)
37%

Good to the last drop. (Maxwell House)
20%

Let your fingers do the walking. (Yellow Pages)
16%

It's the real thing. (Coca-Cola)
13%

Only you can prevent forest fires. (Smokey the Bear)
12%

SOURCE:
Smallbusinesspolls.com

Great Slogans ALSO: ❑ **Appeal to peoples' emotions or sense of pride in a positive manner.** "Known by the company it keeps." (Seagram's Canadian Vodka) *E. Seagram & Sons Incorporated Liquors* ❑ **Direct people to act.** "Take a bite out of Crime." *Crime Prevention Coalition* ❑ **Feature greatest benefit.** "Mends everything but a broken heart." *Fix-All Liquid Cement Co.* ❑ **Invent new concepts.** "Welcome to Miller time." *Miller Brewing Company* ❑ **Invent new words.** "Don't just fertilize . . . Spencerize." *Spencer Chemical Div., Gulf Oil Corp.* ❑ **Mention their company name.** "Everyone needs the Sun." *Sun Insurance Co.* ❑ **Mention their markets.** "America's best read weekly." *Liberty Magazine* ❑ **Mention their products.** "I saw the Haver Lite." (miniature flashlight) *Haverhills* ❑ **Mention their services.** "The greatest show on earth." *Barnum & Bailey Circus* ❑ **Use alliteration.** "Look to Lockheed for leadership." *Lockheed Corp.* ❑ **Use detail.** "99 44/100 % pure." *Ivory soap* ❑ **Use humor.** "Correct mistakes in any language." (erasers) *Eldon Roberts Rubber Co.* ❑ **Use movie titles.** "A diamond is forever." *DeBeers Consolidated Mines Ltd.* ❑ **Use rhymes.** "Takes a licking but keeps on ticking." *Timex Corp.* ❑ **Use the word** *people.* "The can opener people." *Dazey Products Co.* ❑ **Use the word you, yours, or yourself.** "Vote yourself a farm." *Abraham Lincoln (1860)* ❑ **Use puns cautiously.** "A pen is only as good as its point." *C. Howard Hunt Pen Co.*

Writing a Slogan for Your Company or Product

The following is a simplified format for writing a slogan:

Company or Product Name, followed by greatest benefit.

Example: "At ROBERTSON'S, our consultants save you money."

$ucce$$ Story ➡ The "Catalog Queen" Lillian Vernon

Lillian Vernon is the Founder and CEO of the Lillian Vernon Corporation, a leading catalog and online retailer that sells gifts, household items, and children's products (www.lillianvernon.com). Vernon was a refugee from Nazi Germany who came to America in 1937 at the age of ten. In 1951, with only $2,000 in wedding gift money, she placed an ad in *Seventeen Magazine* at a cost of $495. Her first product was a matching monogrammed leather belt and purse. Initially, her goals were modest. She only wished to help supplement her husband's weekly salary of $75. However, her ad generated $32,000 in sales. By 1982, her company had more than 4,000 items in inventory. Today, LVC boasts more than 4,000 employees with revenues of $287 million. In Fiscal 2003, they mailed over 100 million catalogs in 22 editions.

DAY 18 **Worksheets**

Design a business card.
Write a slogan.

Selling Strategies

Brainstorm – Using keywords and phrases, summarize the main points of your selling strategy:

1	
2	
3	
4	
5	

Business Cards

Describe how you want your business card to be perceived. **How** *will you use it? Check "essential" and "optional" information and content you want on your business card. List additional information:*

Essential Content

- ❏ Your name
- ❏ Title or position held
- ❏ Company name
- ❏ Company logo
- ❏ Phone number (personal and/or business)
- ❏ Toll-free 800 number

- ❏ Fax number
- ❏ Pager number
- ❏ Email address
- ❏ Addresses (personal and/or business)
- ❏ URL address

Optional Information/Effects

- ❏ Company slogan
- ❏ Education and/or other qualifications
- ❏ Summary heading of products/services
- ❏ Detailed product and/or services information

- ❏ Special offers; discounts; promotional material
- ❏ White space for handwritten product info
- ❏ Eye-catching graphics
- ❏ Special effects: raised lettering, gold embossing

Additional Information		

Sketch two possible designs for your business card (or design a front and back):

Sketch the final design of your business card:

Company Slogans

Write three slogans using the **company** *or* **product name** + **benefit** *format as shown on page 189:*

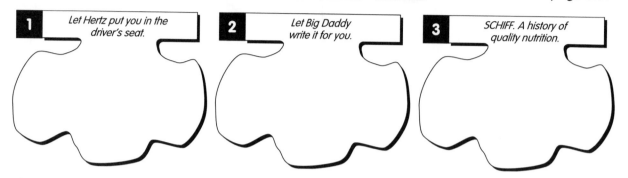

1 *Let Hertz put you in the driver's seat.*

2 *Let Big Daddy write it for you.*

3 *SCHIFF. A history of quality nutrition.*

Write six more slogans using the "Great Slogans" techniques on page 189 (e.g., "invent new concepts," "use detail"). Test your slogans on friends, family, colleagues, and customers. Select the top three:

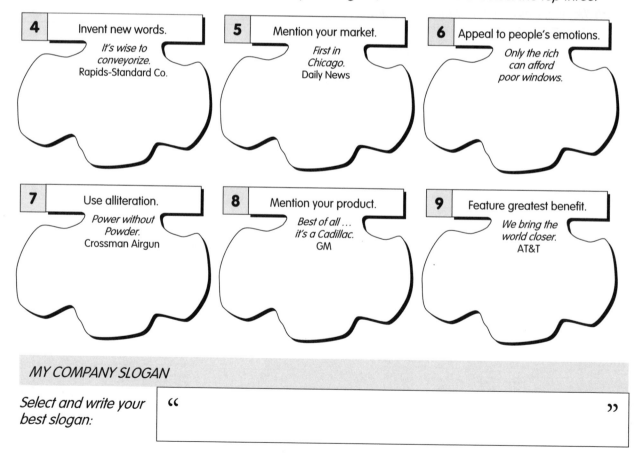

4 Invent new words.
It's wise to conveyorize.
Rapids-Standard Co.

5 Mention your market.
First in Chicago.
Daily News

6 Appeal to people's emotions.
Only the rich can afford poor windows.

7 Use alliteration.
Power without Powder.
Crossman Airgun

8 Mention your product.
Best of all ... it's a Cadillac.
GM

9 Feature greatest benefit.
We bring the world closer.
AT&T

MY COMPANY SLOGAN

Select and write your best slogan:

"   "

DAY 19

Outline your customer service and credit extension plan.

Write a customer service maxim.

Customer Service Plan

Imagine you own a flower shop called *Flora's Boutique*. One day, your bell rings, and in walks a tall elegant woman in her mid-thirties. What do you suppose she is thinking and feeling when she first looks around, talks to one of your staff, buys an expensive crystal vase, and then on her way out trips over your welcome mat and smashes the vase into a thousand pieces? A *Customer Service Plan* attempts to provide answers and guidelines to these and other difficult questions. It also attempts among other things to:

GOAL 1 – Build customer loyalty. View your customer service plan as an opportunity to reward customer loyalty with unquestioning, all-accepting, continuous positive reinforcement. Everyone likes to be treated special (see chart below).

GOAL 2 – Create a positive business environment. Making people feel good about themselves and your company makes it more conducive for them to spend money. Offer free coffee, donuts, and sweets that look like your logo.

GOAL 3 – Establish a marketable company image. "Image is everything." At least that's what we've all grown to believe, conditioned so by companies with huge advertising budgets. These companies feel that if you can't find a need, why not create it by manipulating our primeval urges. These companies recognize that if you create the right image for yourself, you can pretty much sell anything at any price. Cosmetic companies do it. Car companies do it. Beer and soft drink companies do it. So the question remaining is: If others can mold the truth to assist their pursuit of the almighty dollar—and have incredible success doing so—then why not you, as long as you stay within legal and ethical boundaries?

To create a professional image be reliable, courteous, and service orien-

A positive image builds up gradually over many years. A negative one can hit fast and destroy your market position virtually overnight.

More business is lost every year through neglect than through any other cause.
JIM CATHCART

REWARDING CUSTOMERS

The secret to winning and keeping customers for life is to "reward" them.

When a Customer ...	REWARD ...
Appears, calls, or inquires ...	❏ by being prompt and prepared
Is angry or defensive ...	❏ with kindness and empathy
Has special requests ...	❏ by customizing your service
Can't make up his mind ...	❏ with a specific recommendation
Raises objections to buying ...	❏ by empathizing and showing value
Gives buying signals ...	❏ prompt response
Buys ...	❏ by delivering more than you promise
Refuses to buy ...	❏ with polite appreciation
Is going to be disappointed ...	❏ with positive perks
Complains ...	❏ with fast, positive action

tated. Treat each customer with dignity and respect as if each was capable of giving you a thousands dollars in business, even if they only give you a few. This means treating a coal miner, who walks into your jewelry shop with dirt under his fingernails, like any other valued customer. Also, pay close attention to: ✦ appearance and attitude of staff ✦ displays ✦ entrance and parking ✦ location ✦ packaging ✦ prices ✦ publicity from news media ✦ quality of advertising and promotional programs ✦ quality of delivery and after-sales service ✦ quality, appearance, and suitability of stationery, invoices, envelopes, business cards, and logos ✦ store layout ✦ tone of voice on the phone (image is more important in a business of intangibles—e.g., if you sell hair care services, image is more important than if you sell TVs).

GOAL 4 – **Handle complaints right away.** It's hard to remain calm with a hotheaded customer yelling at you. But in such a situation, it is better to let your customer blow off steam, and then calmly solve their problem. This, more than anything else, is a sign of dedication and management sensitivity.

GOAL 5 – **Provide extras that really impress people.** Customizing your services beyond the call of duty shows people you really care, gives you and your team a source of confidence and pride, overcomes customer defensiveness, is great for generating repeat business, and virtually eliminates the competition by establishing you as best customer service provider in your field. Computer printouts, forms, and invoices, for example, can promote customer relations by making customers feel better informed. They don't have to decipher bad handwriting.

Credit Extension Plan

Credit can be extended by your business to clients, companies, or large organizations that usually do business with you on a regular basis, in the form of delayed payments, financing, or charge card services. These forms of credit can be defined respectively as: trade credit, financing, and charge card credit. In all cases, a business that offers such services is engaged in more than providing payment options; the extension of credit and financing is a deliberate marketing strategy designed to stimulate business and give your company a competitive edge.

Pros and Cons of Extending Trade Credit

The advantages of extending trade credit are more customers and increased sales. In fact, most manufacturers and wholesalers find it imperative to offer credit terms to their customers, simply to survive. However, although selling on credit can boost sales, it can also increase direct and indirect costs, which must be weighed against potential benefits. By offering trade credit, you will need more extensive bookkeeping, invoicing, and collection procedures that often demand hiring additional staff just to manage the extra accounts. And what's worse, a definite percentage of the businesses you grant credit to, will not be able to pay.

Guidelines for Extending Credit

Before extending credit to customers, develop a policy with procedures for weeding out potential bad credit risks. Follow these ten steps:

STEP 1 – Become a member of your local Credit Bureau. Credit Bureaus provide the resources to check out all applicants, and the latest up-to-date procedures and polices most companies are using.

STEP 2 – Set policies and standards for screening credit applicants. Not all customers should be allowed to apply for credit. Set a policy that allows you to make sure that credit is warranted before you grant it.

STEP 3 – Devise a credit application form. Before granting credit to a customer, have them fill out an application form. A lawyer can help you in preparing this form. A simple credit application form asks for the customer's name, address, telephone number, place of employment, and bank and credit references.

STEP 4 – Verify the data on the application form. The information provided in the application form should be checked carefully by mail or telephone, and with a bank, credit bureau, or mercantile agency, such as Dun & Bradstreet (sbs.dnb.com).

STEP 5 – Evaluate the "credit worthiness" of applicants. A decision to extend credit to any specific client or company is generally based on *The Five C's of Credit*:

Character – Are they willing to pay bills when due? (credit records must be studied to determine the past behavior of the applicant)

Capacity – Do they have the ability to pay debts? (if a company is suffering a serious cash flow problem, think twice about extending them credit)

Capital – What is the company's net worth? (a company with substantial assets, and a temporary cash flow problem, should not concern you as much)

Conditions – What are the current general economic conditions? Do they speak positively or negatively about granting credit to any customer?

Collateral – What collateral can they pledge to secure credit?

STEP 6 – Set a credit limit. If the application is approved, set a credit limit for the customer (to control your losses in case the account goes delinquent). The limit you choose will depend upon your research and company policies.

STEP 7 – Establish terms of sale. When a firm offers trade credit, it usually offers a discount off the purchase price for early payment (to reduce its average collection

Credit: The lifeblood of commerce.
FRANK MCKINNEY HUBBARD

✱

In business, one way to obtain credit is to create the impression that one already has it.
MIGUEL UNAMUNO

✱

For credit checks on international companies, try:
OWENS.COM

Before establishing your credit policy, check out what your competition is doing. If they are not offering credit, either they don't have the time, human resources, or expertise, or they have lost money on it in the past. However, if they are offering credit, try to get a copy of their policy, copy what works, and then try to innovate on a few issues, particularly, the terms of sale.
PROFIT TIP

PROFIT TIPS

Having a cash-only policy or charging on no-recourse charge cards will prevent bad debts and limit problems associated with extending trade credit. It will also reduce total sales.

✳

Failing to regularly keep track of your bad debts ratio can give you a false sense of net worth and eventually threaten profitability.

period and improve cash flow), and states a limit as to how long the customer has until the bill must be paid. In the case of a wholesaler who ships goods to a retail firm, a typical "terms of sale" might be marked on the shipment's invoice 2/10, net 30. This means that the retailer is permitted 30 days of credit from the date of invoice. If the bill is paid promptly—within ten days—the retailer is entitled to 2% off. Before you establish your terms of sale, check out what your competition is doing. In the least, offer similar terms.

STEP 8 – Set up an accurate efficient invoicing system. Invoices should be prepared and mailed promptly on a regular basis (monthly or bi-monthly) with all payment terms clearly stated. Send invoice with each shipment or invoice within two working days of filling the order.

STEP 9 – Monitor credit usage carefully. Monitoring A/R's allows you to identify problems before they become serious credit risks. This is accomplished by setting up a system for aging all A/R's. Pay particular attention to overdue accounts, not only to make sure that customers have received their bills, but also to stop giving them credit in the future, or until their balance has been paid. When monitoring A/R's, make it a habit of comparing your average collection period (ACP) with industry averages, past experience, and changes to payment terms, as well as your monthly bad debt percentage (as a rule: watch out if your ACP is one-third or larger than your credit period—e.g., if your credit period is 30 days and you have an ACP of more than 40 days, you may have a problem).

A/R Dollar Value = average credit sales per day × average collection period – If a business has credit sales of $500 per day and ACP of 20 days, it will have a total of: $500 × 20 days = $10,000 invested in receivables at any given time (if you are missing the values of certain variables you should be able to make reasonable projections using industry averages).

ACP = A/R Position/Daily Sales – If a business has an A/R position of $2,000, (its customers owe $2,000 at that particular time) and annual credit sales of $40,000, its average collection period is ($2,000)/($40,000/365) or approximately 18 days.

STEP 10 – Establish a bad debts collection policy. Timely and effective debt collections are essential for generating a positive cash flow and increasing profits by diminishing the need for short-term operating loans. All companies extending credit need to implement a systematic collection procedure to follow up on slow accounts. The purpose of this procedure is to help reduce "delinquency" without destroying the goodwill of your best repeat customers. You don't want to avoid losing potentially good customers by giving them a nasty or insensitive collection notice. A bad debts collection policy can be broken down into the following stages: (1) Fax, mail, and/or email a duplicate copy of the invoice of the overdue account. (2) Call the customer and inquire about the delay in payment. (3) Send a form letter requesting payment reiterating any late payment penalties that may be due. (4) Send a series of form letters requesting payment, each one becoming progressively stronger. At some point in this series of form letters, make it clear when you will cease conducting business with the customer until they clear their debt. (5) Hand the matter over to your attorney or collection agency. (6) Take legal action if cost-effective.

Successful
**BUSINESS
PLANNING
30 DAYS**

Outline your customer service and credit extension plan. Write a customer service maxim.

Customer Service Plan

Describe your before-sale and after-sale services. Detail any special policies:

Sample: In our industry, customer service support is critical for success. To help generate customer loyalty and repeat sales, we will provide free delivery within the city area using [UPS, FedEx, own truck fleet]. Our maintenance team is backed by [company] who also have agreed to offer technical support at a cost of $30 per inquiry. Within our industry, a two-week return policy is standard. To further distinguish us from competitors, we are offering a 30-day no-questions-asked return policy.

Handling Complaints – *Check strategies you will use to handle complaints. Describe additional plans:*

Sample: Customer complaints are considered an opportunity to improve our service and hence are treated with great attention. All complaints are handled personally by our sales manager who has five years experience in customer service with [company]. Our policy is to handle complaints immediately or provide solutions within 24 hours.

❑ **Manager Involvement** – Get people at the top actively involved in both listening to and resolving complaints. "Just a second, let me talk to the manager." Is better than, "Sorry the manager won't be back 'til tomorrow."

❑ **24-hour Rule** – If you can't handle complaints right away, handle them within 24 hours.

❑ **Suggestion Box** – Set up a suggestion box in private locations so people won't feel threatened to use it.

❑ **Be Committed** – Take every complaint seriously.

❑ **Make it Easy to Complain** – A great way to get feedback.

❑ **Complaint Handling System** – Use the following technique: (a) listen with understanding and sensitivity; (b) paraphrase what the customer tells you so they know you are listening; (c) find out what the customer wants; (d) propose a solution—if the customer doesn't like your solution, ask what he or she would consider fair; (e) make a follow-up call to insure satisfaction; and (f) whatever else you do, never let the customer lose face.

Customer Maxim – Inspire your customer service policy. Check or write a customer maxim that seems to capture the essence of what you hope your company will become:

❑ **CUSTOMERS** ... ARE human beings first, not business. They need to be treated like friends and guests.

❑ ARE the bosses; we are the employees.

❑ ARE to be treated like lifetime partners; as if we are going to see them every day for the rest of our lives.

❑ ARE ultimately responsible for our business, our profits, and our success.

❑ BRING us their needs; it is our job to fulfill them to the best of our ability.

❑ DESERVE service with a smile.

❑ DESERVE the best value for their dollar.

❑ DESERVE what's best for them, even if it's not necessarily what's best for us.

❑ DO NOT interrupt our work; they are the reason for it.

❑ EXPECT us to make a positive and lasting impression by being committed, attentive to details, and by following up on whatever we promise.

❑ SHALL be rewarded for their loyalty.

❑ SHALL not be argued with, for nobody can ever win an argument with a customer.

Credit Extension Plan

Trade Credit – Check type of trade credit you will extend to customers:

❑ **Open Credit –** Also referred to as open account, open book, or regular credit, this form extends short-term credit to customers without requiring any down payment and without adding either interest or carrying charges to the bill. It is usually extended for a 30-day period.

❑ **Option-terms Credit –** This type of credit permits a customer to charge up to a limit and pay within 30 days of the billing date without penalty. A firm can assign a carrying charge for any amount not paid within that time period and release additional credit (up to the limit) as payments are made.

❑ **Revolving Charge Credit –** Revolving charge credit refers to the continuous releasing of credit to the credit ceiling as payments are made. This type of credit is the most common form of credit given to businesses.

Describe your credit extension plan:

❑ have membership in credit bureau ❑ policies set for screening applicants ❑ credit application form designed
❑ able to verify data on applications ❑ use the "Five C's of Credit" ❑ $[XX] credit limit ❑ terms of sale [2/10, net 30]
❑ A/R's monitored and aged [30 days, 60 days, and 90 days] ❑ bad debts collection policy established

Sample: In the highly competitive lighting fixtures manufacturing industry, it is imperative that we offer trade credit to clients. At [company], we offer wholesalers and retailers with a positive credit profile terms of 2/10, net 30. The industry standard is net 30. Overdue accounts are charged a $5 handling fee, plus 1.5% for each month past due.

Check and describe any additional credit extension polices:

> **Sample:** The ACP for our industry has historically fluctuated between 25 and 28. With market demand rapidly increasing and retailers short of cash, we have projected that our ACP may reach as high as 42. To maintain a positive cash balance, we have included a cash reserve of $[XX] in our startup capital estimate.

- ❑ **We Send** invoices immediately after the sale, rather than wait for the end of the month.
- ❑ **Offer** discounts for quick payments to improve our cash flow position.
- ❑ **Assess** a late payment fee for overdue accounts.
- ❑ **Calculate** [weekly] the percentage of total sales on credit.
- ❑ **Monitor** A/R dollar amounts (A/R position) on an ongoing basis.

- ❑ **Monitor** our average collection period and bad debts ratio.
- ❑ **Project**, monitor, and write off a percentage of bad debts.
- ❑ **Identify** prompt-paying customers and search for more like them.
- ❑ **Have** on file a series of increasingly pointed letters to collect from late or delinquent accounts.
- ❑ **Are** able to show that the costs of granting credit are offset by the benefits of higher sales.

Outline collection procedures for overdue accounts. **What** *is your projected "bad debts" ratio for credit sales?* ❑ duplicate of invoice faxed after [40 days] ❑ customer called after [60 days] ❑ form letters sent after [90 days] ❑ bad debts ratio projected at [X]%

> **Sample:** Based on industry data obtained from [research source], our bad debts ratio for mainland China clients has been projected to be 8.4% of A/R's. To minimize staff overhead, collection of these overdue A/R's will be outsourced to Inter-Credit Pte Co. located in Shanghai.

Other Payment Options – Describe any other credit and selling terms offered:

❑ accept local checks ❑ accept debit cards ❑ accept credit cards ❑ I/We have a merchant account with [company name]. ❑ I/We have Internet credit card verification with [company name].

> **Sample:** We have opened a merchant account with Merchant America at a cost of $19.95 per month. With this service, we can process online credit card payments from national and international customers as well as debit cards at our retail outlet. Our credit card transaction fees are $.30 with a discount rate of 2.14%.

DAY 20

Determine how you will distribute your products or services.

Determine how you will test the market.

Distribution Plan

Cost-effective distribution is fundamental to any marketing effort. You need to be able to deliver your products and services to the right people, at the right time, in the right quantities, and at the lowest cost.

Six Factors for Choosing the Right Distributor

In deciding whether to use agents, wholesalers, brokers, or retailers to distribute your products, consider the six factors as summarized below in the chart. Circle the best descriptive adjective for each factor. The distributor with the most circles is the one most likely to meet your distribution needs.

1) **Number and Types of Customers –** If your manufacturing company deals with a few large customers, you may decide to sell directly to customers using your own sales staff. A toy manufacturer, for example, could sell direct to toy store chains, but would likely need the expertise of an agent to service independent toy stores.

2) **Concentration of Market –** Setting up your own distribution is possible if customers are concentrated in a few areas. If customers are scattered across the nation, it is often more economical to use other distributors.

3) **Price of Product –** The less expensive your product, the more likely that a distributor will be needed. Cheaper items are usually sold in large quantities to intermediaries or wholesalers who then distribute them in smaller numbers to retailers. Expensive, technological products, such as computers or industrial equipment are usually sold directly by the manufacturer or through a specialized agent.

4) **Complexity of Product –** Highly technical items are usually sold directly by the manufacturer. The producer's sales force might be able

> *Distribution is all about getting products to where they are wanted, when they are wanted.*
>
> ✱
>
> *One of the most powerful ways of adding value in the nineties and beyond is understanding that in today's society, wealth is created by distribution.*
>
> **ANTHONY ROBBINS**

Select the Distributor Who Best Matches Your Situation and Needs				
	Sell Directly Yourself	Use an Agent or Broker	Use a Wholesaler	Use a Retailer
1) Number and Types of Customers	Few	Specialized	Hundreds	Diversified
2) Concentration of Market	Concentrated	Concentrated	Scattered	Scattered
3) Price of Product	Expensive	Less Expensive	Inexpensive	Inexpensive
4) Complexity of Product	Highly Technical	Less Technical	Simple	Simple
5) Financial Resources	Extensive	Adequate	Limited	Adequate
6) Need for Control	High	High	Low	Low

to offer pre-sale information and post-sale service, which most wholesalers cannot provide.

5) **Financial Resources –** Most new manufacturers cannot afford to set up a distribution network, grant credit, or provide warehousing for completed products. It is usually more practical and economical to use experienced distributors who already have market contacts.

6) **Need for Control –** Some manufacturers want to maintain control of their product by handling distribution themselves even though the costs are higher. They feel that this way they can maintain a consistent price, provide better service, and maintain higher performance standards. On the other hand, consumer products such as food, clothing, and furniture are usually not sold directly by producers because the need for control over quality of service and price maintenance is less important.

Five More Factors for Choosing a Distribution Method

In addition to the above six factors, the following five factors are also of importance when deciding which distribution methods to use:

Cost of Distribution Method vs. Services Provided – Using intermediaries necessitates building a cost structure to compensate each of the channel members for the part they play in the total distribution process. Intermediaries don't work for free. When choosing a distribution method, factor in the value of the added services an intermediary might provide. Agents, brokers, wholesalers, and retailers, offer different levels of service and cost. Some will do everything for you from packaging to delivery to marketing, while others will provide only a few services. Distributors and selling agencies, despite charging higher fees compared with agents, brokers, and sales representatives, will also stock orders, invoice and carry receivables, place regional advertising, install equipment, train their own sales staff, and provide more extensive after-sales service. The bottom line is if experience shows that your low-cost distributors are unreliable or inconsistent in the quality of service they offer it may be wiser to upgrade.

Distributor Success Rate – Manufacturers trained in *making* products usually have less success distributing them than intermediaries trained in *marketing* products.

Insurance Needs – While in transit, your goods will be subject to many risks, from exposure to the elements, accidents, and damage, to outright theft. This demands that you get sufficient coverage to insure the value of

---

The use of agents, brokers, and sales representatives as intermediaries is usually necessary for a small manufacturing business starting out because of their limited ability to advertise heavily.
PROFIT TIP

Behold the turtle: He only makes progress when he sticks his neck out.
JAMES BRYANT CONANT

*

Co-branding can produce marriage made in heaven ... Barnes and Noble engaged in a co-branding strategy when it began including Starbucks coffee shops inside its bookstores.
ED JOHNS
Brand strategy director for Conrad Phillips & Vutech

MAIL ORDER DISTRIBUTION

To get mail order wholesalers interested in carrying your products, try the following: package products individually in self-mailer containers, ready for the company's address labels; offer the full freight on all orders of 100 lbs. or more along with immediate delivery; offer exclusive protection on space advertising (no one else will advertise the same product); give quantity discounts; explain that they may order samples at your cost price, but should include payment to save you the trouble of invoicing small amounts; include a postage paid envelope for their convenience; and most importantly sell them your product at 55% off the regular suggested price.

your goods while you are liable. Insurance rates will vary with the mode you choose to distribute and transport your goods. A good insurance broker, besides helping you pick the insurance you need at a price you can afford, can also help identify deficiencies in packaging and even production, which can also save you money.

Storage and Warehousing Costs – If you need to store goods, for lists of international warehouse facilities contact the *International Warehouse Logistics Association* (www.iwla.com) or the *International Association of Refrigerated Warehouses* (www.iarw.org).

Transportation and Shipping Costs – Transportation and shipping costs can range from a fraction of an item's selling price—as is the case of transporting grain, coal, gravel, and other bulky commodities—to as much as 40% or more, as in the case of transporting exotic pets from distant regions. Consequently, transportation management must focus on two major objectives: (1) minimizing the costs and effort involved in physically moving products to customers whether by land, air, or water; and (2) ensuring speedy, reliable delivery. To help keep your transportation costs reasonable: ✦ have customers negotiate shipment in cases where they have more leverage with the shipper than you ✦ ship in pieces and assemble in the market ✦ use intermodal shipping (combining two or more modes) ✦ investigate interlining (e.g., switching from U.S. to Canadian carriers once crossing the border) ✦ use freight forwarders or customs brokers as middlemen.

Market Testing Plan

Testing is a way of buying information. It is a powerful research tool used by manufacturers, retailers, service providers, and all other kinds of entrepreneurs to determine the market potential of an idea. It is an activity designed to help you discover what changes, if any, should be made to your product, service, pricing structure, service policy, or advertising promotion before you head into full production or distribution (see page 209 for a list of nine market testing strategies).

Preparing Advertising Records

Advertising records should be incorporated into your daily workflow, not to increase your administrative burden, but rather to increase profits by giving more accurate feedback on the results of promotions. Six methods for monitoring the effectiveness of advertising and promotional efforts, as well as keeping track of how effectively each medium pulls, are as follows:

Survey customers directly. To find out what kinds of advertising customers respond to, conduct a survey, or more simply, ask them directly whenever they are placing an order in person or over the phone. It makes good business sense for you to conduct regular surveys because: (a) *Surveys keep you close to your customers.* This gives you a competitive edge. You can respond more quickly to customer likes, dislikes, and buying habits, than bigger companies. (b) *Surveys help put experience into perspective.* Surveys help you find out what kinds of information has become dated and is no longer relevant to making selling decisions.

Encourage customers to fill out a questionnaire. Questionnaires mailed to customers or left in accessible spots in retail locations can help you get an idea of how effective promotions are. Questions regarding the effectiveness of a promotion can also be incorporated directly onto order forms.

Use an "Advertising Key." An *Advertising Key* is a special code, number, or word added to an ad, coupon, or company address, to help you keep track of your advertising effectiveness and response rates. Every time the key is spotted, it is noted and the promotional media that generated the order is traced. Mail order and direct marketing companies especially, have mastered the art of using advertising keys. To write an advertising key: ✦ add words and/or codes to an advertiser's address—e.g., Studio 62, Suite 6, Room 121, Desk NW2, Dept. GH692, Box Number 512 ✦ add a suffix to your address—e.g., P.O. Box 123-A, 3456-A Hornby St. ✦ use staff names or even fictitious names—e.g., Attention: Pete J. Sanders (*Popular Science*, June) or Attention: Cary Grant (*Car & Driver*).

Design coded order forms. Special codes such as numbers, letters, and words can be added to order forms and coupons to indicate which magazine, newspaper, direct mail, or other promotion they come from. Usually this code includes a date of issue and an abbreviation (e.g., GH603 which means: "*Good Housekeeping*, June 2003"). Likewise, special stick-on labels, or specially produced reply envelopes and BRC's (Business Reply Cards), can be used in mailings to give you keyed information.

Use "Tell Them Joe Sent You Broadcast Ads." You can monitor the effectiveness of broadcast media by asking at the end of your radio or TV ad that customers state a phrase or keyword when visiting your store (this works best if the phrase or keyword entitles them to a special price, discount, or free gift). This technique can also help you discover exactly what areas your customers are drawn from so you can target that area more specifically with other kinds of advertising.

To serve you better, please answer the following:

How did you hear about our product or service?

☐ referral
☐ word of mouth
☐ radio ad
☐ TV ad
☐ billboard
☐ Yellow Pages
☐ magazine
☐ newspaper
☐ direct mail
☐ newsletter
☐ other

DID YOU KNOW?

According to a survey conducted by Cyber Dialogue, 71% of small businesses that accept orders online say the Internet is "essential" to their success. The study also noted that 60% of U.S. small businesses that accept orders online report an increase in sales due to their online presence that amounts to about 23% of total company sales.
Cyberdialogue.com

Use an "Advertising Cost Analysis Chart." Knowing how customers find out about your product or service is not easy. However, you can attempt to gauge the effectiveness of advertising costs by creating models that identify where customers see or hear ads. The "Advertising Cost Analysis" chart shown below, analyzes the results of several different advertising methods. By analyzing this data, you can make better decisions about where to put your advertising dollar and how to direct your sales force. In this example, according to the "Cost per Sale" results, it is obvious that radio and television advertising is inappropriate for this particular product. The "Responses per Sale" is also a useful figure as it indicates the number of people who must be reached by the media to produce a sale.

ADVERTISING COST ANALYSIS

	Daily News	Sunday Insert	Radio 60 Sec Ad	Cable TV 30 Sec Ad	Church Bulletin	Direct Mail	Bulletin Board	Referrals	Unknown	Totals
Circulation	7,500	15,000	10,000	12,000	1,200	1500	40	–	–	47,240
Type of Unit	col. inch	col. inch	minute	minute	page	letter	number	–	–	–
Number of Units	8	16	1	1	1	1	1	–	–	–
Ad Cost	$110	$345	$1,400	$1,900	$35	$300	$120	–	–	$4,210
Cost per Circulation	0.01	0.02	0.14	0.16	0.03	0.20	3.00	–	–	0.09
Responses	190	354	590	498	138	391	97	525	1,458	4,241
Sales	43	76	121	124	43	66	35	48	431	987
Circulation per Response	39	42	17	24	9	4	0.4	–	–	11
Circulation per Sale	174	197	83	97	28	23	1	–	–	48
Responses per Sale	4.4	4.7	4.9	4.0	3.2	5.9	2.8	10.9	3.4	4.4
Cost per Response	0.58	0.97	2.37	3.82	0.25	0.77	1.24	–	–	0.99
Cost per Sale	$2.56	$4.54	$11.57	$15.32	$0.81	$4.55	$3.43	–	–	$4.27
% of Total Responses	4%	8%	14%	12%	3%	9%	2%	12%	34%	100%
% of Total Sales	4%	8%	12%	13%	4%	7%	4%	5%	44%	100%

NOTE An "Advertising Cost Analysis" can also be set up using a spreadsheet program, where circulation, type of unit, number of units, ad cost, responses per ad, and sales per ad are *inputted*, and everything else is *computed*.

Getting the Most Out of a Trade Show

One of the best ways to test the market for a new product or service is to set up a booth at a trade show. At a trade show, you can introduce new ideas, find new partners, make new contacts, instill confidence in potential customers, learn about the market, and overall, generate good public relations. Trade shows are one of the least expensive ways of making multiple sales presentations. They also offer you—and this is very important—the best chance of closing a sale. It has been estimated that each sales contact you make at a trade show has a 54% chance of success—far higher than the 15% success rate of routine sales calls. Trade shows can also be fun. Although many attending are motivated to buy, and quite serious about researching products and services, others are attending simply to get away from the office, socialize, and pick up a few good ideas. If you make your display interesting, informative, and a little entertaining, great interest will be created in your display and you will meet the needs of both types of attendees (see strategies below).

17 Ways to Make Your Trade Show a Big Success

Pre-Show

a) *Book only national trade shows.* Only attend trade shows that have been operating for five years or more. For extensive information on trade shows, visit the *Trade Show News Network* at http://www.tsnn.com.

b) *Rent the best possible display location.* Being big is not as good as being in a good spot. Don't be the first to sign up, be well placed. Try to find out who will be next to you or better yet, who you can be next to.

c) *Publicize your participation in the show to the local press a few months beforehand.* A few months before the show send a press release to all trade publications in your field. This release should describe any new products you intend to introduce at the show.

d) *Send letters to all television and radio stations in the trade show area.* Describe unique facts about your product and offer to appear on any of their talk shows at their convenience.

e) *Write letters or invitations to people who will be interested in your display.* The success of a trade show promotion depends upon *WHO* actually shows up to see your display. Write letters to retailers, wholesalers, and sales representatives, who would have a lot to gain by selling your product or seeing your display.

f) *Write letters or invitations to people who might be interested in your display.* You can improve the results of your trade show promotion modestly or tremendously by writing to fringe accounts—that is people who *might* be interested in your display.

g) *Hit the local press about ten days before the show opens.* Send a press release to newspapers located in the town where the trade show is to be held.

h) *Mail reminder letters.* About a week before the show, send a reminder letter to every person you mailed to previously and remind them to visit your booth. Remember, any positive impressions you make before the show can go a long way to getting your desired result.

i) *Prepare your booth to be different.* A successful exhibit can be summed up in two words—be different. Your booth should look like no other booth. Design your booth so that it will make as much impact as possible. If you have to make some last minute changes, do so.

Show Time

j) *Display as much promotional material as appropriate.* Spread out your product line in as attractive a manner as you can. Have plenty of business cards, letterheads, envelopes, order forms, brochures, and other material on hand to give potential buyers.

k) *Keep a detailed record of everyone who visits your booth.* Record all inquiries. Try to get as many names and addresses as possible. Make notes on casual observers who don't leave their name and even ones who walk by and have no apparent interest in your display. Overall, get as much information as you can on exactly who your target market really is or may become.

l) *Keep a sharp lookout for buyers.* Buyers for large organizations regularly attend trade shows. Buyers may represent themselves, individual businesses, stores, production facilities, or entire chains of stores. Frequently, they will fly long distances to take advantage of the collected assortment of displayed goods relating to their industry. It will be your job to find these people and sell them on any of your ideas or products.

m) *Make a detailed study of all the other exhibitors.* Make a note of who's there, who isn't, who is selling what, which booths are getting the most attention, which products you think have potential, and especially, what the competition is up to.

n) *Approach all related businesses.* Don't hide. Circulate. Talk to other businesses that might be interested in your goods. Who knows, your best contact may be only three booths away.

o) *If the show extends over several days, consider testing your prices, redecorating your booth, or showcasing different products.* Consider using trade shows to get an idea of how response increases or decreases according to changed variables. But, don't go overboard. Test only one variable at a time.

Post-Show

p) *Follow up on all inquiries.* Otherwise, you've wasted your time. People who come to your show are not sure things, but they are highly qualified prospects.

q) *Mail thank-you notes to invited guests.* If you mailed an invitation to someone and they came to see you, make sure to mail a thank you. This is the cheapest PR you're ever going to get.

Determine how you will distribute your products or services. Determine how you will test the market.

Distribution Plan

*Brainstorm – Check marketing and **distribution channels** you plan to use:*

❑ **Brokers, Sales Agents, and Manufacturer Reps –** work independently from the companies they represent. Their business activity consists of buying and selling on behalf of others, thereby earning commissions or fees.

❑ *Brokers –* function as intermediaries between buyer and seller, bringing together the two parties while representing either side (not both at once, of course). They find customers for products and negotiate prices.

❑ *Manufacturer Representatives –* represent manufacturers under contract who are seeking distribution in a selected area and who do not have their own sales forces.

❑ *Sales Agents –* represent any type of business, ranging from service businesses to manufacturing and wholesaling firms while manufacturer's reps (as their name implies) represent only manufacturing firms.

❑ **Distributors and Selling Agencies –** unlike brokers, sales agents, and representatives, distributors and selling agencies are granted extensive authority over the details of prices, terms, customer selection, and marketing decisions. A selling agency is often contracted to sell a manufacturing plant's entire production, and thus often maintains a sizable and effective sales force. Distributors are often charged with buying and selling part of a plant's production in their specific marketing region. The relationship between the distributors and selling agencies and the principal is a close one.

❑ **Wholesalers –** sell primarily to retailers and other wholesalers or industrial users. They do not usually sell goods to end consumers. There are well over 700,000 wholesale establishments in the U.S. More than two-thirds of these firms are merchant wholesalers.

❑ *Cash-and-Carry Wholesalers –* cater to retailers who walk in, purchase needed merchandise with cash only, and take the goods out with them.

❑ *Direct Mail Wholesalers –* offer retailers merchandise for resale, characteristically through the medium of printed catalogs mailed periodically.

❑ *General Merchandise Wholesalers –* sell a variety of different lines of goods much like a general store.

❑ *Industrial Distributors –* wholesale industrial products.

❑ *Industrial Drop-shippers –* supply raw materials or bulky products of a low unit price to industrial users. This type of intermediary, found most frequently in coal, lumber, and metals industries, doesn't take physical possession of merchandise at any point, or put it in a warehouse, but rather arranges for producers to ship the goods directly to customers.

❑ *Merchant Wholesalers –* purchase goods in large quantities, warehouse them, and then break these quantities down into smaller shipments for distribution to customers.

❑ *Rack Jobbers –* distribute a specialized line (e.g., soft-cover books and magazines, toys, health and beauty aids, novelties, household items, and the like) through supermarkets and other high-traffic outlets.

❑ *Single-line Wholesalers –* supply retail clients with a complete in-depth stock in one particular line of goods, such as grocers, hardware outlets, and the like.

❑ *Specialty Wholesalers –* handle a small number of products within a particular merchandise line.

❑ *Truck Jobbers –* service retail outlets directly from a truck with fast-moving products and perishable goods (commonly encountered in the grocery trade). In addition to fresh fruits and vegetables, truck jobbers handle dairy products, cookies, frozen foods, and similar items.

❑ **Retailers –** like wholesalers are intermediaries in the marketing channels who forward goods from the nation's producers through to the final consumers. The retailing industry is a vital sector of the economy and employs more than 20 million people in over three million retail establishments in the U.S. In 2001, total annual retail sales in the U.S. surpassed $3.3 trillion, up from $235 billion in 1967 and $1.8 trillion in 1992. Retail outlets can be approached directly, especially chain outlets, or through their wholesalers and selling agents.

❑ **Trading Houses –** specialize in exporting, importing, and trading goods and services produced by others. They provide a wide range of specialized services to businesses that wish to export, for a fee or commission.

Summarize and detail more specifically how products and services will be made available to customers:

CUSTOMERS BUY ...	
❑ at retail outlets—we sell our goods on consignment ❑ direct from our production plant—no middlemen ❑ direct from commissioned sales staff ❑ from manufacturing reps located across the country ❑ from our vending machines ❑ online 24 hours a day—we offer free shipping for orders over $100 ❑ through our bi-annual mail order catalog ❑ through TV infomercials which run six times a week	_____ _____ _____ _____ _____ **Sample:** [Company]'s primary distribution channels include: [describe channels A, B, C; list company names; distribution method; draw a flowchart if necessary to show how products are shipped and delivered from your company to local/international freight forwarders to final consumers]. We have chosen to use [channel A] because their target market closely matches our customer profile. [Channel B] has exclusive rights to the [area] market. [Channel C] has excellent customer service and the widest coverage in the [area] market.

Summarize other key issues and "factors to consider" in your distribution plan:

FACTORS to CONSIDER	
❑ complexity of product ❑ concentration of market ❑ cost of distribution method vs. services provided ❑ distributor success rate ❑ financial resources ❑ insurance needs ❑ need for control ❑ number and types of customers ❑ price of product ❑ storage and warehousing costs ❑ transportation and shipping costs	_____ _____ _____ _____ _____ **Sample:** The majority of sales in the local Vancouver market will be handled internally by sales representatives working on a commission basis. If we meet our 2006 sales goals, we will recruit 14 additional sales staff members to service the Seattle and Portland markets.

Back up your distribution plan with reports, rate sheets from shippers, and contracts with sales representatives. Also, provide alternative methods of distribution. For example, if your main shipper was FedEx or UPS and they happened to go on strike, who would replace them?

Sample: Although our primary distribution channels are stable, reliable, and able to meet our projected production rate, if a sudden increase in customer demand exceeds their handling capacity, we have access to three secondary distribution channels: [describe; draw a flowchart of primary and alternative channels].	_____ _____ _____ _____ _____

Main Distributors – *List your principal distributors by name and expected sales:*

Distributor	Address	Territory	Terms of Sale	Exclusive or Non-exclusive	Total Expected Sales ($ or Units)

Describe any special arrangements you may have with your most important distributor:

	Sample: Convinced of the marketability of our [products], Wal-Mart has signed an exclusive agreement with us to retail [products] in POP displays in all their chain store outlets. The duration of this contract is for [X] years with the option to renew. Part of our agreement with Wal-Mart is that all POP displays are within 20 feet of checkout counters (see appendix for a copy of this contract).

Main Customers – *List principal customers by name and the amount you expect them to buy:*

Customer	Product	Expected Purchases ($ or Units)	Share of your Sales (%)
	a.		
	b.		
	c.		
	a.		
	b.		
	c.		
	a.		
	b.		
	c.		

Describe any special arrangements you may have with key customers:

Sample: Having always liked my work at [company], Maria Alvarez has expressed interest in moving her account to my new agency. In 2003, she did $[XX] worth of business with my previous employer. Maria has also recommended my services to three of her colleagues.	

Market Testing Plan

Describe methods you will use to test your target market before launching a full-scale promotion:

Sample: Market testing of [product A] for the Germany market has met all of our evaluation criteria for quality, usability, and customer satisfaction. Testing was conducted using an independent research facility [company] located in Berlin. Unit production volume testing in our Dublin plant is scheduled for [date]. Pilot test results have been positive.	

❏ **Alter one variable at a time.** One of the best strategies you can use to test the potential of a promotion is to modify or change one variable of the promotion at a time to find out if that modification or change can significantly improve your results. You can alter, test, or experiment with: ✦ ad copy ✦ ad headlines ✦ ad pictures ✦ ad position ✦ prices ✦ product features ✦ promotional media ✦ seasons of the year ✦ size of ad vs. frequency of repetition ✦ subtle variations of the wording of offers ✦ use of color ✦ use of coupons ✦ use of humor.

❏ **Buy a sample of a product before you stock up on it.** Don't stock a product you haven't first seen, touched, smelled, listened to, used, tried on, handled, or tasted.

❏ **Compare classified and display advertising.** If your promotion can be sold via a classified ad or a display ad, test both media, as one may prove to be substantially more profitable than the other. Classified ads cost less, but produce less. Display ads cost more, but may also produce more, pulling in 40 times more responses than a classified ad.

❏ **Compare consumer response by region.** Different regions of your city, state, country, and the world might have vastly different responses to the same item. A promotion that does well in L.A. might do better in Tokyo, worse in Sydney, and moderately well in New York. A good marketer tests the same promotion in different market regions.

❏ **Compare your product with other similar products on the market.** Conduct a taste test or listening test. Take pictures of your product side by side with the competition.

❏ **Conduct a survey.** Conduct a survey at your retail location, at stores that sell similar products, or by surveying people on the street who look like they might want your product or service. By listening and noting their responses, you can evaluate pricing, appearance of advertising, and other marketing strategies. Mail questionnaire surveys are less expensive than telephone surveys and personal interviews. However, telephone surveys and personal interviews will produce the most immediate response.

❏ **Distribute your product to one store only.** Ask a retailer if they will set up a display of your product in a store at no cost to them unless products are sold. Local privately owned retail outlets are more likely to agree to this than retail chains, as long as your product complements their offerings and has good potential for sales.

❏ **Do a limited advertising run.** Run an ad in one and only one of your chosen advertising media. Limit your insertions until you have analyzed the response rate from this medium and have found it profitable.

❏ **Attend a trade show** (see page 205).

Describe what kinds of analysis and methods you will use to keep track of your advertising. **What** *is your marketing strategy for confirming* **who** *customers are and* **how** *they heard about you?*

TRACKING ADVERTISING RESULTS
❑ advertising keys
❑ after-sale questionnaires
❑ coded order forms
❑ customer surveys
❑ "tell them Joe sent you" broadcast ads
❑ advertising cost analysis charts
❑ track "cost per inquiry"
❑ track "cost per sale"
❑ track "cost per media as a percentage of sales"

<u>Trade Shows</u> – *List trade shows you have attended, results obtained, and/or trade shows you plan to attend. For shows you plan to attend,* **how** *will you make your exhibit stand out? Describe pre-show, show time, and post-show plans. Check strategies below (refer back to page 205):*

Sample: Our participation in the 2004 Dallas International Gift Show in January was more successful than we had expected, bringing in $[XX] worth of orders and [XX] new clients. We followed up all inquiries with thank-you letters, sample products, and our new Summer catalog, bringing in an additional $[XX] worth of sales. We have also rented booths for the March 13–15 Chicago World Trade Show and the March 27–30 Boston Gift Show.

Pre-Show

❑ Book only national trade shows.

❑ Rent the best possible display location.

❑ Publicize your participation in the show to the local press a few months beforehand.

❑ Send letters to all television and radio stations in the trade show area.

❑ Write letters or invitations to people who will be interested in your display.

❑ Write letters or invitations to people who might be interested in your display.

❑ Hit the local press about ten days before the show opens.

❑ Mail reminder letters. ❑ Prepare your booth to be different.

Show Time

❑ Display as much promotional material as appropriate.

❑ Keep a detailed record of everyone who visits your booth.

❑ Keep a sharp lookout for buyers.

❑ Make a detailed study of all the other exhibitors.

❑ Approach all related businesses.

❑ If the show extends over several days, consider testing your prices, redecorating your booth, or showcasing different products.

Post-Show

❑ Follow up on all inquiries.

❑ Mail thank-you notes to invited guests.

DAY 21

Set a pricing structure.

Pricing Policies

Crucial to a good marketing strategy is an effective pricing policy. The prices you charge will affect sales volume, profit levels, and among other things, your company image. To develop a pricing policy: (1) define pricing objectives, (2) establish a simple yet effective pricing structure taking into consideration all business costs, (3) choose a pricing strategy to establish a market presence, and (4) fine-tune and adapt your general pricing policy in response to trends, industry practices, and new innovative pricing strategies to help solidify your competitive position within the marketplace.

Sample Pricing Policy Statements

Product – Before [I/we] established prices for [my/our] [product], [I/we] determined [my/our] per unit costs. [I/We] then researched the market price for similar products. At market price, it was determined that for all but [my/our] lowest sales projections, [my/our] [product] would turn a profit in [time period]. However, since our [product]s offer(s) additional features, including [explain features], [I/we] feel that [I/we] can price it [XX]% above the competition.

To test this price, [I/we] conducted a survey of [XX] users of [product]s. [I/We] first questioned them about the benefits and desirability of [my/our] extra features and then asked them if [my/our] price was acceptable. [I/We] found that [50]% of those polled were interested in [my/our] product. Of this [50]%, [I/we] received [10] firm orders representing approximately [20]% of this group. A breakdown of [my/our] pricing structure is as follows: [describe pricing structure; include price list; clarify pricing objectives].

OR – [I/We] have determined that the market price is $[XX] per unit. If [I/we] charge this price [my/our] margin will equal [XX]%.

OR – [My/Our] unit cost has been figured at $[XX]. [I/We] need a margin of [XX]% to cover our overhead and earn a sufficient profit. [My/Our] selling price will be $[XX].

Service – Before [I/we] set prices for [my/our] [service], [I/we] projected fixed and variable monthly costs to be $[XX]. [I/We] then researched the

---

For most businesses, prices are determined by costs, competition, and industry pricing practices.

✳

In the long run, a profitable sales volume is a much better company goal than maximum sales volume.

PROFIT TIP

Demand-oriented pricing is usually superior to cost-oriented pricing. In the "cost approach," a pre-determined amount is added to the cost of the merchandise. In the "demand approach," prices are based on what consumers are willing to pay.

PROFIT TIP

> *A fair price for oil is whatever you can get plus ten per cent.*
>
> **DR. ALI AHMED ATTIGA**
> Saudi Arabian Delegate to OPEC
>
> ✽
>
> *Business is taking a pile of cash, doing something with it, and winding up with a bigger pile of cash.*
>
> **LEONARD SHAYKIN**
> Managing Partner

market rate for similar services. At market rate, it was determined that for ALL but our lowest sales projections, [my/our] [service] would turn a profit in [time period]. However, since [my/our] service is unique and demands a high level of expertise, [I/we] feel that [I/we] need to bill higher than the competition. A breakdown of [my/our] pricing structure is as follows: [describe pricing structure; include price list; clarify pricing objectives].

Writing "Price Objectives"

Price objectives are qualifying statements about what you want your pricing policy to do, such as keep or build market share, increase profits, meet or prevent competition, introduce new products, and/or increase sales. They give direction to the whole pricing process. Price objectives must closely tie in with your overall business and marketing goals. When setting price objectives, carefully consider what impact prices will have on factors such as sales volume, sales revenue, market share, competitive position, company image, and profitability (see diagram below). Specific examples of price objectives include: ◆ "earn a 15% return on investment" ◆ "increase market share by 30% by end of fiscal year" ◆ "introduce new products at introductory prices to gain a market presence and once established, raise prices."

More "Price Objectives"

- ❏ be perceived as "fair" by current customers and potential customers
- ❏ build store traffic
- ❏ create interest and excitement in a new product
- ❏ desensitize customers to price
- ❏ discourage competitors from lowering prices
- ❏ discourage new entrants to industry
- ❏ enhance the image of the firm, brand, or product
- ❏ help prepare for the sale of the business
- ❏ increase dollar sales, market share, sales volume
- ❏ maintain price leadership
- ❏ match competitor prices
- ❏ maximize long-run profit
- ❏ maintain or build loyalty of distributor and sales representatives
- ❏ maximize short-run profit
- ❏ obtain a target rate of return on investment (ROI)
- ❏ obtain a target rate of return on sales
- ❏ meet ethical or ideological objectives
- ❏ stabilize market or market price
- ❏ use price to make the product "visible"

FACTORS THAT WILL INFLUENCE PRICES

Cost
Demand
Competition
Experience
Customer Perceptions
Profit Goals

Pricing Policy and Strategy

FACTORS THAT PRICE WILL INFLUENCE

Sales Volume
Sales Revenues
Market Share
Competitive Position
Company Image
Profitability

Developing a Price Structure

Developing a systematic approach to setting prices is important to building a successful business. One way to explain and justify your pricing structure is to talk about it in terms of its "price floor" and "price ceiling." The *price floor* is the lowest cost at which you can sell a product to meet all your costs, and still make a small profit. The *price ceiling* is determined by industry practices, what the competition is charging, and the maximum cost consumers are willing to pay based upon their perceived value of your product or service (visit Pricingsociety.com for the latest news on industry pricing strategies).

Calculating Retail Markup

One technique to establish a pricing structure is to mark up goods sold by adding a percentage to their actual cost. Your final price is based on: (a) *the cost of acquiring the goods*, called "cost of merchandise" or "cost of goods sold"—this cost includes the actual price paid for the merchandise plus freight, import duties, and any handling costs minus any quantity and cash discount given to you by the wholesaler; (b) *the cost of operating the business* to sell the goods, called "operating expenses" or "overhead"—this cost includes markdowns, stock shortages, theft, customer discounts, and the salary of the owner; and (c) *desired profit*.

For example: A retailer (Sam's Shirt Shop) purchases a shirt for $20. Using industry averages and a desired profit of 12%, Sam calculates his markup percentage to be 40% based on 15% for wages, 8% for rent, 2% for utilities, and 3% for

Cost of one shirt	$20
Markup amount	$8
Selling price per shirt	$28
Markup percentage	**40%**

advertising. He adds $8 to the price of the shirt for a resale price of $28.

NOTE When first starting a business, it is difficult to determine how much goods should be marked up because a new business has no history of sales on which to base sales projections. It is necessary to research industry trade journals for sales patterns and markup averages.

Expressing Markup as a Percentage of the Retail Price Instead of Cost – "Retail price" rather than "actual cost" is ordinarily used to express markup percentage. The reason for this is that other operating figures

Dollar amount of markup	$8
Retail Price	$28
Retail Markup (dollar markup/retail price)	**29%**

such as wages, advertising expenses, and profit, when expressed as a percentage, are normally expressed as percentages based on retail prices rather than cost of the merchandise. For this reason, most retailers prefer to express their markup as a percentage of retail price (see "Markup Table" on the next page for conversions).

> *Anybody can cut prices, but it takes brains to produce a better article.*
> **P. D. ARMOUR**

Using a Standard Markup Percentage – To maintain your desired level of profit, establish a *standard* or *average percentage of markup*. This markup percentage can be calculated using the formula on the right:

For example, if *Sam's Shirt Warehouse* projects that it can sell 10,000 shirts a year costing $194,000, with shipping costs of $6,000, operating expenses of $53,000, and a desired profit of $27,000, "Initial Markup" would be calculated as follows:

Standard Markup % Formula

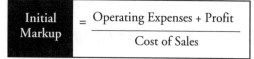

$$\text{Initial Markup} = \frac{\text{Operating Expenses} + \text{Profit}}{\text{Cost of Sales}}$$

$$\text{Initial Markup} = \frac{(\$53,000 + \$27,00)}{(\$194,000 + \$6,000)} = 0.4 \text{ or } \mathbf{40\%}$$

NOTE A business may choose to use a standard markup percentage on all products, or it may have different markups for different goods. The reason for this is standard or average markup percentage does not allow for cost differences in selling different products. For example, if product A costs more to advertise or sell than product B, a standard markup percentage may produce a loss on product A and a greater-than-average profit on product B.

Calculating the Cost of a Service

Services are harder to price than goods. It is more difficult for consumers to determine a fair price for services, and comparative shopping has much less effect in service industries than it does in hard goods industries. Services are also more difficult to price because costs are harder to estimate and it is more difficult to compare prices with the competition. Nevertheless, although more complex, pricing a service is basically calculated in the same way as pricing retail goods:

> **Price (for a service)** = *materials cost + operating expenses* (which include supplies, labor, and overhead) + *the desired profit*

Calculating Materials Cost – *Materials cost* is the cost of materials used directly in a final product, such as sparkplugs and gaskets in the repair of an

"Markup at Retail" and "Markup at Cost" Table

MARKUP AT	
Cost %	Retail %
42.9 =	30.0
45.0	31.0
47.1	32.0
49.3	33.0
51.5	34.0
53.9	35.0
56.3	36.0
58.8	37.0
61.3	38.0
64.0	39.0
66.7	**40.0**
70.0	41.0
72.4	42.0
75.5	43.0
78.5	44.0
81.8	45.0
85.2	46.0
88.7	47.0
92.3	48.0
95.9	49.0
100.0	50.0
150.0	60.0

Markup, also known as markon, is the difference between the cost of the merchandise and its selling price. It can be measured in % or $. Markup is usually figured based on the retail selling price, not the cost price. The following table shows the equivalent percent for markup at cost and retail.

Markup Formula Example: If you want to sell a pair of socks that cost you $3.25 at a 40% retail markup, to arrive at a price, you could calculate it as follows:

Cost = Retail Price – Markup
Cost = 100% – 40% = 60%

Retail Price =
Dollar Cost/Percentage Cost
= $3.25/60% (.60) = $5.42
OR use the markup table:
$3.25 + ($3.25 × 0.667) = $5.42

engine. Supplies such as paper towels are part of overhead, not materials cost. A materials cost list must always be used in preparing a bid or quoting a job. If there are shipping, handling, or storage costs for materials, these must also be included in the total materials cost.

Calculating Labor Costs – Labor Cost is the cost of work *directly* applied to a service, such as a mechanic's work. Work not directly applied to the service, such as cleaning up, is an overhead cost. Direct labor costs are derived by multiplying the cost of labor per hour by the number of hours required to complete the job.

Calculating Overhead Costs – Generally speaking, overhead costs include all costs other than direct materials and direct labor. These costs can also be referred to as the *indirect cost* of providing a service. They include legal fees, supplies, insurance, taxes, rent, accounting, and other labor costs of other people on the company payroll who perform support services that are not charged to direct labor. This cost can be expressed as an hourly rate based on total labor hours per year or as a percentage of direct labor.

Overhead Rate in Total Direct Labor Hours – The following formula can be used in machine shops, repair shops, and design and production shops, where equipment used is inexpensive and there is relatively little difference between skill levels and the hourly wages of employees. It can also be used for small consulting firms.

$$\text{Overhead Rate} = \frac{\text{Total overhead cost}}{\text{Total direct labor hours (per year)}} = \frac{\$40,000}{5,000 \text{ hours}} = \$8 \text{ per hour}$$

Overhead Rate as a Percentage of Direct Labor Cost – In businesses where costly equipment is used by higher paid employees; overhead cost is more closely related to direct labor cost than total labor hours. In this situation, overhead cost can be expressed as a percentage of direct labor.

$$\text{Overhead Rate} = \frac{\text{Total overhead cost}}{\text{Total direct labor cost}} = \frac{\$40,000}{\$50,000} = 0.8 \text{ or } \mathbf{80\%}$$

EXAMPLE As shown in the example on the right, if you calculated your overhead costs to be 80% of your direct labor costs and your employee whom you pay $20 per hour worked for three hours using parts costing $70, your cost to the customer would be $263.38.

> *I don't pay good wages because I have a lot of money; I have a lot of money because I pay good wages.*
> **ROBERT BOSCH**
> German inventor, industrialist (1861–1942)

> *The value of a thing is the amount of laboring or work that its possession will save the possessor.*
> **HENRY GEORGE**

Bill's Auto Shop	
Materials Cost	
Muffler	$70.00
Direct Labor Cost	
Hourly Wages (per hour)	$20.00
Fringe Benefits (30% of wage)	$6.00
Total Cost per Hour	$26.00
# of Hours	3
Direct Labor Total	$78.00
Overhead Cost (80% of direct labor)	
Total	$62.40
Total Costs	$210.40
Profit	
Profit on Materials (30%)	$21.00
Profit on Labor (25%)	$19.50
Profit on Overhead (20%)	$12.48
Total Profit	$52.98
Total Charge to Customer	$263.38

Choosing a Price Marketing Strategy

Every industry has a favorite or common pricing or markup strategy that takes into account "price floors" and "price ceilings" common to the industry. Research your industry to determine what these strategies are and then use them as a guide for your own pricing policies. Keep in mind that it can be disastrous to start artificially low in the attempt to win over market share and then raise prices once established. Use this strategy with caution. In fact, starting out with higher prices might be a better idea. Consumers are notoriously illogical (see page 226 for commonly used pricing strategies).

Fine-tuning Your Pricing Policy

No pricing policy is complete without a little tinkering to help consolidate your strategic position. Use the tips on page 227 to expand and improve your basic pricing policy.

Pricing List

A "pricing list" is the pricing structure or list of prices made available to clients or customers. Outlined below and on page 222 are some samples:

Price List for Computer Chip Manufacturer (Sample #1)

Product Name (1 Ku Tray Units)	Feb '04 (2/1)	Feb '04 (2/15)	% Decrease
Intel® Pentium® 4 Processor 3.4 GHz	$417	$417	–
Intel® Celeron® Processor 2.1 GHz	$69	$69	–
Intel® Xeon™ Processor 2.8 GHz	$3,692	$3,692	–
Mobile Intel® Celeron® Processor 2.4 GHz	$134	$112	16%

Note: Prices subject to change without notice. Prices are for direct customers in 1000-unit tray quantities. Taxes and shipping, etc. not included.

$ucce$$ Story ➜ India's Greatest Foreign Industrialist

Born in Denmark, Henning Holck-Larsen was a greatly respected co-founder and CEO of one of India's greatest companies, Larsen and Toubro Limited (L&T). Holck-Larsen was a large, imposing man, but despite this was considered "the most humble and accessible executive in the organization." When asked the secret of his success as an industrialist in India, he replied: "If you want to belong to a country which becomes a nation, you have to keep the economy growing by creating jobs. And you can only do that by investing in tomorrow, and tomorrow is made by people." Holck-Larsen spent more than 60 years in India. L&T's spectacular record of achievement can be traced to the values he instilled of strong customer orientation and professionalism.

Successful
**BUSINESS
PLANNING
30**in**DAYS**

DAY 21 **Worksheets**

Set a pricing structure.

Pricing Policies

Outline key considerations in your pricing policy: ❏ COGS ❏ overhead ❏ desired profit ❏ market demand

Sample: Our prices are primarily determined by what the market will bear and what competitors are charging. [Competitor A] charges $[XX] per hour and [competitor B] charges $[XX] per hour. With an annual projected overhead of $[XX], we need [XX] billable hours per year to ensure a desired profit of $[XX].	

Price Objectives – *Summarize the main objectives of your pricing policy (review pages 212, 218, 219):*
❏ earn a [XX]% net profit ❏ avoid a price war ❏ match the competition ❏ offer value for the money

Sample: Initially, the objective of our pricing policy is to build store traffic and create interest and excitement in our unique variety of handcrafted antique green gold jewelry. For the first 60 days, we will be offering free engraving for all purchases over $50.	

Factors That Will Influence Prices – *Check the most important factors that will **influence** your **pricing policies** (see next page). List and describe any additional influences that come to mind:*
❏ cost structure ❏ competition ❏ customer expectations ❏ demand ❏ experience ❏ final pricing authority
❏ industry averages ❏ legal concerns ❏ location of business ❏ perceived value to customers
❏ physical appearance of business premises ❏ profit goals ❏ risk

Sample: Before setting prices for our pest control service, we projected fixed and variable monthly costs to be $1,400. We then researched the market rate and for all but our lowest sales projections, calculated reaching profitability within three months from startup. However, since we are using a new delivery technology, which reduces pesticide fumes, our pricing structure is 15% higher than the market average. A breakdown of our pricing structure is shown below.	

Factors that Will Influence Prices

❑ **Cost Structure** – Price your product or service according to costs. A pricing structure should account for all the fixed and variable costs of conducting business, including all marketing and distribution costs.

❑ *Fixed Costs* – Fixed costs generally refer to your operating expenses. They include wages, management salaries, rent, utilities, office supplies, insurance, etc., and usually do not vary with your business volume.

❑ *Variable Costs* – Variable costs generally refer to your cost of goods (inventory costs) as in the case of a wholesaler or retailer and your cost of materials or supplies as in the case of a manufacturer or service provider. Variable costs increase or decrease depending on the amount of goods, materials, or supplies purchased for resale or production. They include the price paid for inventory, materials, supplies, freight charges, handling charges, etc.

❑ **Competition** – Price your product or service according to what the competition is charging. Since your products or services are competing in the marketplace, you must know exactly what the competition is doing before you finalize your pricing policies. To get detailed information about your competitors' pricing polices, send in a friend or go yourself to do some comparison-shopping. Is there discounting? Special sales? Loss leaders? Make some "blind" phone calls.

❑ **Customer Expectations** – Price your product or service according to customer expectations. Some shoppers are very price-conscious; others want convenience and knowledgeable sales staff and will pay more to get it.

❑ **Demand** – Price your product or service according to how many people want it, how badly and how quickly they need it, and how much they are willing to pay for it. Obviously, if there is a large demand for your product or service and you're the only one on the block selling it, you can pretty much charge what you want.

❑ **Experience** – Price your product or service according to what people have paid for it in the past.

❑ **Final Pricing Authority** – Price your product or service according to who has final pricing authority. If you are running a franchise, you may have little say in what you charge for your goods or services. Likewise, be aware that some suppliers and manufacturers attempt to control retail prices by refusing directly or indirectly to deal with nonconforming stores.

❑ **Industry Averages** – Price your product or service according to guidelines set by your industry. Research your industry to determine its average markup percentage and other standard pricing strategies and structures. Trade associations often have pricing schedules for services.

❑ **Legal Concerns** – Price your product or service according to local and national regulations and laws. In some cases, laws may restrict how much you can charge for certain items.

❑ **Location of Business** – Price your product or service according to how good your location is. A business with a prime location can usually get away with charging more for its products or services. For example, consider two similarly equipped hotels, one with a beachfront, the other overlooking a shopping mall parking lot. Which one would you pay more for?

❑ **Perceived Value to Customers** – Price your product or service according to how valuable customers perceive it to be. This will help you establish the upper limit of your price range or "what the market will bear." Perceived value is dependent upon to what extent a product or service saves money, improves the quality of life, is seen as being truly unique, is durable and made of quality parts that are generally understood to cost more, and how well it actually meets needs (if your prices are high, offer more or better service to justify your higher prices).

❑ **Physical Appearance of Business Premises** – Price your product or service according to how much money you have put into interior and exterior renovations. Clients normally expect businesses with posh surroundings to charge higher prices, while those with bare floors and simple shelving to give discounts.

❑ **Profit Goals** – Price your product or service according to profit goals. Prices should motivate customers to buy, be competitive, and cover selling costs. But there's no point starting a business unless you can get a decent return on your investment. Merchandise should always be priced in such a way as to maximize profit taking into account both your short-term and long-term needs.

❑ **Risk** – Price your product or service according to the risks involved in offering certain merchandise or services. Fashionable clothing often carries a higher markup than basic clothing because fashions may suddenly lose their appeal overnight and be replaced by a new fashion craze.

<u>*Factors that Price Will Influence*</u> – *Check important factors that the **price** of your product or services **will influence** (see below). List and describe any additional factors that come to mind:*

❑ sales volume ❑ sales revenue ❑ market share ❑ competitive position ❑ company image ❑ profitability

Sample: A telephone survey of our target wholesale market reveals that purchasing agents are reluctant to order new products with no sales track record. However, we discovered that if we help defray their catalog mailing costs for promoting our product alongside their regular offerings, they are willing to warehouse [XX] units of inventory on a consignment basis. Hence, to enter this market, we have devoted [X]% of our overall marketing budget. If our product sells successfully, we plan to offer 15% discounts to orders over [XX] units to entice wholesalers into making larger purchases and 10% for repeat orders within [time period].

Factors that Price Will Influence

❑ **Sales Volume –** Sales volume is highly dependent on prices. Usually, higher prices mean lower volume and vice-versa. Small businesses can often command higher prices because of the personalized service they can offer. It should be noted that if there is no direct relationship between pricing changes and sales volume, the sale of a product or service is relatively independent of its cost. When this is the case, it is likely that the market is saturated. This situation spells "trouble."

❑ **Sales Revenue –** Setting prices, including credit policies, is a major factor affecting total revenue. If you increase the price of your product, you can expect response to decrease by a certain percentage. However, a one-dollar item may not necessarily get twice as many sales as two dollars. It may get more, or it may get less. To maximize your revenue you must therefore test and research what consumers are willing to pay.

❑ **Market Share –** Your prices will determine to a large extent your percentage of market share compared with your competitors. Lower prices usually mean a larger percentage of the market share.

❑ **Competitive Position –** Prices will affect how your product or service stands in relation to the competition. Occasionally you might use cheaper than normal prices to introduce products or services to get consumer attention and improve your market position. However, if you set prices too low, and the competition is watching closely, you could end up in a price war (in price wars, only the consumer wins).

❑ **Company Image –** Your prices will create an image in your consumer's mind. They will see you as a discounter, general retailer, or overpriced Rodeo Drive type operator. Discounters sell at the lowest possible price and strive for a high volume of units sold while the Rodeo Drive type operator strives for high profit per sale on a lower volume.

❑ **Profitability –** Prices will affect overall profitability. The most profitable price can be found by testing the market with different prices on the same product or service. A high price will give you more profit per sale but less sales. A low price will give you less profit per sale but more sales. Somewhere in between lies the perfect balance between profit per sale and volume of sales.

Elements of Your Selling Price *– Review pages 217, 218, and 219, as well as items on this page and the next. Jot down the most important elements of your selling price:*

_____

❑ **Manufacturing Businesses –** In manufacturing, the most important elements of the selling price are the costs of raw materials, manufacturing overhead (equip.), non-manufacturing overhead, and planned profit.

❑ **Wholesale Businesses –** In a wholesale business, the most important elements of the selling price are cost of goods for resale, overhead, sales volume, competition's pricing and credit policies, and planned profit.

❑ **Retail Businesses –** In a retail business, the most important elements of the selling price are very similar to those of a wholesale business except retailers are also very concerned about how prices affect their "image."

❑ **Service Businesses –** In a service business, the most important elements of the selling price are materials and supplies, labor and operating expenses, competition, and planned profit.

Principal Direct-cost Elements of Your Selling Price

Product and Material Cost – Summarize and describe:

❑ retailers and wholesalers – cost of goods sold including shipping costs
❑ manufacturers – raw materials cost ❑ service providers – materials and supplies costs

_____

Labor Costs – Summarize and describe direct labor costs (for retail and wholesale operations this cost is usually factored into overhead costs):

_____

*Overhead Costs – Summarize and describe overhead costs and how they will affect your pricing. For service providers especially, elaborate upon **how** you factor or calculate overhead into your final price:*

_____

Other Elements of Your Selling Price

Planned Profit – *Discuss gross and net margins for products and service lines. Outline profit goals:*

Competition's Pricing – **What** *are your competitors charging for similar products and services?*

Other Elements – *Summarize other elements of your selling price:* ❑ image desired ❑ inflation pressures

Pricing Structure – *Detail what you plan to charge customers or clients for your products and services:*
❑ Explain how your costs, profit goals, and other elements influenced your decision.
❑ If you plan to operate a retail or wholesale business, explain markup percentages and how you arrived at them.
❑ What exactly is your markup percentage at "retail" and at "cost"?
❑ If you plan to operate a service or manufacturing business, show the method you will use to calculate your prices.
(use worksheets provided on pages 223–225; also visit the Professional Pricing Association website at www.pricingsociety.com)

Sample: To test our pricing structure, we conducted a survey of 24 potential buyers for our shockproof, weatherproof IronSlate™ tablet computers including purchasing agents for FedEx and the U.S. military. We first questioned them about the benefits of IronSlate's durability and then asked them if our prices were acceptable. We found that 75% of those polled were interested in our product. Of those 75%, six placed orders to field-test 80 units.

Describe your schedule for quantity, cash, and other discounts, as well as terms for any credit sales, credit card purchases, returns, etc.:

❑ 10% restocking charge for all returns ❑ bulk purchases of 100 or more will receive a [XX]% discount
❑ buy two, get one free ❑ 3% service charge for all credit card sales ❑ [XX]% discount on Web purchases
❑ free shipping on orders of $100+ ❑ trade-in allowances allowed ❑ [XX]% discount for cash sales
❑ free financing for six months ❑ 10th visit is free ❑ [XX]% discount for early-bird purchases

---

Pricing List for Website Service Co. (Sample #2)

For a free estimate for your website design, please use our free online quote form. If you order the website, half the service fee is due upfront, and the other half is due after the site has been completed:

Basic Services
Initial Set-up Fee........... $75 includes first Web page
Additional Web pages (additional) $30
Banner Ad..$40
Logo design ....$100 and up
Domain name .... $20/year, charged separately
Web hosting..$15/month
Scanned Image...$3
Form e-mailer $50
Secure order form...$150
Shopping cart..$150

Other Services
Small Business Site Package $599
Flash Intro...$250
Online Brochure..$299

Summarize key strategies in your pricing policy (see "Industry Pricing Strategies" on page 226):

❑ Breakeven Pricing ❑ Buying a Market Position Pricing ❑ Competitive Advantage Pricing
❑ Discount Pricing ❑ Full-cost Pricing ❑ Keystone Pricing ❑ Loss Leader Pricing
❑ Matching the Competition Pricing ❑ Multiple Unit Pricing ❑ Odd Pricing ❑ Penetration Pricing
❑ Pre-season Pricing ❑ Price-is-no-object Pricing ❑ Price Lining ❑ Price Skimming
❑ Pricing Above Competitors ❑ Pricing Below Competition ❑ Suggested Retail Pricing

---

Pricing List for Consulting Firm (Sample #3)

ABC Associates provides expert advice, assistance, guidance and/or counseling in support of real, immediate, and enduring business improvements. Please call 1-888-555-5555 to book an appointment. Hourly rates are outlined below (daily rate × 8):

Labor Category	Hourly Rate
Principal Consultant	$162.37
Executive Consultant	$129.80
Senior Consultant	$110.08
Junior Consultant	$70.05
Team Leader	$63.16
Production Assistant	$48.65
Word Processing	$28.12
Graphics Illustrator	$49.82

Pricing Worksheet #1 – Retail or Wholesale Business

Initial Markup:

Operating Expenses for the Year (all fixed and variable operating costs)

Desired Profit for the Year

Cost of Sales (include shipping and handling charges)

A) Markup % = $\dfrac{\text{(Operating Expenses + Profit)}}{\text{(Cost of Sales)}}$ %

Direct Product Cost:

Product Unit Cost

Additional Product Unit Costs (accessories, options, etc.)

B) Total Direct Product Cost $

C) Initial Markup = (A × B) $

D) Product Price (B + C) $

Pricing Worksheet #2 – Service Quote (Contract Bid)

Materials Cost:

Description of Materials (list materials):

A) Total Materials Cost $

Direct Labor Cost:

Hourly Wages (per hour)

Fringe Benefits (30% of wage)

Total Cost per Hour

# of Hours

Other Labor Costs (specify)

B) Total Direct Labor Cost $

C) Overhead Cost [(yearly overhead/yearly total direct labor cost) × B] $

D) Total Direct Costs (A + B + C) $

Profit:

Profit on Materials (_____ %)

Profit on Labor (_____ %)

Profit on Overhead (_____ %)

E) Total Profit $

F) Other Charges $

G) Sales Tax $

H) Total Charge to Customer (D + E + F + G) $

NOTE When submitting a service quote to your customers, "Overhead Costs" and "Fringe Benefits" are factored into "Labor." Profit percentages are factored into "Materials" and "Labor" (see "Service Quote" worksheet on page 224).

SERVICE QUOTE

Company

Date: [ ]

Materials

Description of Materials (list materials):

_____

_____

_____

_____

A) Total Materials Charges $ [ ]

Labor

Cost per Hour

# of Hours

Other Labor Costs (specify)

_____

B) Total Labor Charges $ [ ]

Other Charges (specify)

_____

C) Total Other Charges $ [ ]

D) Sales Tax $ [ ]

E) Total Charge to Customer (A + B + C + D) $ [ ]

Notes:

_____

_____

The above quote is valid until **Date:** [ ]

THANK YOU for Considering our Services

Pricing Worksheet #3 – Manufacturing a Product

Direct Material Costs

Raw Material or Component Part	Description	Supplier	Landed Cost*	x	# or Quantity Required per Unit	=	Cost/Unit Produced
			$				$

A) Total Direct Material Costs per Unit $

* Landed Cost – When importing a product or raw material, a variety of expenses can be incurred that make the item more expensive than the initial price paid to the exporter. These costs plus the original cost are often referred to as the "landed cost." They include: bank charges, bonds to customs (with merchandise above a certain value), brokerage fees, customs duty, currency exchange costs, etc. (see GB📖 #45 "Starting and Operating an Import/Export Business").

Direct Labor Costs

Assembly or Manufacturing Process	Estimated Labor Time per Unit	x	Hourly Rate	=	Labor Cost per Unit
			$		$

B) Total Direct Labor Costs per Unit $

C) Total Direct Manufacturing Cost per Unit (A + B) $

D) Total Estimated Packaging and Shipping Cost per Unit $

E) Total Direct Cost per Unit (C + D) $

F) Fixed Cost per Unit (Yearly Overhead/# of Units per Year) $

G) Other Variable Costs per Unit (Variable Costs/# of Units per Year) $

H) Profit per Unit [(Profit Margin in Percent) $\times$ (E + F + G)] $

I) Final Product Price per Unit (E + F + G + H) $

❑ **Breakeven Pricing** – In breakeven pricing, prices are based on your fixed and variable costs, as well as profit goals. The cost of merchandise (your BE point) will be at one end of your price range, while the level above which consumers will not buy your product or service will be at the other end. Much has been written on breakeven analysis as a means for determining prices. Be warned that it quite often just doesn't work.

❑ **Buying a Market Position Pricing** – Using this form of pricing, you attempt to buy your way into the market by initially offering free samples or "heavy" discount coupons, for example 50 cents off a 99-cent purchase. This pricing strategy is usually reserved for big companies selling repeat goods and having ample cash reserves. It usually takes six months or more before this strategy starts to pay off.

❑ **Competitive Advantage Pricing** – In competitive advantage pricing, prices are set equal to, above, or below your competitors. This strategy requires that you constantly shop the competition. A variation of this is the "we-won't-be-undersold" approach where you offer to meet or beat competitor prices.

❑ **Discount Pricing** – In discount pricing, a retail outlet offers lower prices as a trade-off for sparsely decorated interiors and fewer sales staff. Discount stores depend on greater volume to cover operating costs. They typically work on a 35% to 38% markup compared to 42.5% to 45 % for a department store.

❑ **Full-cost Pricing** – Easy to implement, in full-cost pricing, prices are calculated by adding the costs of the product or service plus a flat fee or percentage as the profit margin.

❑ **Keystone Pricing** – Keystone pricing refers to the practice of setting the retail price at double the cost figure, or a 100% markup. This pricing strategy is most common with jewelry shops, high-ticket fashion shops, specialty shops, and department stores.

❑ **Loss Leader Pricing** – Loss leaders are items sold at a lower price to attract people into your store to buy other regularly priced items. A good loss leader will have a lower wholesale price than other items, look more expensive, sell at other stores at a higher price, be readily available from your suppliers, and/or be a recognized brand or item purchased frequently enough that customers recognize the savings. Loss leaders are more effective if closely associated with other items sold at your regular prices.

❑ **Matching the Competition Pricing** – Using this pricing strategy, you match the prices of other businesses selling comparable products or services.

❑ **Multiple Unit Pricing** – Multiple pricing is the practice of promoting a number of units for a single price. The idea behind it is that you can increase the size of your individual sales by offering a meaningful discount for larger purchases. Example of multiple unit pricing include: ✦ bulk pricing in effect ✦ buy by the truckload ✦ buy three tires, get the fourth free ✦ buy twelve, get one free ✦ cheaper by the carton ✦ six-packs ✦ two for $1.98.

❑ **Odd Pricing** – With odd pricing you use prices that end in 5, 7, or 9 such as $2.99, $4.97, $15.95, or $69. For psychological reasons, consumers tend to round down dollar figures. For example, they round $8.95 to $8 rather than up to $9.

❑ **Penetration Pricing** – In penetration pricing, you introduce your product at a substantially lower price than the competition to gain a share of the market. The purpose of this strategy is to create customer excitement and demand to help establish a strong customer base and discourage competition. However, eventually you will have to raise your prices to start making some profit, and when you do, you will learn a lot about customer loyalty. This strategy works best for repeat goods.

❑ **Pre-season Pricing** – Pre-season pricing is a strategy whereby price discounts are offered as incentives to buy early. This strategy is important to manufacturers because it is advantageous for them to be able to project production requirements and order the right amount of raw materials. Retailers can also use this pricing strategy to even out monthly demand and cash flow.

❑ **Price-is-no-object Pricing** – Using this pricing strategy you charge high prices to create an image of exclusivity and cater only to the cream of society (anybody with money). This strategy will only work if your product or service is: ✦ innovative ✦ in demand ✦ threatened by little or no competition ✦ within a market where price is less important than quality, service, or image (e.g., Beverly Hills, Palm Beach).

❑ **Price Lining** – Price lining is a marketing strategy where you carry products in specific price ranges. A hardware store may carry hammers in good, better, and best categories at $4.97, $7.97, and $9.97, and a professional model at $18.95. The theory behind this strategy is that people buy products with different expectations for quality and length of useful life. This strategy helps meet the needs of customers who are looking for a product at a price they can afford. Advantages of price lining include: ✦ ease of merchandise selection ✦ simplified buying and inventory control. A disadvantage is that by focusing too much on price, you may overlook issues of quality or consumer buying trends. It also limits your ability to meet competitor prices.

❑ **Price Skimming** – Price skimming refers to the practice of charging high prices to maximize profit in the short run. It works best when: ✦ the product is unique ✦ the product targets trendsetters who are easily bored and always looking for something new ✦ you have a strong patent position. The real disadvantage of skimming is that it attracts competition like flies to horse manure. Once your competitors get wind of your profits, they will copy your product and produce "knockoffs."

❑ **Pricing Above Competitors** – Pricing above the competition is possible when non-price consideration are more important to buyers, such as: ✦ convenient or exclusive location ✦ exclusive brands or designer names ✦ free delivery ✦ helpful sales staff ✦ in-home demonstrations ✦ superior product knowledge.

❑ **Pricing Below Competition** – Using this strategy, beat your competitor's price! Because this strategy reduces your profit margins, it can only be effective if it greatly increases sales.

❑ **Suggested Retail Pricing** – Suggested retail pricing is the practice of selling at prices set by wholesalers and manufacturers. The advantage of this pricing strategy is that it simplifies the decision-making process and the trouble of monitoring the competition. It is also convenient because many product lines are already prepackaged and pre-priced.

Fine-tuning Pricing Policies – *Outline any other strategies you will use to fine-tune your pricing policy:*

❑ Since our product is perceived as the market leader, we will charge the highest prices the market will bear.
❑ Creating "perceived value" is one of the best ways for us to secure steady sales and a lasting market share.
❑ Deep discounts can lead to deep trouble, especially if consumers perceive that we are in trouble financially.
❑ Pricing policies based chiefly on profit goals are too rigid and usually fall flat in the marketplace.
❑ We will charge a little more than competitors, because we have the best product. But no one knows it yet.

❑ **Consider allowing trade-ins as part of any purchases.** A trade-in policy is usually important for businesses that sell appliances, televisions, autos, and even musical instruments. The trade-in value is almost always below what the customers could receive if they decided to sell the item themselves.

❑ **Do not lower prices without a good reason.** Dropping prices without an explanation often means that you were unable to compete at the higher price. Consumers catch on to this quickly and may avoid your product or service entirely, being suspicious of your reasons for discounting (they don't necessarily conclude they are getting a bargain). For example, selling a book at a discount suggests that the information in it is not really worth its list price.

❑ **Establish a markdown policy.** A markdown is a reduction in the price of any item. Markdowns are necessary when customer demand is miscalculated, seasonal merchandise is overstocked, merchandise becomes shopworn, personal sales efforts have failed, promotion and advertising efforts have failed, or the competition has lowered their prices. Markdowns are used to avoid being left with old merchandise that is difficult o sell. If properly timed, markdowns can clear out merchandise quickly, thereby increasing cash flow and reducing inventory. In setting a markdown price, the original cost of the merchandise should be recovered if possible. If the original selling price was high enough, a small profit is possible. The markdown price is obtained by subtracting the dollar markdown from the previous retail price. Markdowns are generally taken early in the selling season or shortly after sales slow down.

❑ **Give discounts to distributors or customers who make large orders.** Encourage large orders with bargain bulk purchases. Discounts to distribution channels (brokers, wholesalers, and retailers) may also be needed to get your products distributed to your markets.

❑ **Give discounts for early or prompt payments from credit customers.** Discounts to credit customers can improve collection rates and reduce your average accounts receivable collection period, thereby improving cash flow. Discounts are stated on invoices and sales orders—e.g.: "reduce by 2% if paid 10 days before invoice due date."

❑ **Increase prices when budget projections warrant it.** Random price increases can drive away business and destroy goodwill. However, when your budget projections warrant, it is essential to make increases. Waiting too long to increase prices can destroy your business.

❑ **Issue rain checks for out-of-stock items.** Rain checks should be given to customers who come into your store to buy advertised merchandise recently sold out. This improves customer relations. In some areas, the law requires it. Consult your lawyer or the regional FTC or local trade office for specific advice regarding whether rain checks are needed during advertised sales and under what circumstances.

❑ **Offer a rebate.** If you manufacture goods, overestimate demand, and hence have more goods than you can reasonably sell at present prices, consider offering a manufacturer's rebate to encourage sales. Rebates can also be used to discourage the competition from getting a foothold in the marketplace.

❑ **Re-price all in-stock quantities when your cost of a regularly stocked item goes up or down.** When this is not being done, it is usually an indication that good general business practices are not being followed.

❑ **Split an expensive price into three or four easy payments.** This is a favorite strategy among TV infomercial marketers as it creates the illusion of a cheaper price and allows customers to spread out their payments. A product with a list price of $59.85 can be split into three easy payments of $19.95 plus shipping, handling, and taxes.

To Do List

III. **Marketing Plan**

*Selling
Strategies*

✓ Promotion Plan
✓ Publicity Plan

DAY 22

Develop a promotion plan. Create a promotion budget. Write a news release.

Promotion Plan

A *Promotion Plan* covers all phases of communication between you and your potential customers. It addresses advertising, personal selling, and sales promotion. It is needed to: ✦ acquaint customers with new products ✦ capitalize on the seasonal nature of a product ✦ change or establish a company image ✦ emphasize quality ✦ increase store traffic ✦ inform customers of special services such as delivery or credit extension ✦ introduce new employees to the public ✦ promote consumer awareness of your name and location ✦ promote special events such as a clearance sale ✦ stimulate sales ✦ tie in with a supplier's national promotions.

The Three Basic Components of a Promotion Plan

Although proportions vary depending on the nature of a business, there are three basic components of a promotion plan:

- **Advertising –** Includes newspaper, magazine, flyer, radio, television, billboard, direct mail, poster, newsletter, and Yellow Pages advertising.

- **Personal Selling –** For retail firms, personal selling begins once a shopper enters the store. For service, manufacturing, and wholesale firms, customers must be found. Prospecting outside the company in usually necessary and some kind of internal or external sales force must be created.

- **Sales Promotion –** Sales promotion is a composite of activities that round out your promotion plan. The primary aim of sales promotion is to assist wholesalers and retailers in moving products. Sales promotion *aides* include catalogs, reprints of ads, special displays, window display fixtures, banners, and signs. Sales promotion *activities* also include attending trade shows and conducting demonstrations. **Publicity** is closely linked to advertising and sales promotion, but should be considered a separate forth component (see pages 232 and 239–241).

When developing your promotion plan, think in terms of blending the basic ingredients of advertising, personal selling, and sales promotion, much like mixing a cocktail (refer to chart on the left). This is called your *promotional mix*.

Promotional Mix

Wholesaler

25% advertising

50% personal selling

25% sales promotion

Sock Manufacturer

33% advertising

33% personal selling

33% sales promotion

Catering Service

75% advertising,
referrals, publicity

20% personal selling

5% sales promotion

Sports Shop Retailer

15% advertising

45% personal selling

35% sales promotion

Selecting the Right Ad Media

In selecting media to meet your marketing needs, keep in mind that nowadays, consumers are far more sophisticated and harder to reach than ever before. They have built-in advertising radar and can quickly tune out *bad* advertising quicker than you can lick a stamp. You are faced with the unenviable task of becoming increasingly bold without being intrusive, irritating, or worst of all, boring. You must become more informative, innovative, and responsive to consumer desires, yet at the same time, within budget. Consider the following strategies:

STRATEGY 1 – **Choose a variety of media.** Find out what types of media your target market is most often exposed to. Use common sense, practical experience, and market research. Don't concentrate on one specific source.

STRATEGY 2 – **Collect as much data as you can on each medium.** Research and compare the following for each medium: ❏ cost ❏ circulation ❏ resulting cost per thousand (expressed as cost per M) ❏ error rating for the cost per M either low, medium, or high ❏ market penetration.

STRATEGY 3 – **Examine media from the standpoint of:** ❏ *Audience* (the coverage each enjoys). You need to know an audience does indeed exist, as well as their size and location. ❏ *Acceptance* (the impact of the medium on the audience). The medium must be accepted not only by your target audience but also by potential customers and customers of your competitors. ❏ *Frequency of Exposure* (the ability to expand its impact by being available more than once or twice in a particular time frame). Advertising should reach potential buyers regularly, even daily. Media with a once-a-year or even once-a-month frequency deserves nothing more than a very small part of your budget.

STRATEGY 4 – **Stick to your budget.** Most businesses set aside 10% to 25% of their operating budget for promotion and advertising (this amounts to 2% to 5% of projected sales revenues for retail establishments). Established word of mouth service businesses spend less, while mail order companies, direct-marketing companies, perfume companies, record companies, and beverage companies like Pepsi™ and Coca-Cola™, spend more.

Choosing an Advertising Design Theme

Advertising always works better if you design around a central theme. For example, an *Advertorial* or *News Ad* is a type of ad that announces a new product, something new about an existing product, or states a position on a social, business, or consumer issue. Statements are backed with engaging evidence, an analysis, and most importantly, a product solution. Typically, this type of ad uses a newspaper type headline and a newspaper editorial format. This ad format is especially useful in reaching a segment of the population that shares attitudes or ideologies similar to your own.

A "Promotion Plan" is a marketing tool that answers questions like:

How will you coordinate your billboard promotion to draw attention to your new spring catalog?

✴

In our factory, we make lipstick. In our advertising, we sell hope.
CHARLES REVSON
Founder of
Revlon Inc.

You can fool all the people all of the time if the advertising is right and the budget is big enough.
JOSEPH E. LEVINE

✴

No company that markets products or services to the consumer can remain a leader in its field without a deep-seated commitment to advertising.
EDWIN L. ARTZT

How to Write Advertising Copy

Copywriting is an art that demands talent, experience, and effort to master. Nevertheless, it pays for entrepreneurs to understand key elements every advertisement needs. The following ODaC formula is based on the classic AIDA (Attention, Interest, Desire, Action) formula, and guru copywriter Victor Scwabb's and direct mail marketer Frank Dignan's copywriting formulas. Using the ODaC formula, advertising (1) **O**pens by grabbing attention, (2) **D**evelops by injecting desire, and (3) **C**loses by promoting action.

First and foremost, advertising must jump out and grab attention. A headline should target consumer interests and inject consumers with enough motivation and desire to read more. A TV commercial should make viewers stop munching their corn chips long enough to form a memorable impression. Secondly, advertising should convince consumers they need the product or service being advertised by showing them what worries, shame, drudgery, or other undesirable condition the product will help them eliminate or avoid. Lastly, advertising should encourage consumers to buy, make it easy for them to buy, or even ask them straight out to make the purchase today not tomorrow, and certainly before its "fabulous limited-time offer" EXPIRES!

ODaC – The Advertiser's "Soulmate" (see GB📖 #62 for more details)

OPENERS →	DEVELOPERS →	CLOSERS →
What's it about?	**What's in it for them?**	**What do they do next?**
Open by grabbing attention.	*Develop* by injecting desire.	*Close* by promoting action.
Ask yourself: How can I stand out from competitors and make people want to read, watch or listen to my ad?	Ask yourself: How can I build desire in people to make them want my product or service?	Ask yourself: How can I encourage people to buy my product and what can I do to make it easy for them?
ATTENTION Grabbers	DESIRE Injectors	ACTION Promoters
❏ Ads that look good	❏ Ads that set an appropriate mood	❏ 800 numbers
❏ Balanced layout	❏ Ads that have good jingles	❏ A spectacular offer
❏ Best feature, fact, or benefit	❏ Confusing terms defined	❏ Ask for their order
❏ Catchy slogan	❏ Endorsements	❏ Credit card payment options
❏ Eye-pleasing logo	❏ Feature comparisons	❏ Excellence of customer service
❏ Graphics with human interest	❏ List of benefits backed by facts	❏ Guarantees
❏ Headlines with a twist	❏ List of needs being met	❏ Limited-time offers
❏ Innovative hook	❏ Pain/pleasure images	❏ Postscripts that repeat offer
❏ Photos of target market	❏ Problem/solution statements	❏ Price incentives
❏ Recognizable brand	❏ Success stories	❏ Smooth transition to order form
❏ Strong opening paragraph	❏ Testimonials	❏ Special offers and discounts
❏ Well-thought-out design	❏ Thought-provoking content	❏ Usable order forms

Preparing a Promotional Budget

A *promotional budget* attempts to answer: How much should I spend? When should I spend it? Where should I spend it? What should I spend it on? It includes, in addition to the costs of advertising, the costs of in-store displays, samples, specialty advertising, giveaways, and other non-traditional media efforts (sales goals for promotional budgets can be expressed in dollars, units, or both). Because promotional costs can originate from several sources, it is often a good idea to prepare a master budget broken down into several separate budgets. This way it is easier to closely monitor actual costs and results. Each product or service may also need its own promotional strategy as part of your total marketing plan.

Advertising Budget

The major portion of a firm's promotional budget is often advertising. Budgeting money for advertising encourages consistent promotional efforts and prevents cash flow problems caused by sporadic and unexpected advertising endeavors. Dependable advertising channels include the Yellow Pages, direct mail, flyers, newspaper ads, radio ads, and business cards.

How much should you spend? In general, new retail and manufacturing businesses should be prepared to spend about 5% of projected gross revenues on advertising. An established business should budget 2% to 3%. Service businesses should budget more. In developing your budget, two approaches can be used:

- *The number of dollars projected to successfully promote the sale of a given item or service will go towards advertising.* E.g.: $10 of the $300 selling price for each refrigerator sold will go to advertising so that $3,000 in advertising should sell 300 units and produce $90,000 in sales.

- *A flat percentage of each revenue dollar will go towards advertising.* E.g.: 3% of a projected $100,000 in annual sales will yield an advertising budget of $3,000.

Retail businesses prefer the second approach because it allocates advertising costs for all product lines—all merchandise contributes to advertising costs. More than 50% of the items carried by most stores are never advertised. Their sale is the direct result of customer traffic created by other advertised items.

Comparing Your Advertising Budget with Similar Businesses – Trade associations and other organizations often gather data on advertising expenses and

---

When your advertising asks for the order right out front, with a price and a place to buy and with "NOW" included in the copy, that's hard-sell advertising, and it should invariably be tried before any other kind … Advertising is usually most beautiful when it's least measurable and least productive.
LEWIS KRONFELD

Depending on the type of business you run, 10% to 25% of your operating budget should be pumped back into your business in the form of advertising.

✳

Never skimp on the quality of your advertising or promotional material. Sometimes, as in the case of mail order, advertising is your only salesperson.
PROFIT TIP

> *The business that considers itself immune to the necessity for advertising sooner or later finds itself immune to business.*
> **DERBY BROWN**

> *There are a million definitions of public relations. I have found it to be the craft of arranging the truth so that people will like you.*
> **ALAN HARRINGTON**

publish them as *operating ratios* (expenses items as a percentage of sales). Reconsider your estimated advertising costs if substantially higher or lower than average. To gain a profit, no single expense item should be allowed to get way out of line.

Publicity Plan

Publicity is news about you, your product or your service that appears in a public medium. *Publicists* are people you hire to attempt to control, manipulate, or use to your advantage, public media coverage.

Writing a NEWS RELEASE

The most important form of publicity a small business operator can generate is the *news release*, also called a *press release* or *media release*. A news release can be used to generate positive publicity, inform the world of new products, or update everyone on important newsworthy events regarding your company. A video should accompany any news releases targeted towards TV broadcasting stations.

Parts of a News Release

Address Block and Title – Use your letterhead. Center "News Release" all caps, in a large bold font if possible.

"Release Date" Block – Provide the editor with the date of the release (optional) and exact information concerning the appropriate timing for the release. This information should appear below the title, flush right.

"For Immediate Release" – Releases with no specific time frame are by far the most common type of release.

Releases with Specific Date – An example would be, "For Release January 23 or Thereafter."

Identifying Block – Place below the release date block flush right. Include a contact person with a daytime phone number and an evening phone number. Newspapers don't shut down at night and if an editor needs further information and can't reach you, your release may be dumped.

Headline – Place after the identifying block, flush left or centered. If flush left, the title should not extend beyond the address by more than a few characters (long headlines should be stacked on top of each other, single-spaced).

Body Copy Format – The body of the release begins about one-third of the way down the page allowing some white space for comments, or notes from the editor. The body of the news release is double-spaced—never single-space a news release. Paragraphs are usually indented with normal spacing between paragraphs. Often the city of origin of the news release begins the copy (some media prefer no indention and triple spacing between paragraphs).

Releases More Than Two Pages – If the release runs more than a page, the word "more" is placed in brackets or within dashes at the bottom of the page. Following pages are identified by a slug-line followed by several dashes and the page number at the top, either flush left or right.

End of Release – The end of the release can be designated by the word "end," the number "30" either in quotation marks or within dashes, or the symbol #####.

Photos – Photos should be glossy, B&W (for newspapers), and 8 by 10 inches. Color is better. To save money, take both color and B&W, then mail B&W and add, "color photos available upon request" at the end of the release.

Successful
**BUSINESS
PLANNING
30**in**DAYS**

DAY 22 **Worksheets** ⏱

Develop a promotion plan. Create a promotion budget. Write a news release.

Promotion Plan

*Outline the essential components of your promotion plan. **What** is your promotional mix?*

Sample: Our promotional mix is 20% advertising, 25% personal selling, 15% sales promotion, and 40% publicity. We have decided to devote 40% of our promotion plan to publicity as our research indicates that this is the most effective way for us to inform potential buyers of the unsurpassed quality and benefits of our offerings and build sales. To achieve this goal, we will establish a regular and consistent update program targeting editors of national and local trade and business publications of improvements to our products. We will also strive to open multiple communications channels with sales reps and key management personnel.

Advertising	*%*
Personal selling	*%*
Sales promotion	*%*
Publicity	*%*

Top Marketing Activities – *Summarize the most important activities of your promotional plan. Describe expected impact, any unique promotional activities no one else is doing, and how advertising will be tailored to your target market (refer to charts on page 234 and 235):*

❑ conventions and trade shows ❑ frequent, focused media advertising ❑ informal marketing at social events ❑ networking with colleagues ❑ targeted email prospecting ❑ technical articles to magazines ❑ website

Sample: In addition to publicity, another important marketing activity in our promotion plan is to gain public recognition through trade shows and our website. We also plan to maximize the life of our display ads by targeting monthly magazines.

Brochures – *Outline any requirements for product and service brochures and similar descriptive material. Indicate expected development and production costs:*

Sample: For our scheduled opening day [date], we will be printing 1,000 four-color tri-fold brochures at a cost of $299. [Company] brochures have been professionally designed by [service agency] at a cost of $350 (see Supporting Docs for a sample).

Popular Promotional Media – *Circle media that have an important role in your promotional plan:*

Advantages and Disadvantages of Media				
Media	Audience	Type of Business	Advantages	Disadvantages
Daily Newspapers	Individual communities with some overflow.	General retail and service industries.	Flexible timing. Reaches a large audience.	Can't pinpoint markets. Cluttered. Short life.
Weekly Newspapers	Usually smaller community and neighborhoods.	Retailers and services located within community.	Good local coverage.	Must be used regularly and timed for best results.
Magazines	Business-to-business, consumer, national, regional, special interest.	Retailers and service providers who serve known target markets.	Long life, shared. Aimed at special interest groups.	Long lead-time in preparation.
Radio	Usually community and local area depending on size of station.	Retail and service companies who cater to target groups such as commuters and homemakers.	Reaches a wide market. Good for pinpointing target markets.	Somewhat limited audience.
Television National/Local	Numbers vary with time of day and nature of the show.	Products, services, and retail outlets with a wide appeal.	Creative and persuasive. Large audience. Can target groups, such as kids.	Short exposure. Commonly used. Most expensive.
Cable Community Channels	Varied specific interest groups.	Small retail and service businesses with cable coverage area.	Locally oriented events and programs not covered by traditional media.	Limited audience. Few statistics on viewers to measure results.
Telephone Directories and Yellow Pages	Special consumer groups, businesses.	Service businesses, highly specialized retailers.	Relatively low cost, long life, users are often potential buyers.	Restricted to active shoppers. Ad limited in size and content.
Billboards and Outdoor Advertising	Drivers, passengers, pedestrians.	Adaptable to many products, services, and businesses.	Flexible, repeat exposure. Builds a good corporate image.	Message must be short.
Direct Mail and Email	Business-to-business, household consumers.	General services, retailers, wholesale, manufacturers, small startups, e-stores.	Can be personalized. Flexible timing. Good targeting.	High disposal rate. Negative reactions to junk mail and SPAM.
Printed Promo Materials	Transit passengers, pedestrians, drivers.	Adaptable to many products and service businesses.	Highly visible. Captive audience.	Exterior: short exposure.
Promotional Displays	Pedestrians and retail customers.	Retailers, service businesses.	Helps promote impulse buying.	Requires constant restocking and upkeep.
Specialty Advertising	All kinds of customers and clients.	Retailers, service businesses, consultants.	Builds goodwill, fun, inexpensive.	Freebee sometimes taken for granted.
Websites and Online Ads	Global and local markets (if tied in with other media)	All businesses, especially service providers.	Inexpensive, access to the world.	Need technical expertise. Too much competition.

"Bread'n Butter Advertising Media" – *Select from the following frequently used marketing media:*

❑ **Business Cards** – Low cost; easily distributed; describes product or service; gives address and phone.

❑ **Business Signs** – Very effective; low cost; may be subject to zoning regulations.

❑ **Business Stationery** – Low cost; must be well designed.

❑ **Direct Mail** – Most personalized and pinpointed of all media; tells complete story; rapid feedback; can use coupons, catalogs, letters, brochures, or postcards.

❑ **Interior or POP Displays** – Attractive display of merchandise creates impulse buying; low cost.

❑ **Local Newspapers** – Great flexibility; ad size and position can be varied; great with editorial association, such as food advertisements with cooking column.

❑ **Local Radio** – Expensive but reaches targeted audience; advertisement can be repeated frequently.

❑ **Shopping Bags** – Carry name and message into home.

❑ **Storefront** – Extremely effective; low cost; shows product and price.

❑ **Telephone Solicitation** – Low cost; effective if message is worded carefully.

❑ **Television** – Most expensive; reaches the masses; high visibility; instant exposure of pictures or ideas.

❑ **Vehicles** – Can be effective; low cost; wide exposure.

❑ **Yellow Pages** – Essential for small business; reaches customers who are ready to buy; wide distribution.

How will you integrate promotional efforts? ❑ Will radio ads be supported by newspaper ads? ❑ Will storefront signs match logos on your business stationery? ❑ Will mail order forms look like your website order forms?

Check and describe any additional details regarding your promotional plan: ❑ Will you use cooperative advertising? ❑ Will you implement any sales training programs? ❑ Will you use networking marketing (MLM)?

❑ **Advertising Effectiveness** – How do you plan to measure the effectiveness of each ad medium? Do you have rate sheet data? What is your *Advertising Calendar?*

❑ **Past Marketing Methods** – What past marketing methods have you or other companies found effective? What was the cost per customer or cost per unit of sale? What percentage of your budget was allocated?

❑ **Sales Force** – Will you put together your own sales force? Will you use commissioned sales staff, agents, or independent contractors (putting together a sales force is not recommended for businesses just starting out; it's better to use established intermediaries)?

❑ **Window Displays** – Do you have any plans for in-store sales promotion tools and window displays?

1	
2	
3	

Ad Design Theme – *From the list below, check suitable themes for your advertising promotions. Describe in more detail at least one promotional theme (see GB▭ #55 for 52 ad design themes):*

	Sample: The optimal way for us to reach our target market is to focus our marketing campaign on our advertising theme and slogan. The mood and delivery of our ads will be grace and glamour under pressure.

Problem/ Solution Ad	Presents a problem and then provides a solution or cure.	**Shock Pants off the Consumer Ad**	Tries to shock readers into buying a certain product. Usually shows what would happen if you don't buy their product.
Product:	AIR DRIVEN NAIL HAMMER	Product:	MOTORCYCLE HELMET
Headline:	Tired of Pounding Nails ... Get Sears Nail Driver and Toss Away Your Hammer Forever	Headline:	How Much is Your Head Worth?
Graphic:	A man in tattered overalls with a fat swollen thumb.	Graphic:	A watermelon being thrown out of a car speeding along at 60 miles an hour.

❏ Advertorial or News
❏ Announcing
❏ Before & After
❏ Benefit
❏ Cartoon
❏ Challenge
❏ Clue or Teaser
❏ Command
❏ Comparative
❏ Contest/Sweepstakes
❏ Conversational Letter
❏ Demonstration
❏ Directive

❏ Empathy
❏ Endorsement
❏ Fictional Character
❏ Fictional Place
❏ Free Information
❏ Gimmick
❏ Guarantee
❏ Hornblowing
❏ "How-To" or Advice
❏ Indirect or Curiosity
❏ Informative
❏ Invent-a-Word
❏ Leadership

❏ Location
❏ Meet-the-Advertiser
❏ New Age
❏ Offer
❏ Outlandish Statement
❏ Pain/Pleasure
❏ Pay Less
❏ Plain 'n Simple No- Nonsense
❏ Prediction
❏ Price & Where-to-Buy
❏ Pun
❏ Question

❏ Quotation
❏ Reader Involvement
❏ "Reason Why"
❏ Reward
❏ Rhetorical Question
❏ Selective
❏ Slogan
❏ Steal a Popular Title
❏ Story
❏ Story with a Twist
❏ Testimonial
❏ Tie-in-with-Current-Events

Copywriting Strategy – **How** *do you plan to* **O***pen,* **D***evelop,* **a***nd* **C***lose your ads and promotions?*

O	Grab Attention by ...	
Da	Inject Desire by ...	
C	Promote Action by ...	

Promotional Budget – *Check the following budgeting considerations applicable to your business:*

- ❑ The newer your store, the more advertising is required to make it known.
- ❑ If your store is in a poor location, advertising is required to attract people to go out of their way to shop there.
- ❑ If your store is selling promotional merchandise, you will likely have to spend more on advertising.
- ❑ In order for you to keep your share of the market, expenditures must bear some relationship to what competitors are spending. Aggressive competition usually requires aggressive advertising.

- ❑ If you are operating in a large community, you will likely have to spend more on advertising than a merchant in a small community.
- ❑ Sales days, special promotional events, and holidays important to your business require greater expenditures for advertising to make the event known.
- ❑ Funds from suppliers for media purchase and an availability of prepared ads or commercials through cooperative advertising may allow you to expand your advertising program.

Amount of Funds Available for Advertising – *Select a method for determining how much money to budget for advertising. Describe how you arrived at this budget along with any special considerations that affected your decision (since the cost of adverting must be paid from sales revenue, it usually is expressed as a function of expected sales dollars). Detail other budget considerations:*

❑ Dollar amount will vary according to individual items. ❑ Flat percentage of every anticipated revenue dollar. ❑ Other

Sample: For our startup year, our advertising budget is projected to be $34,000. This works out to be 3% of total projected revenues. This budget is currently 1% higher than industry averages, because [company] feels that the extra expenditure will be needed to help us establish our brand and generate [product/service] interest. For FY 2006, our advertising budget will be reduced to 2.2% to more closely follow industry standards.

	Advertising Budget	
As a % of total sales		%
Industry %		%
Budget in $	$	

Prepare your budget:

Media	Audience Size	Schedule (Advertising Calendar)	Frequency of Use	x Cost of a Single Occasion	= Estimated Cost
				$	$
				Total Estimated Cost	$

Twelve-Month Advertising Budget

Month	Total Sales in % per month	Projected Sales in $ per month	Ad Budget in % of Total Sales/month	Advertising Budget in $ per month	Media 1 ____% of total	Media 2 ____% of total	Media 3 ____% of total	Media 4 ____% of total	Media 5 ____% of total	Reserve Fund (10%)
		Total Sales and Ad Budget Projections			Allocation of Budget					
Jan										
Feb										
Mar										
Apr										
May										
Jun										
Jul										
Aug										
Sep										
Oct										
Nov										
Dec										
TOTAL	100%									

Indicate trade shows you plan to attend to exhibit your product or service. **How** *much will they cost?*

Trade Show	Location	Timing	Estimated Cost
			$
		Total Estimated Cost	$

Describe and project costs for repair, informational, support, or value-added services you plan to offer:

Service	Estimated Cost
	$
	$
	$

Total Costs *– Summarize the total costs of all promotional activities:*

Publicity Plan

Describe any plans to obtain free publicity. Check strategies you plan to use (see GB📖 #66):

Sample: Our publicity strategy is to increase brand recognition among consumers and position [company] as a higher quality alternative to [main competitor]. For this second goal, we are targeting purchasing agents and sales managers using press releases and technical articles to industry trade journals and newsletters.

❑ Bulletin boards at beauty salons, bus stations, service centers, etc.

❑ Car windshields

❑ Donating services or products to the community

❑ Free classified sections

❑ Guest speaking at private functions

❑ Industry directories or professional pages (get your name listed next to a reputable company)

❑ Interview talk shows, TV or radio

❑ Per-inquiry deals where you pay an advertising medium a percentage of your sales or profits

❑ Personal selling at places where people congregate

❑ Promotional goods such as hats, pens, T-shirts, buttons, and pins.

❑ Street seminars and demos

❑ Video news releases

❑ Walking billboards

❑ Word-of-mouth referrals (to get referrals, form reciprocal partnerships with companies that complement your offerings)

Media Kit – A media kit can be sent to newspapers and magazines. It sometimes accompanies a news release. Check items you will include:

❑ backgrounder (additional facts and information about product)

❑ biography (or biographies) and accompanying photos of key personnel in your company

❑ cover letter explaining what the kit is about

❑ feature story or sidebar, if appropriate to the subject matter

❑ table of contents or list of what is in the kit

❑ brochures of product and its uses

❑ annual reports

❑ basic facts sheet outlining the participants at the press conference

❑ clipsheet of illustrations, company logos, and illustrations that can be used by the advertising medium

❑ color product photos (with captions)

❑ color photos of other products made from the manufactured material (with captions)

❑ company magazines or newsletter

❑ cover letter for TV stations

❑ hard copy of the product presentation speeches

❑ in-house magazine article tear sheets on the product

❑ magazine ad folder with sample return order card

❑ press release describing another application of the material

❑ press release on new materials being developed

❑ press release on the product's content (the material used to manufacture the product)

❑ radio and TV scripts

❑ storyboard for TV spot

<u>*News Release*</u> *– Describe any special or innovative news release strategies you may have:*

	Sample: We have prepared a press release for the opening of our new [branch office, retail outlet] at [location], featuring the introduction of our innovative [product/service]. This press release will be distributed to local newspapers and magazines including: [identify mailing list of recipients].

Writing Strategies:

❑ Be believable. Keep your news release factual.

❑ Don't mention advertising possibilities.

❑ Don't try and make an old product sound new.

❑ Incorporate human interest.

❑ Limit the use of adjectives.

❑ Study the format of the medium you are sending the news release to. Research their editorial policies.

❑ Use quotes and reaction statements to give your release news appeal.

❑ Avoid being too controversial, using advertising puffery, or making exaggerated benefit claims.

"Newsworthy Topics:

❑ awards won by your company

❑ case histories of successful applications of your product

❑ charitable acts in the community

❑ joint ventures with other companies

❑ major contracts obtained.

❑ new discoveries or patents

❑ new version of an old product

❑ opening of a new business

Review the following sample news release with cover letter (remember to double-space paragraphs):

Company Name and Address (Letterhead)
Telephone Number

NEWS RELEASE

Date: *Jan 12, 2005*

For Immediate Release

Contact: *Your Name*
Days: *Phone*
Evening: *Phone*

"New Technology Saves Water in Seconds"

Now every homeowner can save gallons of water, every time they use Cromdale's new shower adapter, the Water Miser.

The Water Miser takes only seconds to install and saves gallons of water every time you take a shower.

The portable adapter is about the size of a small grapefruit and fits easily over any standard showerhead, with little fuss and no tools, using a new patented leakproof technology.

"You can take it to a friend's house," says Walter Cromdale, president of Cromdale Innovations. "It's that fast and easy. Plus, turn up the hot water, vary the flow to a fine mist, and PRESTO!" he adds. "You have a steam bath."

Priced at $19.95, the Water Miser is available at hardware stores coast to coast. For further information, phone Cromdale Innovations at (555) 555-5555.

-end-

Company Name and Address (Letterhead)
Telephone Number

COVER LETTER

Date: *Jan 12, 2005*

Dear Member of the Media:

Cromdale Innovations of Vancouver, British Columbia, has recently introduced a brand new product, Cromdale's Water Miser Showerhead, which allows any homeowner to save gallons of water while taking a shower.

Until now, these types of adapters required tedious installation procedures. But now, with the Water Miser, even a child can complete installation in less than 10 seconds.

Because I am convinced that consumers will want to know more about this convenient new device, I am sending you a packet of information and a free sample.

Please call me if you have any questions or if I can be of any help.

Sincerely,

Walter Cromdale

Walter Cromdale
President

(Use Letterhead: which includes company name, address, phone, email, and URL)

NEWS RELEASE

Date: 12/27/98 *(optional)*

For Immediate Release …

Contact: Your Name; Company Name; Daytime Phone; Evening Phone; Email; URL

Headline

Type a descriptive, clever, and catchy headline in capital letters and center it. Lure the editor to read more. Then space down four lines and get into the body of the release.

Issue or problem

The lead paragraph is designed to invite the largest number of people to read the article. It must have broad appeal; make it interesting. The release should be *issue-oriented*; write about the *problem*, not the product or service. The release should begin by stating the problem and telling why this is an important subject. Make it provocative.
(remember to double-space your body copy so editors can make changes if needed)

Development

Write a second paragraph to develop the message. Put the most interesting information first to keep the editor reading. Recite the most important items in descending order so that if some are cut from the end, the most important will remain. Provide interesting facts and statistics.

How the product or service solves a problem

Move from a *what* orientation to a *how* orientation. Tell how your product or service solves a problem. Continue with some background on your product or service and show why it is unique, useful, and timely. Recite benefits. Describe key features. Don't use fluffy language to promote your product or service. Editors won't like it. Don't sell. Inform! Keep in mind that anyone who has read this far will be interested.

Company information

Write a paragraph about your company. Outline its history. Describe important events.

Ordering information

Include the price of your product or service and mention where it is available and in which stores. List your address so readers will know where to send inquiries. Code your address so you can keep track of inquiries.

End the release with the newspaper termination sign: -30-

News Release Worksheet

Company Name, Address, Phone, URL, and Email

NEWS RELEASE

Date:

For Immediate Release ...

Contact: Company: Phone: D N Email:

Headline

Lead Paragraph (Attract Readers – *State Problem*):

Development (Explain the *What*):

How the Product/Service Solves the Problem (Explain the *How*):

Company Information (*History, Interesting Facts, etc.*):

Ordering Information (Include *Address, Price, Website, etc.*):

-30-

DAY 23

Develop a packaging concept. Write your warranty.
Summarize your marketing approach.

Packaging Concept

Successful packaging is the result of feedback and input from marketing managers, salespeople, manufacturing reps, distributors, graphic and product designers, and customers. In developing your *packaging concept*, explain how your packaging better positions your product in the minds of your target customers. Show how you have considered their tastes. Talk about its size, shape, color, material, wording, and how your packaging meets or exceeds FDA and FTC regulations.

To Do List

III. **Marketing Plan**

Selling Strategies

✓ Packaging Concept
✓ Strategic Alliances
✓ Service and Product Mix Strategy
✓ Timing of Market Entry
✓ Warranty Policies

Marketing Approach

✓ Marketing Approach

Packaging is a competitive tool to help influence your customer's buying decisions. It helps make your product stand out from others and acts as a silent salesperson to all those who pass by.
PROFIT TIP

Designing the Perfect Package in "Seven Steps"

Putting a widget in a box, covering the box with a few pictures and labels, and calling it *packaging,* is dangerous. Packaging is more than that. Packaging has protective, distributive, and promotional functions. It makes products convenient to use, safe to use, and easy to ship. It also performs an integral role in all advertising and marketing efforts, and more than any other single factor is responsible for creating a company's image. In fact, some people prefer to think of packaging as an exact science. To design a package:

STEP 1 – Gather information. To create a package that is unique, aesthetically pleasing, and meets the needs of your company, consumers, and distributors, shop the competition, and gather as much information as you can. In-store research can be useful, along with information gleaned from books, periodicals, and brochures.

STEP 2 – Develop a preliminary concept. Make at least 10 to 25 sketches. Indicate typestyles and logos. Make sure sketches are neat and clear and keep them in your portfolio for future reference and for use as presentation material.

STEP 3 – Prepare a "comprehensive." Plan the structural design of the package to take into account potential production and manufacturing problems. Its size and shape should also make it easy for employees, distributors, and customers to handle. Materials used must also protect contents during shipping and handling.

STEP 4 – Design a box cover. Use markers to prepare a layout showing what you want the final box cover to look like. Construct a mock-up of this layout and take a Polaroid of it. Do several variations if needed. When satisfied, have a pre-production meeting with your photographer. At this meeting: present your layout; describe your ideas about the set, lighting, mood, and the appearance of models (if required); and review your budget. Once the photo shoot is under way, let the photographer shoot as many rolls of film as needed to cover every possible situation and angle. After processing the film and choosing the best results, scan the photos into a computer. Here, words, logos, and other information can be added, as well as images retouched and imperfections removed.

STEP 5 – Construct a prototype. Build a prototype/mock-up as close as possible to the final design. Use the prototype to further test the viability of the design.

STEP 6 – Test the prototype. Evaluate the package from an engineering, artistic, consumer, and cost effective point of view. If the packaging is not durable enough, attractive enough, or too expensive, improve it or scrap it and start all over again.

STEP 7 – Prepare a production mechanical. A production mechanical incorporates all final art, photographs, illustrations, and type onto one sheet, which will later be attached to the cardboard, glass, or plastic container.

Sample Packaging Concept

The competitive advantage of *Bradley's Whole-wheat Mini-buns* is that they are an all-natural product that appeals to the health-conscious. Because of their quality, customers must see the mini-buns through the package. Therefore, *Bradley's Whole-wheat Mini-buns* will be boxed in clear material. The positioning statements, "For real bun eaters who know the difference" and "It's all natural" will appear on the face of the package. Across the left corner of the package will be a red slash that reads, "Keep the goodness. Keep us in the fridge."

Strategic Alliances

A *Strategic Alliance* or *Partnership* is an agreement made with another company or companies to undertake R&D, marketing, financing, sales, distribution, or other business endeavors and activities to each other's mutual benefit. They are particularly important for Internet based businesses and service providers. In this section, you might also discuss your network of contacts and how they are able to assist you in referring clients or perhaps negotiating favorable supply contracts. Make sure to outline any well-known experts in the field who have expressed interest in your proposal and have offered to help build sales.

Service and Product Mix Strategy

If you plan to sell both products and services, each should complement each other to increase overall sales. For example, a beauty salon, in addition to providing hairstyling services, may also find it profitable to retail hair care products.

Timing of Market Entry

A company can be started any time. However, the *act* of entering the marketplace—that is, opening doors for business or launching a new product—must be carefully timed. Having your products and services available at the right time depends upon industry conditions, buying habits of consumers, recent trends, and the local and national economic outlook. "Timing" must be *market driven*. It should NOT be a decision based solely on your internal planning schedule.

Warranty Policies

A *warranty* tells customers you will correct any problems arising within a specified period following the performance of a service or sale of a product at no charge. Warranties build trust and promote repeat business. A typical service warranty might be 30 days on parts and 90 days on labor (see examples on the right).

Marketing Approach

One final area of your *Marketing Plan* that deserves special attention is a summary description of your marketing approach. Your *Marketing Approach* describes how you ultimately plan to satisfy the needs of your target market by combining your marketing research, competitive analysis, and marketing strategies. It acts like a mission statement for your marketing plan.

Comparing the "Old" Marketing Approach with the "New"

There are two specific ways in which the "old" classic, or "sales" approach to market planning differs from the "new" marketing approach:

In the "old" marketing approach, management tells designers and engineers to create a product, which once produced, is given to salespeople, who are then told to find customers to buy the product. In the "new" marketing approach, management *first* determines what customers really need or want, then pass that information on to designers and engineers who develop and produce a suitable product. When sales staff is given the finished merchandise, they already have leads on potential customers. The "old" marketing approach *ends* with the customer, while the "new" marketing approach, *begins* and *ends* with the customer.

WARRANTY POLICIES

Our standard 1-year limited warranty covers the original hardware for a period of one year from the date of purchase. Lifetime technical support is provided for the original hardware configuration only.

OL Computer Online

✱

For a period of five years after the date of original shipment from our factory, products manufactured by [XYZ company] are warranted to function properly and be free of defects in materials and workmanship. Should a [XYZ company] instrument fail during the warranty period, return it freight pre-paid to our factory. We will repair it (or at our option, replace it) at no charge, and pay the cost of shipping it back to you.

Seabird Electronics

Most business activities including advertising are dedicated to solving the firm's problems. Success, however, is more likely if you dedicate your activities exclusively to solving your customer's problems.
SBA

Under the "old" marketing approach the customer exists for the business, while under the "new" marketing approach, the business exists for the customer.

Brand strategies provide clear and consistent differentiation in a given marketplace.
ROBERT WOYZBUN
Marketing
Consultant

✦

Brand is mission. Brand is marketing. Brand is business.
MICHAEL PUCCI, Ph.D.
Brand Consultant

The second major difference between the "old" marketing approach and the "new" is the *focus* of management. The "old" marketing approach focuses on *volume* and *sales* while the "new" marketing approach focuses on *profit*.

The two above distinctions can be simplified into two rules of thumb:

- **Focus on the needs of your customers, not products.** All company policies and activities should be aimed at satisfying customer needs.

- **Focus on making a profit, not increasing sales volume.** Profitable sales volume is a better company goal than maximum sales volume.

Getting the Most Out of Your Marketing Approach

To further develop your marketing approach: ✦ identify specific markets you now serve ✦ determine the needs and wants of your present customers ✦ determine what you are doing now to satisfy those needs and wants ✦ prepare a marketing plan to meet customer needs you are presently not meeting ✦ find out which advertising is the most effective at reaching old and new customers ✦ test to see if your new strategies are yielding results ✦ periodically analyze your firm's competitive advantage to find out what you do best ✦ capitalize on this strength.

Brand Promise

A fundamental strategy to guide your marketing approach can be the nurturing and building of brand name recognition. A *brand statement* is an elaboration of your company's *brand promise* to your customers. Its purpose is to help create a "mental image" in your target market of how your business will meet their needs. Your brand becomes the sum total of all expectations that a customer or client has when they buy or use your products or services or deals with your company. A brand promise can be so powerful that it replaces your mission statement as the fundamental driving force behind your company. Management legend Tom Peters argues that, "Real branding is personal. Real branding is integrity. Real branding is why I/you/we[all] get out of bed in the morning." However, building a brand name can be quite costly, and it doesn't happen overnight. It will take years of effort and the consistent implementation of your brand strategy.

To write a brand statement, answer the following: ❏ What do you want your customers to think when they think of your company? ❏ How are you going to achieve consistency in your products and services so customers will never forget you, and in fact, will grow to depend on you—and only you?

Successful
**BUSINESS
PLANNING
30 in DAYS**

Develop a packaging concept. Write
your warranty. Summarize your
marketing approach.

Packaging Concept

Describe factors that have influenced your packaging. Summarize your "packaging concept" (see factors on page 248): ❑ bubble packs ❑ custom boxes ❑ poly bags ❑ reusable glass jars ❑ shrink wrap

Sample: To convey a unique selling proposition in the marketplace, we will not use industry standard shrink wrap packaging. Our packaging concept is to use materials that are environmentally friendly and reusable. For this reason, we are using custom biodegradable boxes, with popcorn as protection for goods in transport.

Estimate costs for developing packaging and per unit costs. **How** *has this been factored into pricing?*

Sample: We have obtained quotes from three branding and package design agencies: [list]. Development costs range from a low of $[XX] to a high of $[XX]. [Company A] has quoted a unit cost of $[X] per 1,000. [Company B] has quoted $[X] per unit.

Explain how your packaging design will increase sales (add photos to your "Supporting Documents"):

❑ Metric conversion measurements have been included to avoid confusion for [Asian, European] customers.

❑ New packaging design has eliminated [breakage, spoilage] during transport.

❑ New production methods have reduced our packaging costs to [3%] of total product costs.

❑ Our packaging stands out from the crowd on a shelf.

❑ Packaging is easy to open even for the elderly.

❑ Product packaging will not harm the environment.

❑ Product packaging can be reused around the house. Some customers will buy our products just for the packaging.

Sample: Although our packaging is similar to competitors, by using distinctive colors and art print images, we hope to preserve our unique identity on display shelves. Our packaging is also more durable, which should reduce breakage.

Brainstorm – Check factors below important to your package design:

❑ **Art and Beauty Needs** – Beauty of package design is essential. People buy what they like the looks of. Some people even collect packaging (wine bottles, jars).

❑ **Budget** – For most products, packaging should not add more that 5% to the total cost of the product.

❑ **Company Needs** – You must connect your company to the buying public or market in a way that attracts customers and keeps them coming back.

❑ **Competitive Pressures** – 75% of all goods purchased by consumers in the United States are distributed in packages, all of them vying for consumer attention. How will your package stand out?

❑ **Consumer Needs** – Package design is molded by the needs, preferences, tastes, purchasing power, and buying habits of your consumers.

❑ **Distribution and Shipping needs** – Design packages so they can fit on top of each other to allow for more compact shipping. Design packaging to be as light as possible to reduce shipping costs. This is especially necessary if the product is to be mailed.

❑ **Environmental Concerns** – More than 20 million tons of plastic a year is produced in the U.S. alone. The cubic volume of plastics has surpassed that of steel, copper, and aluminum combined. Plastic material currently in use will take up to five centuries to degrade. It is no wonder that more companies are seriously looking at how their packaging is disposed, whether it's biodegradable, reusable, or environmentally green. They also debate about whether they should use recycled paper or switch to biodegradable protective filler (like popcorn) instead of using environmentally hazardous Styrofoam chips.

❑ **Future Trends in Marketing** – Consider new production and distribution techniques, as well as new marketing techniques and procedures.

❑ **Government Regulations** – Packaging attracts a great deal of government attention. Regulatory agencies such as the Food and Drug Administration (FDA) have strict procedures for the labeling of items falling within its jurisdiction. The Federal Trade Commission (FTC) through its *Fair Packaging and Labeling Act*, also regularly enforces strict safety and strength standards on all packaging. In Canada, research: The *Food and Drug Act*, the *Consumer Packaging and Labeling Act*, and the *Hazardous Product Act*. In Europe, research: the *Packaging and Packaging Waste Directive*. Also see Dun & Bradstreet's *Exporters' Encyclopedia*.

❑ **Industry Standards** – Government regulations and industry standards are designed to protect users of a carton. There are laws pertaining to shipment method, such as rail, airfreight, truck, and regular parcel post. Common tests involve subjecting packaging materials to drops, jolts, shock, and vibration.

❑ **Input from Professional Package Designers** – A package designer can help you with graphic and structural design concerns, as well as package production, printing, and the modeling process.

❑ **Labeling Requirements** – On your principal display panel (usually 40% of the total front display area), include the product's name, manufacturer, and packer or distributor. The manufacturer's name and address may appear anywhere on the package. Quantity statements, descriptions of contents, and safety warnings must also appear somewhere within the lower 30% of the label, be parallel to the base of the package, and be separated above and below from other printed matter. If multiple products are further packaged in a corrugated shipping box, this box must include a *Box Certificate* specifying weight, paper content, puncture and bursting test strength, and gross width.

❑ **Marketing Needs** – Package design must also be tied in effectively with newspaper, magazine, and television advertising so that consumers can easily identify a product by its packaging. More and more packaging also includes the company's URL.

❑ **Message Desired** – Packaging can deliver messages about your product, brand, product category, target market, or benefits offered. It can also project uniqueness, create an image, and even send subliminal messages (e.g., color, shape, size, and texture can be used to suggest luxury).

❑ **Packaging Equipment and Production Techniques** – What packaging and filling equipment do you have or have access to in your area?

❑ **Product Needs** – Size, weight, shape, and fragility, are obvious design concerns. You wouldn't put perfume in a plastic container if you could afford glass, and you wouldn't shrink wrap expensive china.

❑ **Wholesaler and Retailer Needs** – Consider the needs of the people who will sell and distribute your products. You may need special promotional and display materials to complement packaging for supermarkets, department stores, boutiques and so on (e.g., make sure your packaging fits easily on retail shelving).

Strategic Alliances

Describe any partnerships you have with other companies to help sell, distribute, or promote products. Also, clarify your network of contacts: **Who** *are they?* **What** *industry?* **How** *can they help build sales?*

Sample: [Company] has strategic alliances with Vistaprint.com and eLance.com. These alliances allow us to utilize the services and expertise of these firms at no additional cost to us. To increase website traffic, we are also pursuing strategic relationships with Yahoo, About Inc., and Business.com.

❏ **Bundled Products and Services** – Include your product or service with another company's product or service as part of a special promotional package (e.g., software with a book, massage therapy with health products, hotel accommodation with an airline ticket).

❏ **Cooperative Advertising** – Two or more companies can share costs for the same promotion. Manufacturers can share advertising with suppliers. Merchants in a mall can produce a joint catalog or flyer.

❏ **Distribution Agreements** – Let another company carry or distribute your product or service line, or do the same for them.

❏ **Joint Venture** – Team up with another company or group of companies to develop new software, launch a new product, or research and develop new technology.

❏ **Licensing Agreements** – Give another company permission to sell or make/deliver your product or service or use your company name or trademark in exchange for a fee or the rights to do the same.

❏ **Piggyback Inserts and Promotions** – Piggyback your flyers with products from other companies. You might also offer small ads on your product packaging.

❏ **Referrals** – Refer clients to retail outlets that offer products related to your services and vice versa.

Service and Product Mix Strategy

Describe how key products and services will complement each other to increase overall sales:

Timing of Market Entry

State when you plan to enter the market and how you arrived at this decision. Describe special buying trends or patterns that have influenced this decision: ❏ first entrant advantage ❏ fast-follower advantage

Sample: Although [competitor] may enjoy a unique advantage as first entrant into the [market], it is doubtful they will be able to quickly recoup their investments made to kickstart this new market. As a fast follower, we will be able to leapfrog into earlier profitability.

Warranty Policies

Describe your product or service guarantee (see page 245 for more examples): ❑ 30-day Money Back Guarantee ❑ Standard 1-year Limited Warranty ❑ guaranteed to be free from defects in materials and workmanship ❑ no refunds after two weeks ❑ will replace it free of charge for three weeks from purchase date ❑ We warrant against [describe] but we do not warrant [describe].

> **Sample:** Eastern Digital external hard drives carry a Standard Warranty Period of one (1) year. ED Caviar® SE EIDE hard drives carry a Standard Warranty Period of three (3) years. ED Raptor™ hard drives carry a Standard Warranty Period of five (5) years. No warranty service is provided by ED Digital unless your ED Product was purchased from an authorized distributor or authorized reseller.

Marketing Approach

Describe ways you have been able to focus on **needs** *and* **profits** *rather than products and sales volume:*

> **Sample:** At Shinko Securities our marketing goal is to enhance customer loyalty by: ensuring our sales and marketing approach is truly focused on customers; making sure our advice correctly reflects clients' investment preferences; and reexamining employee mannerisms and behavior during customer contact. To meet this final goal, we have set up "Good Behavior Working Group" training.

<u>*Brand Statement*</u> *– Elaborate on your "brand promise" (review page 21): Brand is built by:*

❑ quality ❑ price ❑ trust ❑ service ❑ packaging ❑ logos ❑ jingles ❑ advertising ❑ goodwill

BRAND AREAS of CONCERN and STRATEGY STATEMENTS		
❑ *Brand Equity* – How much "goodwill" do you have? ❑ *Brand Perception* – How well will your company be perceived at startup?	❑ *Brand Loyalty* – We have developed such a strong relationship with our customers that it will be difficult for others to compete.	❑ Our [product, service] brand has been consistent in [quality, price, user benefits] for the last five years, creating a loyal following.

Part IV

FINANCIAL PLAN

TEGuS Cartoons   *Peter J. Patsula*

"You worry too much Harry. Signing bank documents in your own blood is not the least bit unusual."

> Rule #1: Never lose money.
> Rule #2: Never forget rule number one.
>
> ∝ **Warren Buffett**

In this section . . .

- 📄 Capitalization Plan
- 📄 Uses of Funds Statement
- 📄 Pro Forma Financial Statements
- 📄 Current Financial Statements
- 📄 Business Financial History
- 📄 Profit Planning
- 📄 Risk Assessment
- 📄 Closing Statement

Calculate startup costs.

Summarize sources of capital, loans required, and uses of funds.

FINANCIAL PLAN

IN THIS section, provide details for all aspects of your *Financial Plan*. Show past, current, and projected financial needs. Prepare both pro forma (projected) and current financial statements. In this section, also provide a business financial history statement, outline a profit plan, assess the risks investors and lenders face, show how you plan to lessen those risks, and write a closing statement to summarize your business proposal.

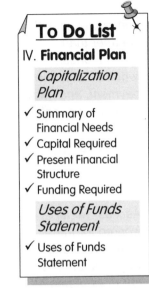

To Do List

IV. **Financial Plan**

Capitalization Plan

✓ Summary of Financial Needs
✓ Capital Required
✓ Present Financial Structure
✓ Funding Required

Uses of Funds Statement

✓ Uses of Funds Statement

Capitalization Plan

A *Capitalization Plan* summarizes your capital requirements and whether you need a loan or investment capital. It tells potential lenders or investors how much money you're trying to borrow or raise, for lenders, what collateral you have to offer and your loan repayment plan, and for investors, what percentage of the company they will own in return for their investment.

Begin this section with a half or full-page summary addressing all the key areas of your financial plan.

Summary of Financial Needs

This is a brief outline usually in the form of chart indicating why you are applying for a loan and how much you need. This summary should be placed at the front of your capitalization plan. A *Summary of Financial Needs* can be taken straight from your *Executive Summary*.

Capital Required (Startup Costs)

Estimating capital required is the first step in developing a financial plan. With as much precision as possible, estimate initial startup costs along with monthly operating expenses. More specifically, describe facility, equipment, materials, and inventory costs. You should also factor in any estimates and quotes from contractors and suppliers. Invariably, most startups underestimate the real costs of starting and running a business. Unforeseen expenses can quickly add up putting you into a cash flow crunch that inevitably worsens, especially if sales projections also fall short. A good strategy is to overestimate expenses and factor in a generous cash reserve.

According to a survey conducted by INC. Magazine, 56% of all entrepreneurs begin with their own seed money, 41% receive bank loans, and only 2% obtain venture capital.

✳

Money never starts an idea; it is the idea that starts the money.

W. J. CAMERON

Sample Capital Requirements Statement

[Company name] has estimated [initial, startup, first year, total] capital required at $[XX]. These requirements will allow us to cover all initial startup costs and provide us with enough operating capital for [XX] [number of months, years] until operations break even. This estimate also provides us with a [surplus, safety margin] of $[XX] to handle unforeseen [expenses, drops in sales].

Renting, Leasing, Buying, and Financing Options

Every business will find itself in a situation where it has to choose between renting, leasing, buying, or financing capital acquisitions, such as vehicles, buildings, computers, machinery, or land. Your decision will depend upon the particulars of your situation and the pros and cons of each form of capital acquisition.

What is a rental or a lease? A *rental* is a short-term agreement or contract under which capital property is rented from one person to another on an hourly, daily, weekly, or monthly basis with rates tending to decrease the longer the rental period. On the other hand, a *lease* is a long-term agreement or contract, under which capital property is rented from one person to another for a fixed period of time (usually one year or more) at a specified rate. Any equipment you require can often be rented or leased from the company that sells the equipment.

Why Rent or Lease? *Rent* for convenience, flexibility, to "try before you buy," and to avoid locking yourself into a long-term lease. *Lease* because it's cheaper than renting, doesn't require a big down payment, and helps control your cash flow. *Rent* or *lease* because its easier than getting financing, because you lack the funds to buy, to avoid taxing cash reserves, to avoid maintenance and repair responsibilities, to avoid obsolescence and depreciation, to improve asset liquidity, and to get immediate tax deduction benefits.

Present Financial Structure (Capital Sources)

Describe how much capital you have available to capitalize your business and the sources of these funds. Detail the amount of your initial investment and the investment of others. Bankers and investors like to know exactly what you and other owners have at risk. Your chances of raising money are better if you can show a considerable personal level of commitment to financing your business.

Funding Required

State the amount of loans or additional funds required (if any), when they are required, and your preferred terms. Support the amount requested with information such as purchase orders, supplier estimates, advertising rate sheets, and marketing results. If necessary, include detailed reports in your *Supporting Documents* section. Also, provide a summary of collateral offered, credit rating, present and past financing, and your repayment schedule.

Finding Capital

Many businesses never blossom into mature ventures due to one serious but common problem: *lack of capital*. It is a common plight for startups to end up scrounging around for funds, not only to meet basic startup costs but also to cover operating costs needed to keep the business alive long enough to break even and earn a profit. To make matters worse, banks and investors usually want nothing to do with a new business unless its owners can personally guarantee loans with collateral of equal or greater value. An "I'll pay you back as soon as I can" is simply not good enough (see GB📖 #81 for a list of 50 possible sources of capital).

What Investors Look for When You Apply for Capital

Banks favor emerging and developing businesses that have a proven track record and need additional capital for expansion, NOT startup operations. The reason for this is simple: many startups fail. Why should they take a risk? Would you? Whoever you choose to help fund your proposal, pick someone you can live with. Because they will be around for a long time making sure their investment is safe (see page 264 for factors lenders and investors look favorably upon).

Loan Application

If interested in obtaining a business loan, the institution considering the loan will often supply you with an application. The format may vary, but generally will require the types of information as shown on page 263 (also refer to page 307). To improve your chances of getting your application approved by a particular lender, research their interests and areas of expertise. Find out if they fund businesses like yours, at what stage of development they like to provide funding, and whether they have any "hidden" agendas—e.g., they prefer funding environmentally friendly businesses and avoid dot.com startups (see page 263 for more financing tips).

Banks are here to help the people who want to come up in the world.
DAVID ROCKEFELLER
Investment Banker

✳

In 2000, the U.S. Small Business Administration (SBA) gave out nearly $50 billion in small business loans, of which $12 billion went to minority-owned businesses.

✳

The entrepreneur is like an eagle ... he soars alone, he flies alone and he hunts alone.
DR. MICHAEL SMURFIT
Irish Independent

The most attractive types of personal collateral from a lender's point of view are real estate, marketable securities, and the cash value of life insurance plans.
BANKING TIP

Uses of Funds Statement

If the main reason for writing your business plan is to obtain a loan, include a *Uses of Funds Statement* (also called a *Loan Fund Dispersal Statement*). This statement is brief and specific. It describes: (1) how loan funds will be distributed among fixed assets and working capital; and (2) how purchases and expenditures will help increase production and sales thus making it easier to make interest payments and pay back the loan. It may also include (3) your loan repayment schedule. Give valid reasons for all purchases and expenditures. Make sure any support data and research are easy to locate in your *Supporting Documents*. If this information is not well organized and retrievable, a loan officer examining your application may refuse it for the simple reason that your backup material could not be found. In this section, you may also wish to outline any backup plans you have, in case you are not able to secure the full amount of the loan requested.

NOTE A *Sources and Uses of Funds Statement* at one time was commonly used by large firms to show how changes in cash or working capital (WC) were achieved as related to items on the balance sheet. For a startup, however, it is more meaningful to distinguish between: *sources* of funds (WC increases) and *uses* of funds (WC decreases) for your startup or new project.

Sources of Funds	WC +
Company Investment	$30,000
Mortgage Loan	$45,000
Equipment Loan	$25,000
Total Funds Needed	$100,000
Uses of Funds	**WC −**
Building Renovation	$60,000
Equipment Purchases	$30,000
Working Capital	$10,000
Total Project Costs	$100,000

Sample Uses of Funds Statements

The money invested in [company] will be used for the following purposes:

- ❏ Inventory; raw materials ($115,000)
- ❏ Purchase of (machine), Model # 627899 plus installation ($50,000)
- ❏ Working capital ($30,000)
- ❏ Leasehold improvements (estimate $25,000)
- ❏ Delivery truck (Ford Ranger, $13,000)
- ❏ Office equipment and supplies ($1,000).

- ❏ Computers – Four IBM NetVista X Pentium 4's, Flat Panel Displays ($6,000)
- ❏ Startup costs – legal fees, filing fees ($5,000)
- ❏ Initial office expenses, lease deposits, phone, fax, office furniture ($2,000).
- ❏ Software – Four Order Entry, MS Office XP, QuickBooks ($1,500)

The above cash outlays, totaling $248,500, will allow us to purchase the above items outright rather than lease or finance them. This will enable us to lower our overhead and meet sales projections for the first year.

DAY 24 **Worksheets** ⏱

Calculate startup costs. Summarize sources of capital, loans required, and uses of funds.

Financial Plan

List financial statements you will include in your business plan (those checked must be included; others are optional and depend on the stage of development of your business):

☑ Capital Required (Startup Costs)

❑ Uses of Funds Statement

❑ Asset Sheet

☑ Income Projection
  - 1st year detailed by months
  - 2nd and 3rd year detailed quarterly
  - Three-year Summary

☑ Pro forma Balance Sheet

☑ Breakeven Analysis

☑ Cash Flow Projection
  - 1st year detailed by month
  - 2nd and 3rd year detailed quarterly

❑ Detailed Expense Budgets

❑ Market-value Balance Sheet

❑ Deviation Analysis (see page 303)

❑ Statement of Change in Financial Position (see page 303)

❑ Balance sheets and income statements for past three years

❑ Historical reports ❑ Tax returns

Capitalization Plan and Summary of Financial Needs

Summarize capital needs. If a loan is required, state amount needed, reason why, and collateral offered:

Sample: We have estimated startup and working capital requirements for the first year of operation to be $125,000. We currently have $75,000 and are seeking a loan of $50,000. To secure the loan, we are offering property with a market value of $268,000 and an equity position of 35% ($95,000).

Capital Required (Startup Costs)

Pre-opening Legal and Professional Fees – Include money spent on incorporation, the writing up of partnership contracts, review of lease agreements or purchase contracts, and the setting up of an accounting system.

Pre-opening Promotion Costs – Include Yellow Pages listing, business cards, flyers, newspaper ads, catalogs, brochures, newsletters, signage, and any other advertising costs.

Renovations, Repairs, and Decorating of Business Site – Include electrical rewiring, ventilation, air conditioning, partitioning, painting, carpeting, and other expenditures that improve the operating site but are not considered removable.

Other Initial Startup Costs and Services – Include any miscellaneous pre-opening expenditures entered nowhere else, such as training of staff, travel to suppliers, logo design, etc.

Initial Startup Costs – *Estimate one-time financial requirements in column C. Use columns A and B if you have already purchased or financed items or if you've already lined up capital sources for specific startup costs, such as a loan for an automobile or equipment purchase, or credit (A/P's) for supplies:*

Item	A Total Cost	B (Equity) Capital Attained	C = A – B Capital Needed	D Capital Sources
Examples: *Land and Building*	$150,000	$150,000	$0	asset already paid for
Opening Inventory	$50,000	$0	$50,000	savings
Leasehold Renovations	$40,000	$20,000	$20,000	short-term bank loan
Computer	$1,500	$1,125	$375	12-mth. store financed
Land				
Buildings				
Renovations and Repairs *(construction)*				
Improvements *(mechanical, electrical)*				
Machinery and Equipment *(include installation costs)*				
Shop Tools and Supplies				
Fixtures and Equipment *(shelves, wall brackets, tables, chairs, cabinets, etc.)*				
Office Supplies *(include stationery costs)*				
Vehicles *(include cars, trucks, vans)*				
Opening Inventory *(include any materials needed for the manufacturing of products)*				
Utility Hookup and Installation Fees				
Licenses and Permits *(include association and membership fees)*				
Pre-opening Legal and Professional Fees				
Pre-opening Promotions and Advertising				
Security Deposits *(advance money required for rent, utilities, telephones, leased equip.)*				
Accounts Payable *(accounts already owed)*				
TOTALS	$	$	$	
Cash reserve *(for unexpected capital purchases)*			$	
OTHER Initial Startup Costs			$	
TOTAL Estimated Initial Startup Costs			$	

Monthly Startup Operating Expenses – *Estimate monthly expenses for* _____ *months (it is recommended that you include at least three months of operating expenses in your startup capital projections):*

Item	Estimate of Monthly x Expense	Number of Months Before Breakeven =	Total Cash Required
Variable Operating Costs	$		$
Advertising and Marketing			
Auto and Travel			
Interest on Loans			
Inventory *(includes opening inventory purchases required to meet supply demands)*			
Legal and Professional Fees			
Office Supplies/Purchases *(include purchases planned once business is underway)*			
Repairs and Maintenance			
OTHER Variable Monthly Expenses			
Fixed Operating Costs	$		$
Wages of Owner [1]			
Employees' Salaries, Wages, Benefits			
Rent or Lease Payments *(building)*			
Rent or Lease Payments *(computers or any other piece of leased or rented equipment)*			
Insurance *(include home owner's, fire, life, theft, personal, and product liability coverage)*			
Loan Payments *(include monthly payments on outstanding loans)*			
Membership Fees *(include association dues)*			
Phone			
Subscriptions *(to business periodicals)*			
Utilities *(include power, water, and gas installation and hookup charges)*			
OTHER Fixed Monthly Expenses			

Total Cash Required to Cover Monthly Operating Expenses	$
PLUS: **Total Estimated Initial Startup Costs** (from previous worksheet)	$
Total Cash Required for Startup	$
Recommended Startup Capital Required (add 25%) [2]	$

[1, 2] See notes on the next page.

[1] **Wages of Owner –** Personal living expenses are one of the most important and often overlooked expense items. Normally, it is figured as the salary you pay yourself. Don't forget to add any withdrawals anticipated during prep-startup time.

[2] **Recommended Startup Capital Required (add 25%) –** Startup costs can vary greatly depending on the size and scope of your business, the length of time it takes to produce marketable products or services, competition pressures, and many other variable factors such as unforeseen expenses, delays, inflation, strikes, supplier bankruptcies, and even personal emergencies. For this reason, it is recommended by many financial advisors that in addition to whatever calculation you come up with, to add a 25% to protect yourself from the unexpected.

Detail startup capital requirements (use results from the last two worksheets). Discuss implications. Summarize important considerations or assumptions made when making startup capital estimates:

❑ How much money do you have in reserve? ❑ How long can you operate if sales projections fall short?

Sample: Because it may take up to a year to build a profitable customer base, in calculating our startup capital needs, we have factored in a working capital safety margin of $85,000 to allow us to continue operations for at least six months even if sales growth is 50% lower than projected. We've also included a surplus fund of $25,000 to handle unforeseen expenses.

Leasing – State reasons for choosing to rent or lease equipment, land, etc., rather than buy or finance:

Sample: Our largest purchase requirement is for production equipment used for making [products]. After pricing equipment at a cost of $[XX], to preserve capital for materials if demand exceeds projections, we have decided to lease equipment instead at $[XX] per month over five years with [company].

Compare the costs of renting, leasing, financing, and purchasing a major capital acquisition, such as land, a building, a vehicle, or equipment:

Description of Item:				
	Renting	Leasing	Financing	Purchasing
Length of Lease or Loan:				
Interest Rate Charged:				
Down Payment/Deposit:				
Cost per Month:				
Cost per Year:				
Cost for Three Years:				
Total Cost:				
% of Costs Tax Deductible:				

Present Financial Structure (Capital Sources)

Current Capital Sources – *Provide an overview of the current financial structure of your business.* **What proportion of total startup requirements have you obtained to date? What funding have you obtained?**

Sample: To date, Rokisa Inc. has obtained $6.25 million in startup capital from founding members. To launch Buddha-Blues.com, we need an additional $3 million loan by May 2006. While seeking additional sources of long-term capital to support growth initiatives, we will continue to work within our current capital sources.

Detail the amount of your initial investment and the investment of others to date:

Sample: Dr. Emilio Robba, president of [company], has invested $2.5 million for 20,000 shares (20% of the original stock issue). The other three founding members, Sita Kim, Phillip Sarver, and Jet Li, have each invested $1.25 million for 10,000 shares each.

Source of Funds	Amount	Debt or Equity	Repayment Schedule
Personal savings	$		
Friends, neighbors, relatives			
Banks, credit unions, other financial institutions			
Mortgage and insurance companies			
Credit from suppliers			
Government grants and loans (SBA Loans)			

Other Capital Sources – *Describe any additional sources of capital (see checklist on the following page):*

Sample: If we fail to obtain loan funds for development and expansion by May 2006, we will consider a profit-sharing joint venture with [company A or company B] who have expressed interest. However, as part of the agreement among founding members, additional shares will not be issued until Buddha-Blues.com is ready for an initial public offering.

Check other possible sources of capital to further finance your business (see GB⬚ #81 for 50 sources):

❑ Advance payments from contracts ❑ A/R financing ❑ Business credit cards ❑ Cash value of life insurance ❑ Conditional sales agreements	❑ Commercial banks ❑ Contra bartering ❑ Credit unions ❑ Equipment financing ❑ Equipment leasing ❑ Factoring companies ❑ Financing with accruals ❑ Floor financing	❑ Government sponsored programs ❑ Home equity loans ❑ Installment financing ❑ Inventory financing ❑ Issuing stock (IPO) ❑ Joint ventures ❑ Letters of credit	❑ Licensing agreements ❑ Limited partnerships ❑ Pension plan withdrawals ❑ Private investors ❑ Selling unnecessary assets ❑ Venture capital

❑ **Credit Capital (vendor financing)** – Credit capital, also called trade credit or vendor financing, can be obtained from suppliers or credit card companies who give you a grace period before payment is due or interest charged. Many suppliers, if convinced of the soundness of your venture, will strongly consider granting you credit in their own efforts to find new customers and expand their business. Credit capital is often overlooked as a means of financing a startup.

❑ **Debt Financing** – Debt financing is a direct obligation to pay interest to someone (an investor or lender), in exchange for having lent you the money. The biggest advantage of debt financing is that it allows you to retain, for the most part, control of your company. You're entitled to all company profits and have ultimate decision-making authority. After you have repaid the borrowed money, the lender has no further claim on your business. On the other hand, the biggest disadvantage of debt financing is making those monthly loan payments. If you miss a payment or are late, the lender may impose severe penalties, such as additional fees, a poorer credit rating, or the possibility of calling the loan due.

❑ **Equity Financing** – Equity financing requires selling a partial interest in your company. In effect, all new equity investors become new business partners. The advantages of equity financing are no monthly loan payments and no direct obligation to pay back any funds (i.e., there is no debt!). In addition, you will likely have more freedom to explore more creative capitalization ideas with an equity investor than with a debt investor. On the other hand, the biggest drawback, besides the fact that you have to share the profits, is the loss of control over your business. Quite often, your equity investors will not agree with your short- or long-term plans, and since you have given them a share in your business, you will have to listen to their point of view. Another drawback is that equity financing tends to be very complicated and invariably will require the advice of attorneys and accountants.

❑ **Cash Capital (personal financing)** – Cash capital is capital that you pay no interest on and you have ready access to. It is derived from personal savings, cashed-in equity, or borrowing from future cash contracts. Using cash capital is certainly the easiest, if not the best way to finance your business.

Funding Required

Loans Needed – State amount of new funding required (if any), when required, and desired terms:

	Sample: To increase equity through property ownership, [company] is seeking a loan of $[XX] to purchase the warehouse and parcel of land currently being leased at $[XX] per month. [Company] has $[XX] in investment cash and requires $[XX] in additional loan funds. To finance this purchase, we are looking for a 30-due-in-7 balloon payment mortgage at a fixed rate of [X]% with a conversion option.

Loan Application – *Research financing institutions you will approach to request a loan. What are the requirements for each lender? Do they have special interests? Will you have to:* ❑ fill out an extensive loan application form? ❑ provide personal net worth statements for each partner? ❑ obtain reference letters?

Financing Institution	Loan Officer	Application Requirements / Comments	Types of Loans / Terms Offered
Cape Cod Bank & Trust	Fletcher G. Boyle (555-3421)	two-page Commercial Loan Application form; Personal Financial Statement form	Business Installment Loan; SBA Loan; Fixed rate, 1–5 years

Check information you need to complete loan applications:

❑ *Assets, Liabilities, and Net Worth* – Find these on your balance sheet.

❑ *Contingent Liabilities* – List debts you may come to owe in the future.

❑ *Inventory Details* – Summarize your inventory status, current policies, and methods of evaluation.

❑ *Income Statements* – You may be required to compile several years of income statements on one sheet.

❑ *Real Estate Holdings, Stocks, and Bonds* – Banks love collateral.

❑ *Sole Proprietorship, Partnership, or Cooperation Information* – Provide information on your legal structure.

❑ *Audit Information* – You may be asked about other prospective lenders you are seeking credit from and when your books were last audited.

❑ *Insurance Coverage* – Banks are very interested in seeing that you have covered key insurance risks.

Check general strategies you can use to obtain bank financing:

❑ Avoid asking a bank for "working capital." Banks prefer giving loans for tangible assets.

❑ Compare your business financial status and needs with other similar businesses.

❑ Find out beforehand what kind of loan best suits your needs. Research options for financing.

❑ Have a written detailed business plan and a short summary business plan.

❑ In your interview, listen. Let your plan do the talking (and don't expect a bank to finance your entire business).

❑ Open a separate business checking account before asking for a loan.

❑ Research government grants and loans.

Check factors that will make investors look favorably upon your loan application (see page 264). List additional factors that may put your application in good standing:

❑ Ability to Serve a Debt ❑ Adequate Owner Investment ❑ Attractive Return on Investment
❑ Collateral ❑ Company Stability ❑ Equity Position ❑ Financial Ratios ❑ Industry Performance
❑ Liquidity of Company Assets ❑ Management Experience ❑ Potential for Involvement in Key Decisions
❑ Potential Growth ❑ Proven Credit Rating ❑ Regular Financial Reporting

❑ **Ability to Serve a Debt** – Banks and investors want to know how well you can service a debt—i.e., carry interest charges and eventually repay the loan in full. They need reassurance and proof that earnings will cover interest payments and the principal covered by the liquidation of whatever it is the money is going to be used for.

❑ **Adequate Owner Investment** – Most proposals will be rejected flat-out unless the owner has risked a substantial amount of the business's capital needs. Investors and banks want to see that you have a serious level of commitment to your business and that you are sharing the risk. There is no fixed percentage for this equity contribution, but most lenders require at least 25% of the total amount required to establish the business.

❑ **Attractive Return on Investment** – Investors can obtain returns of up to and exceeding 10% with relatively safe investments in mortgages and bonds. For them to consider investing in your enterprise, which carries a greater degree of risk than mortgages, your business must promise better financial returns. Since equity investors usually take a greater risk, they also expect to earn more on their investment than do debt investors.

❑ **Collateral** – Anything of value owned by your company or owed to you and contributes to the worth of your business is an asset and can be pledged as collateral for a loan, property, or equipment purchase. Common types of collateral include accounts receivable, real estate, equipment, and inventory. On the other hand, soft assets which include such intangibles as goodwill, patents, formulas, and capitalized research and development are not always accepted as collateral; they are, in fact, thought to distort a business's value and are regarded as a danger signal if given too high a value.

❑ **Company Stability** – Bankers and investors need to believe your company will be around for a while. They prefer companies that issue stock purchasable on the stock market and have a life of their own. Public companies provide greater liquidity and easier opportunities for obtaining equity capital since their shares can be sold to anyone. Bankers and investors will also look at your retained earnings, company profits, equity, and dividend payments to determine your overall stability.

❑ **Equity Position** – Bankers will review the current and projected equity position of a business. The important aspect of equity is not so much the dollar amount but the ratio of equity to assets or debt. A growing business usually shows an equity position of 30% to 50% in relation to total assets. This means that the owners own 30% to 50% percent of the company.

❑ **Financial Ratios** – Bankers and investors use financial ratios to determine the relative health of a business. The data for ratio analysis comes from your company's *Balance Sheet* and *Income Statement*. One of the most important ratios is your total debt to total assets ratio, also known as your "equity position." This ratio is calculated by dividing total debt or liabilities by total assets. It looks at the ability of a business to repay long-term debt and is given special focus in the American Bankers Association guidelines for evaluating a business.

❑ **Industry Performance** – Bankers and investors will also examine the current state of the industry, including its past, recent, and future performance.

❑ **Liquidity of Company Assets** – Banks and investors need to know how fast current assets, such as inventory and receivables (used as collateral for short-term loans), as well as fixed assets, such as land, buildings and equipment (collateral for long-term loans) can be converted into cash, in case your business goes bankrupt.

❑ **Management Experience** – A vital ingredient of every startup loan application is management expertise. Lack of management expertise is the single biggest cause of business failures. Loan officers and investors will also look at your reputation and integrity (have you kept your promises in the past), your proven ability and experience (have you previously managed or owned a successful business), as well as the reputation and experience of all key individuals in your company.

❑ **Potential for Involvement in Key Decisions** – Although not always the case, many investors want to be involved in key management decisions and may also want to function as directors or officers of the company.

❑ **Potential Growth** – Banks and investors will also analyze your expected rate of growth. They don't like to see companies growing too slow or too fast.

❑ **Proven Credit Rating** – Banks and investors like to invest in companies with solid credit ratings. They need to know you will make interest and principal payments on time. Records and references for loans previously paid provide excellent proof. Banks and investors may also want to know your personal credit history.

❑ **Regular Financial Reporting** – Banks and investors usually want to see tight financial controls in place and prompt financial reporting. They like to see cash flow budgets updated monthly and lists of aged receivables and payables (preferably prepared by outside accountants). They also like to know about major changes in advance, new and large orders anticipated, plans for expansion, and when loan payments might be late.

Collateral Offered – *List collateral—assets and possessions—to be offered as loan security. Estimate the present market value of each item and include any other important information about owners and supporters and their collective ability to pay back loans:*

Credit Rating – *If asking for a loan, outline your history at repaying debts. Include a copy of your personal credit record obtainable from a local credit bureau. Give reasons why you are a good credit risk:*

Sample: All founding partners of [company] have excellent credit ratings and a long reliable loan repayment history. A copy of each partner's credit profile from [credit bureau] and list of fully paid loans and outstanding personal loans are included in the Supporting Documents section at the end of this proposal.

Present and Previous Financing – *List present and previous financing (if any). Include term loans outstanding (balance owing, repayment terms, security held); lines of credit applied for (security offered); and current lines of credit (amounts, security held). Include letters of credit in supporting documents:*

Sample: [Company] has a current outstanding loan of $[XX] with [lender]. Monthly principal and interest payment are $[XX]. This loan is being fully serviced by company revenues and will be repaid by mid-2005. [Company] also has a $[XX] revolving line of credit with [bank] that has been active for [X] years.

Repayment Schedule – *Write a statement indicating how loan funds are to be repaid. Include repayment sources and time required, copies of cash flow schedules, budgets, and other appropriate information (in your "repayment schedule" investors like to see at least two different sources of repayment):*

Sample: At projected rates of cash flow, [company] will be able to service a monthly interest and principal payment of $[XX] to repay the loan within [XX] months. Loan repayments can be made monthly, preferably on the third day of each month.

Type of Loan Required – *What type of loan do you require? Describe what you will be using the loan for:*

❑ **Business Installment Loan –** Generally used to finance fixed assets from one to five years depending on the useful life of the asset.

❑ **Growth Capital Loan –** Used to meet needs that are to be repaid with profits over a period of years, usually not more than seven.

❑ **Working Capital Loan –** Used to meet fluctuating needs that must be repaid in cash during the business's next full operating cycle.

Other Types of Loans
❑ Commercial Loan
❑ Construction Loan
❑ Line of Credit
❑ Short-term Loan
❑ Term Loan ❑ SBA Loan

_____

_____

_____

_____

Sample: [Company] is seeking growth capital of $[XX] to meet the following expansion goals: (1) renovate and expand existing west-end branch; (2) augment company staff to sustain planned growth; and (3) increase budget for research and development. The following growth activities will increase cash flow through increased sales and reduce production inefficiencies [explain how].

Review and check the following factors that speak positively and negatively about any loan applications you need to make. Clarify weaknesses and how you plan to rectify them:

Factors Your Lender May Use to Positively Evaluate Your Application:

❑ Your character, integrity, and overall management experience and skills.

❑ Your company's track record (e.g., sales, profits).

❑ Your product and its relative importance to the market and industry.

❑ Your financial statements preferably accompanied by a CPA's review and assessment.

❑ A clear description of the purpose of the loan.

❑ Your company's ability to provide data to the bank both accurately and in a timely manner.

❑ The primary and alternative sources of repayment.

Factors Your Lender May Look Negatively on in Approving Your Loan:

❑ Accounts receivable past due, indicating that cash is coming in too slowly.

❑ Accounts payable abnormally extended.

❑ Poor inventory operation, such as low turnover, large back orders, out-of-date stock.

❑ High debt-equity ratio—signifying large outstanding loans.

❑ Large withdrawals of profits by company owners.

❑ Need to borrow short-term funds to meet long-term needs.

❑ Insufficient financial data.

❑ Poor credit rating for principal business owners/officers.

❑ Personal problems of executives.

_____

_____

_____

_____

Sample: [Company] is a good loan risk for the following reasons: Financial statements will be audited quarterly by Coopers and Lybrand and will be made available upon request to lender for review, and status reports on cash flow and sales can also be made available upon request. Furthermore, loan repayment can be serviced from [company]'s working capital or from owner's equity during unexpected periods of negative cash flow.

Uses of Funds Statement

Summarize use of loan funds. Provide a back-up statement describing reasons for dispersal:

Select name for statement: ❑ Uses of Funds Statement ❑ Use of Loan Funds ❑ Loan Fund Dispersal Statement

USE OF LOAN FUNDS	Loan Fund Dispersal Statement
I. Funds Required a. HPS Inc. will need a business installment loan of $25,000 to purchase three pieces of equipment.	I

II. Dispersal of Loan Funds
 	
b. The equipment needed is as follows:
 	
  1) Munson Rotary Batch Blender ($14,000)
  2) Used APM Bag Loader VLS-2000 ($7,700)
  3) Two Vita-Mix Blenders ($1,800)
 	
c. The remaining $1,500 will be used to market the new product and contribute to the first loan installment.
	II

III. Back-up Statement d. The equipment purchased will support $50,000 in additional sales during the first year (a 20% increase in total revenues). This will result in a net profit increase of $10,000 per year sufficient to repay the loan and interest within three years.	III

Describe in more detail any major purchases or expenditures you plan to make with funds obtained:

Sample: Currently, all [company]'s manufactured dog food products are bagged by hand. Using the VLS-2000 automatic form, fill, seal, and discharge bag loader, up to a 60% reduction in labor cost is possible. There is a further 54% savings on materials compared to using pre-made bags or special perforated bags on a roll. The operator's only function is placement of product into the automatically made bag.	

Prepare a 12-month and three-year income projection.
Prepare a cash flow statement. State assumptions made.

Pro Forma Financial Statements

The purpose of preparing pro forma financial projection statements is to show lenders and investors that you have researched your market and profit potential in relation to costs. Since a new business does not have a track record, this analysis must be thorough, critical, logical, and probable—not just possible. Any inconsistencies will be quickly spotted leaving a bad impression on lenders who may lose faith in your entire proposal regardless of its merits. The following five statements belong in every business plan and are by far the statements most lenders want to see. They should be prepared in the order shown below as each one builds on the one done previously:

12-month Income Projection	Three-year Income Projection	Cash Flow Statement	Breakeven Analysis	Pro Forma Balance Sheet

Basic Budgeting Terminology

The ability to know your cash flow status at any particular moment in time, as well as make accurate income projections on a regular basis is an essential business survival skill. You must know HOW MUCH and WHEN cash is needed to pay bills, buy inventory, etc. To this end, the following terminology is helpful:

Budget

A budget is a forecast of all cash sources and expenditures. It follows an income statement type format covering a 12-month period, month by month. At year's end, the projected income and expense figures are compared with actual performance of the business as recorded in the financial statements. The two most important budgeting tools are the *Cash Flow Statement* and the *Income Projection*.

Income Projection

An *Income Projection* examines all revenue and expense items (including depreciation) to determine the monthly and yearly profitability of a venture.

> *Everything someone does on a daily basis should be traceable back to an annual or quarterly plan.*
>
> **RICHARD E. GRIGGS**
>
> ✱
>
> *A budget is the way to go broke methodically.*
>
> **ANON**
>
> ✱
>
> *The largest determining factor of the size and content of this year's budget is last year's budget.*
>
> **AARON WILDAVSKY**
> Political Scientist

Cash Flow

The term *Cash Flow* refers to the amount of funds readily available to make purchases and pay current bills. Over a specific period, it is the difference between cash receipts (money you take in) and cash disbursements (money you spend).

Cash Flow Statement

A *Cash Flow Statement* (also known as a *Cash Flow Projection*) refers to an estimate of anticipated cash sales, as well as anticipated cash payments of bills. These estimates are usually scheduled on a weekly, monthly, or quarterly basis and are frequently used to help project the amount of money required to finance your operations on a yearly or even day-to-day basis.

NOTE *Cash Flow* and *Income Projection Statements* are not the same. The difference between the two results from how principal payments and depreciation are recorded. Loan principal payments are included as cash outflow in a cash flow statement but are not recorded on the income statement. On the other hand, depreciation is included as a business expense on the income statement but not as cash outflow on the cash flow statement.

Breakeven Analysis

A *Breakeven Analysis* determines at what point your income matches your expenses and overhead. This information can help you project the profit potential of your venture, as well as point out the necessity for controlling your costs.

Working Capital

Working Capital is the difference between current assets and current liabilities. It measures the amount of liquid assets a company has available to expand and improve operations. A positive working capital balance is desirable. Working capital includes items such as cash, marketable securities, accounts receivable, inventories, accounts payable, accrued wages, and unpaid taxes.

Working capital management, like cash flow management, is primarily concerned with the day-to-day operations of a business rather than long-term business decisions. Working capital policies deal with decisions related to types and amounts of current assets and the means of financing them. These decisions involve: ◆ the management of cash and inventories ◆ credit policy and collection of accounts receivable ◆ short-term borrowing and other financing opportunities, such as trade credit ◆ inventory financing ◆ accounts receivable financing.

Profits are the lifeblood of the economic system, the magic elixir upon which progress and all good things depend ultimately. But one man's lifeblood is another man's cancer.

PAUL A. SAMUELSON
Professor of Economics, Harvard University

DID YOU KNOW?

Small businesses tend to have a limited number of financing opportunities and less access to capital markets. This requires them to rely heavily on short-term credit such as accounts payable, bank loans, and credit secured by inventories and/or accounts receivable. The use of any of these financing sources reduces working capital by increasing current liabilities.

Since the average firm has about 40% of its capital tied up in current assets, decisions regarding working capital greatly impact the success of a business. This is especially true for smaller businesses, which often minimize investments in fixed assets by leasing rather than buying, but which cannot avoid investing in inventories, cash, and receivables.

Working Capital Cycle

The *Working Capital Cycle* involves the steps a business takes from the time it makes the first cash commitment towards providing a product or a service, to the point when it receives cash payment for its sales (accounts receivable). An individual cycle ends when the full cash amount for the sale is received.

Calculating the Working Capital Cycle – The Working Capital Cycle may be calculated by using the following formula:

$$\text{WCC} = \text{ICP} + \text{RCP}$$

ICP – (Inventory Conversion Period) refers to the length of time between purchase of raw material, production of the goods or service, and the sale of the finished product.

RCP – (Receivable Conversion Period) refers to the time between the sale of the final product on credit and cash receipts for the accounts receivable.

Capital Cash Conversion Cycle

The *Capital Cash Conversion Cycle*, also referred to as the *Cash Flow Cycle*, is defined as the length of time between the payment of what a business owes (payables), and the collection of what a business is owed (receivables). During this cycle, a business's funds are unavailable for other purposes. Cash has been paid for purchases but cash has not been collected from sales.

Calculating the Capital Cash Conversion Cycle – The *Capital Cash Conversion Cycle* may be calculated by using the following formula:

$$\text{CCC} = \text{ICP} + \text{RCP} - \text{PDP}$$

PDP – (Payable Deferral Period) refers to the time between the purchase of raw material on credit and cash payments for the resulting accounts payable.

For example, if it takes 35 days after orders are placed to receive and process raw materials into finished products, the ICP is 35 days. Assuming that 25 days after the arrival of raw materials, the firm pays for them, the PDP would be 25 days. If the firm receives cash payment for the sale of its product or service in 30 days, the RCP is 30 days. The CCC can then be calculated as: 35 + 30 – 25 = 40 days.

Reducing the Capital Cash Conversion Cycle – Since there is always a cost to financing, a goal of almost any business is to minimize the length of time funds are "tied-up" in order to reduce the amount of working capital needed for operations. Strategies include: ✦ reducing the ICP by processing the raw materials to produce the goods as quickly as possible ✦ reducing the RCP by speeding up collection ✦ lengthening the PDP by slowing payments.

Assumptions Made

Believable projections are critical to getting bankers and investors to support your idea. Properly derived, they turn **qualitative** company goals and marketing strategies into **quantitative** reality which in turn fosters credibility and defensibility of your proposal. However, more importantly, making accurate projections is critical to your survival as an entrepreneur. In fact, startup financial statements become pretty much useless unless based on real figures and the best possible operating and financial assumptions you can determine (see "Categories of Assumptions" on the next page).

- **Creating an Assumptions Made Sheet –** An *Assumptions Made* or *Financial Assumptions Sheet* can be used to detail and summarize important numbers you have arrived at in the development of your financial statements. Preparing an assumptions made sheet is a process that keeps your numbers objective and helps you avoid the temptation of becoming too creative. Start by listing important financial statement categories along with your estimations, percentages, or ratios and a brief explanation of how you came up with them (see samples on pages 272 and 365). It is usually easiest to create this sheet after you have prepared your statements and have thoroughly researched, experimented, wrangled with, and worked out the numbers. State assumptions by: (1) summing up in a paragraph or two at the beginning of your *Financial Plan* or *Pro Forma Financial Statements* section; (2) adding explanations at the bottom of affected statements; or (3) adding to your *Supporting Documents* section.

- **Strategies for Making Assumptions –** (a) *Record them as you make them.* While preparing each statement, jot down any assumptions made along with an explanation. (b) *Always choose the highest value for a debt or expense item.* Be conservative. Estimate fixed operating expenses by researching similar businesses. Estimate variable expenses as a percentage of sales. Research average markups from suppliers and industry trade associations. Estimate wages by multiplying hourly wages by 30% to 60% to cover health plan and other benefits. (c) *Always choose the lowest value for an asset or revenue item.* Estimate sales volume or market share by reducing it to the lowest value you think you might achieve and then dividing that by two or three. (d) *Be comprehensive.* Make assumptions for worst case, conservative case, and best case scenarios.

When making financial projections, you will never have all the necessary information. Thus, assumptions must be made. However, if assumptions aren't realistic, perhaps then neither is your plan.
PLANNING TIP

False assumptions can be very dangerous for companies especially when they lead to so-called conventional wisdom or result in competitive blind spots.
DR. PAUL TIFFANY
Hass Business School
✳

In a startup company, you basically throw out all assumptions every three weeks.
SCOTT MCNEALY
✳

It is important not to ignore forecasts that are uncongenial.
JIB FOWLES

❑ **general** (A/R's and A/P's, cash flow changes, competitor reactions, fixed asset purchases, spoiled or damaged inventory, government policies)

❑ **revenues** (seasonal patterns, joint venture profits, federal grants)

❑ **variable expenses** (advertising, raw materials, R&D, inventory, taxes)

❑ **fixed expenses** (bad debts, leasing, returns)

❑ **inflation rate** (cost of living, deflation)

❑ **loans received** (loan payment, interest rates)

❑ **payroll increases** (new employees, out-sourcing)

❑ **product lines** (selling price increases, gross profit margins, markup %)

❑ **recession** (expansion)

Be prepared to defend your assumptions more rigorously when meeting with bankers and investors. They want to be convinced your figures are as accurate and as realistic as possible.

✳

By utilizing the financial assumption process, you will be developing your plan the right way.

LINDA PINSON
Anatomy of a
Business Plan

Use your 12-month income projection to develop your three-year income projection. Use both these statements to develop your cash flow projection and breakeven analysis.

Sample Assumptions Made

[Company name]'s financial projections are based on the assumption that we will generate [revenues, profits] of $[XX] within [years/months]. Initial market share penetration is anticipated to be $[XX] for [product, service] at a margin of [X]%, and increase to $[XX] by the end of the first [quarter, year] and $[XX] by the end of [year]. We are assuming that costs, including [labor, raw materials, COGS] will increase by the general inflation rate at [X]% per year, based upon [research source]. [New equipment] will further reduce costs by $[XX], thereby increasing our profit margin by [X]%. The cost of [supplies] will be reduced by [X]% by taking advantage of [early payment discounts].

12-month Income Projection

A *12-month Income Projection* shows sales and receipts, cost of sales, gross profit, expenses, and net profit for the entire year. All of these can also be expressed as a percentage of sales making the values easy to compare year to year.

Sample Sales and Income Projections and Assumptions

Sales have been forecast at the following growth rates:

	Year 2	Year 3
[Product/Service] 1:	[XX]%	[XX]%
[Product/Service] 2:	[XX]%	[XX]%

Returns and discounts are estimated at 5% of total sales. This rate is based on operating ratios from [source]. We are offering a range of quantity discounts, plus an early payment discount to trade credit customers.

Cost of goods sold will increase at 0.25% per month or 3% per year. This rate is equivalent to this year's projected inflation rate [source].

Freight will be paid by customers.

Preparing a 12-month Income Projection

A *12-month Income Projection* is valuable as both a planning and management tool to help control and monitor business operations. It allows you to make projections of income generated each month and for the business year, based on reasonable predictions of monthly levels of sales, costs, and expenses. It looks similar to a cash flow projection, but it keeps track of ALL expenses and revenues (not just cash-based ones), and also factors in depreciation. The real value of an income projection becomes more apparent when projections are compared with actual results. This comparison enables you to make more accurate future projections and take steps to correct problems. To complete the "12-month Income Projection" shown on page 285, follow these steps:

a. **Find out industry percentages.** Industry figures serve as useful benchmarks against which to compare cost and expense estimates. These percentages can be obtained from trade associations, accountants, or banks. Also, your reference librarian might be able to refer you to documents that contain these figures. Increasingly, these figures can also be found online. Visit www.bizratios.com for helpful resources and links (see pages 308 and 309 for more sources).

b. **Project total gross sales (revenues).** Estimate your total number of units of product or services delivered that you realistically expect to sell each month at the prices you expect to get. Make sure to subtract any returns or markdowns, as well as sales tax.

c. **Calculate cost of sales.** Estimate all *direct costs* of selling your product or service. Project how much you will pay for inventory (include shipping, raw materials), as well as direct selling costs for any services provided (e.g., direct labor, contract labor, client materials, and transportation costs). The cost of goods sold (COGS) is often expressed as a percentage of sales. Once again, check with your trade association to get the best ratio for your business.

d. **Calculate gross profit.** Subtract the total cost of sales from monthly gross sales to arrive at your gross profit. For example, with a cost of sales operating ratio of 59.4%, and January revenues of $100,000, your January gross profit would be $40,600.

e. **Estimate variable (controllable) and fixed expenses.** Estimate all *indirect costs* of selling your product or service. Include depreciation (*variable costs* change with the amount of sales—many can be controlled at your discretion—while *fixed costs* do not change).

NOTE You should depreciate any individual item of equipment, furniture, fixtures, vehicles, etc., costing over $100. In general, to do this, divide the cost of each fixed asset item by the number of months over which it will be depreciated. For complete information on allowances for depreciation, request free publications and assistance from your local tax bureau.

f. **Calculate operating profit.** Subtract total operating expenses from your gross profit.

g. **Project other income and expenses.** Other income and interest expenses are usually factored in at the end of an income statement to facilitate easier analysis of these important items.

h. **Calculate net profit before taxes.** To calculate your net profit, subtract other expenses from your operating profit and add other income (also referred to as net income before taxes).

i. **Estimate tax payments.** Include all federal, state, and local income taxes.

j. **Calculate net profit after taxes.** Subtract taxes from net profit (net income after taxes).

k. **Total monthly columns.** Sum each of the monthly sales and expense items across the table.

l. **Calculate annual percentages.** Compare this figure to the industry percentage in the first column. Use the following formula:

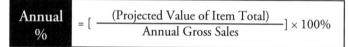

$$\text{Annual } \% = \left[\frac{\text{(Projected Value of Item Total)}}{\text{Annual Gross Sales}} \right] \times 100\%$$

m. **Compare your projected 12-month Income Statement with actual sales and expenses.** On a regular monthly basis, fill out a second 12-month income statement using actual results. This final step is the most important step of the entire process. As a business owner, any reliable feedback you can get is as good as gold.

Three-year Income Projection

A *Three-year Income Projection Statement* shows your income and deductible expense projections (such as depreciation), for the next three years of your operations (see pages 282 and 286). To prepare a three-year income projection, for the first year, use the figures from your 12-month income projection. Base your second and third year's figures on these projections, as well as any projected increases or decreases of expenses (due to inflation or changes in the market) and increases in sales. Make sure to note any assumptions made.

Cash Flow Statement

A *Cash Flow Statement*, also called a *Cash Flow Budget*, is a key part of every business plan. It is the only tool you have to assure that you can meet your financial obligations and show lenders you have sufficient cash to carry a loan. A cash flow statement identifies when cash is expected, how much cash will be received, when cash must be paid out, and exactly how much cash is needed to pay expenses. Overall, it helps present a clearer picture of your monthly cash inflow and outflow for your next year of operation and assess profits after taxes.

Preparing a Cash Flow Statement

The primary concern of a cash flow projection is to help anticipate cash receipts and cash expenditures so at the end of each month you will have a good idea of how much money you have or won't have to pay bills (see the next page for cash flow tips). Three basic steps for preparing a *Cash Flow Statement* are:

FIRST – Estimate sales and all incoming revenue. Sales from previous years of similar companies can be used as a guide. Be sure to consider seasonal trends that may affect sales volume at different months (use the "Sources of Cash Worksheet" on page 284).

SECOND – After projecting cash receipts from all sources, estimate the expenses necessary to achieve anticipated sales. Operating expenses can be expressed in dollars or as an operating ratio in the form of a percentage of sales. Industry operating ratios can be found at your trade association (use the "Cash to Be Paid Out Worksheet" on page 284).

THIRD – Subtract projected cash expenditures from revenue. The remaining sum will indicate a negative or positive cash flow. A positive cash flow at the end of the year is good, especially if occurring in all 12 months and generating a nice profit. But this is unlikely. Most startup companies will have a negative cash flow initially, with a breakeven point occurring at some point in the future (hopefully after a few months). A negative cash flow after one year is not good; unless you have ample financial reserves, investors with deep pockets, and/or evidence that your cash flow position will eventually improve.

NOTE A cash flow statement deals ONLY with cash transactions. All sales and expenditures listed are actual cash sales and cash expenditures. A cash flow statement does not consider depreciation, amortization of goodwill, or other non-cash expense items. Prepaid items, such as insurance and supplies contracts, affect cash flow only in the period they are actually paid. A/R's and A/P's are not included unless cash is actually received or paid out during the period.

A person's treatment of money is the most decisive test of his character, how they make it and how they spend it.
JAMES MOFFATT

Unfortunately, small businesses regularly experience cash flow problems. When cash flow becomes problematic, small business owners should assess their individual situations. Above everything, small business owners must understand the nature of their business' problem.
C.D. HEINEN
Senior VP for small business banking at Comerica Bank-Texas

Avoiding the Cash Flow Crunch

❑ Avoid grand-opening posturing, overblown staffs, grandiose ads, and ALL poorly thought-out expenses.

❑ Carefully monitor rapid increases in credit sales. Uncollected A/R's can quickly deplete your cash reserves.

❑ Carefully monitor your highest costs. Keep a tight rein on inventory.

❑ Don't expand too rapidly. Cash flow generated by increased sales may not be sufficient to pay increased costs.

❑ Don't withdraw excessive cash for living expenses. Reduce owner compensation if cash flow is tight.

Strategies

❑ Fine-tune your sales and expense projections by: (a) comparing your projected operating ratios with those of other companies; (b) learning to recognize seasonal sales patterns; (c) improving your accuracy by comparing *projected* cash flows with *actual* cash flows.

❑ Lease equipment instead of buying.

❑ Monitor the length of your accounts receivable average collection period (ACP). The shorter it is the better. Be wary of slow collections.

❑ Negotiate the "payment time" of any contracts, in addition to the price.

❑ Reduce your CCC by offering discounts for early payment.

❑ Research credit customers carefully to reduce your bad debts ratio.

❑ Keep costs within industry averages.

❑ Use short-term financing when needed by establishing a credit line with a bank. But only borrow to the extent needed.

❑ Use customer funds by charging purchases on their credit card and having a cash only policy (this may reduce overall sales but will improve cash flow).

Preparing a 12-month Cash Flow Budget

Cash flow projections are best made on a spreadsheet. Not only does this allow you to change variables and projections and have the results automatically calculated, but it lessens the need to list similar expenditures repeatedly. The sample cash flow statement on page 287 can be used as a guide to set up a spreadsheet, or as a worksheet to customize your own personalized cash flow statement. To prepare a cash flow statement, follow the steps outlined below (it is a good idea to do separate cash flow budgets for worst, average, and best case scenarios):

To me the important thing is not how much money I have, but what the money is doing.

J. PAUL GETTY

✱

A budget tells us what we can't afford, but it doesn't keep us from buying it.

WILLIAM FEATHER

1.   ❑ *Projected* – Check this box if you are preparing a projected cash flow statement.

   ❑ *Actual* – Check this box if you are preparing a cash flow statement based on actual results. Preparing this kind of statement is a good way to sharpen future projections.

   Type – State whether projection is a worst, average, or best case scenario.

2. **Beginning CASH BALANCE** – Start with the first month of your business tax year. Enter your startup capital or cash on hand balance from the previous month's end (also referred to as your opening cash balance, surplus cash, or total cash in the bank at the first of the month). If you don't know this exact figure, estimate it.

   NOTE If your business is new, base your projections on market research and industry trends. If you have an established business, also use previous financial statements.

3. **CASH IN** – Estimate all cash revenues your company expects to take in during the month (use industry operating ratios if needed).

3a. *Cash Sales* – Estimate all cash revenues your company expects to take in specifically from the sale of your goods or services. Include cleared checks and credit card slips. Omit accounts receivable sales unless cash is actually received. Also omit orders taken and invoices sent out where no cash has been received. If necessary, divide this section into several categories depending on how useful you think this information is (e.g., sales of widgets, sales of shoes).

NOTE The primary source of cash revenue in your business will be from sales, but sales will vary from month to month due to seasonal patterns and other factors. It is thus necessary to project whether monthly sales will produce enough income to pay each month's bills. Bear in mind that it is much easier and more accurate to project expenditures than to project sales. Because sales projections are critical to the success of your company, and often quite inaccurate, serious research and extra precautions should be evident and reflected in your determination of them.

3b. *A/R Collections* – Estimate the amount your company expects to collect from its sales on account. Some statements further break down this category into: (a) collections from last month's sales, (b) collections of sales from two months ago, and (c) collection from sales more than two months ago. This is a good idea if the majority of your sales are on credit.

3c. *Interest Income* – Estimate interest from investments, securities, and bank accounts.

3d. *Sale of Fixed Assets* – If you plan to sell any fixed asset your company owns, such as a car, building, or office furniture, estimate the amount you expect to receive.

3e. *Loans Received* – Project any borrowed funds you may receive during the month.

3f. *Other Cash Sources* – Estimate all other sources of cash you expect to receive over the month. Include items like rent income, capital gains on shares sold, and stock dividends received.

4. **CASH OUT** – Project all fixed and controllable expenses for the month. Include any amounts that will be written by check, bearing in mind that if you write a check in January for the full year's insurance, the full amount of the check is put in the January column and nothing else is entered for the rest of the year (this procedure is quite different when you post the payment to your accounting records). Some of the expense items listed in this cash flow statement may not be applicable to your business, and some may be missing. Add and subtract where necessary. Try to make all categories as appropriate to your situation as possible and connected to your bookkeeping system.

NOTE A bill, mailed check, or purchase order placed with a supplier is not a cash expenditure. A check that clears your bank account is a cash expenditure. By keeping all of the above in mind you can forecast cash flow in a reasonably intelligent manner. Remember, depreciation of machinery, buildings and other equipment and furniture should not be included in a cash flow statement.

4a. *Inventory and Raw Material Purchases* – Estimate inventory purchases intended to be resold to the public during the month. Also, include any parts and materials used to manufacture goods intended for sale. You may find it useful to further break down this section to keep track of key items and further control costs.

The person who doesn't know where his next dollar is coming from usually doesn't know where his last dollar went.
ANON

✳

Why is there so much month left at the end of the money?
JOHN BARRYMORE

PROFIT TIPS

Cash flow problems can result from poorly adjusted markups, pilferage, and incorrect tax reporting.

✳

A/R collections can kill you. Even if you turn a profit every month after startup, if you don't have a sufficient cash cushion to ride out the payment period, by the time your customers actually pay you, you will be flat broke and out of business, with not even one cent to buy your next month's stocks.

Additional worksheets, forms, and business letters are available online at BFORMS.COM.

✳

4b. *Staff Salaries and Wages* – Estimate all base salaries and wages, as well as overtime or bonuses paid. You may want to break down this category further to keep track of administrative, manufacturing, and selling labor costs.

4c. *Payroll Expenses* – Estimate payroll expenses including paid vacations, paid sick leave, health insurance, unemployment insurance, and payroll taxes. This figure is usually between 10% and 45% of the amount for "Staff Salaries and Wages."

4d. *Outside Labor and Services* – Estimate expenses, if any, for outside labor or temporary services for specialized or overflow work, as well as subcontracting and consulting needs.

4e. *General Supplies* – Estimate expenses for office and operating supplies (supplies are items purchased for use in the business but are not for resale).

4f. *Repairs and Maintenance* – Estimate amounts needed for periodic expenditures such as painting or decorating.

4g. *Advertising* – Estimate expenses for marketing your products or services. Amount should be adequate to maintain sales volume.

4h. *Car and Travel* – Estimate expenses for use of company vehicle if any. Include parking charges, gas, oil, maintenance, insurance, and other related expenses.

4i. *Shipping and Delivery* – Estimate shipping, delivery, postage, and freight costs.

4j. *Legal and Accounting Fees* – Estimate expenses for legal and bookkeeping services.

4k. *Rent and Lease Payments* – Estimate rent or leasehold payments. Enter payments only when you pay them. If you pay in three-month chunks, enter payments every three months. Do not split them up as you would on an income projection.

4l. *Telephone* – Estimate phone charges, including long-distance and modem charges.

4m. *Utilities* – Estimate water, heat, light, and power consumption charges.

4n. *Insurance* – Estimate amounts needed for coverage on business property and products including fire and liability, as well as workers' compensation. Exclude executive life insurance. This should be included in owner's withdrawal.

4o. *Licenses and Permits* – Estimate amount needed for licenses and permits.

4p. *Interest Charges* – Estimate interest charges on loans, bank overdrafts, lines of credit, and accounts payable. Bear in mind that if the purpose of your cash flow statement is to help you figure out how much money your want to borrow, this interest figure may be difficult to estimate. Consequently, you may decide to leave it blank for now and fill it in later when you have a better idea how much loan funds you need to borrow. Of course, you will then have to update your statement.

4q. *Income Tax Payments* – Enter estimated quarterly tax payments to the IRS. Note that if yours is a new business, no quarterly payments may be necessary until after your first fiscal year, since the IRS has no information to calculate your payments. Nevertheless, funds should be set aside to meet these payments.

4r. *Other Taxes* – Estimate real estate taxes, inventory taxes, sales tax, and excise tax.

4s. *Other Operating Expenses* – Estimate any other operating expenses for which separate accounts would not be practical such as dues and subscriptions, packaging costs, and miscellaneous expenses incurred prior to first month projections and paid for after startup.

4t. *Loan Principal Payments* – Estimate monthly principal repayment amounts for any operating loans, vehicle loans, or mortgages on buildings or property. For example, if you borrow $43,000 at 6% over five years to partially finance a land purchase, and your monthly payment is $831.31, then following your amortization schedule, you would enter $516.31 here for your first monthly payment and $315.00 as an interest charge in 4p. For your second monthly payment, you would enter $518.89 here and $312.42 in 4p, and so on (for simplicity, you may wish to combine finance charges and principal charges and title this category *Loan Payment*).

4u. *Fixed Asset Payments* – Estimate any monthly amounts paid for renting, leasing, or financing equipment.

4v. *Capital Expenditures and Startup Costs* – Enter your startup costs here. As well, estimate money spent over the course of the year for the purchase of fixed depreciable assets such as vehicles, leasehold improvements, filing cabinets, or computers. List the amount when cash disbursements are actually made or checks written.

4w. *Owner's Withdrawal* – Estimate here the amount you need to live on, the amount you pay yourself, or the amount you expect to withdraw from the company bank account for whatever reason. Include payments for such things as owner's income tax, social security, health insurance, executive life insurance premiums, as well as cash dividends paid to stockholders.

5. **Total CASH OUT** – Total all cash payments for the month.

6. **CASH FLOW** – Cash flow is calculated by subtracting *Total CASH IN* by *Total CASH OUT*. If the result is a loss, put it in brackets, use a red pen (black for a gain), or use a negative sign. If the *deficit* is large, an operating loan will be required or increased to cover the deficit. If the *surplus* is large, excess funds should be applied to any existing operating loans.

   NOTE Some owner-managers also like to include a *Cumulative Cash Flow* entry. *Cumulative Cash Flow* adds the previous month's total to the new month's total.

7. **CASH Balance** – *Cash Balance*, also referred to as "closing cash balance" or "cash position," is calculated by adding your *Beginning Cash Balance* to your *Cash Flow*. This result is then automatically posted to the next month as your beginning or opening cash balance.

8. **Essential OPERATING DATA** – The following estimated data totals are NOT part of a cash flow statement but they do provide important information for management decision-making.

8a. *Sales Volume* – Estimate sales volume for the month. This figure also includes expected accounts receivable sales. Estimated sales volume is a very important figure and should be projected carefully, taking into account the size of your facility and employee output, as well as realistic consumer demand.

A "Cash Flow Statement"—your "Yearly Budget" — becomes more useful to you as a business owner if you use it to regularly evaluate actual figures compared with your projections. A "Quarterly Cash Flow Budget Analysis" can help you gain more control over your business operations (see page 369). You can use this worksheet to compare "projected" cash flow with "actual" results, and also determine if any loans are needed.

✳

Effort means nothing without results.

JOE COSSMAN

DEPRECIATION
can be a tricky expense to estimate. FIRST, there is "management depreciation," where an owner distributes the cost of a capital asset over its useful life less salvage value. For example, a $12,000 machine, projected to last ten years before it must be replaced and having a salvage value of $2,000, might be depreciated at $1,000 a year using the straight line method. SECOND, there is "income tax depreciation." This is the amount the government will allow you to depreciate and claim as an expense.

8b. *Accounts Receivable* – This figure includes previous unpaid credit sales plus current month's credit sales, less amounts received that month. Don't forget to deduct anticipated bad debts.

8c. *Bad Debts* – Your bad debts ratio can be projected using industry standards as a percentage of your total accounts receivable. Bad debts should be subtracted from 8b in month anticipated.

8d. *Inventory on Hand* – This figure is estimated by taking your estimated last month's inventory plus merchandise received and/or manufactured in the current month minus the amount sold in the current month.

8e. *Accounts Payable* – This figure is estimated by taking your previous estimated accounts payable plus current month's payable minus amount paid during month.

8f. *Depreciation* – This figure is established by your accountant, or can be estimated by taking the value of all equipment and dividing it by its useful life (in months) as allowed by the IRS.

8g. *Loan Required* – If cash flow is negative, estimate any loans that may be required.

Sample Cash Flow Assumptions

[I/We] project that we will be able to generate sufficient revenues from operations to meet our initial needs after receiving a loan of $[XX]. A positive cash flow is anticipated after [five] months of operation. However, our projections have been made in industries that have never been fully addressed. They are based upon our experience and an analysis of market conditions. Should sales not meet initial projections, adjustments will be made to inventory levels and other long-term commitments decreased or postponed. Other changes include [describe other cash flow strategies].

$ucce$$ Story ➡ Joe Cossman: The "Messiah" of Marketing

Joe Cossman grossed more than $30 million selling mail order ant farms, toy soldiers, garden sprinklers, fly-poison, potato spud guns, and shrunken heads. He is the all-time "master" at securing marketing rights for unusual, even failed products, and turning them into winners. The *Wall Street Journal* has called him "The Messiah of the free enterprise system." After World War II, Cossman started working in his kitchen after hours from his $35-a-week job. His first successful product made him $30,000 in less than one month. In his book, *How I made $1 Million in Mail Order*, Cossman describes how someone once brought him an unsuccessful mail order product and offered to sell him the rights. The product consisted of earrings with little bells attached. Cossman renamed the product "mother-in-law earrings," targeted them to newlyweds, and managed to turn this mail order loser into a mail order winner. Cossman claims he spends at least one full day a month at the library.

Prepare a 12-month and three-year income projection. Prepare a cash flow statement. State assumptions made.

Pro Forma Financial Statements

Collect facts and figures you need to prepare the following five financial statements:

| ❑ **12-month Income Projection** – Summarizes profit and loss projections for 12 months. Also known as a Pro Forma Profit & Loss Statement. | ❑ **Three-year Income Projection** – Summarizes your profit and loss projections for the next three years. | ❑ **Cash Flow Statement** – Summarizes cash flow projections for the next year of operation and annually for another two years. | ❑ **Breakeven Analysis** – Projects the amount of revenues your company needs to break even. | ❑ **Pro Forma Balance Sheet** – Summarizes balance sheet projections annually for each of the next 3 to 5 years. |

12-month Income Projection

Using the worksheets on pages 283 and 285, estimate sales and receipts, cost of sales, gross profit margin, expenses, and net profit for the next 12 months. Summarize results below:

Sample 12-month Projection		
XYZ Supply Company Inc.		
Sales	523,063	100%
Cost of Goods	366,144	70%
Gross Profit Margin	156,919	30%
Operating Expenses:		
Advertising	3,605	0.7%
Depreciation	4,000	0.8%
Insurance	2,900	0.6%
Legal and accounting expenses	4,412	0.8%
Office expenses	2,995	0.6%
Rent	24,000	4.6%
Repairs and maintenance	437	0.1%
Salaries	34,650	6.6%
Telephone and utilities	6,683	1.3%
Miscellaneous	8,507	1.6%
Total operating expenses	91,919	17.6%
Net profit (before taxes)	65,000	12.4%

State any assumptions made in your projections (refer to page 272):

Sample: In preparing a 12-month income projection for [company], we made the following assumptions: Revenues would increase by $[XX] after we land the Chrysler account. Based on a CPI of 6%, variable costs would increase by 0.5% per month.

Three-year Income Projection

Using the worksheet on page 286, estimate sales and expenses for the next three years. Summarize results below. State any <u>assumptions made</u> *(refer to page 272):*

SAMPLE 3-YEAR INCOME PROJECTION (YEAR 1)		
Three-year Projection FOR: *Sam's Pizza Palace* As OF: 12/31/2004		
	YEAR 1	
GROSS SALES (less returns and allowances)	$490,000	
LESS Cost of Goods Sold (COGS)	200,000	
GROSS PROFIT	$290,000	
LESS VARIABLE Expenses (controllable) (selling)	165,000	
LESS FIXED Expenses (overhead) (administrative)	95,000	
TOTAL Operating Expenses (fixed + variable)	270,000	
ADD OTHER INCOME (dividends and interest):	500	
LESS Interest Expense	3,000	
NET INCOME (Before Taxes)	$17,500	
LESS Estimated Tax Payments	1,900	
NET INCOME (After Taxes)	$15,600	

<u>*Brainstorm*</u> *– Using the "Business Operating Expenses" form on the next page, check expense items applicable to your business. Write an account number for each to coincide with your accounting system (see page 109). Clarify any important expense variables:*

Sample: Providing sales reach $490,000, a key success factor in our first year is to keep variable selling and PT labor costs below 38% of sales and preferably less than 34%. To control labor costs, we hire PT college students.

Cash Flow Statement

Using the "Period Ending Cash Flow Projection" form on page 284, estimate YEARLY sources of cash flowing INTO and OUT OF your business. After completing this form, complete the 12-month Cash Flow Statement on page 287 (this form is also available online at bforms.com). Summarize results below:

Sample: After receiving a loan of $[XX], we project being able to generate sufficient revenues from operations to generate a positive cash flow after eight months of operation. However, our projections have been made in industries that have never been fully addressed. They are based upon an analysis of market conditions and our experience. Should sales not meet initial projections, adjustments will be made to inventory levels and other long-term commitments decreased or postponed until our total loan obligation is paid in full.

Expense Accounts
500–599

Operating Expenses are all the costs associated with supporting your product or service—your *Cost of Goods Sold* is not considered an operating expense.

When preparing your financial statements, you can break down operating expenses into **fixed costs**, also known as "overhead," "administrative," or "general and administrative" expenses, and **variable costs**, also known as "controllable," "selling," or "sales and marketing" expenses. It is not necessary to do this, but depending on your business, it can provide you with more useful information.

To get ideas for the best expense categories for your business, review as many worksheets as you can. Make sure you select categories related to your accounting system. The more careful you are about this now, the easier it will be to record expenses, prepare financial statements for analysis, and determine your tax liability.

Strategies

1. *Select expense categories based on*:
   ❑ the categories commonly used within your industry ❑ the categories your accountant recommends ❑ the categories that best help you understand your financial position ❑ the categories that match your accounting software ❑ the categories outlined as accepted business deductions by tax authorities.

2. *Don't have too many accounts*. It is not the case that the more accounts you have the better. Too many accounts means too much accounting. Find a balance between choosing the LEAST number of accounts to give you the MOST useful information for financial analysis and year-to-year comparisons.

3. *Select general headings for your expense items that really capture what your business is about*. Keep related expenses together, such as meals and entertainment, vehicle and travel, and shipping and delivery. NOTE: Get an accountant to review your expense accounts.

Variable Expenses

Variable expenses are closely related to the sale of your product or service. They vary and are usually directly proportional to your volume of business. Divide these costs into subcategories customized to your business.

AC#	Variable Cost	Summary
	❑ Variable Expenses	
	❑ Controllable Expenses	
	❑ Selling Expenses	
	❑ Sales and Marketing	

AC#	Variable Cost	General
	❑ Advertising and Marketing	
	❑ Costs of Goods Sold (not an operating expense)	
	❑ Dues and Subscriptions	
	❑ Interest Charges	
	❑ Legal and Accounting	
	❑ Meals and Entertainment	
	❑ Repairs and Maintenance	
	❑ Sales Wages and Salaries	
	❑ Shipping and Delivery	
	❑ Supplies	
	❑ Vehicle, Gas, and Oil	
	❑ Other Expenses	

AC#	Variable Cost	Subcategories
	❑ Depreciation Expense for Production Equipment	
	❑ Education and Training	
	❑ Factory Labor	
	❑ Fulfillment of Orders	
	❑ Inventory Holding and Storage Expenses	
	❑ Investment Expenses	
	❑ Payroll Expenses	
	❑ Postage and Shipping	
	❑ Promotions	
	❑ Research and Development	
	❑ Sales Commissions	
	❑ Software Purchases (may need to be depreciated, and if so, cannot be listed as expense)	
	❑ Trade Shows	
	❑ Travel	
	❑ Web Hosting Fees	

Fixed Expenses

Fixed expenses remain the same regardless of how many products or services you sell, even during slow periods. These costs can be divided into subcategories customized to your business.

AC#	Fixed Cost	Summary
	❑ Fixed Expenses	
	❑ Overhead	
	❑ Administrative	
	❑ General and Administrative	

AC#	Fixed Cost	General
	❑ Bad Debts	
	❑ Depreciation	
	❑ Employee Benefits	
	❑ Income Tax	
	❑ Insurance	
	❑ Licenses and Permits	
	❑ Office Salaries	
	❑ Office Supplies	
	❑ Rent	
	❑ Telephone	
	❑ Utilities	
	❑ Miscellaneous Expenses	

AC#	Fixed Cost	Subcategories
	❑ Depreciation Expense for Buildings and Renovations	
	❑ Depreciation Expense for Displays and Fixtures	
	❑ Depreciation Expense for Office Equipment	
	❑ Deprec. Expense for Vehicles	
	❑ Domain Name Expense	
	❑ Equipment Rental or Leasing	
	❑ Factory Overhead	
	❑ Furniture and Equipment Purchases (these must usually be depreciated, and if so, cannot be listed as expenses)	
	❑ Mortgage Expenses	
	❑ Pension Plans	
	❑ Profit Sharing Plans	
	❑ Property Tax	
	❑ Software Leasing	
	❑ Software Tech Support	
	❑ Telecommunications	

<u>*Period Ending Cash Flow Projections*</u> – *In preparation to complete the 12-month Cash Flow Statement on page 287, estimate YEARLY sources of cash flowing INTO and OUT OF your business (put an asterisk * by any monthly estimates made; multiply by 12 to get yearly estimates):*

Sources of Cash Worksheet	Cash to Be Paid Out Worksheet
Cash Flowing INTO Your Business	**Cash Flowing OUT OF Your Business**

Sources of Cash Worksheet — Cash Flowing INTO Your Business

From _____ *to* _____

Cash on Hand (beginning of period)

Sales and Revenues
- Sales
- Service Income
- Deposits on Sales or Services
- A/R Collections

Other Income
- Interest Income
- Sale of Long-term Assets

Liabilities
- Loans Received

Equity
- Owner Investments (sole-p, part.)
- Contributed Capital (corp.)
- Sale of Stock (corp.)
- Venture Capital

Other Cash Sources

_____

TOTAL CASH AVAILABLE

* *monthly estimate*

What *will your cash flow be at the year's end?*
When *will your company turn a profit? If your business has a negative cash flow for more than three months, how will you avoid cash flow problems (see page 276)? Will you still be able to make loan payments? State any* <u>*assumptions made:*</u>

Cash to Be Paid Out Worksheet — Cash Flowing OUT OF Your Business

Startup Capital Expenditures
- Business License (annual expense)
- DBA Filing Fee (one-time cost)
- Other Startup Costs:

_____

Inventory
- Cash Out for Items for Resale
- Raw Materials Purchases

TOTAL Startup Expenses
- Variable Expenses (controllable)
- Advertising
- Car and Travel
- Shipping and Delivery
- General Supplies
- Legal and Accounting Fees
- Outside Labor and Services
- Packaging Costs
- Payroll Expenses
- Repairs and Maintenance
- Sales Salaries
- Miscellaneous Direct Expenses

TOTAL Variable Expenses

Fixed Expenses (overhead)
- Administrative Salaries
- Insurance
- Interest Charges
- Licenses and Permits
- Rent Payments
- Telephone
- Utilities
- Miscellaneous Indirect Expenses

TOTAL Fixed Expenses

Long-term Asset Purchases
- Fixed Asset Payments
- Liability Payments
- Debts, Loans and A/P's
- Income Tax
- Other Taxes

Owner Equity
- Owner's Withdrawal

TOTAL CASH to be PAID OUT

* *monthly estimate*

12-month Income Record or Projection

	Industry %	Jan	Feb	Mar	Apr	May	Jun	Jul	Aug	Sep	Oct	Nov	Dec	Annual Total	%
Gross Sales (revenues)	100%													$	100%
Cost of Goods Sold (COGS)														$	
Gross Profit															
Controllable Expenses															
Salaries and Wages															
Payroll Expenses															
Legal and Accounting															
Advertising and Marketing															
Automobile															
Office Supplies															
Dues and Subscriptions															
Meals and Entertainment															
Repairs and Maintenance															
1.															
2.															
3.															
Miscellaneous														$	
Total Controllable Expenses															
Fixed Expenses															
Rent															
Depreciation															
Utilities															
Insurance															
Licenses and Permits															
1.															
2.															
3.															
Miscellaneous														$	
Total Fixed Expenses														$	
Total Expenses														$	
Operating Profit															
Other income (interest income)															
Other expenses (interest expense)														$	
Net Profit (loss) Before Taxes															
Taxes (Federal, State, Local)															
Net Profit (loss) After Taxes														$	

Three-year Projection FOR: **As OF:**

	YEAR 1	YEAR 2	YEAR 3

GROSS SALES
    LESS Returns and Allowances

$		

    LESS Sales Tax (if included in sales)

    LESS COST OF GOODS SOLD:
        Inventory at Beginning of Fiscal Period
        ADD Cost of Goods Purchased During Fiscal Period
        ADD Freight and Delivery Charges
        LESS Purchased Returns
        LESS Inventory at the End of the Fiscal Period

    TOTAL Cost of Goods Sold

GROSS PROFIT (GS – COGS)

$		

Gross Profit (as a percentage of sales)

		%

    LESS VARIABLE Controllable Selling Expenses
        Accounting and Legal Fees
        Advertising and Marketing
        Fulfillment (Packaging and Shipping)
        Meals and Entertainment
        Motor Vehicle Expenses (except Depreciation Allowance)
        Office Supplies
        Repairs and Maintenance
        Sales Salaries and Wages
        1.
        2.
        Other Variable Expenses

    LESS FIXED Overhead Administrative Expenses
        Administrative Salaries and Wages
        Bad Debts
        Business Tax, Fees, Licenses, Dues, and Subscriptions
        Depreciation
        Insurance
        Rent Payments
        Payroll Expenses and Taxes
        Property Taxes (list here or include in Estimated Tax)
        Telephone and Utilities (Heat, Hydro)
        1.
        2.
        Other Fixed Expenses
    TOTAL Operating Expenses (fixed + variable)

OPERATING PROFIT (GP – OE)

$		

    ADD OTHER INCOME:
        Interest from Bank Accounts
        Royalties and Dividends on Stock
        Gains from Sale of Fixed Assets
        Misc. Income
    LESS Interest Expense (from loans or credit)

Net Profit Before Taxes (OP + other income – int. exp)

$		

    LESS Estimated Tax Payments (federal, state, local)

NET PROFIT After Taxes

$		

Net Profit After Taxes (as a % of sales)

		%

CASH FLOW STATEMENT

Name of Business: _____ ☐ Projected ☐ Actual Type: _____ Date: _____

	Jan	Feb	Mar	Apr	May	Jun	Jul	Aug	Sep	Oct	Nov	Dec	T
										FIRST OF MONTH			
Beginning Cash Balance													

CASH IN

	Jan	Feb	Mar	Apr	May	Jun	Jul	Aug	Sep	Oct	Nov	Dec	T
Cash Sales													
A/R Collections													
Interest Income													
Sale of Fixed Assets													
Loans Received													
Other Cash Sources													
Total CASH IN													

CASH OUT

	Jan	Feb	Mar	Apr	May	Jun	Jul	Aug	Sep	Oct	Nov	Dec	T
Inventory, Raw Mater.													
Staff Salaries and Wages													
Payroll Expenses													
Outside Labor													
General Supplies													
Repairs and Maintenance													
Advertising													
Car and Travel													
Shipping and Delivery													
Legal and Account. Fees													
Rent and Lease Payments													
Telephone													
Utilities													
Insurance													
Licenses and Permits													
Interest Charges													
Income Tax Payments													
Other Taxes													
Other Operating Exp.													
1.													
2.													
Loan Principal Payments													
Fixed Asset Payments													
Capital Expenditures													
Owner's Withdrawal													
Total CASH OUT													

	Jan	Feb	Mar	Apr	May	Jun	Jul	Aug	Sep	Oct	Nov	Dec	T
										END OF MONTH			
CASH FLOW													
CASH Balance													

(non-cash flow info)

	Jan	Feb	Mar	Apr	May	Jun	Jul	Aug	Sep	Oct	Nov	Dec	T
										OPERATING DATA			
Sales Volume													
Accounts Receivable													
Bad Debts													
Inventory on Hand													
Accounts Payable													
Depreciation													
Loan Required													

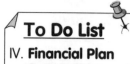

DAY 26

Prepare a breakeven analysis and a pro forma balance sheet.

Breakeven Analysis

A *breakeven point* occurs when fixed and variable expenses exactly match total revenues generated; there is neither profit nor loss. This point can be expressed in total dollars or total units of production (cost of which exactly equals the income produced from its sales). This analysis can be shown mathematically or graphically. Most of the figures needed for a breakeven analysis can be derived from your three-year income projection statement.

Preparing a Breakeven Analysis

Once you have determined all fixed and variable business operating costs, use this information to prepare a *Breakeven Analysis*. In preparing this analysis, you will need to make several assumptions. These **assumptions** often include: (a) selling prices will not change; (b) total fixed expenses will remain the same; and (c) variable expenses will increase and decrease in direct proportion to sales. Following are five methods and examples for preparing a breakeven analysis for retail, service, and manufacturing businesses.

Using the Basic Breakeven Formula

All breakeven formulas are derived from the following *Basic B.E. Formula*:

Basic Breakeven Formula

$$\text{Sales} - \text{Cost} = 0$$

EXAMPLE 1 – Clara Shoemaker plans to start a widget manufacturing company with $40,000 in startup capital. Presently, her competitors are selling similarly featured widgets for $140 per widget. Clara calculates that each widget will cost $80 to manufacture including materials and labor. She also estimates additional variable costs for each widget, including delivery, storage, and returns, to be $10 per widget. Estimating her annual fixed operating expenses to be $10,000 (not including her own salary), she calculates her breakeven point to be:

$$140W - \$10,000 - 90W = 0$$
$$50W = \$10,000$$
$$W = 200$$

The "Basic Breakeven Formula" says that for any business, its breakeven point occurs when sales minus costs equal zero.

＊

Since your breakeven point is not reached until total sales equal total fixed and variable expenses, in the calculation of your breakeven point, you will need to project revenues and expenses far enough ahead, until revenues are greater than expenses. For some startups this might be one month, for other startups, it might be two to three years.

Clara needs to sell 200 widgets to break even. However, if she wants to make a salary of $30,000 to equal her old salary and a profit of $6,000 (15%) on her startup investment of $40,000, she must sell an additional 720 widgets.

$$140W - \$10,000 - 90W = \$36,000$$
$$50W = \$46,000$$
$$\mathbf{W = 920}$$

If, on the other hand, Clara finds out from her market research that it is nearly impossible to sell 920 widgets annually and that a more realistic volume would be 800 widgets, and if she still wants to maintain her profit and salary level, then she has to either increase her selling price or find ways of reducing her variable and fixed costs. To solve this problem, she might decide to make the following four changes: ✦ increase her selling price to $147 per widget ✦ decrease her variable costs by $8 per unit by locating cheaper suppliers ✦ add an extended warranty service to justify her higher prices at a cost of $5 per widget ✦ increase her advertising budget by $2,000. The result would look like this:

$$147W - \$12,000 - 87W = \$36,000$$
$$60W = \$48,000$$
$$\mathbf{W = 800}$$

Calculating the B.E. Point Using Gross Margin

The basic breakeven formula says that for any business, its breakeven point occurs when sales minus cost equal zero. This formula can be expanded upon to include both fixed and variable costs as follows:

$\boxed{\textbf{Sales = FC + VC}}$	S = Sales in dollars at breakeven point FC = Fixed Costs or operating expenses VC = Variable Costs or cost of goods

This formula looks easy enough to use, but substituting values directly into it is impractical, since for a retail business, for example, variable costs (cost of goods sold) cannot be known until the end of the year when inventory levels are taken.

To project a breakeven point, you must instead use a variation of this formula that asks you to first calculate gross profit, change this value to gross margin (also known as the contribution margin), and then substitute

Although a breakeven analysis is a helpful analysis tool to assess a startup operation, it is not essential for every business plan. Bankers are more concerned about whether you can make loan payments and what collateral you can offer. Investors want to know how much shares will appreciate.

A man visiting a small boomtown called Cisco, Texas, noticed a lot of activity at the town's little hotel. Thinking that it was likely that ALL boomtown hotels did exceptionally well, he was immediately intrigued. This young man had always wanted to be a banker but put this idea on hold. His name: Conrad Hilton.
SUCCESS STORY

If your plan is not workable, it is better to learn it now than to realize six months down the road that you are pouring money into a losing venture.

this value back into the original breakeven formula. By calculating your gross margin for all merchandise sold, the price structure that generates a level of revenue to purchase goods, pay operating expenses and make a profit for you, can easily be determined. Using a little math wizardry, this simpler and more practical breakeven formula can be derived as follows:

Since gross profit (GP) is equal to sales (S) minus the cost of sales (VC)

$$GP = S - VC \quad or \quad VC = S - GP$$

And, gross margin (GM) is equal to Gross Profit (GP) divided by sales (S)

$$GM = GP/S \quad or \quad GP = GM \times S$$

And, sales (S) must equal FC plus VC, according to our basic breakeven formula

$$S = FC + VC$$

Then, by substituting the second formula into the first and the first into the third, the following equality results:

$$S = FC + [S - (GM \times S)]$$

Simplifying this equation leaves us with: $FC = GM \times S \quad or \quad S = FC/GM$

$$\boxed{\text{B.E. Point}} = \frac{\text{FC (operating expenses)}}{\text{GM (gross margin)}}$$

EXAMPLE 2 – To get a feel for this formula, let's look at the following example. Suppose Jane Bundy opens up a shoe store and sells shoes for $40 a pair. If her cost is $25 per pair then her gross margin per pair is $15 or 37.5% of the total.

Selling price = $40 or 100%
Cost of shoes = $25 or 62.5%
Gross Margin = $15 or 37.5%

If she calculates her operating expenses (fixed costs) to be $75,000 per year, her breakeven point would be:

FC ($75,000)/GM (37.5%) = **$200,000**

Sales of $200,000 means Jane must sell 5,000 pairs of shoes at $40 per pair to break even. However, she projects that this is unlikely. Instead, she decides to raise her price, which will in turn raise her gross margin. However, a question remaining is: How much will she have to raise her price to break even?

Cost of Goods Sold
(COGS) = inventory at beginning of period plus purchases during the period minus inventory at end of period.

✱

Gross Margin *(GM) is the same as Gross Profit Margin (GPM), which is the same as Contribution Margin (CM). These terms are defined as the average percentage of gross income realized after COGS, that is, the portion of sales available to pay fixed costs expressed as a percentage.*

Determining that she can sell shoes for $50 a pair, she calculates her new breakeven point as follows:

Selling price = $50 or 100%
Cost of shoes = $25 or 50%
Gross Margin = $25 or 50%

With operating expenses of $75,000, the sales volume to break even is:

FC (75,000)/GM (50%) = **$150,000**

At a price of $50 per pair, Jane now has to sell 3,000 pairs of shoes to break even. She is confident she can sell this volume; however, she will not make a profit selling at $50 a pair. Therefore, she has to again rethink her strategy. She decides she would like to realize a profit of 10% on her operating or fixed costs ($75,000 × 10% = $7,500). To calculate the volume of sales required to earn this profit, she adds the profit to the fixed costs. If she holds the price at $50 for a gross margin of 50%, the sales needed to realize this profit are:

FC + profit ($75,000 + $7,500)/GM (50%) = **$165,000**

To generate $165,000 in sales, she must sell 3,300 pairs of shoes at $50 per pair. This level of sales will cover her variable expenses (cost of goods), her fixed expenses (operating expenses), and generate a profit of $7,500. However, if she is still not confident she can sell this volume of merchandise, and realizes that she has little or no competition, then she may instead decide to raise her gross margin to 55%. She would then calculate her new pricing strategy as follows:

Unit selling price = Unit Costs of Shoes/VC% =
($25)/VC% (.45) = $55.56 or **$56** selling price

Unit selling price = 100% = $56
Variable cost = 45% = $25
Gross margin = 55% = $31

With total sales of $150,000 and cost of sales of $67,500, her gross margin is $82,500. With fixed costs of $75,000, her profit margin is $7,500.

Calculating the B.E. Point Using Markup Percentage

The formula used in the previous example can be easily modified to use markup percentage instead of gross margin as one of the unknown vari-

To get profit without risk, experience without danger, and reward without work, is as impossible as it is to live without being born.

A. P. GOUTHEY

Reducing business overhead costs, such as rent, utilities, and interest, immediately lowers your breakeven point. When your breakeven point is lowered, you can reach profitability sooner.

PROFIT TIP

ables. Since markup percentage is virtually the same as gross margin, the breakeven point can be determined as follows:

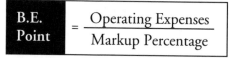

$$\text{B.E. Point} = \frac{\text{Operating Expenses}}{\text{Markup Percentage}}$$

EXAMPLE 3 – If your operating expenses are $50,000 and average markup is 30%, then your required sales to break even can be calculated as follows:

B.E. Point = $50,000/30% = **$166,667**

Calculating the B.E. Point for a Service Provider

Another variation of the *Basic B.E. Formula*, as shown below, can be used to calculate the breakeven point of a service provider—or any other business for that matter—by adding up enough projected revenues and expenses beyond a point or fiscal year's end that you know revenues are greater than expenses.

EXAMPLE 4 – Jan London plans to open a beauty salon. She estimates her fixed costs after one year to be $17,000, variable costs to be $21,000, and total sales to be $51,000. To calculate the *Volume of Sales* she needs to break even, she uses the following formula:

$$\text{B.E. Point} = \frac{\text{Fixed Costs}}{[1-(\text{Variable Costs}/\text{Sales})]}$$

B.E. Point =
$17,000/[1 – ($21,000/$51,000)] =
$17,000/(1 – 0.41) =
$17,000/0.59 = **$28,813**

B.E. Point = volume of sales to break even
Fixed Costs = administrative, depreciation, rent, insurance, loan interest, etc.
Variable Costs = selling, inventory purchases, advertising, packaging, wages, etc.
Sales = the corresponding sales volume or income from the sale of goods and services over the same specified period as used to determine your variable costs

Calculating the B.E. Point for a Manufacturer

Using still another variation of the *Basic B.E. Formula*, a manufacturer can calculate the number of product sales required to break even.

EXAMPLE 5 – James Billings plans to start a tennis racquet manufacturing company. He calculates his fixed costs to be $80,000 per year and his variable costs to be $40 per racquet. His selling price to suppliers and retailers is $90. To calculate the *Number of Units* he needs to sell to break even, he uses the following formula:

$$\boxed{\begin{array}{c} \textbf{B.E.} \\ \textbf{Point} \end{array}} = \frac{\text{Fixed Costs}}{\text{Selling Price} - \text{Variable Cost/Unit}}$$

B.E. Point =
$80,000/$90 – $40 =
$80,000/$50 = **1,600 units**

B.E. Point = # of units to break even
Fixed Costs = rent, salaries, depreciation, etc.
Variable Cost/Unit = your costs per unit
Selling Price = what you charge suppliers

What to Do With Your Results

Once you have figured out your breakeven point, stop and evaluate how realistic it is. If it's too high, review your cost figures and breakdown of yearly expenses on your *12-month* and *Three-year Income Projection*. Compare them with industry operating ratios. If any of your cost items seem too low or too high, change them. With your revised figures, work out a new breakeven analysis.

If it still doesn't look right, think about ways of decreasing variable and fixed costs, as well as whether you can raise your per unit selling price (as long as it won't drastically affect sales volume). If it looks better, don't pat yourself on the back just yet. Get an accountant, SCORE counselor, or business consultant familiar with the type of business you are planning to start to take a good look at your figures. They may see something that you have missed out completely. The bottom line is don't back your startup plan with your life's savings until your breakeven point is truly reachable.

Drawing a Breakeven Graph

To graph the results of your breakeven analysis, use the worksheet on page 297 or some graph paper. Use the horizontal axis to represent sales volume in dollars (or number of units sold), and the vertical axis to represent expenses in dollars (refer to graph #1 and graph #2 on the next two pages).

EXAMPLE – In *example #4* on page 292, Jan London knows her fixed costs are $17,000 per year and variable costs are $21,000 for $51,000 of sales. To prepare a breakeven graph, the following needs to be done:

Line 1 – Draw a straight line to represent the dollar value of all fixed costs.

Line 2 – Starting from zero, draw a sloping line to a point towards the end of the graph where total sales equals total expenses (e.g., $45,000 in "total sales" = $45,000 of "total revenues"). This line represents total revenues.

The basic principle of turning ideas into big money is to seize every money building idea and work with it until the idea fits your purpose, decide on the steps needed to make it work, and then proceed to do it as soon as possible.
DUANE NEWCOMB

The worst crime against working people is a company which fails to operate at a profit.
SAMUEL GOMPERS
✳
Having more money does not insure happiness. People with ten million dollars are no happier than people with nine million dollars.
HOBART BROWN

Line 3 – Starting from the fixed costs line, draw a sloping line to a point where the amount of variable expenses derived from a certain amount of sales is known (e.g., $51,000 in sales yields $17,000 + $21,000 = $38,000 in expenses). This line represents total expenses. The intersection of lines 2 and 3 is the breakeven point and should agree with your mathematical calculation ($28,813, see page 292). The shaded triangular area below that point represents company losses, while the shaded triangular area above represents potential profits.

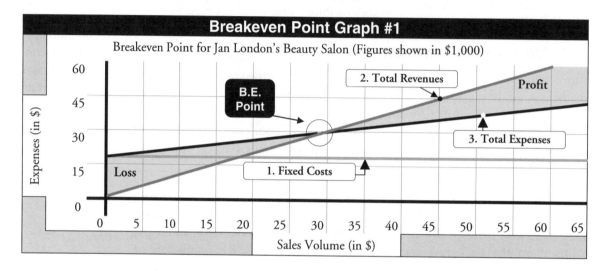

Sample Breakeven Statement

The following table shows our breakeven point:

Profit	Revenue	Fixed Costs	Variable Costs
$0	$45,000.00	$11,400.00	$33,600.00

It is projected that [company name] will break even by [month] of [20XX]. Sales are projected to be $[XX] above breakeven by [month, 20XX]. The gross profit margin for our first year is [X]% totaling $[XX]. If we do not reach our breakeven point as projected, we will implement the following cost-cutting strategies: [describe]. In addition [company name] will [describe additional sources of cash OR new sources of revenues].

Using a GM, BE, ROI, and Projected Profit Sheet

A GM, BE, ROI, and Projected Profit Sheet can be used to determine the breakeven point for a single item (see page 299). Follow steps 1 to 34. Explanations of key terms are provided as needed. Use the results to then draw a graph as shown on page 295.

A rush to market with complex solutions that fail to provide business benefits at reasonable costs for small businesses will, in fact, increase near term opportunity, but severely reduce the long term potential of the technology.

ANTHONY PICARDI
Senior VP of Global
Software, IDC

Pro Forma Balance Sheet

Worthy of inclusion in a business plan is a *Pro Forma Balance Sheet* reflecting sources and uses of equity funds and borrowed funds before your company begins operations. Pro forma balance sheets may have a variety of components, but all have a common format (see pages 298, 301, 302, and 314). If requesting a loan, you may find it prudent to ask your banker for the form they use. It will make it easier for them to evaluate the health of your business using a form they are familiar with. A summary statement of your balance sheet should also be included (see sample below).

A *Balance Sheet* examines **Assets** (anything within your business of monetary value); **Liabilities** (debts to creditors); and **Net Worth** (the owner's claim).

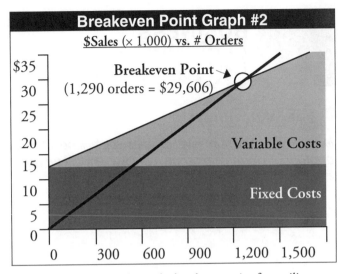

The following graph shows the breakeven point for mailing 6,000 brochures for Jack's Jewelry Warehouse promoting a gold chain that sells for $22.95. Fixed costs are $12,500. Gross Margin is $9.69/unit (B.E. = FC/GM = 1290).

Net Worth = Assets – Liabilities

- **Projected Balance Sheet –** In addition to requiring a *Pro Forma Balance Sheet* for "day one," lenders or investors may also require a *Projected Balance Sheet* for the "end-of-year" or key target dates in the life of your business (you can use the form on page 298 or 314). It is important to show how any infusions of capital from a lender or other sources will affect your financial position.

Sample Pro Forma Balance Sheet Summary Statements

Initially, [company name] books will be kept using [an Expense Journal and an Income Journal]. For FY [20XX], [I/we] will be upgrading to a computerized accounting package to better monitor our financial performance. Information for current financial statements will be compiled monthly and reviewed against our pro forma statements. If we find that we are consistently over budget, appropriate actions will be taken to adjust costs and other budget projections. Our next step will be to [recheck our cost structure] and [reevaluate our markup percentage on products] to make certain we are obtaining the best balance of sales and profits.

Even if you plan to spread the purchase of some assets through the year, for the purposes of your pro forma balance sheet, assume that all assets will be provided at startup.

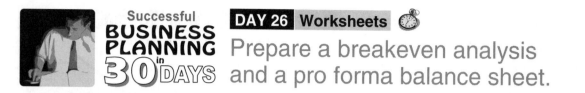

Prepare a breakeven analysis
and a pro forma balance sheet.

Breakeven Analysis

*Indicate the minimum level of sales you will need to cover all fixed and variable costs (choose an appropriate formula as shown below). Project **when** your breakeven point will occur:*

Sample: With a projected gross margin of 56.3% and fixed costs at $72,400, it is estimated that Hawaii Massage Supply will achieve its breakeven point of $128,600 by March, 2005. Sales are projected to be $200,000 above breakeven by January, 2006. HMS's gross profit margin for FY 2006 is estimated to fall to 47% once initial inventory loan has been fully paid. If 2005 sales fall short of projections, we will implement the following revenue building and cost cutting strategies: [describe].

Breakeven Point in *Sales Dollars* or *Units* =

See Examples 2 and 3	*See Example 4*	*See Example 5*
Fixed Costs	Fixed Costs	Fixed Costs
[GM]	[1 – (Variable Costs/Sales)]	[Selling Price – Variable Cost/Unit]

=

B. E. Point =

Explain any assumptions made *in making your breakeven calculations (see pages 290–292):*

Sample: Revenue projections for FY 2006 are based on acquiring and maintaining client contracts with [company A, B, and C], as well as labor and materials costs increasing at the rate of inflation. If such costs increase by [X]% over the CPI, we will adjust hourly rates and materials charges accordingly. However, if we fail to acquire the above clients, we will need to rethink our profit centers and business model to remain viable.

Graph your breakeven point:

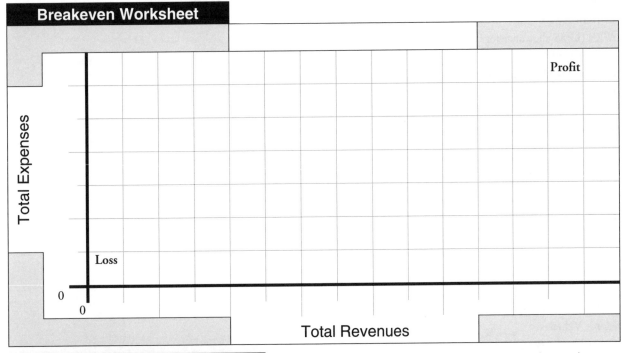

Breakeven Worksheet

Profit

Total Expenses

Loss

0

0

Total Revenues

GM, BE, ROI, and Projected Profit Sheet – *If your business is based on marketing single products, use the breakeven worksheet on page 299. Describe any assumptions made:*

Pro Forma Balance Sheet

Prepare a Pro Forma Balance Sheet using the form on page 298. Outline any estimations or assumptions made, as well as procedures followed. Estimate sources and uses of equity and borrowed funds. Provide proof of equity in Supporting Documents:

NOTE: If seeking a loan, find out if a projected balance sheet, for the year's end or after capital has been injected, is also required.

Sample: Information for current financial statements will be compiled monthly and reviewed against pro forma statements. If we find that we are consistently over budget, we will adjust costs and other projections. Our next step will be to rethink markup percentages on products to make certain we are obtaining the best balance of sales and profits.

PRO FORMA BALANCE SHEET

Balance Sheet FOR: As OF:

Current Assets

A/R's (LESS allowance for bad debts)

Cash in Bank

Cash on Hand (includes Petty Cash)

Inventories (Merchandise)

Prepaid Expenses

Short-term Investments

Long-term Investments

Supplies

Other Current Assets

Total Current Assets   A $

Fixed Assets

Buildings

Land

Furniture and Fixtures

Leasehold Improvements

Materials and Equipment

Motor Vehicles

Other Fixed Assets

Total Fixed Assets   B $

Total Assets (C = A + B)   C $

Current Liabilities

Accounts Payable

Interest Payable

Taxes Payable

Short-term Loans Payable

Other Current Liabilities

Total Current Liabilities   D $

Long-term Liabilities

Long-term Loans Payable

Mortgages

Other Long-term Liabilities

Total Long-term Liabilities   E $

Total Liabilities (F = D + E)   F $

Total Net Worth (G = C – F)   G $

Total Liabilities and Net Worth (H = F + G)   H $

GM, BE, ROI, and PROJECTED PROFIT SHEET

PROMOTION: **Date:**

Notes

Line 11 – Make sure you include return charges and losses usually a factor of .03 to .05 × total sales (i.e., 3% to 5% of total sales).

Line 22 – To determine your total variable costs accurately, anticipate other costs of doing business including: ✦ future markdowns for goods that do not sell quickly enough ✦ shrinkage (theft or disappearance) ✦ miscellaneous transportation and delivery costs ✦ cost of doing any alterations that may be requested by your customer.

Line 23 – Calculating your total variable costs is pretty much the same as calculating your cost of goods sold except that the former is used to calculate the costs for one individual item while the latter is used to calculate the costs of your entire inventory.

Line 28 – Collectively referred to as gross profit, GM (gross margin) is the difference between sales income and the cost of the goods sold before any fixed expenses have been taken out for an individual item. GP (gross profit) is the term used to refer to the total of all gross margins. GP = Sales – Cost of Goods Sold. GM = Total Selling Price – Total Variable Costs.

Line 29 – A list of fixed operating costs can be found on an income projection.

Line 30 – The breakeven point is equal to your overhead or fixed operating costs (O) divided by the difference of your unit sales price (P) minus your unit variable costs (V). B.E. = O/(P – V).

Lines 31–32 – ROI refers to Return on Investment or Net Income = Revenues – Expenses. In graph #2 shown on page 295, Jack's Jewelry Warehouse would have to sell 2,580 units to have a 100% return (net income) on an investment of $12,500.

Item	Description	Formula	Subtotal	Total
	Variable Costs (per unit) and Fixed Operating Costs			
1	Selling Price of Product or Service (do not include sales tax)			
2	ADD Other Charges (postage and handling, etc.)			
3	TOTAL PRICE OF PRODUCT OR SERVICE	1 + 2	$	
4	Owner's Cost of Product or Service			
5	Handling Expense and Order Processing			
6	Package Expenses (mailing carton, tape, etc.)			
7	Shipping (postage or UPS charges)			
8	"Premium" Costs Including Handling (if premium offered)			
9	Special Business Sales, Hidden, or Use Tax, if any	3 × ( ) %		
10	TOTAL COSTS OF FILLING THE ORDER	add 4 to 9	$	
11	Estimated % of Returns (expressed as a decimal)			
12	Postage and Handling of Returns	5 + 7		
13	Refurbishing Returned Merchandise	10% of 3		
14	Total Costs of Handling Returns	12 + 13		
15	CHARGEABLE COSTS OF HANDLING RETURNS	11 × 13		
16	Estimated % of bad debts (expressed as a decimal)			
17	CHARGEABLE COSTS OF BAD DEBTS	3 × 16	$	
18	Estimated % of Sales via Credit Cards (as a decimal)			
19	Credit Card Processing Charge	( ) % of 3		
20	CHARGEABLE COST OF CREDIT	18 × 19	$	
21	ADMINISTRATIVE OVERHEAD PER UNIT		$	
22	OTHER COSTS PER UNIT		$	
23	TOTAL VARIABLE COSTS	10 + 15 + 17 + 20 + 21 + 22	$	
24	Unit Profit After Variable Costs	3 – 23		
25	% of Final Sales (expressed as a decimal)	1.0 – (11)		
26	Net Unit Profit	24 × 25		
27	Credit for Returned Merchandise	4 × 11		
28	GROSS MARGIN (NET PROFIT PER ORDER)	26 + 27	$	
29	TOTAL FIXED OPERATING COSTS (Mailing, Advertising, etc.)		$	
	Profit Calculations			
30	NUMBER OF ORDERS TO BREAK EVEN	29/28		
31	NUMBER OF ORDERS TO OBTAIN 50% ROI	1.5 × 30		
32	NUMBER OF ORDERS TO OBTAIN 100% ROI	2.0 × 30		
33	PROJECTED PROFIT IF ? # OF ORDERS RECEIVED	(# of orders × 28) – (29)	$	
34	PROJECTED PROFIT IF [XX] # OF ORDERS RECEIVED	(# of orders × 28) – (29)	$	

Comments:

DAY 27

Prepare a current income statement, balance sheet, and asset sheet. Calculate financial ratios.

Current Financial Statements

If your business has already been in operation for a year or more, include actual performance statements reflecting your business activities. Specifically, include a current (1) *Income Statement*; (2) *Balance Sheet*; and (3) *Asset Sheet*. You might also consider adding a *Deviation Analysis* and *Market Value Balance Sheet*.

How Detailed Should Financial Statements Be?

Income statements and balance sheets should be limited to a page. For large companies with many accounts, financial schedules can be used to provide details for any summary accounts used. These schedules can be added to your *Supporting Documents* section. For income statements, financial schedules can be used to break down selling expenses, general and administrative expenses, and cost of goods sold. For balance sheets, they can break down asset and liability accounts such as Property Owned and Loans Payable.

Current Income Statement

The *Income Statement*—also referred to as a *Profit and Loss Statement, Income and Expense Statement*, or *Operating Statement*—summarizes the results of all business activity for a specified period. It is the most important financial statement you will prepare each year, as its totals are used to determine your tax liability. It shows all income sources for your business, all expenses incurred in obtaining the income, and the profit or loss resulting. It can also help reveal things like whether you're paying too much rent, whether you need to schedule work to use your truck fleet more efficiently, whether mail should be used instead of telephones, or whether you need to reduce inventory. Analyzing your income statements can also help you pick out strengths and weaknesses of ad campaigns and inventory management practices (see example on the next page and worksheet on page 313; common income statement terms are defined on page 273).

Allocating Depreciation Costs to the Period of Time Covering the Statement – One difficulty in developing an income statement is in properly allocating

If your business has already been in operation for some time, provide income statements and balance sheets for your current year and the last three in your "Supporting Documents" section.

depreciation costs to the period of time covering the statement. Since fixed assets, such as equipment and building costs, cannot be included under *expenses*, to allocate these costs properly, their purchase price must be divided by the expected life in years or months, whichever corresponds to the period covered by the income statement. Using the straight line method of calculating depreciation, purchase prices are charged uniformly over the life of the asset. Ask your accountant for the best method of depreciation for your type of business factoring in tax reporting and management requirements.

> *It sounds extraordinary but it's a fact that balance sheets can make fascinating reading.*
>
> **MARY ARCHER**

Current Balance Sheet

The *Balance Sheet* summarizes the financial position of a business at the time of the report (usually the ending of an accounting cycle). It looks at assets, liabilities, and net worth (owner's equity). If your business possesses more assets than it owes to creditors, your net worth is *positive*. If you owe more money to creditors than you possess in assets, your net worth is *negative*. The balance sheet is useful for purposes of control, management direction, and decision-making. To fill out the balance sheet provided on page 314, use the following steps:

NOTE Figures used to compile your balance sheet are taken from previous balance sheets, as well as your current income statement.

1) **Title the balance sheet.** At the top of the page fill in the legal name of your company and the day the balance sheet was prepared.

2) **List all current assets.** List anything of value that is owned or legally due to your business and can be converted into cash within 12 months of the date of the balance sheet (or during one established cycle of operations).

   Inventories – When listing your inventory, include raw materials on hand, work in progress, and all finished goods either manufactured or purchased for resale.

   Short-term Investments – When listing your short-term investments, list them at either cost or market value, whichever is less (be consistent).

3) **List all long-term investments.** These include all long-term assets such as stocks and bonds that you intend to keep for longer than a year.

Accepted Income Statement and Balance Sheet Formats

INCOME STATEMENT

INCOME from Sales (Gross Sales)
   a. *Net Sales* (gross sales – returns and allowances)
   b. *Cost of Goods Sold*
   c. *Gross Profit* [a – b]

EXPENSES (expenses do not have to be split)
   a. *Selling Expenses* (direct, controllable, variable)
   b. *Administrative Expenses* (indirect, fixed, overhead)
   c. *Depreciation Expense*

INCOME from OPERATIONS (Operating Profit)
(Operating Profit = gross profit – total expenses)
   a. *Other Income* (interest and dividend income)
   b. *Other Expenses* (interest expense)

NET PROFIT (loss) Before Income Taxes
   a. *Taxes* (federal, state, local)

NET PROFIT (loss) After Income Taxes

BALANCE SHEET

ASSETS
   a. *Current Assets*
   b. *Long-term Investments*
   c. *Fixed Assets*

LIABILITIES
   a. *Current Liabilities*
   b. *Long-term Liabilities*

NET WORTH (Assets – Liabilities)
In the case of a *Proprietorship or Partnership*, net worth is equal to the owner's original investment plus earnings after withdrawals. In the case of a *Corporation*, net worth is equal to the sum of contributions by owners or stockholders plus earnings retained after paying dividends.

4) **List all fixed assets.** Fixed assets are listed at cost less depreciation. This is called their net value. However, land is listed at its original purchase price irrespective of its market value.

Accumulated Depreciation – Instead of listing their fixed assets at their "net value," some balance sheets list them at their "original value." However, an additional Accumulated Depreciation account must be added to this kind of balance sheet. The total here is then subtracted from the total of the fixed assets.

Other Fixed Assets (Leased Assets) – If any of your fixed assets are leased, depending on the leasing arrangement, both the value and the liability of the leased property may need to be listed on your balance sheet.

5) **List all current liabilities.** This includes all debts, monetary obligations, and claims payable within 12 months or one cycle of operations.

Short-term Loans Payables – When listing your short-term loans payable, list the balance of principal due on all short-term debt and the current amount due of total balance on notes or loans whose terms exceed 12 months.

Taxes Payable – This account can be split into federal and state income tax, self-employment tax, property tax, and sales tax. Income taxes incurred during the accounting period and yet to be paid can be estimated by your accountant.

6) **List all long-term liabilities.** All long-term liabilities such as loans payable, contracts payable, and mortgages are listed at their outstanding balance less the current portion due (which is listed in short-term loans payable).

7) **List your net worth.** In a proprietorship or partnership, *net worth* is each owner's original investment (capital invested) plus any earnings after withdrawals. In a corporation, *net worth* is usually reflected in a capital stock account, current year earnings less dividends paid, and retained earnings (accumulated earnings up to the period).

8) **Compare your total liabilities and net worth.** The sum of these two amounts must always match that for total assets.

Current Asset Sheet

A *Current Asset Sheet* lists all assets currently in use by your business, how much investment each required, and the source of funds used to capitalize them (see sample on page 306).

Other Financial Statements

Although it may not be sensible to include page after page of financial statements and analysis, it is worth considering what's out there and how they might add to the defensibility of your plan. Three statements of immediate consideration as additions to your *Financial Plan* are described on the next page (more statements are summarized on page 307):

- **Deviation Analysis** – A *Deviation Analysis*, also referred to as *Horizontal Financial Statement Analysis*, usually compares differences in actual income and expenses to projected income and expenses on a month-to-month basis. It helps you spot strengths and weaknesses in your projections and budgeting.

- **Market-value Balance Sheet** – One of the problems in a growing business is that the existing equity or collateral position can be artificially low because of accelerated depreciation. Using accelerated depreciation results in a *Book-value Balance Sheet* that has less equity or collateral than a market-value balance sheet. The former shows assets at their depreciated value whereas the latter shows the assets at their current market value. To develop a *Market-value Balance Sheet*, present your current book-value balance sheet with an additional column for the market value. Documentation of market value can be provided through appraisals or advertisements that include prices on similar equipment or assets. The market-value balance sheet usually increases the equity dollar amounts and the equity-to-assets ratio. This should result in a banker's willingness to loan a larger amount for growth activities.

- **Statement of Change in Financial Position** – This document shows how changes in working capital occur over a specific period. It is not a requirement of the *Tax Act* but management is increasingly using it as a tool to cultivate better profits and cash flow. Accountants and bankers are also placing increasing emphasis on this statement.

Business Financial History

A *Business Financial History* is a summary and analysis statement of financial information about your company from its inception to the present. The information compiled here can be used to complete loan application forms that lenders and investors often require (see page 307 for the types of information most often asked for). Of particular importance in this section is the calculation and record of key financial ratios (derived from financial statements), as well as other performance indicators and benchmarks useful for making future projections and comparisons. Understanding "what" these numbers mean and exactly "how" they are derived is a great way to assess the financial health of your business and hone your skills of financial statement analysis to ensure you have what it takes to improve profitability and recognize danger signals. Lenders also utilize this information along with a credit history report and cash flow analysis to determine loan risk.

What creditors consider profitable depends on the type of business being assessed. A 2% profit margin for a grocery store is considered normal. But less than 10% for an accounting firm is quite low.
PROFIT TIP

DID YOU KNOW?

The new North American Industry Classification System (NAICS) has replaced the old 1987 Standard Industrial Classification (SIC) system for classifying industries. Knowing your NAICS and SIC code can help you find the best operating ratios.
www.naics.com

PI's should be ...

Related to your mission statement.

Cost-effective (not too expensive to derive or monitor).

Relevant to stakeholders, such as management, bankers, and investors (if the response to the PI is "so what," then don't use it).

Verifiable and *replicable* by external investigators wishing to audit your performance.

Financial and Operating Ratios

The relationships between amounts of invested capital, sales levels, various cost categories, inventory turnover, and other items, form what are often referred to as *Financial* or *Operating Ratios*. Bankers and investors use financial ratios to determine the relative health of a business. Management can also use them to provide valuable checkpoints allowing for better control over key aspects of a business before it's too late to make adjustments. The basic data for ratio analysis is contained in your balance sheet and income statement.

NOTE Industry financial and operating ratios useful for making projections for various types of businesses can be found in the publications listed on page 308 and trade journals particular to your industry. These publications should be available at your public library. You can also find business ratios online and at local business centers and SBA offices. Bizratios.com has a list of online sources, as well as a sampling of business ratios for several types of companies.

Analyzing Financial Statements

Outlined below are six basic ways to analyze your financial statements:

Profitability Analysis – The ability to make a profit as measured by your gross profit margin, operating profit margin, and net profit margin.

Liquidity Analysis – The ability to meet financial obligations as measured by your current ratio, quick ratio, and net working capital.

Debt Analysis – Sum of outside loans/funds being used to generate profits as measured by your debt to assets and debt to equity ratios.

Investment Analysis – The return on your investment (ROI) as measured by net profits to total assets and profits to net worth.

Vertical Analysis – A percentage analysis of components in a single financial statement to show their relationship.

Horizontal Analysis – A percentage analysis of changes in values in items on a financial statement from one year to the next.

Performance Indicators

Performance Indicators, also referred to as *Key Financial Indicators* or *Benchmarks*, are statistics, costs, ratios, and other forms of information, which illuminate or measure progress in achieving your mission and financial objectives. They are important tools you can use to assess and monitor the health and performance of your business. A number of them should be unique to your type of business, while others can be more general, such as financial ratios extracted from your statements. In developing this section, it is best to create a chart or table to summarize past, present, and future key PI's (see page 312 for a list of PI's).

Sample Financial Ratios and Key PI's Statement

[I/We] have based our financial statement projections on data compiled by [name source—e.g., Robert Morris Associates, Bizminer.com, *Business and Industrial Financial Ratios* 20XX edition, XYZ Trade Association].

The following [chart, table] indicates our [key financial indicators, key PI's, benchmarks] for the [first three years]. We foresee major growth in sales and operating expenses, accompanied by a lengthening of our average collection period during expansion. Note that margins and expenses are consistently controlled and net profit increases nicely. Inventory turnover slows down somewhat in the [third year] due to the burden of higher inventories for increasing [product] sales.

> *Any financial ratio can be used as a key performance indicator.*
>
> ✳
>
> *Use PI's that are easy to compile and monitor, and provide truly useful information to evaluate your business.*
>
> ✳
>
> *Study the past, if you would divine the future.*
>
> **CONFUCIUS**

$ucce$$ Opportunity ➡ China: The 1.3 Billion Market

According to WorldBank.org, China's GDP was 946.3 billion in 1998. By 2003, this rose to 1.33 trillion. Real GDP growth over the past six years has ranged from a low of 6.8% to a high of 8.0%. Within this time period, population has stabilized at a market size of approximately 1.3 billion people.

Dansk Industri (2003), in a workshop on "Critical Factors for Success in China," reported that "for the past eight years, China has been the second largest recipient of foreign direct investment (FDI) in the world after the United States." They added that "growth in China has been impressive, the economy stable and exporters and producers are being attracted like bees to honey." A similar article in *Business China* (1996) also available in *China: The Consumer Revolution* by Conghua Li (1998), pointed out that the most important success factors for new businesses entering China were business vision and strategy, human resources, products tailored to market, cost controls, and product quality. Also important were strength of relationships with Chinese partners, market information, choosing the right Chinese partner, and reliability of infrastructure. Surprisingly, government access and tax incentives had a much lower priority and impact on success. Another key factor to success in China is understanding the Chinese way of doing business, their business behavior, mindset, and negotiating techniques, as well as the strong influence of Confucianism. For example, in Chinese business culture, humility is a virtue. Brash claims are regarded with great suspicion.

Prepare a current income statement, balance sheet, and asset sheet. Calculate financial ratios.

Current Income Statement

Discuss positive and negative aspects of your current income statement (see page 313). List any special concerns, as well as areas important to profitability (this is no place to try and hide from the facts):

> **Sample:** For fiscal year 2004, [company] had net sales of $678,500, with COGS at $410,000. Selling, administrative, and depreciation expenses totaled $190,000. Adding other income of $1,500 and interest expenses of $3,000, [company] earned a net profit of $77,000 before taxes and $45,900 after taxes. One area of concern is an increase in selling and administrative expenses by 15% over fiscal year 2003 with only a 3% increase in net sales. This increase has been attributed to inflation, rising leasing costs of $450 per month, a staff training program of $4,000, and a salary increase of $300 per month to three key staff members. To regain lost profitability, we are currently [describe].

Current Asset Sheet

<u>*Sources and Costs of Assets*</u> *– List all current assets (refer back to page 62):*

Asset	Cost	Source of Funds	Asset	Cost	Source of Funds
	$			$	
			Cash	$4,500	Personal Savings
			Accounts Receivable	5,000	From Profits
			Inventory	4,000	Vendor Credit
			Pickup Truck	6,000	Previously Owned
			Packaging Machine	12,000	Installment Purchase
			Office Desk and Chair	600	Previously Owned
			Calculator	80	Personal Cash
			Personal Computer	3,000	Personal Savings

Current Balance Sheet

Discuss positive and negative aspects of your current balance sheet (see page 314). List special concerns:

Sample: Our cash available is $[XX]. Our Quick Ratio is 2 to 1. Our Current Ratio is 3 to 1. With these two balance sheet ratios well above averages of 0.6 and 1.2 for the greeting card industry, [company] is in an excellent position to meet any new short-term or long-term loan obligations.	

Other Financial Statements

List other financial statements you will include and why they are relevant:

❑ Business Financial History Form or Loan Application (as provided by a potential lender or investor)

❑ Capital Expenditure Projections

❑ Depreciation Schedule (needed if you have lots of buildings and equipment)

❑ Detailed Business Costs (projected and actual)

❑ Detailed Cost of Sales (outlines production, marketing, pro-rated, and administration costs)

❑ Detailed Sales Projections (quarterly, annual, and three-year projections; sales volume can be indicated in units and dollars)

❑ Deviation Analysis of Income Statements

❑ Financial Statement Analysis Summary (summarizes historical and projected ratios and statement values compared to industry standards such as: sales, cost of goods, interest expense, assets, inventory, net worth, net working capital, current ratio, quick ratio, gross profit margin, and ROI)

❑ Market-value Balance Sheet

❑ Statement of Change in Financial Position

❑ Vertical Balance Sheet Analysis (items listed as a % of Total Assets or Liabilities + Net Worth)

❑ Vertical Income Statement Analysis (items listed as a % of Total Sales)

Business Financial History

Check financial information needed to complete any loan forms required (obtain forms from lenders):

❑ **Asset Holdings** (real estate, stocks and bonds)

❑ **Assets, Liabilities, Net Worth** (from balance sheet)

❑ **Audit Information** (Who audits your books and when? Has the IRS?)

❑ **Contingent Liabilities** (debts you may owe in the future—e.g., letters of credit, suits pending)

❑ **Insurance** (coverage for merchandise, machinery, buildings, earthquakes)

❑ **Inventory Details** (amount, value, valuation method, purchase terms)

❑ **Legal Structure** (years as a proprietorship, names of partners, names of board of directors)

❑ **Financial Ratios** (ROI, debt to equity, debt to assets, gross profit margin, operating profit margin, net profit margin, quick ratio, current ratio, net working capital)

Loan Form Information – *Summarize financial information about your company from start to present:*

S-Prop. / Part. Capitalization Info		Corporate Capitalization Info		Product/Market Info		
Number of Years in Present Businesses		Date Incorporated		Product/Service Revenues of	$	
Date of Organization		Under Laws of State/Province of		Product/Service Net Profit of	$	
Date of Filing Fictitious Name (DBA)		Number of Shares Authorized		Current Inventory Value	$	
Businesses You Are Connected With		Number of Shares of Stock Outstanding		Number of Clients Developed		
Net Worth of Business	$	Par Value of Stock	$	Markets Developed		
Names of Partners		Owner(s) Number of Shares Owned		Market Share Secured		%
Amount Each Contributed		Date Acquired Capital Contributions		Categories Market Share Secured in		

Financial and Operating Ratios

Where to Find FINANCIAL and OPERATING RATIOS – *Visit your library and consult the publications listed below. List sources you will use to make your financial statement projections and other estimates:*

❑ **Dun & Bradstreet Information Services** – *Industry Norms & Key Business Ratios.* Desktop Edition. New York (annual), also available on diskette. Gives balance sheet and income statement statistics, as well as financial ratios for over 800 lines of business. Arranged by four-digit SIC industries. D&B also publishes *Key Business Ratios*, which contains over 700 pages of British financial ratios for some 378 SIC industries in the U.K.

❑ **Financial Research Associates** – *Financial Studies of the Small Business*, P.O. Box 7708, Winterhaven, FL 33883-7708 (annual). Contains financial ratios for about 50 lines of small business (those with capitalization under $1 million—retail, wholesale, services, contractors and professional services, and manufacturers—by asset size categories).

❑ **Bizminer.com** – 19,000 industry profiles online.

❑ **Robert Morris Associates** – *Annual Statement Studies*, One Liberty Place, Philadelphia, PA 19103. Contains financial and operating ratios for more than 360 lines of business (by four-digit SIC number). Includes manufacturers, wholesalers, retailers, services, and contractors.

❑ **Tryo, Leo Ph.D.** – *Almanac of Business & Industrial Financial Ratios*, Englewood Cliffs, NJ: Prentice-Hall (annual). Lists operating ratios for over 160 industries arranged by a four-digit industry classification similar to SIC. Features IRS data on 3.7 million U.S. corporations.

❑ **U.S. Bureau of the Census** – *Quarterly Financial Report for Manufacturing, Mining, and Trade Corporations*, Washington, DC: U.S. Government Printing Office. Contains quarterly income statement and balance sheet data, as well as selected financial and operating ratios. Also see *Business Expenditures Survey* at:
http://www.census.gov/csd/bes/

Research financial and operating ratios for your industry and list them here:

Selected Operating Ratios for Small Businesses – (Source: compiled from "Almanac of Business and Industrial Financial Ratios" 1996 edition; available at most libraries).

Type of Business	Cost of Sales	Gross Profit	Operating Expenses	Operating Profit
MANUFACTURING				
Electronic components	62.1	37.9	34.4	3.5%
Bread, bakery products	59.4	40.6	37.9	2.7
Sporting and athletic	56.7	43.3	34.5	8.7
Jewelry, precious metals	61.1	38.9	32.5	6.5
Women's dresses	61.4	38.6	33.8	4.8
Commercial printing	59.6	40.4	35.6	4.7
WHOLESALERS				
Stationery supplies	66.5	33.5	31.2	2.3
General groceries	77.0	23.0	21.1	1.9
Jewelry	70.1	29.9	26.1	3.8
Sporting goods and toys	68.5	31.5	29.2	2.3
Fresh fruit, vegetables	78.2	21.8	19.3	2.5
RETAILERS				
Jewelry	54.0	46.0	41.2	4.8
Books and stationery	61.5	38.5	36.7	1.8
Women's ready-to-wear	59.3	40.7	37.7	3
Gasoline service stations	77.7	22.3	19.6	2.7
Groceries and meats	76.3	23.7	21.7	2.0
Sporting goods, bikes	66.2	33.8	30.1	3.7
SERVICES				
Travel agencies			98	2
Accounting			86.5	13.5
Leasing equipment			90.8	9.2
Motels and hotels			96.5	3.5
Computer programming			95.7	4.3
YOUR BUSINESS				

Detailed Operating Ratios for Book, Greeting Cards, and Miscellaneous Publishing Businesses (Source: "Almanac of Business and Industrial Financial Ratios" 1996 edition; available at most libraries).

Performance Indicator (%)	All	$100,000 to $250,000 in Assets	Your Business
Cost of Operations	39.5	30.0	
Rent	2.3	3.4	
Taxes Paid	3.0	2.4	
Interest Paid	4.4	1.1	
Depreciation, Amortization	4.1	3.4	
Pension and Other Benefits	2.5	1.4	
Other	42.3	41.6	
Operating Margin	1.9	16.7	
In Thousands of Dollars:			
Average Total Revenues	$2,952	$527	
Net Receivables	$672	$10	
Inventories	$309	$31	
Total Assets	$3,494	$176	
Notes and Loans Payable	$1,157	$54	
Selected Financial Ratios:			
Current Ratio	1.2	1.5	
Quick Ratio	0.6	0.7	
Net Sales to Working Capital	14.6	22.5	
Inventory Turnover	3.5	5.2	
Receivables Turnover	4.1	–	
Total Liabilities to Net worth	2.2	1.2	
Financial Factors (%):			
Debt Ratio	68.9	53.7	
Return on Assets	7.9	18.5	
Profit Margin Before Income Tax	5.5	5.1	
Profit Margin After Income Tax	4.0	4.9	
# of Enterprises Compared	10,864	1,644	

Discuss any relevant or unusual findings, as well as trends. **How** *have ratios changed over the years?*

Sample: Financial ratios for [type of industry] have been quite stable over the last five years. However, in order to adopt new technologies needed to remain competitive, many companies have had to increase long-term debt to update equipment, resulting in a debt ratio increase from 65% in 2003 to 85% in 2004. In the short term, this has reduced profitability. Companies unable to finance retooling are currently losing sales. [Competitor A and B] have recently filed for bankruptcy.

Business Ratios – *The following financial ratios play an important role in the granting or denial of loan requests. Review and select those needed to monitor the financial health of your business:*

Profitability and Investment

☑ **Net Profit to Total Sales** – This ratio, (a.k.a.) *Profit Margin* ratio, is derived from your Income Statement, as is *Gross Profit Margin* and *Operating Profit Margin*. To calculate it, divide net profit by total sales. Of course, the larger the ratio, the better.

☑ **Return on Investment** – This ratio is one of the most frequently calculated investment return ratios. To calculate it, divide your company's net profit (after tax) by total assets as found on your financial statements.

☑ **Profits to Equity** – This ratio shows your return on equity (ROE) and is considered one of the best criteria for profitability. To calculate it, divide net profit (after tax) by equity or tangible net worth. *Tangible Net Worth* is the true worth of a business (assets minus liabilities) minus intangible assets such as goodwill or incorporation costs.

Debt

☑ **Debt to Assets (Debt Ratio)** – This ratio looks at the ability of a business to repay long-term debt. It is given special focus in the American Bankers Association guidelines for evaluating a business. To calculate it, divide total liabilities by total assets. For example, if you owe $100,000 and have total assets of $200,000, then your debt to asset ratio would be 1:2 or 50%. This means your assets are twice as large as the debts. Your company presents a healthy financial picture. The higher the ratio, the more risk of failure.

Debt (continued)

☑ **Debt to Equity** – This ratio shows the relationship between what is "owed" and what is "owned" by owners. It is calculated by dividing total long-term debt by owner's or shareholders' equity. Bankers like to see this ratio well under "1" which means there is lots of equity to carry debt. Investors like to see higher ratios to increase their leverage and boost potential profits.

❏ **Times Interest Earned Ratio** – This ratio is calculated by dividing net profit before interest and income tax by interest expense. Anything near "1" means almost all profits are paying off debts.

Liquidity

☑ **Current Ratio** – This ratio is used to assess your company's solvency—i.e., its ability to pay off debts promptly. A current ratio of 2 to 1 or higher is looked upon well. It means you have more than enough cash on hand—and assets such as inventory that can be quickly converted into cash—to meet all debts due within a year's time. To calculate it, divide current assets by current liabilities.

☑ **Quick or Acid-test Ratio** – This ratio is calculated by dividing current assets less inventory, by current liabilities. It measures liquidity and reveals whether a firm can meet its maturing obligations. A ratio of 1 to 1 or higher is recommended.

☑ **Net Working Capital** – The surplus of current assets over current liabilities is net working capital. It is calculated by subtracting current liabilities from current assets as found on your balance sheet. The higher the amount the better.

Activity

❏ **Cost of Sales to Total Inventory** – This ratio is used to assess how well your company has used its resources. To calculate it, divide the total cost of sales by total inventory.

❏ **Sales to Fixed Assets** – This "asset utilization" ratio shows what sales are generated by each dollar invested in plant and equipment. To calculate it, divide total sales by total assets. For example, if sales are $400,000 and assets $150,000, your sales to fixed asset ratio would be 2.76. This means that $2.76 of revenue is generated from $1 of assets.

❏ **Sales to A/R's** – This ratio is used to find the number of days money is tied up in credit sales to determine the average collection period (ACP). It tells you (and your banker) how much it will cost to run your business for the number of days A/R's are tied up, and thus how much money you need to have on hand or to borrow. As a general rule, the greater A/R's the more capitalization you need to tide your business over until accounts are paid. To calculate this ratio, divide A/R's by daily sales. For example, if annual sales totaled $400,000 of which $100,000 were A/R's, and your business was open for 300 days, making your average daily sales $1,333, then your sales to A/R's ratio would be 4 to 1 and your ACP would be 75 days.

❏ **Sales to Inventory** – This ratio gives the average turnover of your inventory and is useful for comparing your company's performance with others within the industry. To calculate it, divide annual sales by current inventory. For example, if annual sales are $600,000 and current inventory $75,000, your sales to inventory ratio would be 8 to 1. This means that your inventory turns over eight times a year.

Financial Statement Analysis – *Calculate projected values. Compare with past values or current industry ratios:*

Key Ratios and Formulas		☐ Industry ☐ Historical:		Projected Year:	
Profit and Investment	Net Profit Margin = Net Profit / Net Sales	Net Profit	$	$	
		Net Sales	$	$	
		Net Profit Margin	%	%	
	Operating Profit Margin = Operating Profit / Net Sales	Operating Profit	$	$	
		Net Sales	$	$	
		Operating Profit Margin	%	%	
	Gross Profit Margin = Gross Profit / Net Sales	Gross Profit	$	$	
		Net Sales	$	$	
		Gross Profit Margin	%	%	
	Return on Assets = Net Profit / Total Assets	Net Profit	$	$	
		Total Assets	$	$	
		ROI	%	%	
	Return on Equity = Net Profit (after taxes) / Tangible Net Worth (Equity)	Net Profits	$	$	
		Tangible Net Worth	$	$	
		ROE	%	%	
Liquidity	Current Ratio = Current Assets / Current Liabilities	Current Assets	$	$	
		Current Liabilities	$	$	
		Current Ratio			
	Quick Ratio = Current Assets – Inventories / Current Liabilities	Current Assets – Inventory	$ –	$ –	
		Current Liabilities	$	$	
		Quick Ratio			
	Net Working Capital = Current Assets – Current Liabilities	Current Assets	$	$	
		Current Liabilities	$	$	
		Net Working Capital	$	$	
Debt	Debt to Assets = Total Debt / Total Assets	Total Debt	$	$	
		Total Assets	$	$	
		Debt to Assets	%	%	
	Debt to Equity = Total Long-term Debt / Owner's Equity	Total Long-term Debt	$	$	
		Owner's Equity	$	$	
		Debt to Equity	%	%	

Summarize conclusions of your ratio analysis and how it will affect future management decisions. **How** *regularly will you monitor ratios as part of your working capital management policy?*

Sample: [Company] has a high debt to assets ratio of 93.2%. Despite this, in its first year of operation, it has maintained a positive cash balance of $65,000. Net sales were less than projected, at minus 4%, but due to effective management and cost control by Janice Noori, net profits were 10% higher than projected.	

Performance Indicators

<u>Key PI's</u> – *Select and list PI's you will use to evaluate and monitor the performance of your business. Table the values of or create a pie or bar chart for:* ❑ past PI's ❑ current PI's ❑ projected PI's

Activity PI's
- ❑ Accounts payable turnover
- ❑ Average collection period
- ❑ Average number of staff
- ❑ Back orders filled
- ❑ Days of inventory on hand
- ❑ Employee turnover
- ❑ Inventory turnover
- ❑ Machine downtime
- ❑ Number of clients
- ❑ Number of complaints
- ❑ Number of returns

Sales
- ❑ Ratio of sales to calls
- ❑ Sales growth
- ❑ Sales per employee
- ❑ Sales of key products

Website Related PI's
- ❑ Page hits
- ❑ Repeat visitors
- ❑ Unique visitors
- ❑ Visitors who spend money
- ❑ Visitors who abandon their order

PI's Derived from Statements
- ❑ Net worth
- ❑ Interest expense
- ❑ Total assets

Liquidity
- ❑ Current ratio
- ❑ Net working capital
- ❑ Quick ratio

Debt
- ❑ Debt to equity ratio
- ❑ Debt to net worth
- ❑ Total debt

Expenses
- ❑ Advertising expenses
- ❑ Cost of goods sold
- ❑ Operating expenses
- ❑ Overhead as a % of sales

Profitability and Investment
- ❑ Earnings per share
- ❑ Individual item markup
- ❑ Net profit margin
- ❑ Net profit per owner
- ❑ Profit per sale
- ❑ ROI and ROE

Key PI's (Benchmarks)	Past			Current Year (20___)				Projected	
	–3	–2	–1	0	+1	+2	+3	+4	+5

Summarize why the above PI's were chosen. Provide explanations for variations in benchmark values:

Sample: The following financial indicators, shown in Table 4, are based on data compiled by Robert Morris Associates, and an analysis of our company's past performance. For the first three years after loan infusion, we foresee major growth in sales and operating expenses, accompanied by a lengthening of our average collection period for the first two years. For 2006, advertising expenses will increase by 15% as we launch an extensive marketing campaign for [product]. We are closely monitoring our debt ratio, ACP, and overhead as a percentage of sales [explain why].

INCOME STATEMENT

Statement of Income for: **As of:**

(A) AC#[1]   **GROSS SALES**   100%[2]

       LESS Purchased Returns and Allowances

       LESS Sales Tax (if included in sales)

       LESS COST OF GOODS SOLD:

       Inventory at Beginning of Fiscal Period

       ADD Cost of Goods Purchased During Fiscal Period

       ADD Freight and Delivery Charges

       LESS Purchased Returns

       LESS Inventory at the End of the Fiscal Period

(B)   **TOTAL** Cost of Goods Sold

(C)   **GROSS PROFIT** (A – B) $

       LESS OPERATING EXPENSES:

       Accounting, Legal, and Professional Fees

       Advertising and Marketing

       Bad Debts

       Commissions and Fees

       Depreciation (Capital Cost Allowance in Canada)

       Employee Benefit Programs

       Insurance

       Meals, Entertainment, and Travel

       Motor Vehicle Expenses (except depreciation allowance)

       Office Expenses

       Payroll Taxes (Payroll Expenses and Taxes)

       Pension and Profit Sharing Plans

       Permits, Fees, Licenses, Dues, and Subscriptions

       Property Taxes (list here or include in Estimated Tax)

       Rent or Lease Payments

       Repairs and Maintenance

       Salaries and Wages

       Supplies (Office Supplies)

       Telephone

       Utilities (Heat, Hydro)

       Other Operating Expenses:

(D)   **TOTAL** Operating Expenses

(E)   **OPERATING PROFIT** (C – D) $

       ADD OTHER INCOME:

       Interest from Bank Accounts

       Royalties and Dividends on Stock

       Gains from Sale of Fixed Assets

       Misc. Income

       LESS Interest Expense (from loans or credit)

                     NET PROFIT Before Taxes $

       LESS Estimated Tax Payments (federal, state, local)

                      NET PROFIT After Taxes $

[1] **Note:** Add account numbers (see pages 109 and 362).
Use accounts applicable to your business.

[2] **Note:** All percentages based on Gross Sales.

BALANCE SHEET

Balance Sheet FOR: _____   **As OF:** _____

AC# [1]	**Current Assets**			% of Assets
	Accounts Receivable			
	LESS allowance for bad debts	( )		( )
	Cash in Bank			
	Cash on Hand (includes Petty Cash)			
	Inventories (Merchandise)			
	Prepaid Expenses			
	Short-term Investments			
	Supplies			
	Other Current Assets			
	Long-term Investments			
	Fixed Assets			
	Land			
	Buildings			
	Furniture and Fixtures			
	Leasehold Improvements			
	Equipment			
	Auto/Vehicles			
	Other Fixed Assets			
	LESS Total Accumulated Depreciation [2]	( )		( )
	TOTAL ASSETS	$		100 %

AC#	**Current Liabilities**			% of Liab.
	Accounts Payable			
	Interest Payable			
	Taxes Payable			
	Wages and Salaries Payable			
	Short-term Loans Payable			
	Other Current Liabilities			
	Long-term Liabilities			
	Long-term Loans Payable			
	Mortgages			
	Bonds Payable (applies to corporations)			
	Other Long-term Liabilities			
	TOTAL LIABILITIES	$		100 %

Owner's Equity (Use 1 and 2 for Prop. or Part.; Use 2, 3, and 4 for Corp.)   % of Equity

AC#			
	1. Proprietorship *or* Partnership Earnings		
	2. Capital Stock *or* Capital Invested (Startup Capital)		
	3. Retained Earnings		
	4. Current Year Earnings Less Dividends Paid		

[1] **Note:** Add account numbers (see pages 109 and 363). Use accounts applicable to your business.

Total Owner's or Stockholder's Equity = **NET WORTH** $ _____   100 %

TOTAL LIABILITIES and NET WORTH $ _____

[2] **Note:** To coordinate with your accounting system and provide more useful information for balance sheet analysis, consider breaking down *Total Accumulated Depreciation* for each fixed asset (e.g., *Furniture acc. depr., Auto acc. depr.*)

AC# 160	Buildings		$208,300		15.1%
AC# 160	1. Cost	250,000			
AC# 161	2. Less Building Accumulated Depreciation	41,700			

DAY 28

Describe how you will maximize profits and cut costs.

Outline your exit, investment, retirement, and tax plans.

Profit Planning

A *Profit Plan* outlines ways to reduce costs and lower your tax burden. It blossoms as strategies are developed for investing in short-term and long-term investments, as well as developing personal and company retirement plans to secure profits. Cash should never be idle. Cash must work for you as hard as you did to earn it.

To Do List

IV. **Financial Plan**

   Profit Planning

   ✓ Cost Reducing Measures
   ✓ Exit Strategy
   ✓ Investment and Retirement Plans
   ✓ Tax Plan

Cost Reducing Measures

There is one cardinal rule known to every successful business operator:

"The quickest way to increase profits is to reduce costs."

To boost profits and increase the amount of cash available for expansion and further investment, implement cost-cutting strategies that control and reduce expenses. Consider the following: If you're operating at a 10% profit ratio, for every $100 you spend, an additional $1,000 is needed in increased sales to balance these expenditures. Remember, overhead *kills* profits. As Ben Franklin once said: *Beware of little expenses: A small leak will sink a ship.*

All-time Biggest Money Wasters

Anyone can spend a million dollars (large corporations do it all the time). But it takes patience, determination, planning, and research, to spend it wisely, and even more, NOT to spend it at all. To get into the proper frame of mind for cost cutting, consider the following *All-time Biggest Money Wasters* (how many have you fallen victim to?): ❑ buying a new car every few years ❑ buying anything new and improved without asking yourself if it *really is* new and improved ❑ buying anything on sale you don't really need ❑ buying designer clothing ❑ eating at fancy restaurants ❑ keeping money in low interest savings accounts ❑ playing the lottery ❑ taking expensive vacations ❑ using a *gold card* because it makes you feel successful! The "33 Scrooge Strategies" on page 326 are further aimed at helping you find ways to reduce your business and personal living costs.

A man is the richest whose pleasures are the cheapest.
HENRY D. THOREAU

❋

Every increased possession loads us with a new weariness.
RUSKIN

Most of the money a businessman calls profit is merely money that has not been wasted.
JOSEPH COSSMAN

❋

Getting money is like digging with a needle; spending it is like water soaking into sand.
JAPANESE PROVERB

Exit Strategy

An *Exit Strategy* gives your mission and company goals a finish line. It clarifies what will happen when you decide to move on and leave your business. All businesses need an exit plan or *Payback Strategy*, especially those looking to woo investors who quite understandably want to know how and when they will get their money back (see page 321 for possible "Exit Strategies").

Investment and Retirement Plans

Any profits left over after you've paid business and personal living expenses, planned for growth, and contributed to your retirement plan, should be invested in one or a combination of the following investment products:

❑ *Cash Investments* ❑ *Bonds and Debt Instruments* ❑ *Equities* ❑ *Mutual Funds*

The Four Major Categories of Investments

Summarized below are the four major types of financial investment vehicles available to you to help build your investment portfolio. The investment vehicle you choose depends upon liquidity needed, rates of return desired, and risk involved (see charts on page 317 for historical rates of return).

Cash Investments – Savings accounts, money market certificates, term deposits, short-term investment certificates, and T-Bills are generally seen as very low risk investments. Except for term deposits and investment certificates, which are usually cashable after three months to five years, cash investments are very liquid (cashable), but offer low rates of return (4% to 8%). Having part of your portfolio in cash gives you the flexibility to react quickly to investment opportunities or emergencies and makes your portfolio less exposed to market volatility.

Bonds and Debt Instruments – Debt instruments are contracts between people who want to borrow and people who want to lend. They include investments such as bonds, debentures, mortgages, and personal loans. The contracts involve the borrower paying certain amounts of money in the form of principal and interest at certain times in the future, once the loan has been made. Debt instruments usually earn interest at a predictable rate (5% to 9% or more). However, if you sell them before maturity, there is the potential for capital gains or losses. If interest rates go up, your contract is valued less by the market. If interest rates go down, your contract, with its higher rate of interest, becomes more attractive. Bonds are usually purchased at a $25,000 minimum in multiples of $1,000.

Equity Investments (Stocks) – Equities are shares of a company or organization that increase or decrease in value depending on the market's perception of the company's future earnings prospects. This group includes stocks, equity, and shares of private companies. It also includes real properties and collectibles. Equity investments are expected to grow in value over time and may even provide some income in the form of regular dividends. Historically, they have achieved the best returns but are also the most risky, because their value is based on market demand.

Mutual Fund Investments – Mutual funds pool resources to invest solely or in a combination of cash investments, debt instruments, or equities. The variety of mutual funds available to investors is almost limitless. To find top funds try:

http://money.cnn.com/funds/
http://biz.yahoo.com/p/top.html

Rate of Return for $100 Invested in 1950

Investment	Value	Rate
Consumer Price index (cost of Living)	**$728**	4.4%
90-Day Canada Treasury Bills	**$1,889**	6.5%
Scotia McLeod Long-term Bond index	**$2,395**	7.1%
5-year Guaranteed Investment Certificates	**$3,511**	8.0%
Toronto Stock Exchange 300 Total Return Index	**$11,291**	10.7%
U.S. Stock Total Return Index in Cdn. $	**$30,179**	13.1%
U.S. Small Stock Total Return Index in Cdn $	**$51,296**	14.4%

| $100 | $1,000 | $10,000 | $20,000 | $30,000 | $40,000 | $50,000 | $60,000 |

1950 **1996**

The above chart shows how much a $100 investment made in 1950 would have grown if it were invested in any one of the above seven investment vehicles.

Source: Canadian Government Document (values quoted in Cdn$)

Annualized World Market Rates of Return*

Country	Period	Equities	Bonds	Treasury Bills	Inflation Index
Canada	1950-1996	10.7	7.1	6.5	4.4
Germany	1954-1988	11.8 (14.5)	7.0	5.3	3.1
Japan	1971-1992	11.6 (16.0)	7.8	6.6	5.0
New Zealand	1931-1992	10.1	5.9	6.6	5.7
Sweden	1919-1990	9.5	5.2	5.7	3.5
U.K.	1919-1998	12.1	6.5	5.6	4.1
USA	1925-2000	11.0 (12.4)	5.3	3.8	3.1

*The above compound annualized rates of return assume reinvested dividends and do not account for taxes. For real rates of return, subtract the inflation index. The "Equities" rates of return column lists figures for large company stocks and where data was available small company stocks in parentheses. Sources: [1] Dimson, E., & Marsh, P. (2001). UK Financial Market Returns 1955–2000. *Journal of Business, 73.* [2] Ibbotson Associates (2000). *Stocks, Bonds, Bills, and Inflation 1999 Yearbook.* [3] Barclays Capital (1999). *Equity-gilt Study.* [4] Canadian Government Document.

Four Ways to Save $100,000

Monthly Deposit required to accumulate		
$100,000		
(with an average return of 10%)		
Monthly Deposit	*# of Years*	*Total Invested*
$44.24	30 years	$15,926.40
$131.69	20 years	$31,605,60
$488.17	10 years	$58,580.40
$1,291.37	5 years	$77,482.20

Investment Risk vs. Returns

Asset	Volatility	Return	RISK
Cash Investments	Low	Low	Low (but may not earn more than inflation)
Debt Investments (Bonds)	Moderate	Moderate	Moderate (but may not beat inflation; or interest rates may rise creating capital losses)
Equities (Stocks)	High	High	High (market may fall)
Mutual Funds	Low to High	Low to High	Low to High (depends on type of mutual fund)

Choosing the Best Investment Mix for Your Age

Number of Years to Retirement	**20+ years**	**15–20**	**10–15**	**5–10**	**0–5 (retirement)**
Short-term Investments	10%	10%	10%	15%	15%
Income	15%	20%	30%	40%	55%
Growth Income	15%	20%	30%	25%	20%
Growth	60%	50%	30%	20%	10%

There are essentially five different kinds of portfolio mixes to choose from, depending on your age to retirement. The above investment mixes are recommended guidelines. They factor in the need for capital conservation and appreciation.

Retirement Planning

The *first* part of your retirement plan is to take advantage of the federal government's deferred tax sheltered savings plan by opening an individual retirement account. This is an essential strategy for reducing your taxes and increasing your net worth. In fact, the sooner you start contributing, the more rewards you will reap in the future. Compounding is the key (see charts on page 319). In the U.S., open an IRA (Individual Retirement Arrangement). In Canada, open an RRSP (Registered Retirement Savings Plan). The *second* part of your retirement plan is to start a company retirement plan for both yourself and your employees.

Personal Retirement Plans: The IRA and RRSP – In the U.S., you can contribute to a deductible IRA if you received taxable compensation during the year, such as income from self-employment, and will not reach age $70^1/_2$ by the year's end. As of 2002, you can contribute a maximum of $3,000 of your taxable compensation ($3,500 if over 50; $4,000 from 2005 to 2007; $5,000 in 2008). This amount is deducted from your taxable income and you won't have to pay interest until you make a withdrawal. A new type of

A "deferred tax sheltered savings plan" is the long-term investment most favored by financial planners. It offers safety, interest reinvestment, and tax deferment. With earnings compounding tax-free annually, it can easily make you a millionaire if you start early enough.
PROFIT TIP

IRA, called the Roth IRA, provides no deductions for contributions, but as long as you meet the requirements, *all earnings are tax-free* when you or a beneficiary withdraws them. You can start a "traditional" IRA or a Roth IRA even if you are covered by another retirement plan. In Canada, the maximum RRSP contribution is the lesser of 18% of earned income or $14,500 (2003 budget; increasing to $18,000 by 2006). However, if you did not use your entire RRSP deduction limit from previous years, you can carry it forward.

Tax Sheltered Growth

Years in Plan	5%	10%	15%
10	$13,207	17,531	23,349
20	$34,719	63,002	117,810
30	$69,761	180,943	499,957

(for a $10,000 lump sum)

Company Retirement Plans – Company retirement plans offer you tax advantages to set aside money for yourself and your employees' retirement. They can be funded entirely by company contributions or by a mix of company and employee contributions. Employer contributions are generally deductible within certain limits. In the U.S., the most popular plans for small businesses are SEPs, Keoghs, 401(k)s, and SIMPLE Plans. In Canada, the most popular plans are Group RRSPs, RPPs, and DPSPs (see page 323).

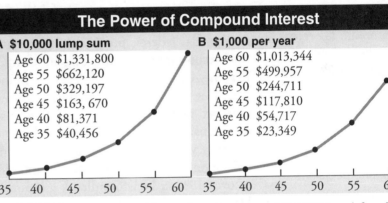

The Power of Compound Interest

A $10,000 lump sum

Age 60	$1,331,800
Age 55	$662,120
Age 50	$329,197
Age 45	$163,670
Age 40	$81,371
Age 35	$40,456

B $1,000 per year

Age 60	$1,013,344
Age 55	$499,957
Age 50	$244,711
Age 45	$117,810
Age 40	$54,717
Age 35	$23,349

Example A shows a 25-year-old investing a lump sum of $10,000 in a deferred tax sheltered savings plan and getting an annual rate of return of 15%.

Example B shows the same 25-year-old investing $1,000 each year for 30 years and getting an annual rate of return of 15%.

Note: In example A, if you invest an additional $2,000 at the end of each year, by age 65 you will have over $8 million dollars!

Tax Plan

The tax levy imposed by each governmental entity is the single most important impediment impacting upon company financial goals. To make matters worse, taxing agencies are notorious for writing confusing tax laws that often require years of experience and education, even with the help of trained professionals, before you fully understand what you can retain. It's as if taxing authorities are hoping to intimidate you with complex rules and regulations to prevent you from actively seeking legal ways to reduce your tax liability. However, with knowledge and careful planning, you can legally save tens of thousands, if not hundreds of thousands of dollars over your lifetime. A tax planning strategy is your first step to beating the taxman.

A good retirement plan can help attract quality staff.

*

Anything that you do to increase job security automatically does work for you. It makes your employees a closer part of the unit.
ROGER SMITH

Tax Liabilities in the U.S.

Hundreds of guides on every conceivable tax problem are available at local IRS field offices or in the *Freedom of Information Reading Room*. Most are also available online at http://www.irs.gov. In general, federal corporate tax rates vary from 15% for taxable income under $50,000 to 35% for taxable income over $18.3 million. Proprietorship and partnership tax rates vary from 15% to $39.6% depending on your income. In addition to this, the state may levy a tax that varies from 0% to 12% depending on the state.

Tax Liabilities in Canada

In Canada, federal, provincial, and municipal governing bodies have distinct responsibilities and taxing authority. The federal government's *Canada Revenue Agency* (www.CCRA.ca) levies income tax, capital gains tax, excise tax, sales tax, and customs duties. Individual provinces levy income tax, sales tax, and resource royalties. They also charge for permits and licenses. Municipalities levy taxes upon real estate and business, usually based on property value and type of business conducted. In 2002, the total combined federal and provincial tax rates for individuals ranged from 39% in Alberta to over 48% in Newfoundland. Corporate rates ranged from 35% to 43%. However, to attract foreign investment and stimulate economic growth, Canada has adopted an aggressive *Five-year Tax Reduction Plan* to make its corporate tax rate the lowest in North America—its largest tax cut in history. Under this plan, personal income taxes will be reduced and other tax measures put in place to reward entrepreneurship. By 2008, the average combined federal and provincial corporate tax rates, including capital taxes, is targeted for 33.8% by 2008, which is more than 7% lower than the current U.S. average corporate tax rate of 40%.

Tax Liabilities Around the World

If you are hoping to expand globally, the "big four" accounting firms PricewaterhouseCoopers, Ernst & Young, KPMG, and Deloitte & Touché provide taxation and business guides for countries worldwide. At least one of these series should be available at your public library (see page 324).

Corporate Tax Rates	Sources: KPMG, OECD, PricewaterhouseCoopers, CCRA, Worldwide-tax.com (rates include average local taxes)		
Australia 30%	China 30%	India 48%	Singapore 22%
Bahamas (none)	Germany 38%	Ireland 20%	Switzerland 21%
Canada 36%	Hong Kong 16%	Japan 41%	U.K. 30%
Cayman Islands (none)	Hungary 18%	Mexico 32%	U.S. 40%

Successful
BUSINESS PLANNING
30 in **DAYS**

Describe how you will maximize profits and cut costs. Outline your exit, investment, retirement, and tax plan.

Cost Reducing Measures

Outline how you plan to cut costs (see "Scrooge Strategies" on page 326):

MORE WAYS to REDUCE COSTS and BUSINESS OVERHEAD		
❑ Avoid downsizing, cutting corners, and reducing customer service. ❑ Develop skills. Skilled workers build profits.	❑ Don't play "hardball" with suppliers. Develop a win-win relationship. ❑ Eliminate errors by developing simpler work strategies.	❑ Train workers in new cost-saving technologies. ❑ Use Total Quality Management (TQM) tools to reduce wastage.

Exit Strategy

Check exit strategies you may have for leaving your business once you have reached your goals:

❑ **Sell All or Some** – You can sell all or a portion of your business to an independent buyer.

❑ **Franchise** – Although franchising is legally complicated and expensive, if your concept is easy to replicate and profitable, you might just be the next McDonald's.

❑ **Get Acquired** – Plan from day one to be acquired by a larger company. Study possible interested corporations and target your development goals to coincide with their expansion goals and marketing plans.

❑ **Go IPO** – Investors like to see companies plan for an Initial Public Offering (i.e., get traded on the stock exchange). It's a good way for them to get their money back. However, IPO's require extensive planning and high legal costs.

❑ **Liquidate** – In some cases, it is best to break up a company and sell all its assets. This will give the least return, especially if you operate a consulting business whose main value is tied into the reputation of its owners and other intangible assets such as goodwill.

❑ **Merge** – Find a willing competitor or industry-related horizontal or vertical partner and team up with them (e.g., you sell, they make; you make, they supply).

❑ **Start an ESOP** – You can set up an *Employee Stock Ownership Plan*. An ESOP has tax advantages and is good for building employee morale.

❑ **Transfer Ownership** – You might wish to turn over your business to a family member or heir. Plan to do it in a way that minimizes estate taxes.

Describe your exit plan in more detail. Explain: ❑ **Where** are you going? ❑ **How** long will it take? ❑ **What** happens when you get there? Make it clear how investors will get their money back:

	Sample: From 1993 to 1999, the number of key suppliers in the automotive supply chain has drastically shrunk from 30,000 to 3,000. [Research source] has forecasted that within the next five years, there could be as few as 300 suppliers serving automotive assembly lines. It is anticipated that to become one of the 300 remaining "mega" suppliers, there will be competition for the acquisition of a modern alloy wheel production plant such as [company]. We have scouted three companies who are likely to be interested in acquiring our facility. These include: [list and explain why these companies will be looking to acquire].

Investment Plan

Outline investment goals and strategies. Describe investment vehicles and reasons for choosing them:
❑ Cash Investments ❑ Bonds and Debt Instruments ❑ Equities (Stocks) ❑ Mutual Funds ❑ Real Estate

	INVESTMENT STRATEGIES		
	❑ Avoid GIC's that tie up your funds for one year or more. ❑ Buy bonds for the long term. ❑ Buy income producing real estate.	❑ Buy "value stocks" when interest rates are low or when the stock is "out of favor" with investors but has a good PE ratio and dividend.	❑ Diversity your portfolio. ❑ Never let money sit idle in your checking account. ❑ Seek a 10% to 15% rate of return.

Retirement Plan

*Detail your **personal** retirement plan. State monthly contributions (in $ amount or % of sales or profits):*
❑ IRA ❑ ROTH IRA ❑ RRSP ❑ Other _____

*Detail your **company** retirement plan. State monthly contributions (in $ amount or % of sales or profits):*

	Sample: Although the 401(k) is more common in our industry, [company] has decided to set up the easier-to-administer Simplified Employee Pension (SEP) plan for owners and employees. SEPs allow contributions of 13.0435% of net earnings to a maximum of $22,173. Contributions are tax deductible. [Company] will limit contributions to [X]% of net earnings or a maximum of $[XX] per year.

USA and Canada Company Retirement Plans – *Check retirement plans appropriate for your business:*

USA See publication IRS 560 *Retirement Plans for Small Business (SEP, Simple, and Qualified Plans)* www.irs.gov

❑ **Keogh (HR-10) Plans –** Available to FT or PT proprietorships or partnerships. A *Keogh Profit Sharing Plan* lets your employees share in your profits.

❑ **SIMPLE Plan –** The *Savings Incentive Match Plan for Employees* can be used by self-employed individuals and employers with less than 100 employees.

❑ **401(k) –** Appropriate for businesses with 25 employees or more.

❑ **The Simplified Employee Pension –** A retirement plan for proprietorships, partnerships, or corporations. Under a SEP, you make deductible contributions to an IRA that is owned by you or your common-law employees. Mutual funds can be excellent investments for SEPs.

❑ **Stock Bonus Plan –** This plan is similar to a profit-sharing plan, but only a corporation can set it up.

CANADA See publication T4040 *RRSPs and Other Registered Plans for Retirement* www.ccra-adrc.gc.ca

❑ **Registered Pension Plans –** An RPP is a trust registered with CRA (Canada Revenue Agency) and established by a company to provide pension benefits for employees when they retire. RPPs are not required by law, but once set up face stringent provincial and federal regulations.

❑ **Group RRSP –** Is like an individual RRSP but with additional benefits: low annual fees, improved reporting, flexible investment vehicles, easy to set up and maintain.

❑ **Deferred Profit Savings Plan –** Employers may contribute any amount out of profits, up to legislated maximums, into an employee DPSP account or trust fund. Contributions and earnings are sheltered from income tax until withdrawn. A DPSP can help focus employee attention on your bottom line and the method for allocating funds is flexible. No contributions are needed in years without profit.

Tax Plan

Tax Liability Estimate – *Estimate your tax liability for your first three years of operation:*

❑ U.S. tax information can be found at www.irs.gov ❑ For Canada, visit www.ccra-adrc.gc.ca or *www.fin.gc.ca*
❑ For links to international tax information, try www.taxsites.com OR www.worldwide-tax.com (see next page)
❑ A useful tax estimating tool for U.S. taxes is available at www.quicken.com/taxes/taxslashing/estimator/

Federal Tax		%	State or Provincial Tax	%	Other Taxes	%
1st Year	20		Total Federal, State, and Others	%	Tax Liability in Dollars	$
2nd Year	20		Total Federal, State, and Others	%	Tax Liability in Dollars	$
3rd Year	20		Total Federal, State, and Others	%	Tax Liability in Dollars	$

Tax Strategies – *Describe any strategies you have for legally reducing your small business taxes:*

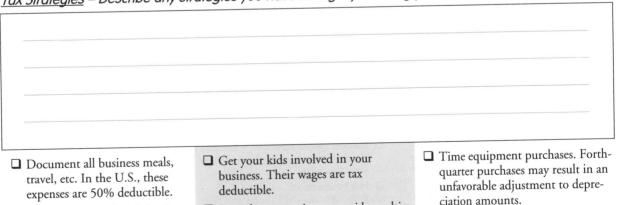

❑ Document all business meals, travel, etc. In the U.S., these expenses are 50% deductible.

❑ Claim a home office deduction.

❑ Get your kids involved in your business. Their wages are tax deductible.

❑ Pay sales tax on time to avoid penalties.

❑ Time equipment purchases. Forth-quarter purchases may result in an unfavorable adjustment to depreciation amounts.

Tax Liabilities and Retaining Tax Documents – Review tax liabilities. How long will you keep tax files?

USA Order the *Small Business Resource Guide* CD-ROM Pub. www.irs.gov

❏ **Income Tax –** All businesses except partnerships must file an annual income tax return. Partnerships file an information return. Partners are taxed personally on their share of business income. Corporations are taxed separately from shareholders. Proprietorships and partnerships can generally deduct the same expenses as corporations. Federal income tax must be paid as you earn or receive income during the year. This means, paying an estimated tax. For sole proprietors, partners in a partnership, or shareholders of an S-corporation, installments must be made by the 15th day of the 4th, 6th, 9th, and 12th month. Generally, each installment must equal 25% of the required annual estimated tax. If a corporation or an individual fails to pay by the due date, they may be subject to a penalty.

❏ **Self-Employment Tax (SECA) –** The SECA tax (SE tax) is a social security and Medicare tax for individuals who work for themselves. It provides business owners with retirement benefits, disability benefits, and medical insurance. The SECA tax rate on net earnings for 2003 was 15.3% on the first $87,000 of which 12.4% was for social security (old-age, survivors, and disability insurance), and 2.9% was for Medicare (hospital insurance).

❏ **Employment Taxes –** Business owners who are employers must pay employment taxes. These taxes include social security, Medicare, and Federal unemployment taxes.

❏ *Social Security and Medicare Taxes (FICA)* – The Federal Insurance Contributions Act (FICA) requires employer and employee to each pay 6.2% of the employee's income for social security and 1.45% for Medicare (2003).

❏ *Federal Unemployment Tax (FUTA)* – FUTA provides unemployment payments to workers who have lost their jobs. The FUTA tax rate is 6.2% on the first $7,000 of wages (2003).

❏ **Excise Taxes –** An excise tax is a tax imposed on the selling price of particular types of goods manufactured or produced in the U.S., such as luxury cars, coal, and gas. You may have to pay this tax if you manufacture or sell certain products, operate certain kinds of businesses, or use various kinds of equipment, facilities, or products.

CANADA For *more* information visit: www.ccra-adrc.gc.ca/tax/business/

❏ **Corporate Income Tax –** A corporation must pay at the end of each month of its fiscal period either one-twelfth of its estimated tax for the year, or one-twelfth of the tax paid in the previous taxation year. After its fiscal year-end, the corporation calculates its actual tax for the year and within two months of the year-end, pays any balance owing in addition to the monthly installment. If there is no tax owing, the corporation has up to six months after the fiscal year to file its return. Corporate tax returns must be filed both federally and provincially.

❏ **Proprietorships and Partnerships Income Tax –** Sole proprietors and partnerships must remit quarterly tax payments on all business income in advance, after making allowances for deductions. The four installments are made: Mar. 31, June 30, Sept. 30, and Dec. 31. Each installment must be equal to one-quarter of the taxpayer's estimate of taxes owed. The taxpayer calculates his or her actual tax for the year on or before April 30 of the following year and pays the amount he or she owes in excess of the installment or claims a refund.

❏ **G.S.T. –** In 1990, the 7% Goods and Services Tax (G.S.T.) replaced the Manufacturer's Sales tax. It is strongly recommended that all business owners carefully assess the impact of the G.S.T. on all aspects of their operation.

INTERNATIONAL Large accounting firms produce a series of international booklets on accounting, taxation, and company law information. Highly recommended.

❏ **PricewaterhouseCoopers –** Publishes a "Doing Business Guide: [Country]" series.

❏ **Ernst & Young –** Publishes a "Doing Business in [Country]" series.

❏ **KPMG –** Produces an "Asian Pacific Taxation" series. Available online at www.kpmg.com.hk. Click "Services" > "Tax" > "Publications."

❏ **Deloitte Touché Tohmatsu –** Publishes a "Doing Business" series available online at www.deloitte.com

❏ **HLB International –** Taxation guides available at www.hlbi.com/DBI_list.asp

Documents Suggested length of time for retaining tax files:

Retain Two Years ❏ general correspondence ❏ requisitions

Retain Three Years ❏ bank reconciliation statements ❏ expired insurance policies (no cash value) ❏ personnel files on departed employees ❏ petty cash vouchers

Retain Seven Years ❏ A/P's and A/R's ledgers ❏ all canceled checks indicating outlays of money ❏ all expense vouchers, such as rent and advertising ❏ asset records ❏ bad debt deductions ❏ capital expenditure records ❏ charitable donations ❏ employee disability benefits records ❏ employee taxes and withholding statements ❏ inventory records ❏ invoices and sales records ❏ monthly trial balances ❏ old contracts and leases ❏ payroll records and time sheets ❏ purchase orders ❏ remittances of unemployment insurance premiums and pension plan contributions (where applicable) ❏ vouchers for payments to vendors, employees, etc.

Retain Indefinitely ❏ audit reports and financial statements ❏ canceled checks for taxes, capital purchases, and important contracts ❏ capital stock and bond records ❏ income and sales journals ❏ contracts and leases that are current ❏ copyright, patents, and trademark registrations ❏ corporation charters, minute books of meetings, and bylaws ❏ correspondence on legal and tax matters ❏ deed, mortgages, easements, and other property records ❏ general and private ledger sheets ❏ general journals if they are essential to the understanding of the general ledger entries ❏ insurance records ❏ property appraisals ❏ share records ❏ special contracts and agreements ❏ tax returns, including supporting records, and work papers

Review when annual and quarterly tax payments are due. **How** *have these payments been factored into your income projections and cash flow statements? Describe any assumptions made:*

Sample: Based on projected revenues of $[XX], our estimated quarterly tax payments for 2005 are $[XX]. These have been factored into cash flow projections for January, April, June, and September.	

Business Calendar for U.S. Federal Taxes for Which You May Be Liable

FY			SP = Sole Proprietor P = Partnership SC = (Subchapter) S Corporation C = Corporation		SP	P	SC	C
1*	**Jan**	15	Estimated Tax	Form 1040-ES	✓	✓	✓	
		31	FICA (Social Security Tax) and Income Tax Withholdings	Forms 941, 941E, 942, and 943	✓	✓	✓	✓
		31	Information on FICA and Income Tax Withholdings	Form W-2 (to employee)	✓	✓	✓	✓
		31	FUTA (Federal Unemployment Tax)	Form 940-EZ or 940	✓	✓	✓	✓
		31	FUTA (only if tax liability exceeds $100)	Form 8109 (to make deposit)	✓	✓	✓	✓
		31	Annual Information Returns for Certain Payments Made	Form 1099 (to recipients)	✓	✓	✓	✓
2	**Feb**	28	Annual Information Returns for Certain Payments Made	Form 1099 (to IRS)	✓	✓	✓	✓
		31	Information on FICA and Income Tax Withholdings	Form W-2 and W-3 (to S.S. admin)	✓	✓	✓	✓
3	**Mar**	15	Income Tax (corporate)	Form 1120, 1120-A, or 1120S			✓	✓
4	**Apr**	15	Estimated Tax	Form 1040-ES or 1120-W (C-corp.)	✓	✓	✓	✓
		15	Self-employment Tax	Form 1040 (Schedule SE)	✓	✓		
		15	Income Tax (individual, partner, S-Corp. shareholder)	Form 1040	✓	✓	✓	
		15	Annual Return of Income	Form 1065		✓		
		30	FICA (Social Security Tax) and Income Tax Withholdings	Forms 941, 941E, 942, and 943	✓	✓	✓	✓
		30	FUTA (only if tax liability exceeds $100)	Forms 941, 941E, 942, and 943	✓	✓	✓	✓
6	**Jun**	15	Estimated Tax	Form 1040-ES or 1120-W (C-corp.)	✓	✓	✓	✓
7	**Jul**	31	FICA (Social Security Tax) and Income Tax Withholdings	Forms 941, 941E, 942, and 943	✓	✓	✓	✓
		31	FUTA (only if tax liability exceeds $100)	Form 8109 (to make deposit)	✓	✓	✓	✓
9	**Sep**	15	Estimated Tax	Form 1040-ES or 1120-W (C-corp.)	✓	✓	✓	✓
10	**Oct**	31	FICA (Social Security Tax) and Income Tax Withholdings	Forms 941, 941E, 942, and 943	✓	✓	✓	✓
		31	FUTA (only if tax liability exceeds $100)	Form 8109 (to make deposit)	✓	✓	✓	✓
12	**Dec**	15	Estimated Tax	Form 1120-W				✓

* If your tax year is NOT January 1st through December 31st, then simply follow the above calendar, but move the 1st month of your fiscal year to **FY - 1** (e.g., if your fiscal year is May 1st to April 30th, then do everything in May as required above for Jan, Jun for Feb, etc.). If the 15th day of the month falls on a Saturday, Sunday, or a legal holiday, the due date is the next day that is not a Saturday, Sunday, or legal holiday.
Calendar Source: IRS Publication 509 *Tax Calendars for 2002*

33 Scrooge Strategies *– Check strategies you will use to lower your business and living overhead:*

Business Overhead

☐ Attend free IRS-sponsored workshops to reduce taxes.

☐ Buy in small quantities at first. You can always reorder.

☐ Buy inventory and supplies in larger quantities to get volume discounts, once you have a clear understanding of your markets.

☐ Buy quality to save over the long run. Cheap fixtures, equipment, and furniture wear out faster and become obsolete quicker.

☐ Carefully consider all new technology before spending any money on it.

☐ Develop a good relationship with your suppliers and service providers. Not only can this lead to better discounts and terms, but suppliers and service providers are often your best link to keeping up with the latest trends.

☐ Follow the 80/20 rule. Your profits lie in the 20% of your customers who give you 80% of your business.

☐ Follow the two-thirds rule. Always put two-thirds of your energy into reducing costs and one-third into increasing income.

☐ Join a local, state/provincial or national barter exchange and swap for items you need to run your business.

☐ Lower your thermostat. Heat is money. For each Fahrenheit degree above 68 degrees, your fuel consumption goes up an average of 2.5%. If you permanently lower your thermostat from 72 degrees to 68 degrees, you will save 10% on your annual fuel consumption.

☐ Make holidays partially tax deductible as business trips.

☐ Minimize transportation costs. Driving to and from your business is a daily expense. If you drive less, you can save on gas, parking, maintenance, and repairs.

☐ Reduce meals out. If you're like most people, you spend about $5 a day on lunch and snacks. If you bag it from home, you can easily save $50 to $100 a month.

☐ Send faxes after 11 P.M. Rates can be 60% lower.

☐ Stay at budget motels on business trips.

☐ When starting out, try not to hire. Do the work yourself, especially if your business is small or home-based.

☐ Yearly reassess your own insurance needs and deductibles to see if you can't reduce these costs.

Personal Living Expenses

☐ Always think of ways NOT to spend your money.

☐ Avoid buying convenience foods. Convenience foods not only cost more, but in the end are bad for your health (and contribute to higher medical bills).

☐ Be wary of get-rich-quick seminars. Much of the advice get-rich-quick schemers have to offer is simplistic, deceptive, wrong, and quite often harmful.

☐ Buy a used car. With new cars depreciating by 20% after one year, and 50% after three years, should you be spending $15,000 to $20,000 on a new car?

☐ Buy only the clothes you need and when you do, buy quality. The wealthy can't afford to waste time buying cheap things over and over again. Why should you?

☐ Clean with natural products. Use baking soda, ammonia, boric acid, vinegar, and lemon juice. Not only is this cheaper but it's better for the environment.

☐ Cut down or give up tobacco and alcohol. Cutting down on tobacco and alcohol can save the average heavy drinker and smoker over $3,000 a year.

☐ Don't buy more furniture than you need. The less you have, the more spacious your rooms will look.

☐ Drastically reduce the amount you spend on beauty products. The best-kept beauty secrets are almost free.

☐ Enter contests you have a good chance of winning. Many company-sponsored promotional contests offer excellent chances of winning. Some people even claim to make a living on these contests.

☐ Get rid of your second car. Cutting out that extra car payment, along with its insurance and maintenance costs, could easily save you $300 to $600 a month.

☐ Keep all warranties and bills of major purchases. You never know when clock radios, hair dryers, and the like will suddenly expire for no good reason.

☐ Make it a habit of reviewing newspaper ads, newsletters, and supplier circulars for special discounts.

☐ Reduce personal long-distance calls. Write letters instead, fax, or better yet, send email.

☐ Settle for a smaller house to keep your mortgage payments reasonable.

☐ Take in boarders or rent a basement suite.

DAY 29

Anticipate the reactions of your competitors.

Develop an insurance and risk management plan.

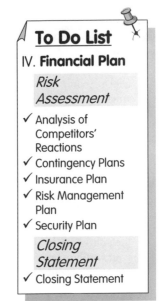
Risk Assessment

Investors want to know how much money they can make if they invest in your business. But they also want to know what their risks are—*worst* and *best* case scenarios—and what evidence you can provide to show them you have anticipated potential problems and have come up with solutions.

Analysis of Competitors' Reactions

Competitors aren't going to just sit around while you steal their market share. In fact, if management is on their toes, they too have developed "contingency plans" for new competition. In this section, address "what if" scenarios specific to key competitors—e.g.: What will you do if competitors start a "price war?"

Contingency Plans

A *Contingency Plan* addresses and provides solutions for "what if" scenarios. It follows the format: "If [problem] happens, we will [solution, strategy, counter measure]. It is quite similar to a *Risk Management Plan* accept that it focuses more on "solutions to high-risk problems" specific to your business or industry, rather than "more generic low-risk problems" particular to all businesses such as "acts of God" or other unforeseen circumstances.

Insurance Plan

Almost all businesses need insurance of some kind. Manufacturers need product liability. Service industries need personal liability. Security-related businesses require bonding. Bankers especially want to see that you have adequate coverage to safeguard any loans you might be asking for. For most small business owners, coverage is needed for property, liability, business interruption, and Worker's Compensation. When negotiating rates with agents, take full responsibility for understanding all conditions and terms, including price, coverage, and deductible. Many agents work on commission and will be more than happy to sell you something you don't need.

How do you insure yourself against insurance premiums?
PETER CORRIS

Partners in a business will often purchase life insurance on each other in order that, on the death of one partner, the others will have the funds to purchase all of the business.
INSURANCE TIP

Important Types of Business Insurance

- *Automobile* – Purchasing commercial vehicle and collision insurance, allows a company to insure its cars, trucks, and other vehicles against the possibility of theft, accidental damage, and bodily injury to others.

- *Business Interruption* – Compensates you for revenue lost due to a fire or during a temporary halt in business caused by theft or illness.

- *Business Life and Health* – Business life polices can be written to you, your family, or partner(s), against financial loss due to death or serious injury.

- *Fidelity and Surety Bonds* – Fidelity bonds protect against loss due to employee dishonesty. Useful where employees have access to large sums of money or inventory. Surety bonds are often issued to guarantee performance from contractors.

- *General Liability* – Protects you from financial loss when customers, employees, or anyone from the public claims bodily injury or property damage sustained on your premises, during business-related activity, or through use of your product.

- *Group Life and Health* – A benefit you might offer employees.

- *Property (Fire and Theft)* – All businesses need to insure against fire. Property insurance can be categorized under comprehensive, all-risk, and inside-outside packages that may or may not include fire, theft, flood, crime, vandalism, or inland marine coverage. The "Storekeeper's Burglary and Robbery Policy" is an example of a comprehensive crime insurance policy available to retailers.

- *Workers' Compensation* – Employers must have insurance to compensate employees for loss of income or medical expenses that result from work-related injury or disease.

Risk Management Plan

When applying for a loan, banks will require certain types of insurance, depending on the nature of the business and the type of loan.

A *Risk Management Plan* is the heart of your *Risk Assessment*. Here is where you show how you plan to deal with specific events that may cause losses to your company. In this section, explain *causes* and *effects* of potential problems and your *strategy* to reduce the risk. More specifically, describe any risk reducing measures you have taken or plans developed if there is a strike, recession, new technology, bad weather, supplier problems, or shifts in consumer demand. Likewise, describe any risk reducing measures or plans you have if sales projections are off by 30%, sales double, workers quit, or if a key manager becomes ill. Other types of risks experienced by small business startups include: ❑ loss of financing ❑ legal disputes ❑ intellectual property infringement ❑ new government policies ❑ unexpected competition ❑ loss of key staff ❑ bad debts ❑ fire and water damage ❑ data loss ❑ theft and vandalism ❑ market saturation ❑ environmental damage ❑ bad publicity.

It requires a great deal of boldness and a great deal of caution to make a great fortune, and when you have got it, it requires ten times as much wit to keep it.
RALPH WALDO EMERSON

Sample Risk Management Statements

Seasonal buying patterns have been considered in our projections. However, the current [economic slowdown, recession] could heighten deviations and adversely affect cash flow. For this reason, all sales forecasts have been kept conservative.

[State and local ordinances, zoning laws] that may affect our [product, business] are [describe]. To overcome this [company name] has [describe solution]. [I/we] will stay on top of any future legal issues through the services of [list consultant] and by monitoring [list publications and other research sources].

[Company name] has purchased product liability insurance from [insurance company]. This policy [describe terms, conditions, and period of coverage]. However, future increases in insurance premiums, as estimated by our agent, [name], could make it prohibitive for us to maintain adequate coverage leaving us exposed to [describe possible threats of legal action related to your product].

[Company name] has also purchased [describe type of insurance] to protect against [fire, floods, theft]. Despite this precaution, a major natural disaster could affect our business and cause [list and describe types of risks].

Security Plan

A *Security Plan* lists ways you protect your business from employee dishonesty, accidental destruction of property, and among other things, theft and vandalism. It is also becoming increasingly important to establish a backup security plan for computer data and procedures for dealing with Internet-related computer virus attacks.

Closing Statement

A *Closing Statement* at the end of a business plan can be used to reinforce the purpose of your plan and help direct readers to the conclusion you want. It can also be used to legally validate the contents of your plan.

Sample Closing Statement

[I/We], the undersigned, declare that the statements made herein are for the purpose of obtaining business financing and are to the best of [my/our] knowledge true and correct. [I/We] consent to the bank making any inquiries it deems necessary to reach a decision on this information about [company name] to any credit-reporting agency or to anyone with whom [I/we] have financial relations. Current financial statements have been validated by [CPA, accounting firm].

_____   _____
      Date   Signature

If you're successful, people are going to sue you. So be prepared and get yourself a good lawyer now. Lawsuits are part of the business game today.
RON POPEIL
✳
Some businesses fail because they become too successful, too soon. If your company becomes inundated with orders, what contingency plans do you have for hiring additional staff and contacting additional suppliers?

If a man will begin with certainties he shall end in doubts; but if he will be content to begin with doubts he shall end in certainties.
FRANCIS BACON

DAY 29 **Worksheets** ⏱

Anticipate the reactions of your competitors. Develop an insurance and risk management plan.

Risk Assessment

Types of Risks – *List and evaluate the "severity" and "potential for" business risks your company will face:*

❑ industry volatility   ❑ heavy reliance on a few clients   ❑ poor performance of key personnel   ❑ political instability

❑ **Customer Attitudes**
What if your customers no longer want your fancy designer hats ever since the latest pop idol claimed that they "make my head look too big!"

❑ **Economic Uncertainty**
What happens to your restaurant if rising unemployment keeps people eating at home?

❑ **Government Regulations**
What happens if a new local ordinance invalidates your license or rezones your property?

❑ **Greedy Suppliers**
What do you do if your supplier decides to raise their prices and you are forced to pay because they are the ONLY supplier in the region?

❑ **Industry Too Expensive**
The startup costs of some industries—such as shipbuilding—are so high that cash reserves can be quickly depleted if sales are slow.

❑ **Labor Problems**
What happens if you lose your top sales person to a competitor or all your Web techs go on strike?

❑ **Product Cycle Ends**
Product market expands, matures, and then shrinks. What if you find out you started at the wrong time?

❑ **Slow-moving Inventory**
A camera shop might not be able to move old cameras once the latest digital camera makes everything else obsolete.

Note: "Degree of Risk Severity" is measured from 1 to 10 with 10 being the highest. "Weight of Risk" is measured in percent. The total should add up to 100%.

		Degree of Risk Severity	Weight of Risk	TOTAL Risk Factor
1			%	
2			%	
3			%	
4			%	
5			%	
6			%	
7			%	
	Overall Risk		100 %	

Sample: Table 5 shown [above, below] outlines seven sources of risk than may impact [company] over the next five years. Each area of risk has been assigned a "Degree of Risk Severity" from 1 to 10 (with 10 being the highest) and a "Weight of Risk" measured in percent of total risk. The value of both measures are based on [research source] and our experience in the industry. Even though risk severity of water damage to our plant is quite high, we have estimated that the total risk factor is quite low. On the other hand, the most serious risk facing [company] is the threat of poor market acceptance. Although high-grade digital cameras have sold successfully in the past to [market], there is no assurance this will continue. Demand for 1 megapixel camera phones has begun to erode sales of lower-grade digital cameras. This trend could impact our sales.

Analysis of Competitors' Reactions

Detail how competitors might react to the entrance of your business into the market. Will they try to squeeze you out? Will they drop prices below cost? Will they start a publicity war?

Sample: As they have done in the past with new competitors, upon our entry into the market, [competitor A] may drop their prices. In anticipation of this risk, we have set aside a reserve fund of $[XX] to operate at a loss of $[XX] for eight months.

Contingency Plans

*Describe strategies you will implement to reduce risk in the event your original assumptions are incorrect. **What** happens if you can't turn a profit after a year? Do you have a "Plan B" or some kind of safety net?*

Sample: If [company] experiences a slower growth rate than projected, we will implement the following strategies to reduce risk to investors: (1) limit expansion investment to [X]% of working capital; (2) pursue other marketing channels including [describe]; and (3) stop recruitment of new staff until sales levels pick up.

Insurance Plan

<u>*Insurance Coverage Sheet*</u> *– Summarize your insurance protection. **What** kind of coverage is it? **What** is the cost? Are there special terms? **Who** is the carrier? (see* GB📖 *#31 "Getting Insurance"):*

❑ Automobile ❑ Business Interruption ❑ Business Life and Health ❑ Crime ❑ Disability ❑ Employee Benefit Coverage ❑ Fidelity, Surety Bonds ❑ General Liability ❑ Key-person Losses ❑ Product Liability ❑ Personal Liability ❑ Group Life and Health ❑ Property (Fire and Theft) ❑ Workers' Compensation ❑ Water Damage

Type of Insurance	Company	Contact Person	Coverage	Deductible	Annual Cost
General Business Policy (see supporting documents for copy)	Fast Insurance Inc. 678 W. Quick Street, Boston 12345	Jim Joy, Jr. (432) 555-4321	$1,000,000	$1,000	**$ 1,582**

Monthly Insurance Cost $ Total Annual Insurance Cost $

Risk Management Plan

Identify the most "severe" business risks your company faces and how you plan to deal with them:

Risk 1

cause

effect

strategy

Risk 2

cause

effect

strategy

Risk 3

cause

effect

strategy

Security Plan

Describe security measures you have taken to discourage theft and vandalism, protect inventory, and safeguard important documents. Do you have an alarm system? Do you have a fireproof safe?

Sample: [Company] is insured for theft and vandalism by [insurance carrier]. Insurance premiums are $[XX] annually for $3 million in coverage with a $1,500 deductible. We have also installed a [brand name] alarm system at a cost of $[XX]. Our website and database server is backed up every 24 hours. A copy of our Internet and staff security policy is available upon request.

Closing Statement

Jot down keywords and phrases to summarize any points you wish to make in your closing statement:

Sample: Supported by an innovative product line and strong financial projections validated by Ernst & Young-Sydney, Banyo World believes that this opportunity is a sound business investment. To proceed we are looking for venture capital of US $2.6 million by May 2006 for an ownership stake of [X]%.

Part V

SUPPORTING
DOCUMENTS

TEGuS Cartoons   *Peter J. Patsula*

"I'm afraid you have the wrong number . . .
But wait just a moment! Would you mind if
I asked you a few survey questions?"

> If you don't design your own life plan,
> chances are you'll fall into someone else's
> plan. And guess what they have planned
> for you? Not much.
>
> ☞ **Jim Rohn**

In this section . . .

- 📄 Documents Required
- 📄 Other Documents
  and Support Plans

DAY 30

List documents needed to support research.

SUPPORTING DOCUMENTS

EXCESSIVE documentation, exhibits, and appendices should not be part of the main business plan. As separate appendices, they make your proposal look less formidable. In your *Supporting Documents* section, include all records that back up the statements and decisions made in previous sections of your business plan. This section can also include items such as brochures, magazine articles, reviews, technical papers, and summaries of market research studies.

NOTE Compile your list of supporting documents as you work through this guide. For example, while writing your *Location Analysis*, you might decide to include a copy of your "lease agreement." Write "lease agreement" in the worksheet on page 339.

To Do List

V. **Supporting Documents**

Documents Required

✓ Contracts and Lease Agreements
✓ Credit Reports and Income Tax Returns
✓ Legal Documents
✓ Letters of Reference
✓ Personal Financial Statements
✓ Résumés

Other Documents and Support Plans

✓ Other Documents and Support Plans

Documents Required

Bankers and investors often require the support documents listed under this heading. If needed, include them in an appendix at the end of your business plan. If your appendix is quite large, break it up into several smaller appendices each grouped under a logical heading.

Contracts and Lease Agreements

Include all business contracts and agreements, both completed and currently in force, such as insurance policies, property and vehicle titles, purchase agreements, service contracts, mortgages, and debentures. Include all lease agreements currently in force between your company and leasing agencies.

Credit Reports and Income Tax Returns

Business credit reports can be obtained from suppliers or wholesalers. *Personal* credit reports and rating can be obtained from credit bureaus (refer to page 108), banks, and companies who you have dealt with on a credit basis. Depending on the purpose of your business plan you may also want to include copies of federal, state, and local income tax returns for the prior year.

Be careful not to go into too much detail in this section.

∗

Make sure that the information contained in this section does not contradict anything you said earlier.

Legal Documents

Include all legal papers pertaining to your legal structure such as articles of incorporation, partnership agreements, and franchise agreements. Also, include proprietary rights, such as copyrights, trademarks, and patents.

Letters of Reference

Include business or personal letters recommending you as a reputable and reliable businessperson. List the names, addresses, and phone numbers of: ❏ banks or other institutions with whom you have had financial dealings (state branch, type of account, type of loan, terms, etc.) ❏ accountants, lawyers, or other professionals with whom you have had business relationships ❏ other creditors including long-term relationships with suppliers.

Personal Financial Statements

Banks often require personal financial statements from all owners. They are an important part of your financial package because they: (1) verify your company financial statements; (2) identify hidden liability or equity; and (3) reveal other activities vying for your attention. Prepare a current *Personal Net Worth Statement*, outlining personal assets and liabilities, for yourself, each partner, or each stockholder owning 20% or more of the stock of your corporation. You should also prepare a *Personal Income Statement*.

Both statements should be limited to one page (see pages 340 and 341). For new ventures, put these statements in your *Business Financial History* section, especially if they warrant detailed explanation.

Résumés of Management and Key Individuals

Include your résumé if a sole proprietor, a résumé for each partner if a partnership, and résumés of all officers if a corporation. Include other individual(s) who will play a key role in making decisions and building profits. Limit résumés to one or two pages (see page 342). Include the following:

- **Overview –** Highlight your most relevant skills and qualifications.

- **Experience –** List previous businesses owned and related employment at other companies. Include duties, responsibilities, and related accomplishments.

- **Special Skills** – List personal strengths—e.g., strong knowledge of highway contracting, highly organized, five years experience with QuickBooks.

- **Education** – List dates, schools, fields of concentration, and related projects.

- **Affiliations and Interests** – List organizations you belong to that enhance your credibility. Also, include related awards you or your business has received.

Other Documents and Support Plans

Include only documents and materials that will be of immediate interest to readers. Keep others where they can be made available on short notice. Under this heading, you might want to list additional information and documentation available to lenders and investors and who should be contacted to obtain it (see page 338 for a list of "other documents").

Support Plans

Support Plans provide summaries and details of key projects in your *Operations Schedule* (see pages 26 and 140). They should be kept separate from your business plan, unless a particular project has great significance to the success and profitability of your business.

The best preparation for good work tomorrow is to do good work today.
ELBERT HUBBARD
✳
To be prepared is half the victory.
MIGUEL DE CERVANTES
✳
I'm just preparing my impromptu remarks.
WINSTON CHURCHILL
✳
Success depends upon previous preparation, and without such preparation there is sure to be failure.
CONFUCIUS

$ucce$$ Story ➡ Founder of STAR Television, Li Tzar Kai

In 1990, Richard Li Tzar Kai dreamed up STAR Television, the satellite cable-television network that revolutionized Asia's electronic media overnight. STAR broke through several government television monopolies, introduced soap operas to housewives from Punjab to Pusan and turned on a nation of teens to heavy metal and rock 'n roll. It also made Li Tzar Kai a fortune: he sold STAR to Rupert Murdoch's News Corp. in 1995 for $950 million. Li now wants to do for telecommunications what he did for television. He has stated that he wants "to provide Asians with the same very basic access to services that the West now takes for granted." Through his new company, Pacific Century CyberWorks (PCCW), Li Tzar Kai provides telecommunications and Web services across the Asian region. Born in Hong Kong in 1966, at only 37 years old, he has been listed in *Forbes'* World's Richest People.

List documents needed to support research.

Documents Required

Check documents to be included in your Appendix:

- ❑ Articles of Incorporation
- ❑ Contracts
- ❑ Credit Reports
- ❑ Income Tax Returns
- ❑ Lease Agreement

- ❑ Franchise Agreements
- ❑ Partnership Agreements
- ❑ Proprietary Rights (copyrights, trademarks, patents, licenses, distribution rights)
- ❑ Letters of Reference

- ❑ Personal Financial Statements (Net Worth and Income Statement)
- ❑ Financial Statements of Partners
- ❑ Résumés of Management and Key Individuals
- ❑ Your Résumé

Other Documents and Support Plans

Brainstorm – Check other documents and materials that you may include in your business plan:

- ❑ A/P's Summaries (include schedule of payments)
- ❑ A/R's Summaries (including aging schedules)
- ❑ Appraisals (property, equipment)
- ❑ Backup Research on Competitors
- ❑ Bank Statements
- ❑ Benefit and Features of Products
- ❑ Brochures, Printed
- ❑ Business Model
- ❑ Charge Account Statements
- ❑ Company Investment Portfolio
- ❑ Competitor Comparison Profiles
- ❑ Consulting Reports and Surveys
- ❑ Drawings (product designs, floor plans, logos, production process)
- ❑ Financial Statements for Associated Companies (if applicable)
- ❑ Focus Group Analyses

- ❑ Industry Information
- ❑ Industry Pricing Structure
- ❑ Job Descriptions for the Management Team
- ❑ Letters of Intent (potential orders, customer commitments, letters of support)
- ❑ List and Description of Major Liabilities (including mortgages)
- ❑ List of Fixed Assets (description, age, serial #s)
- ❑ List of Inventory (type, age, value)
- ❑ List of Leasehold Improvements (description, date made)
- ❑ List of Prospective Customers
- ❑ Location Plans
- ❑ Magazine, Newspaper, and Trade Journal Articles About Your Company, Product, or Service
- ❑ Marketing and Demographics Studies

- ❑ Mock-ups of Actual Marketing Brochures Describing Your Product or Service
- ❑ Names of Suppliers or Possible Suppliers
- ❑ Personal Property Values (to substantiate the value of your personal guarantee if required)
- ❑ Photos (location, buildings, facilities, products)
- ❑ Pricing Lists (to support cost estimates)
- ❑ Pricing List Breakdown (further clarifications of costs and fees)
- ❑ Product Specifications
- ❑ Product Test Results
- ❑ Promotion Calendar
- ❑ Publicity Articles and Promotional Pieces
- ❑ Technical Drawings
- ❑ Technology Backgrounders

List agreements, documents, reports, research studies, and other materials that **must be** added to support key statements in your business plan:

Write a summary list of **other** documents, support plans, and materials that you may or may not include (e.g., brochures, reviews, ABC product plan):

Personal Financial Statements

Prepare a Personal Net Worth Statement for yourself, key owners, and investors (see page 340). Provide a brief summary statement of your personal Net Worth. Highlight key figures:

Sample: Personal net worth statements of all founding partners have been included in the Supporting Documents section. The combined net worth is $[XX]. These statements have been verified by [accountant].

Prepare a Personal Income Statement for yourself, key owners, and investors (see page 341). Provide a brief summary statement of your personal disposable income. Highlight key figures:

Sample: My current disposable income is $[XX] (see Personal Income Statement in Appendix). To cover loan payments, personal expenditures can be further reduced by [X]%, leaving a disposable income of $[XX].

Résumés of Management and Key Individuals

Prepare a résumé, along with those of management, owners, and key individuals (see page 342). Provide a brief summary of your résumé. Highlight key skills and experiences:

PERSONAL NET WORTH STATEMENT

Name: Date:

ASSETS

Cash

Cash on Hand	
Checking Accounts	
Saving Accounts	
Money Owed to You	

Investments

Mutual Funds	
Stocks and Bonds	
Savings Bonds	
Other	

Cash Surrender Value

Annuities	
Life Insurance	
Pension Fund	
Retirement Plans	

Personal Property

Real Estate	
Furniture/Antiques	
Art/Jewelry	
Vehicles	

Other Assets

Accounts and Notes Receivable	
A.	
B.	
C.	

LIABILITIES

Unpaid Bills

Credit Cards	
Income Taxes	
Insurance Premiums	
Other Unpaid Bills	

Installment Loans

Automobile	
Other	

Long-term Loans

Bank	
Education	
Home Equity	
Other	

Real Estate Loans

Home	
Other	

Other Liabilities

Alimony Payments	
Accounts Payable	
Notes Payable	
Contracts Payable	
A.	
B.	
C.	

TOTAL ASSETS	$	TOTAL LIABILITIES	$

NET WORTH $

PERSONAL INCOME STATEMENT

Name: **Date:** **Period:**

INCOME

Gross Salaries	
Bonuses and Commissions	
Spouse's Gross Salaries	
Rental Income	
Annuities and Pensions	
Dividends and Interest	
Sale of Personal Capital Items	
1.	
2.	
TOTAL Gross Income	

Less Taxes

Personal Income Tax	
Other Taxes	
A) TOTAL NET INCOME	

Household

Rent/Mortgage Payments	
Household/Apt. Insurance	
Property Taxes	
Utilities (telephone, power, etc.)	
Maintenance and Repairs	
Furniture and Appliances	
Stereos, TVs, and Computers	
Day Care Services	
Other Household Expenses	

EXPENSES

Transportation

Auto Loan/Lease Payments	
Auto Insurance	
Gas and Oil	
Repairs and Maintenance	
Licenses, Fees, and Parking	
Other Transportation Expenses	

Personal

Food	
Clothing	
Laundry and Cleaning	
Music, Movies, and Theatre	
Drinking, Dining, and Dancing	
Sporting Activities	
Vacation and Travel	
Gifts, Donations, and Dues	
Education, Books, and Magazines	
Medical/Dental/Life Insurance	
Doctor and Dentist Fees	
Prescription Medicines	
Loans, Debts, and Credit Payments	
Investment and Savings Plans	
Other Personal Expenses	
1.	
2.	

B) TOTAL LIVING EXPENSES

TOTAL DISPOSABLE INCOME (A – B) $

Owner's Résumé

Name:

Address:

Contact:

Overview

Dates/Headings

Experience

Special Skills

Education

Affiliations and Interests

CONCLUSION

TEGuS Cartoons   *Peter J. Patsula*

> Whatever failures I have known, whatever errors I have committed, whatever follies I have witnessed in private and public life have been the consequence of action without thought.
>
> ᴄᴈ **Bernard M. Baruch**

In this section . . .

- Business Plan Writing Strategies
- Why Businesses Succeed or Fail
- Sample Cover Letter
- Sample Business Plan
- Idea Sheet, Daily Planner, Quarterly Cash Flow Budget Analysis
- Index
- The 30 Day Business Plan™ Checklist

Conclusion

CONGRATULATIONS! You've completed your business plan! Now, type it out and seek professional counsel. If located in the U.S., set up a meeting with a Service Corps of Retired Executives volunteer or get some FREE advice via email at www.score.org. There are SCORE chapters in every state. Next, have your business plan reviewed by people who regularly work with business owners and have come to recognize characteristics of ventures that succeed or fail. Show your plan to a small business banker or accountant. If you already know people who are running their own successful business, have them look at it. Whatever you do, don't let your plan sit on your desk and collect dust. You've put in long hours and hard work to get it finished. Don't let that work go to waste.

Business Plan Writing Strategies

Before typing your business plan, ask yourself the following four questions:

- What should my business plan look like?
- How long should it be?
- Who will read my business plan?
- What's the best way to get started?

APPEARANCE – **A business plan should look good.** Although you may have limited time and limited resources, and should put your efforts where there is the most reward—there is no excuse for a sloppy-looking business plan. Put your best foot forward: this commands respect. Copies of your business plan should be printed on quality paper and placed in a blue, black, brown, or clear duo-tang folder or binder, or professionally bound at a local print shop. There should be no typing, spelling, punctuation, or grammar errors. Number your copies: "copy 1 of 5", "copy 2 of 5," etc.

NOTE A skillful graphic designer can polish a business plan to the point that its appearance shines more than its content. Every entrepreneur should be cautioned to avoid losing sight of the real purpose of a business plan. Keep it straightforward and clear. Save the glitz for your marketing campaigns.

LENGTH – **Don't make your business plan too long or too short.** A 200-page business plan makes a dandy fire, while a three-page business plan makes

---

The Effective Business Plan ☑

1. Are goals tied to your mission?
2. Are customers clearly defined?
3. Are buying objections overcome?
4. Are strengths and weaknesses assessed?
5. Have future opportunities been clarified and threats prepared for?
6. Are strategies in place to learn from your competitors?
7. Does your marketing strategy make sense?
8. Is your competitive advantage clear?
9. Are your numbers believable?
10. Is there innovation in your company, marketing, and financial plans?

You have five minutes to convince a banker or investor to seriously read your plan. After that, all they need is one good reason to toss it aside. Don't give it to them.
FUNDING TIP

three dandy paper airplanes. A plan being used as a management tool should be at least 10 pages (see our "sample business plan"). As a general rule, if you are going to a bank or an individual investor, prepare no more than 30 to 40 pages, preferably 15 to 20 pages, including the *Supporting Documents* section. Rarely should your plan exceed 50 typewritten pages.

AUDIENCE – **Have a good idea WHO will be reading your business plan.** There are two main types of business plans: (a) those intended as "roadmaps" for starting, operating, and growing a business; and (b) those intended as "sales documents" for raising capital, attracting investors, securing bank loans, or securing lines of credit from suppliers. In each of the above cases, the intended reader has different expectations and needs. Although the information contained in either plan might be essentially the same, the emphasis is different. A plan intended as a roadmap—with the targeted audience being management or owners—wouldn't need to include extensive biographies of key management figures. However, a plan intended to be used as a sales document for raising capital or obtaining a loan—with the intended audience being bankers or investors—would. In fact, the background and experience of management may be what investors consider the most important part of your plan. They want to be convinced that your company is in control of its future before they put their money on the line.

When typing your business plan, also consider the specific needs of each audience group. Investors, for example, want to know how much capital you are asking for, how much risk is involved, how much potential for profit there is, and whether you are credible, trustworthy, and committed. On the other hand, a banker is more interested in knowing how much money you have at stake, how you will make loan payments, and if you go bankrupt, what personal guarantees you are able to offer.

OUTLINE – **Start by rethinking your table of contents.** You could complete your business plan by typing out the entries made into this guide using similar section titles and headings as shown on page 42. This guide has been carefully organized into a clear yet comprehensive outline. Depending on the purpose of your business plan, you may also decide to cut and rearrange your content to better examine "Key Areas" unique to your business, and as a result, more effectively meet your needs and the needs of your target audience. If you are seeking a loan from a particular bank or organization, find out the *exact* order they like content to be presented. Loan officers read hundreds of business plans and like to keep things the same so they can find important data quickly!

To structure a new outline:

- *Create a heading structure two levels deep.* Write down on a piece of paper all the sections you want to discuss making sure to leave enough room under each second-level heading for a list of third-level headings. Use the table of contents checklist on page 42 to assist in this task. If needed, raise second-level headings to the first level to emphasize important areas.

- *As you research and outline new sections in your first- and second-level headings, make a list of additional "Key Areas" or third-level headings that need to be researched further.* Express each "Key Area" as one word or a phrase. Organize related "Key Areas" into a logical sequence under each of your second-level headings. Go down as many levels into each "Key Area" as needed; however, one additional level should be more than enough.

- *To start building paragraphs, write concise informative sentences about each "Key Area" by describing the "who," "what," "where," "when," "why," "how," and "how much."* For example, if writing about a unique business location, describe *what* kind of building is on the site, *where* it's located, *why* you chose it, and *how much* it costs to rent, lease, or purchase. Use the ideas and information entered into this guide, as well as the sample paragraphs provided, as starting points. Be concise and clear. Eliminate words you don't really need. If your writing lacks vigor and clarity, consult online guide GB 📖 #57 "Writing and Editing Like a Pro."

Instead of writing your business plan yourself, you have the option of having someone else do it for you. But this can be expensive. The cost can easily exceed $30,000 if you use a professional consulting firm. Furthermore, the resulting document is not your plan, and as a result may have little operational value to you. If someone else develops your business plan, it becomes THEIRS, not YOURS.

Making Your Business Plan Sell

GRAPHICS – *Use well-designed illustrations, graphs, charts, and photos.* A picture may be worth a thousand words, but in a business plan, it might be worth an extra $1,000 or $1 million in venture capital. If a photo or chart can be used to ease assimilation of your plan's content, USE it! If you have to, contract a specialist to design it right. However, don't clutter your business plan with too many visuals. You can always include detailed product diagrams, photographs, charts, etc., in your *Supporting Documents* section.

ADJECTIVES – *Avoid the use of self-promoting adjectives.* Adjectives like "leading" and "superior" belong in advertising, not a business plan. Although you may use such words in your mission or vision statement, do not say things like: "It is the best product ever." Instead say: "Our product features [A, B, and C] and sells for 15% less than brands [X, Y, and Z]."

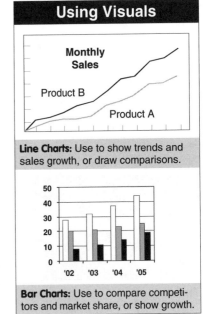

Using Visuals

Monthly Sales

Product B

Product A

Line Charts: Use to show trends and sales growth, or draw comparisons.

Bar Charts: Use to compare competitors and market share, or show growth.

*A good plan today
is better than a
perfect plan
tomorrow.*
GEORGE S. PATTON

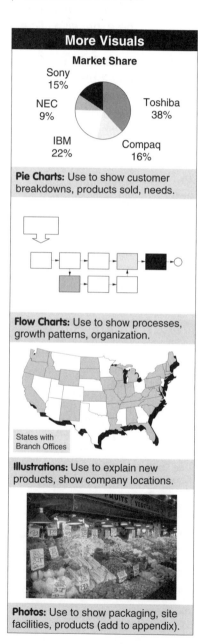

More Visuals

Market Share

Sony 15%
NEC 9%
IBM 22%
Toshiba 38%
Compaq 16%

Pie Charts: Use to show customer breakdowns, products sold, needs.

Flow Charts: Use to show processes, growth patterns, organization.

States with Branch Offices

Illustrations: Use to explain new products, show company locations.

Photos: Use to show packaging, site facilities, products (add to appendix).

BULLETS – *Use bullet points to break up complex information.* Bullets allow for faster reading and greater comprehension. Using bullets also makes it easier to grab ideas for PowerPoint presentations with potential investors or partners. However, don't overuse them. Keep bulleted lists to seven items or less, preferably one line for each item.

BUSINESS TERMS – *Use appropriate business terms and "buzzwords."* Make sure you have correctly used industry terms and catchphrases, especially those "popular" with your targeted reader. However, don't fill your plan with too much technical jargon that few readers will understand.

COVER LETTERS – *Include a cover letter for specific readers.* If submitting a business plan for funding or other specific objective, it is essential to introduce yourself first, summarize your proposal, and point out aspects of your business plan the reader might be most interested in (see page 350).

FACTS and NUMBERS – *Use facts and numbers to support your information and add to your credibility.* Nothing sells a business idea like good solid realistic numbers. Don't say: "Our expenses are less than others." Say: "By sharing leasing costs with ABC Inc., we have cut overhead by 33%."

MARGINS – *Make sure margins are wide enough.* There is no need to double-space your business plan. However, formatting ample left, right, top, and bottom white space not only makes your business plan more inviting, but also leaves room for readers to jot down notes and ideas.

ONE SIDE ONLY – *Print on one side only.* Printing on both sides of a business plan is not a good idea. You do not want reverse print to show through from the other side.

THIRD-PARTY SUPPORT – *Use positive comments from outside sources.* If you say your company is "great," it's worth about two cents. But if Bill Gates says, "Microsoft is projecting a 250% growth in the XYZ industry," or C-NET has rated your company website as, "the #1 content provider for animal medicine," or 25 surveyed customers said your brand of coffee, "tastes better than their favorite national brand," then make sure you strategically place these comments to add credibility to your claims.

Why Businesses Succeed or Fail

Outlined below are some critical factors that may lead to the success or failure of a new business venture. For 90+ additional tips, see online guide GB📖 #12 "Learning Why Companies Succeed and Why they Fail":

Companies Succeed Because They …

Adopt effective communication systems. Excellent companies believe in the importance of informality between management and employees to enhance communication.

Are quality driven. Excellent companies strive to make things that work fast and last. Their fundamental goal is to create products and services that add value to the lives of their customers.

Believe in productivity through people, not things. Excellent companies treat the rank and file as the root source of quality and productivity gain. They encourage happiness and a sense of community.

Innovate all aspects of their business. Excellent companies seek to be innovative in almost every aspect of their business including pricing, HR policies, distribution, sales promotion, stationery, signs, etc.— not just in their products and services.

Companies Fail Because They …

Are badly managed. Bad managers believe bigger is better, like to analyze everything, and among other things, have narrow-minded business philosophies.

Borrow more money than they should. Companies fail because they borrow money unnecessarily or at a rate higher than they can afford to pay back. They fail to understand that interest and repayment schedules can severely constrict cash flow.

Cater to the wrong kind of client. Companies fail because they are afraid of not getting enough clients and thus end up courting overly demanding time-hogs and reluctant payers.

Don't make the effort to develop a loyal customer base. Companies fail because they make the mistake of negotiating every deal or making every sale like they'll never see or need the customer again.

$ucce$$ Story ➡ SBA's 2003 Business Persons of the Year

Sharon and Martin Bennett started a pet products business in 1989. With a $5,000 loan, they purchased two refurbished sewing machines and began making dog collars in a spare bedroom. Sharon developed all the first products herself, sourced raw materials, handled A/R's and A/P's, packaged and shipped orders, and mastered financial analysis. By the end of 1998, their operation Premier Pet Products had grown from a two-person operation to over $2.4 million in sales and 40 employees. Partnering with manager and marketer Evan Wooton in 1999, Premier continues to expand. Premier's dedication to quality and education, as well as a sincere concern for the welfare of people and their pets, has earned them the trust of top pet supply retailers, veterinarians, and pet trainers around the world. Premier now services over 10,000 accounts with annual sales of $10 million. Their slogan, "Your Pets, Our Passion™" (more success stories at www.sba.gov/success/success.html).

Successful businesses require hard work and a business plan.
JAMES FROMMEL
Chairman of SCORE of Memphis, *Business Review*

✳

Entrepreneurs, the successful ones, have on average nine failures for every success. It is only the successes that you will hear about, the failures they credit to experience.
CHARLES HANDY
The Age of Unreason

✳

A Japanese research study found that the top managers knew 4% of the problems in their company, supervisors knew 74%, and workers in the trenches knew 100%!

A cover letter must be included with any plan you send or email to a potential funding source. Clarify:

1. How do you "know" or "know of" the recipient?

2. How did you get their name?

3. Who else is supporting your

Connect a credible person with your plan. Plans that come from a credible source are more likely to be read.

If you don't have an intermediary or credible supporter, state the name and nature of your company and why you have chosen to send your plan to the recipient.

4. Why have you chosen this particular funding source or investor?

5. Why is the recipient an appropriate funding source for your proposal?

The 30 Second Elevator/Email Pitch

Use Your Company Letterhead
[Your company] [Street address] [City], [Postal code]
[Phone] [Fax] [Email]

[Date]

[Addressee name]
[Addressee company or Organization]
[Street address]
[City], [Postal code]

Dear [Addressee name] (double check that you are sending your plan to the right person):

I am currently seeking [an investor, funding] for [company], an [established, startup] [type of business]. You were referred to me by [name] of [company, organization].

OR … [Name of intermediary] suggested I get in touch with you with regard to my business, [company], a [type of business] that [describe what you do/sell].

Based on your interest in [industry, product, service] I believe the [enclosed, attached] business plan for [company] may interest you.

Knowing of your interest in funding [business type], I have [enclosed, attached] a copy of the business plan for [company], an [established, startup] [describe type of business] now seeking financing to enable us to [describe reason—e.g., expand operations, open new outlets].

NEXT (describe the nature of your business and its development stage)

[Company] is a [startup, leader] in the [production, field] of [product/service]. Our mission is to [briefly describe]. We have targeted [market] for our [product/service] because of [state reason and/or trend]. Our competitive advantage is [describe]. We also have a strong management team, including [state a few names, titles in company, and main qualifications].

OR … [Company] offers/sells [describe what you do or sell]. We serve [describe market]. We make our money by [describe more specifically "what" and "how" you sell]. Our company is like [describe similar companies]. Our strategy for success is [describe "keys to success"]. One of our main goals is to [describe your vision].

ADD (if necessary, the amount of investments or loans sought, terms, equity offered)

We are seeking $[XX] in return for [XX]% equity in our company. The funds will be used for [marketing, expansion, training staff, product R&D].

OR … We are seeking a credit line in the range of $[XX] to assist [company] in [describe how funds will be used]. We are offering [describe collateral, e.g., A/R's, inventory] to secure the loan.

END

Thank you for considering [company]. I will [contact, telephone] you within [seven days] to answer any questions you might have, as well as provide additional information if needed. If you would like to discuss matters sooner, please contact me at [state phone] or [include email].

Sincerely,

[Name]
[Title]
Attachments: [list]

All Health No Hype™ Company (AHC)
P.O. Box 123
San Diego, CA 92101
(619) 555-2225

BUSINESS PLAN

Nutriva Sports Nutrition Shake
allhealth-nohype.com
Custom Fitness & Nutrition Solutions

Robert Jackson, President
P.O. Box 123
San Diego, CA 98765
(Email) info@allhealth-nohype.com

Sample Plan

Plan prepared by
Robert Jackson July 28, 2002

copy 1 of 3
(Private and Confidential)

The following is a sample plan for *Nutriva Sports Nutrition Shake* developed by AHC, a recently established service provider owned and operated by freelance exercise consultant and trainer Mr. Robert Jackson. Bob has accumulated $50,000 in growth capital.

The purpose of Bob's plan is to seek an additional $50,000 loan from a successful marketing consultant and college friend, who has previously expressed interest in his idea and who may or may not become a second managing partner. The targeted reader, Ms. María Covas, wants to make sure Bob has carefully thought through all aspects of his idea and that the numbers make sense.

Disclaimer! Although every attempt has been made to make this business plan as realistic as possible, the names, concepts, and numbers are for educational purposes only. They do not reflect an actual financial history. Do not use it as a source of research for your own company.

NOTE – It is not the intention of this sample plan to find fault with reputable products and companies. This plan is a learning tool. Where appropriate, fictional names and companies have been used to protect the innocent.

Feedback – A table of contents is usually included as a separate page, especially if your plan is 20 pages or more.

TIP – For 15 pages or less, consider putting your table of contents on your cover page to give readers quick access to their "hot buttons."

Table of Contents
allhealth-nohype.com
Custom Fitness & Nutrition Solutions

Executive Summary

Attention-grabbing Introduction

Medical costs have gone through the ceiling. Aging baby boomers are refusing to submit to the idea of living out their golden years inactive and disease-ridden. More than ever, people are questioning treatments of diseases—pharmaceutical, radiation, and surgical—that do not always lead to better health. Alternatives are needed. Holistic nutrition consultants and solution providers are well positioned to service the growing needs of the general public as they increasingly seek to become more attuned to connecting their mind, body, and spirit to achieve optimal health. With preventative practices gaining rapidly on conventional medical wisdoms, never before has there been a better time to enter the nutrition and fitness industry.

Company Description

AHC was formed as a proprietorship in January of 2001 in San Diego, California by Robert Jackson to meet the growing demand for personal trainers and nutrition experts.

Development Stage; Mission and Goals

In its first year of operation, AHC generated a net profit after taxes of $31,600 and developed Phase I of its informational website allhealth-nohype.com, which currently receives more than 20,000 page hits per month. Over the next five years, AHC wishes to expand into the sports nutrition industry using Robert Jackson's client base, connections within the industry, and its interactive health and information website.

Company Facilities ☑ location advantage

AHC is located within ten minutes' walking distance to three of San Diego's largest fitness centers. With 1,000 sq. ft., it offers sauna, training, and massage facilities. AHC has leased its second level to Fabian's Hair, a hair treatment, skin care, and beauty shop that services clientele matching AHC's customer profile.

Products and Services; Accomplishments ☑ major contracts secured

AHC offers personal training and massage services in-home and on its premises. As part of their training sessions, AHC clients receive an end-of-session sports nutrition shake—Nutriva. Response to Nutriva has been overwhelmingly positive. Gracie Ellen of Juice Boosters Inc. has agreed to retail Nutriva. AHC has also secured an order for 1,000 samples for the All Company Inc.'s annual corporate retreat April 17, 2003.

Target Market

AHC clients include executives, athletes, celebrities, service workers, and retired couples with a high interest in a healthy lifestyle and preventative medicine. Nutriva will extend AHC's customer base by servicing the fast-paced life of the ordinary individual who wishes to build lean muscle mass, slim down, and acquire healthier eating habits.

Competition ☑ competitive advantage

Although the health and fitness industry is jam-packed with commercial interests, there are few facilities offering customized fitness and nutrition solutions. AHC has expertise, an excellent location, a fast-growing website, and low overhead.

Management Team ☑ stage of product creation ☑ other businesses owned

Known for his charismatic training style and ability to produce client results, Robert Jackson has been active in the fitness and nutrition industry for over ten years. He has been formally trained in holistic nutrition, has won prestigious competitive events, and has personally trained over 100 private clients. He has been developing Nutriva for more than five years with extensive client testing over the past year.

Funds Required

$50,000 has been raised to bring Nutriva to market. An additional $50,000 in working capital is needed by January 1, 2003 for three years @10% secured by real estate.

Executive Summary

Feedback – The following executive summary has been created using the worksheets on pages 47 to 49. It lacks narrative flair beyond the first paragraph and reads a little dry, but it doesn't waste words.

Bob has determined that María Covas —his main target reader—is a no-nonsense person who prefers straight-forward information. She has already expressed interest in Bob's idea, so doesn't need to be impressed much with product and profit claims. She does, however, need to be satisfied that Bob can crunch the numbers.

Bob might consider adding a few more facts and numbers to preview the depth of the research in the remaining parts of his plan.

TIPS – If you add an attention-grabbing introduction, don't make it too long (100 words is plenty).

You don't have to include headers— such as *Company Description, Development Stage, etc.* They have been added here as learning guides.

1.1 Vision

Within the next five years, grow AHC into a $5 million a year online retail health outlet specializing in an all-in-one sports nutrition shake for athletes, bodybuilders, professional entertainers, weekend fitness types, and the aging baby boomers. AHC will also provide personalized nutrition and exercise solutions based on blood type, body weight, metabolism, age, genetic makeup, activity level, lifestyle, and fitness goals. We want to get rid of all the nonsense surrounding health claims and provide REAL information, value, and sensible solutions to our clients and customers. We also want to be regarded as the gurus of health: honest, knowledgeable, healthful ourselves, and compassionate. Our ten-year plan is to build our own production facilities and see Nutriva in every supermarket across the globe, right next to milk, rice, and tofu. With the nutrition industry maturing and consolidating, small companies are carving out workable market niches. On the other hand, large companies are increasingly participating in healthy and functional foods by acquisition—e.g., Kellogg recently bought *Worthington*; Kraft bought *Balance Bar* and *Boca Burger*; and Nestle bought *PowerBar* (source: *Nutrition Business Journal*). After seven years of successful operations, Nutriva will begin preparations to be acquired by a large food manufacturer—OR go IPO.

1.2 Mission

Our mission is to provide the highest quality sports nutrition shake on the market for a reasonable price made from all natural ingredients that come as close as possible to the nutrient power of whole foods. We believe that no body is the same and everybody deserves the best health they can achieve.

1.3 Company Goals

- Dedicate ourselves to the continuous self-improvement of our clients.
- Be role models ourselves. Live the lifestyle we teach.
- After one growth year, fully bring the "Nutriva Sports Nutrition Shake" to market.
- After two years, self-publish: *All Health No Hype – Myths and Facts*.
- After three years, develop free workshops for disadvantaged inner-city youths: "How to Live the Good Life on a Budget." Distribute free Nutriva 4-packs to participants.
- After four years, aggressively expand into Canada and the Pacific Rim.

1.4 Financial Objectives

- Generate $600 in service revenues 200 workdays a year for FY 2003 revenues of $120K.
- Attract at least three Fortune 1000 companies as clients by 12/2003.
- Get one new client a week to establish a client base of 200 clients by FY 2004.
- Generate $20,000 in Nutriva revenues from online affiliates for FY 2004.
- Sell at least 10,000 books by 12/2005 for revenues of $40,000.

Five-Year Projections	2003	2004	2005	2006	2007
Nutriva Sales	$37,200	$203,000	$712,300	$2,137,000	$5,542,000
AHC Net Profit (After Taxes)	$29,000	$52,700	$126,400	$288,600	$619,200

1.5 Company Facts

- AHC generated a net profit after taxes of $31,600 for FY 2001. Available capital for Nutriva expansion: $50,000. Seeking an additional $50,000 in working capital.
- Phase I of website finished 6/2001: 20,000 page hits per month 6/2002.
- Contract for 1,000 orders of Nutriva from All Company Inc. secured for April 17, 2003.

Company Plan

2.1 Company Description

In January, 2001, All Health Company (AHC) was formed as a proprietorship to provide customized fitness and nutrition services for individuals and small groups in the San Diego area. Initial capitalization of $87,500 came from owner assets and savings.

AHC has been very successful in generating and increasing sales, as well as effective in achieving profitability. This is due to the following reasons:

- Robert Jackson produces results with his clients. Word-of-mouth referrals are high.
- AHC has access to expert marketing and financial advice.
- AHC has an excellent location with sufficient parking and room for growth.

AHC operates at 345 [street name omitted] near the CBD area. This location is desirable because there is no direct competition and it is exceptionally convenient for our clients. Our clients have frequently complimented us on the appearance of our building, lighting, and facilities. The building was originally used as a private home and was purchased for $310,000 at an estate auction. This price was well below market value. The lower level has large display windows, street front walk-in access, and a secure private back entrance. Our location was financed 1/2001@6% for $280,000 over 30 years and was recently appraised at $410,000. No renovations are currently required. We are leasing the second level for $1,200 per month to Fabian's Hair. The property is zoned for commercial and residential use.

2.1.1 Development to Date (R&D)

AHC has already spent a considerable amount of time researching and developing Nutriva within a budget of $10,000. So far, we have been able to perfect our formulation to provide a superior protein, antioxidant, fiber, and omega-3 fatty acid formulation. The largest achievement to date is the use of a relatively new process that allows us to remove moisture from the product without damaging nutrient content. This will allow us to distribute Nutriva in a concentrated form to reduce packaging and shipping costs. All Company Inc. has placed an order for 1,000 samples for April 17. Two other corporations have expressed similar interest. Natural Health Foods Inc. has also expressed interest in retailing Nutriva.

2.1.2 Keys to Success

- *Build High-traffic Location*: AHC has a steady stream of walk-ins from Fabian's Hair and nearby fitness firms. Fabian gives referrals in return for a favorable lease agreement.
- *Build High-traffic Website*: AHC provides the best "All Health, No Hype" advice, free. This approach has helped build our credibility. Our website regularly receives positive remarks. Over 40% of our new clients found us on the Web.
- *Low Overhead*: AHC leases it upper level to subsidize its mortgage. Facilities cost is low, freeing up more funds to pay off growth or working capital loans if needed.
- *Leverage Service Success into Product Success*: AHC seeks clients looking for long-term programs and thus are likely to be loyal repeat customers. We develop relationships, not clients. AHC is well positioned to leverage its goodwill into product sales.

2.1.3 Legal Structure

To keep focused on product development and marketing, AHC will remain a proprietorship. Once Nutriva sales surpass $500,000 (targeted for FY 2005), AHC will retain the services of a lawyer and incorporate for the following year. Incorporation is necessary to make it easier to secure additional growth or working capital if needed and reduce product liability risk. AHC has all necessary permits and licenses to distribute its services and bring Nutriva to market.

-5-

Company Description

Feedback – Bob is sticking to a clear straightforward company description. This is no place for exaggeration. Some small photos of his location and facilities might've been a nice addition.

Important! Your "Keys to Success" (i.e., what you need to do to succeed) should be carefully thought out. This is where your reader can really tell if your business concept has enough merit and uniqueness to succeed in the marketplace.

TIPS – Using bullets is a great way to condense information. But too many bullets can leave your plan riddled with point form statements that become tedious to read. Visual and narrative variety is needed. Each page should be composed with the idea that page design builds excitement and helps maintain reader motivation. Although a well-formatted plan won't sell a lousy idea, it will help get a good business plan read.

Bob has added "Licenses and Regulations" information to his "Legal Structure" section. Throughout this sample plan, you will notice that section titles have been moved around and combined as needed. This is okay. Make changes that you think best presents the information particular to your business proposal.

Feedback – Rather than use his opening paragraph to summarize his sales plan, Bob has decided to direct attention to two critical details: (1) his key sales strategy and (2) recent third-party approval.

He repeats this strategy throughout his plan. In general, he doesn't use summary headings to summarize. Rather, he uses them to capture the essence of why his business proposition will be successful.

Writing Style – Should you write in third person (he, she, AHC) or first person (I, we, us)?

Bob has written some sections of his business plan in third person and some other sections in first person. And other times, he combines both in the same paragraph. First person is more personable. Third person can sound rather stuffy and pretentious, but some people consider it more formal and business like. Get feedback on which is more appropriate for your proposal. Tell your test reader who you are submitting your plan to and what they think about your approach.

Think about the impact of "we" or "I" on your reader.

TIP – Bob has not prepared a confidentiality or non-disclosure agreement (NDA) for his submission to María. However, if she requests Nutriva's ingredients and production process, he will request that she sign one.

2.2 Sales Plan

AHC will leverage its proven fitness and nutrition services to gain market recognition for Nutriva. Nutriva has been evaluated by Research Labs and exceeds all FDA labeling and safety requirements under the 1994 *Dietary Supplement Health and Education Act* (DSHEA).

2.2.1 Products and Services

- *Fitness and Nutrition Consulting and Training* – AHC offers fitness and nutrition solutions including Power Yoga classes, kick boxing, and therapeutic massage (see website for a complete list). AHC has also partnered with Dr. Ted Graves who offers colon hydrotherapy and supervised natural fasting cleanses, and Dr. Sally Lowe who offers chiropractic care specializing in deep active release sports massage.

- *Nutriva Sports Nutrition Shake* – "No supplement can replace the power of food. No matter all the hype, FOOD is the real elixir of life" (Jackson, 2000, *Magazine*). Nutriva will combine the best of EAS's *Myoplex Ready-to-Drink Nutrition Shake*, MegaFood's *Essentials for Life*, HerbaLife's *Active Fiber*, and Dr. Sear's *OmegaRx Pharmaceutical-Grade Fish Oils*. Nutriva drinkers will experience "The Nutriva Advantage™" due to high quality, wholesome ingredients, omega-3 boosters, and pure Whey protein isolate. Nutriva is not supplementation. It IS food. It will NOT be sold in powdered form. It will be distributed with 50% of its original production moisture removed. An expiration and freshness date will be clearly stamped on packaging. Nutriva has an estimated shelf life of one year, longer if refrigerated. Nutriva has been lab-tested by Research Labs for protein (42g), carbohydrate (25g), fat (7g), fiber (5g), and calories (331 cal). A detailed vitamin, mineral, and other nutrient breakdown is available upon request.

- *Nutriva Client Feedback* – "The vitamin pill is an unnatural product. Unsupported by enzymes and other nutrients researchers haven't even discovered yet, it is metabolized very inefficiently, and in large doses, overtaxes the kidneys" (Dr. Ted Graves, 1999, *Medical Journal*). Bob has surveyed that most of his clients dislike popping vitamins. He takes Nutriva wherever he goes. At the end of client sessions, he mixes Nutriva with a battery-operated blender along with some pure vanilla extract, a piece of fruit, and 4 oz of distilled water. Clients consistently ask: "Where can I buy this stuff? I feel great after I drink it." Nutriva also has a unique satisfying taste all by itself.

- *Bob's Nutriva Recipe Book and Expansion* – Important to the Nutriva product usage strategy is Bob's personal shake recipe book. Currently, Bob has over 100 recipes complete with nutrient content analysis for different body, age, and blood types. Within the next two years, Bob will self-publish a book: *All Health, No Hype*, based on his website articles, recipe book, and client experiences. Bob's market research indicates that book sales increase credibility, which in turn will increase Nutriva sales.

2.2.2 Production and Distribution Plan

After five years of experimentation, Bob has created a nutrient mix that is pleasant tasting and mixes easily with added flavorings. Nutriva is concentrated but smooth, unlike competing products that tend to clump. AHC has received quotations from Company Labs, Factory Inc., and Drink Manufacturing for the initial production of 4,800 samples ranging from $1.54 to $1.87 per sample. Set-up charges start at $4,600. Details of the production process are being kept a trade secret. AHC intends to initially market through its facilities, partners, AllHealthNoHype.com website, and local health food stores, fitness firms, and juice bars. AHC may also recruit the services of an independent sales rep to reach out-of-state markets. However, the long-term plan is to distribute Nutriva direct to retailers from Nutriva.com (Phase III of AHC's Web strategy). Packaging has been designed by Greg Burns, former employee of General Mills. AHC has 288 cubic feet available for storage (room for 6,000+ samples).

2.3 Operating Plan

All Health No Hype™, Nutriva™, and The Nutriva Advantage™ are trademarks of AHC. Nutriva's proprietary nutrient blend is a trade secret and is not being released to any third party without the signing of a non-disclosure agreement. This agreement was prepared by AHC's legal consul, Bob Ashton of National Legal Services.

2.3.1 Accounting, Order Entry, Banking, and Inventory Plan

Currently, AHC is using a double-entry cash based income and expense journal accounting system to meet tax record needs. Prior to startup, AHC set up a chart of accounts with the help of Ted Green, a retired CPA. AHC will computerize and adopt a double-entry accrual based system for 2004. Our current system will easily transfer to QuickBooks Pro or MYOB, two software choices we are currently testing.

Fitness and nutrition services are billed by sales receipt. Most AHC clients pay by cash or credit card, and less than 10% by check. AHC has a retail merchant account with RBC Centura. The average cost of this service is 2.4% per transaction. A Nurit Wireless Unit, leased at $39.95 per month, enables us to process credit cards on and off location. The same rate and service is also available for online transactions. AHC has a CitiBank business checking account with 24/7 online access. With a Fair, Isaacs Co. FICO credit rating of 735, Bob negotiated $1,000 overdraft protection and an unsecured credit line of $10,000 @8%.

Nutriva inventory will initially be monitored using an inventory "in-stock" record and a period ending inventory record. For income tax purposes, the "identified cost method" and "FIFO method of identification" will be used for valuing inventory. Online orders will be processed by credit card payment. Offline orders at the AHC location will be cash or credit only, billed with a sales receipt (see pricing policies on page 10). Trade credit will be offered to Nutriva wholesalers and retailers with terms 2/10 net 30. An invoicing system and bad debts policy is already in place. Fast Fulfillment Services will be handling storage and fulfillment for the third quarter of 2003. Inventory carrying, shipping, fulfillment, and handling costs have been quoted at $7.85 per case ($0.33 per product).

2.3.2 Technology and Communications Plan

AHC currently uses a Pentium 3, with 256MB of RAM, a 20 GB hard drive, a CD-RW, and a 17-inch flat panel screen. AHC has a cable connection to the Internet. Website and data are backed up monthly by recordable CD's. AHC also has a digital answering and fax machine that functions as a printer, photocopier, and scanner. Bob can be reached by cellular phone and keeps his appointments using Microsoft *Outlook*, synced with a Compaq Pocket PC. When off location, AHC phone calls can be forwarded to his cell phone. Bob answers email for half an hour each day. He also receives 10 to 15 calls a day and will be hiring a part-time assistant/trainer/receptionist to assist in service and product inquiries. To update the AHC website, Bob uses *Front Page 2000*, *Dreamweaver 4.0*, and *Photoshop 6.0*.

2.3.3 Web Strategy

AllHealth-NoHype.com is being developed to provide information to the health-conscious community in San Diego, the U.S., and the world, and to promote Nutriva Sports Nutrition Shake. The development of this site will occur in two phases. Phase I has positioned All-Health-NoHype.com as an authoritative holistic fitness and nutrition resource that gives pure heath facts supported by industry research, and without the hype and misinformation that often accompanies commercial websites. Current contributors to AllHealth-NoHype.com include Robert Jackson, Dr. Ted Graves, and Dr. Sally Lowe. Phase I was completed January 2002. Phase II will be completed January 2003.

Feedback – Bob's *Operating Plan* lacks clarity regarding his fulfillment and shipping process and the costs associated with it for his first six months of 2003. Although it is clear he will be using a sales receipt based system (and he does comment on website back-end development on page 7), it isn't clear how orders will be processed, where inventory will be stored, and how orders will be packed and shipped.

It also isn't clear what capacity Fast Fulfillment Services can operate at and whether they can handle, for example, sales of $700,000 as projected for 2005.

TIP – Whenever you think your plan is missing something or needs an additional fact or more research, then IT DOES. If you feel that it might be too much trouble to get all of these details sorted out, eventually these compromises will all add up and your credibility will be shot.

FICO – FICO scores tell lenders whether a consumer is a good credit risk. Scores can range from 300 to 850. The higher the score, the better the credit risk. According to E-LOAN, a California-based Internet lending institution, a consumer with a FICO score of 580 will pay around $495 per month for a five-year $20,000 car loan, while another borrower with a FICO score of 700 will pay $382.

2.3.3 Web Strategy (continued)

- *Business Model* – Our business model is based on building customer loyalty by providing quality information. AllHealth-NoHype also acts as a virtual business card and portfolio showcasing AHC services, success stories, and location facilities, thereby reducing marketing costs. Revenues are generated from associate and referral programs, targeted advertising towards equipment stores and fitness gyms, and Nutriva sales.
- *Site Positioning* – AHC's website is dedicated to providing honest fitness and nutrition information that is in no way compromised by marketing motives.
- *Building Traffic* – Website partnerships have been formed with [*names omitted*]. The All Health No Hype monthly newsletter has 15,000 subscribers growing at 20% per month.
- *Front-end Development* – Interface is fast, easy to use, and appealing to users. Most pages download in 10 seconds or less with a 56K modem. Users are able to discuss, give opinions, and rate products. Online ordering is simple and secure.
- *Back-end Development* – Site hosted by Tierranet.com for $35 per month (99.9% uptime). Includes unlimited traffic, 150 MB of storage, and shopping cart. Shipping is handled by UPS ground at $6 per case. After 2ndQ, fulfillment will be handled by Fast Fulfillment Services at $7.85 per case. Site updates and maintenance handled by Bob. HitBox is used to track Web stats including unique visitors and sales per visitor at a cost of $25 per month.
- *Future* – The Nutriva.com portal will be created for Nutriva retailers and consumers.
- *Resources Needed* – AHC has budgeted $5,000 for 2002 and $2,000 for 2003 for design and tech support to complete Phase II. Phase II will be 95% completed by 12/1/02.

2.3.4 Nutriva Milestones

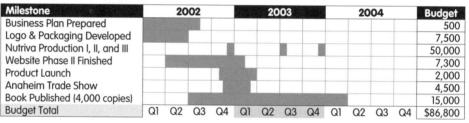

Milestone	2002				2003				2004				Budget
Business Plan Prepared													500
Logo & Packaging Developed													7,500
Nutriva Production I, II, and III													50,000
Website Phase II Finished													7,300
Product Launch													2,000
Anaheim Trade Show													4,500
Book Published (4,000 copies)													15,000
Budget Total	Q1	Q2	Q3	Q4	Q1	Q2	Q3	Q4	Q1	Q2	Q3	Q4	$86,800

2.4 Management, Advisors, Key Staff, and Gaps in Team

Robert Jackson is a well-known fitness expert, exercise therapist, and holistic health educator in the local area. He has trained competitively with top-place finishes in the Ironman Triathlon and U.S. National Biathlon (see résumé page 16). Presently, AHC is a one-person operation with three advisors. Contract workers and part-time college workers are hired as needed.
- <u>Gerald Lim</u> of Big Accounting Inc. assists in tax preparation and quarterly budgeting. Service costs for FY 2001 were $1,200. • <u>Ted Green</u> is a retired CPA from Price Waterhouse. He's been a board member for three corporate startups, one within the nutrition industry. He has been a regular client of Bob's for over three years and has helped Bob develop a pricing strategy, set up an accounting system, and meet FDA labeling and safety requirements. He is well connected within the legal industry. • <u>Gracie Ellen</u> owns and operates a chain of five juice bars located across the city. She has a business degree from UCLA and has been helping Bob test market Nutriva. • <u>Oscar Baker</u> handles advanced JavaScript, cgi scripting, and php coding. Service costs for FY 2001 were $2,100. • <u>Gaps in Team</u>. A PT assistant will be hired 10/1/2002 to assist in training and order processing. A FT marketing expert is needed for FY 2004 or earlier who will be responsible for marketing and distribution of Nutriva to NHF and MM markets. Bob is willing to offer a partnership opportunity to a candidate with the right mix of skills, experience, and industry connections.

Marketing Plan

3.1 Market Analysis

The *Nutrition Business Journal* estimates the global nutrition industry at $150 billion, $53 billion from the U.S. alone (2001). Part of the $18 billion dietary supplements sector, the sports nutrition, weight loss, and meal replacement market carries the torch with annual sales of $9.9 billion and projected growth rates of 12% to 15%—double the 6.2% growth rate of the industry as a whole. Although some trade publications are of the opinion that the DS industry has begun to mature, high growth rates are still predicted in the foreseeable future. In the recent past, some have estimated industry sales growing at the rate of 20% to 30% a year. In the U.S., there are 1000+ manufacturers in the DS sector and 300+ distributors.

3.1.1 Market Trends
– The general online demographic right now in the U.S. is in sync with the types of people who buy nutrition supplements: young males and females in their 20's and 30's with discretionary income and Internet connections. Supplementation has also become more popular with teenagers looking to body build. As they get older and get jobs, they will have more discretionary income to purchase Nutriva. Other trends include:

- *Health Portal Sites* – In the last seven years, numerous content/commerce portal sites have been launched for fitness and nutrition markets: including iTownhealth.com and FitnessSite.com. Invariably, with many commercial interests and contributors, offerings at these sites have become fragmented. Overloaded with information choices, consumers are now increasingly looking for niche markets (source: *Nutrition Business Journal*).
- *Whey Protein* – Early nutrition shakes used egg protein (albumin) and milk protein (casein). Cross Pro was the first commercially available Whey protein Isolate in 1995. Whey protein has a better taste, is more easily utilized by the body, and mixes well.
- *Manufacturing E-Commerce* – According to the Department of Commerce, 94% of e-commerce is B2B. Manufacturing leads all industry sectors with shipments that account for 18.4% ($777 billion) of the total value of manufacturing. In 2000, 12.6% of food manufacturing revenues were generated from online sales, up from 10.7% in 1999.

3.1.2 Target Market
– AHC customers are sensitive to quality and convenience. They are looking for personalized service and nutrition solutions. They seek knowledgeable staff, ease of purchase, and trainers they can emulate. AHC targets 18- to 80-year-olds wishing to improve their health, and who are tired of products and services that promise benefits without results. Nutriva targets users looking for a permanent nutrient shake to add to their diet. Our most important markets for Nutriva for 2003 will be site visitors, natural health food stores (NHF), corporate HR departments, fitness firms, and juice bars. For 2004, Nutriva will expand into the mass market (MM) representing grocery, drug, and convenience stores.

3.1.3 Market Segmentation and Market Share
– After successfully completing our entry phase into the local NHF market, we will expand into national NHF and MM markets using email, direct mail, telephone, and one-on-one marketing strategies. To foster continued growth, we will exhibit at two trade shows per year, form strategic Web partnerships, and establish an affiliates program. AHC conservatively estimates that under current market conditions, it can achieve a 0.05% U.S. market share of $5 million within five years.

Nutriva Segmentation (100%)	2003	2004	2005
Non-retail Internet	35%	71%	66%
Non-retail ACH Location	15%	8%	4%
Non-Retail Health Food (NHF)	50%	19%	22%
Retail Mass Merchandiser (MM)	0%	2%	8%

U.S. Supplement Sales by Distribution Channel
2001 Total Sales ($17.6 Billion)

Retail MM 33%
Non-Retail 33%
Non-Retail NHF 33%

Breakdown
Multilevel – **57%**
Practitioner – **19%**
Mail Order – **19%**
Internet – **5%**

Feedback – Bob should add more detailed strategies for approaching each market segment. For example, Bob already has a corporate client. How did he get this client? How will he get more?

Often, sales forecasts end up functioning more like goal statements and benchmarks, rather than true projections. It's nearly impossible to predict sales with any degree of accuracy, especially if you have no experience in the industry and are starting up in a relatively new or rapidly changing industry or sector. If possible, find someone who has started a company similar to yours and can give you an idea of what kind of numbers to expect.

TIP – Getting the facts is tough. Getting one little piece of information on market growth for instance to support your sales projections could take days and even weeks of searching. But, this research can make all the difference.

If you need your business plan for investment capital, you must get your facts straight. However, if you are using your plan for your own internal purposes, don't let one little fact halt your planning process. Projections are just that, "Projections." The projections themselves are not as important as the process of trying to find them.

359

Feedback – At two
pages, Bob's marketing
plan is insufficient. Al-
though he wants to
keep his business plan
size down, an additional
two pages with charts,
sales figures, etc.,
would be more appro-
priate. Marketing is a
tough business, but it is
also one of the most
important determinants
of success and not to be
taken lightly. Any strategies you work out here,
will help you better
prepare for reality,
when nothing you
planned works, or
something you didn't
plan takes off.

Things to Add –
Although Bob has a
good understanding of
his service costs, he
lacks comparative
information on his
product costs. Bob
needs to compare
costs with his competi-
tion to find out if he has
a cost advantage or
disadvantage.

He should also conduct
some in-depth research
on competitor pricing
strategies. Although he
already has ideas of
this based upon his
experience and use of
nutrition products, he
should put it down on
paper. Bob also needs
to find out the average
markup for sports nutri-
tion shakes for NHF
and MM retailers.

Don't include every idea
you come up with. A
business plan is a plan-
ning tool that takes you
through a discovery
and development proc-
ess. Your final proposal
will be a "snapshot" of
that journey.

3.2 Competition Analysis

Planet Muscle Magazine lists the top four protein manufacturers in the world as Met-Rx, Beverly International, MD Labs, and Worldwide Sport Nutrition. Companies consistently meeting or exceeding label claims include Beverly International, EAS, Met-Rx, Twinlab, and Weider. Recently, EAS has established itself as one of the fastest growing nutrition companies in the world with sales of $[number omitted] for 2001. The main reason for this is Bill Phillips—the charismatic author of *Body for Life* and originator of the *Million Dollar Body for Life Challenge*. By bringing the concept of bodybuilding to the masses, and produc-ing results, Bill has created a loyal following for his products. EAS strengths include market penetration, competitive pricing, and worldwide distribution. To its disadvantage, EAS has a poor website, weak sense of online community, and fragmented product line.

3.2.1 Competitive Advantage – AHC has a prime location and lower-than-average overhead allowing more profits to be funneled back into operations to help avoid high debt ratios and lost sales opportunities. AHC will also emulate the Bill Phillips success formula by featuring online contests and success stories. More than that, AHC will reward loyal cus-tomers with discount coupons, free training, and uncompromising Nutriva quality.

3.3 Selling Strategies

Although offline marketing is important, it has been proven more effective after a dot.com has become established online. Amazon.com does not use TV commercials. AHC is follow-ing Amazon's Internet distribution strategy by building a solid online community.

3.3.1 Promotion and Publicity Plan – The production cost of "Nutriva" will be higher than those of our competitors, considering the quality of our ingredients. To make a profit, offline marketing costs must be kept low. Nutriva will be marketed using online ad-vertising, brochures, direct mail, displays, personal selling, and word of mouth. A media kit has been prepared to target local periodicals for Nutriva's launch date. In 2004, magazine advertising in *Flex* and *Health* will be tested for response. Marketing slogans include: "The Nutriva Advantage™," "Taste Nutriva! Feel the Nutriva Buzz," and "I'd walk a mile for a Nutriva." At AHC, we want Nutriva to be perceived as a low-pressure sell. We are selling lifestyle, not protein. Our promotional budget is $14,500 to 2004 and 5% of sales thereafter.

3.3.2 Pricing Policies – (1) Fitness and nutrition services are priced at $100 an hour per person (with 30% to 50% discounts for groups), $1,000 for three-hour group train-ing sessions, $2,000 for a full day, and $10,000+ for corporate weekend packages. Custom-ized fitness and nutrition makeover packages start at $2,500. (2) Nutriva will be priced at the upper edge of what the market will bear, competing with the top name brands. This pricing fits with the general positioning of Nutriva as the "Best Quality Nutrition Shake on the Mar-ket." Nutriva will be sold in singles for $3.95, in 4-packs at $14.95, and by the case, 24 for $79.95 (see "Assumptions Made", page 15 for more pricing details).

3.3.3 Packaging and Positioning Strategy – Nutriva will be sold in a cool blue and gray 11FL oz recyclable container. To disassociate itself from its product class—"Real food, Ready-to-Drink" and "Concentrated Natural Energy"—positioning statements will be used.

3.3.4 Strategic Alliances – AHC has partnered with Dr. Graves, Dr. Lowe, and Gracie Ellen and has also made arrangements to sell exercise products online from Exercise U.S.A. AHC is also working to bundle a case of Nutriva with yearly membership dues at Fit House.

3.3.5 Brand Promise – Nutriva will communicate healthy living, as good as food, con-venience, versatility, pure and natural ingredients, and integrity.

Financial Plan

4.1 Capitalization Plan

To bring Nutriva to market, AHC has budgeted $80,000 for 2003, plus $30,000 for 2001 and 2002. Loan funds of $50,000 are being requested for January 1, 2003, with a commitment needed by October 31, 2002.

4.1.1 Capital Required

To fund Nutriva production and promotion costs for 2002 and 2003, as well as meet loan obligations, AHC estimates capital requirements of $110,000. With projected Nutriva sales at 14,400 units for 2003 and total production at 38,440 units, AHC estimates an additional $37,200 in Nutriva revenues, with 24,000 units in inventory available for 2004 sales.

Nutriva 2001/2002/2003 Budget	2001	2002	2003	
Legal, Accounting, and Product Liability Insurance Costs	500	2,000	4,000	
Nutriva Logo Design, Package Design, Case Design, B-plan	7,500	0	0	
Production One-time Setup Charge	0	4,600	0	
Production I 200 cases, 4,800 samples ($1.54 per unit)	0	7,392	0	
Production II 400 cases, 9,600 ($1.26 per unit)	0	0	12,096	
Production III 1,000 cases, 24,000 ($1.09 per unit)	0	0	26,160	
Anaheim Trade Show (March 8–10, 2003)	0	0	4,500	
Promotion (brochures, travel, letterhead, media kit)	0	3,000	7,000	
Loan Payment ($50,000 @10% over three years)	0	0	19,363	
Website Development Phase II, Fulfillment Costs*	0	5,000	7,172	
Total Capital Required (Nutriva Budget)	$8,000	$21,992	$80,291	$110,283.00
Revenue AHC Location (15%) 2,160 at $3.56** each			7,690	
Revenue Website (35%) 5,040 at $3.33** 10% discount			15,105	
Revenue (50%) 7,200 at $3.33** 40% discount			14,386	
Total Projected Nutriva Revenues for 2003 (14,400 samples)			$37,181	

* 2003 fulfillment costs projected at 25% of production cost ($4,872); website ($2,300). ** See p. 15 *Nutriva Sales*.

4.1.2 Sources of Capital

AHC has a current cash capital balance in excess of $50,000. With an additional injection of $50,000 in loan funds, AHC will be able to meet all 2003 Nutriva budget projections plus add $20,000 towards a growth reserve fund. The creation of a reserve fund is essential to AHC's long-term expansion strategy. It will give the Nutriva division flexibility to meet rapidly increasing production costs if sales are greater than projections, as well as ride out any unexpected periods of slow sales. The loan funds also provide AHC with enough operating capital to maintain a positive cash flow balance during all periods of expansion.

Capital Sources and Loan Injection	2003
Cash in Bank	50,000
Loans	50,000
Total Capital Available to Fund Nutriva Division	$100,000

4.2 Uses of Funds

AHC will use the $50,000 in loan funds to produce 1,600 cases (38,400 units) of Nutriva and cover promotion costs for 2003. The funds will also allow us to have adequate inventory for the start of 2004 and prevent cash flow problems if sales are higher or lower than projected. Even if sales are 0% of projections, AHC will be able to fulfill its loan obligations.

Uses of Loan Funds	2003
Production of 1,400 Cases of Nutriva (Working Capital)	38,500
Anaheim Trade Show and Promotion (Working Capital)	11,500
Total	$50,000

Feedback – Bob has simplified his budget and other financial statements to focus on items that matter the most. He might also consider adding some graphs to summarize his projections. Although tables present data more accurately, a graph can provide visual relief to keep readers from suffering from *cognitive overload*— that is, "too many dang numbers!"

NOTE! Many statement figures In this section have been rounded off and simplified to the nearest thousand (000's). For the most part, this is due to space limitations in the design of this sample plan. However, without such restrictions, it is usually better to use full numbers—e.g., $19,363, instead of $19.4.

TIP – You may find it difficult to decide how many expense items, accounts, growth figures etc., you need to analyze in your financial plan. Too many numbers can take away from your most important figures, while not enough numbers can leave large gaps in your analysis. Remember, detailed financial schedules can always be added in your appendix to fill in the gaps.

4.3 Financial Analysis

AHC's financial analysis is based on the assumption that service revenues will grow 15% annually, expenses will increase 5% due to inflation, and initial market penetration for Nutriva will be $37,200*. Nutriva sales are projected to increase 450% for 2004 and 250% for 2005. These later projections are based on Nutriva gaining shelf space in NHF markets, and increasing web traffic generating online sales. Although these growth projections may seem high, they are actually quite conservative considering current interest and preliminary feedback from market testing. All sales and expense projections are cash-based. AHC will be changing to an accrual-based accounting system for 2004.

* The following financial statements and projections have been reviewed by Gerald Lim of Big Accounting Inc. Detailed assumptions are listed on page 15. Detailed expense breakdowns are available upon request.

4.3.1 12-month Income Projection

A before tax net profit of $42,300 is being projected despite a 110% increase in overall costs from 2002. High sales are expected in March and April due to trade show participation.

AHC 2003 Income Projection in Thousands (000's)

AC#		Jan	Feb	Mar	Apr	May	Jun	Jul	Aug	Sep	Oct	Nov	Dec	Total
4000	**AHC Total Sales**	12.6	12.0	12.4	22.7	12.7	10.6	9.8	10.4	12.3	13.0	12.7	12.2	153.4
4100	Service Sales	11.8	10.9	10.4	13.8	9.8	7.7	7.5	7.9	9.7	10.1	9.5	8.7	117.8
4200	Nutriva Sales	0.8	1.1	2.0	8.9	2.9	2.9	2.3	2.5	2.6	2.9	3.2	3.5	35.6
5000	Direct Cost of Goods	0.22	0.20	0.54	12.78	0.30	0.32	0.34	0.37	0.41	0.42	26.7	0.6	43.2
	Gross Profit	12.38	11.8	11.86	9.92	12.4	10.28	9.46	10.03	11.89	12.58	–14.0	11.6	110.2
6100	Administrative Expenses	2.2	1.8	1.7	1.7	1.7	1.9	2.1	1.7	2.1	1.7	1.7	1.8	22.1
6200	Selling Expenses	1.8	1.6	1.0	2.0	0.5	1.6	0.6	1.1	1.7	0.9	0.9	2.4	16.1
6300	Nutriva Expenses	4.3	4.5	1.8	0.5	0	0	1.6	2.0	0.7	0	2.4	0	17.8
6150	Depreciation Expense	0.8	0.8	0.8	0.8	0.8	0.8	0.8	0.8	0.8	0.8	0.8	0.8	9.6
6000	**Total Operating Costs**	9.1	8.7	5.3	5.0	3.0	4.3	5.1	5.6	5.3	3.4	5.8	5.0	65.6
7030	Other Income (lease + interest)	1.50	1.50	1.51	1.51	1.53	1.54	1.54	1.54	1.55	1.56	1.51	1.51	18.3
8010	Other Expenses (loan interest)	1.78	1.77	1.76	1.75	1.73	1.72	1.71	1.70	1.69	1.68	1.66	1.65	20.6
	Net Profit (Before Taxes)	3.0	2.83	6.31	4.68	9.2	5.8	4.19	4.27	6.45	9.06	–19.95	6.46	**42.3**

4.3.2 Three-year Income Projection

AHC is projecting Nutriva revenues of $37,200 in 2003, $203,500 in 2004, and $712,300 in 2005. Based on 2001–2002 growth, service revenues are projected to increase 15% per year. Nutriva expenses will increase in 2004 and 2005 as a full-time marketer is hired and website and promotion costs increase. Service sales for 2005 include $40,000 in book sales.

AHC Three-year Projection with Horizontal and Vertical Analysis in Thousands (000's)

AC#	Industry Ratio*	%	2001	%	2002	%	2003	%	2004	%	2005	%
4000	**AHC Total Sales**	100	89.1	100	102.5	100	153.4	100	339.0	100	908.1	100
4100	Service Sales	–	89.1	100	102.5	100	117.8	76.0	135.5	40.0	195.8	21.6
4200	Total Nutriva Sales	–	–	–	–	–	35.6	23.2	203.5	60.0	712.3	78.4
4210	ACH Location Sales	–	–	–	–	–	7.7	–	16.3	–	28.5	–
4220	Website Sales	–	–	–	–	–	15.1	–	144.5	–	470.1	–
4230	NHF Sales	–	–	–	–	–	12.8	–	38.7	–	156.7	–
4240	MM Sales	–	–	–	–	–	0.0	–	4.0	–	57.0	–
5000	Direct Cost of Goods	64.4	–	–	7.4	7.2	43.2	28.2	119.0	35.1	463.0	51.0
	Gross Profit	35.6	89.1	100	95.1	92.8	110.2	71.8	220.0	64.9	445.1	49.0
6100	Administrative Expenses	–	6.4	7.2	10.1	9.9	22.1	14.4	37.3	11.0	46.8	5.2
6200	Selling Expenses	–	16.7	18.7	17.5	17.1	16.1	10.4	19.3	5.7	20.3	2.2
6300	Nutriva Expenses	–	8.0	9.0	14.6	14.1	17.8	11.6	82.5	24.3	147.0	16.2
6150	Depreciation Expense	2.0	6.7	7.5	9.6	9.4	9.6	6.2	9.6	2.8	9.6	1.1
6000	**Total Operating Costs**	26.3	37.8	42.4	51.8	50.5	65.6	42.8	130.7	38.6	223.7	24.6
7030	Other Income	0.6	15.3	17.2	15.4	15.0	18.3	11.9	18.5	5.4	20.2	2.2
8010	Other Expenses	–	16.7	18.7	16.5	16.1	20.6	13.4	18.8	5.5	16.8	1.8
	Net Profit (Before Taxes)	6.5	49.9	56.0	42.2	41.2	42.3	27.6	89.0	26.0	224.8	24.7
6900	Taxes (Federal, State, Local)	–	18.3	36.7	13.5	32.0	13.3	31.4	36.3	40.8	98.4	43.8
	Net Profit (After Taxes)	–	31.6	35.5	28.7	28.0	29.0	18.9	52.7	15.5	126.4	13.9

* From 1998 Almanac of Business and Industrial Financial Ratios SIC 2096 "Other Food and Kindred Products."

4.3.3 Cash Flow Budget

AHC projects sufficient revenues from operations to make loan payments and end the year with a positive cash balance of $103,512. Positive cash flow is anticipated in all months except February and November. However, should Nutriva sales not meet initial projections, adjustments will be made to production levels and other long-term commitments decreased or postponed. Projections have been adjusted for seasonal sales patterns. The table below shows cash accumulation from a beginning balance of $49,000 and infusion of $50,000.

AHC 2003 Cash Flow Budget

	Jan	Feb	Mar	Apr	May	Jun	Jul	Aug	Sep	Oct	Nov	Dec	Total
CASH IN (Beg. Bal.)	49,200												
Service Sales	11,800	10,900	10,400	13,800	9,800	7,700	7,500	7,900	9,700	10,100	9,500	8,700	117,800
AHC Location (15%)	440	480	1040	640	550	420	540	680	720	640	720	820	7,690
Website Sales (35%)	360	360	720	3,720	1,006	1,006	1,078	1,078	1,150	1,364	1,578	1,722	15,142
A/R Collections (50%)	0	240	240	4,560	1,344	1,440	720	672	768	912	912	960	12,768
Lease Revenue	1,300	1,300	1,300	1,300	1,300	1,300	1,300	1,300	1,300	1,300	1,300	1,300	15,600
Interest Revenue	202	199	207	212	227	234	237	241	252	261	210	211	2,693
Loans	50,000	0	0	0	0	0	0	0	0	0	0	0	50,000
Total Cash In	64,102	13,479	13,907	24,232	14,227	12,100	11,375	11,871	13,890	14,577	14,220	13,713	221,693
CASH OUT													
Admin Expenses	2,180	1,740	1,730	1,720	1,720	1,900	2,130	1,690	2,050	1,710	1,720	1,810	22,100
Selling Expenses	1,750	1,600	1,000	2,000	480	1,630	640	1,100	1,680	950	850	2,420	16,100
Nutriva Production	0	0	0	12,096	0	0	0	0	0	0	26,160	0	38,256
Nutriva Fulfillment*	220	200	540	670	300	320	340	370	420	420	500	600	4,900
Nutriva Promotion	2,000	4,500	1,000	500	0	0	0	2,000	0	0	1,500	0	11,500
Wages, Legal, Ins.	1,550	0	0	0	0	1,550	0	0	0	0	900	0	4,000
Website Phase II	800	0	800	0	0	0	0	0	0	700	0	0	2,300
Taxes	2,952	2,255	0	0	0	0	0	0	56	1,203	2,255	0	8,721
Mortgage	1,679	1,679	1,679	1,679	1,679	1,679	1,679	1,679	1,679	1,679	1,679	1,679	20,148
Loan Payment	1,613	1,613	1,613	1,613	1,613	1,613	1,613	1,613	1,613	1,613	1,613	1,613	19,356
Asset Purchases	0	0	0	0	0	0	0	0	0	0	0	0	0
Owner Withdrawal	1,500	1,500	1,500	1,500	1,500	1,500	1,500	1,500	1,500	1,500	1,500	35,00	20,000
Total Cash Out	16,244	15,087	9,862	21,778	7,292	8,642	9,452	9,952	8,998	9,775	38,677	11,622	167,381
Cash Flow	47,858	−1,608	4,045	2,454	6,935	3,458	1,923	1,919	4,892	4,802	−24,457	2,091	54,312
CASH BALANCE	97,058	95,450	99,495	101,969	108,884	112,342	114,265	116,184	121,076	125,878	101,421	103,512	103,512

* For 2003, fulfillment and other costs are projected at 25% of yearly production cost (see page 14 for 2004 and 2005).

4.3.4 Nutriva Breakeven Analysis

With Nutriva sales up to 2005 projected at $951,961, fixed costs at $277,981, and variable costs at $632,600, AHC's Nutriva division will reach its breakeven point at $828,557 in sales, sometime within the first month of the fourth quarter of 2005.

Total estimated Nutriva Sales (up to 2005) = $36,161 + $203,500 + $712,300 = $951,961. Nutriva fixed startup and selling costs for this period are budgeted at $8,000 + $14,600 + $17,800 + $82,500 + $147,000 + $8,081 in interest = $277,981. Variable costs are projected to be $7,400 + $43,200 + $119,000 + $463,000 = $632,600. Using the formula, *Sales at BE Point = Fixed Costs divided by [1 – (Variable Costs/Projected Sales)]*, AHC will break even at:

$277,981 divided by [1 – ($632,600/$951,961)] = $277,981 divided by (1– 0.6645) = $277,981/0.3355 = $828,557

4.3.5 Current and Projected Balance Sheet

The following analysis shows a healthy growth of net worth and a strong financial position.

AHC Current Financial Position for 2001 and Projected Financial Positions for 2002 and 2003 ($000's)

AC#		Performa	2001	2002	2003	AC#		Performa	2001	2002	2003
1100	Cash in Bank	22.5	51.1	49.2	103.5	2100	A/P's	0.0	0.0	0.0	0.0
1200	A/R's	0.0	0.0	0.0	1.6	2250	Taxes Payable*	0.0	13.8	(1.6)	1.4
1300	Inventory	0.0	0.0	7.4	26.2	2300	Loans	0.0	0.0	0.0	35.0
1400	Other Current*	0.0	0.0	0.0	0.0	2400	Mortgage	280.0	276.6	272.9	269.0
1500	Land	160.0	160.0	160.0	160.0	2000	*Total Liabilities*	280.0	290.4	271.3	305.4
1600	Building	150.0	146.4	142.7	138.9	3100	Invested Capital	87.5	87.5	87.5	87.5
1900	Other Fixed	35.0	31.9	26.2	20.4	3200	Earnings	0.0	11.5	26.7	57.7
1000	*Total Assets*	367.5.0	389.4	385.5	450.6	3000	**Net Worth**	87.5	99.0	114.2	145.2

*California "sales tax collected" and "sales tax payable" have been omitted from AHC's financial analysis.

-13-

Feedback – Bob could have provided more analysis of his cash flow budget and financial position. Numbers can mean very little without interpretation.

Warning! To make your income, breakeven, and cash flow projections look better (especially if seeking loan or investment capital), you will be tempted to underestimate costs and overestimate sales. Don't do this! As a planning tool, your financial analysis will become next to useless. Furthermore, bankers and investors have seen every trick in the book and will be able to quickly spot where you've become too creative. Once this happens, your credibility is lost.

TIP – It bears repeating that despite your best research, sales projections are quite often little more than educated guesses. They function more like budget goals and targets rather than business science. For this reason, it is very important to clarify your sales assumptions and risks. This way lenders and investors can better assess their risk and gain confidence in your ability to assess and prepare for the unknown.

Note! Don't include account numbers in your statements. They've been added here to show how they might be used in your accounting system. These numbers are based on QuickBooks Pro software.

363

4.4 Business Ratios and Performance Indicators

To assess the financial health of AHC and its new Nutriva division, AHC will monitor the business ratios and activity measures shown below, as well as perform quarterly vertical, horizontal, profitability, and liquidity analysis of financial projections. If we find that we are consistently over or under budget, appropriate actions will be taken to adjust costs and other budget projections, as well as reevaluate our pricing structure. AHC will pay close attention to website sales per visitor and the level of retail sales in NHF and MM markets to evaluate whether our long-term vision is feasible. Operating margins will decrease towards industry averages as Nutriva sales increase in revenue contribution. AHC projects its debt ratio to fall below 60% by FY 2005. Service division sales are projected to peak after 2004.

AHC and Nutriva Benchmarks

	SIC Code 8980*	2096*	2001	2002	2003	2004	2005	2006	2007
AHC Total Sales (000's)	100%	100%	89.1	102.5	153.4	339.0	908.1	2,337	5,542
Service Sales (000's)	–	–	89.1	102.5	117.8	135.5	195.8	200.0	200.0
COGS + Operating Costs (%)	82.8%	90.6%	42%	58%	71%	74%	76%	79%	81%
Operating Margin (%)	17.2%	9.4%	58%	42%	29%	26%	24%	21%	19%
Net Profit (000's)	7.4%	6.5%	31.6	28.7	29.0	52.7	126.4	288.6	619.2
Nutriva Sales (000's)	–	–	–	–	37.2	203.5	712.3	2,137	5,342
Nutriva Sales Growth (%)	–	–	–	–	–	450%	250%	200%	150%
MM and NHF A/R Sales	–	–	–	–	50%	21%	30%	56%	72%
Total Website Sales	–	–	–	–	35%	71%	66%	41%	26%
Nutriva % of Total AHC Sales	–	–	–	–	24%	60%	78%	93%	97%
Page Views (000's)	–	–	–	120	500	1,500	2,200	2,700	3,000
Unique Visitors (000's)	–	–	–	60	150	400	650	820	1,000
Total Unique Customers (000's)	–	–	–	–	0.21	2.0	6.5	12.3	20.0
Sales per Visitor (%)	–	–	–	–	0.14	0.5	1.0	1.5	2.0
Debt Ratio % (Debts to Assets)	54.8	27.9	74.6	70.4	67.8	68.0	53.9	–	–
Notes and Loans Payable	127.0	26.0	276.6	272.9	304.0	283.3	260.5	255.9	251.0
Return on Equity % (ROE)	–	29.2	31.9	25.1	20.0	34.9	44.3	–	–
Net Worth (000's)	157.0	293.0	99.0	114.2	145.2	151.0	285.6	–	–

* Industry ratios from *1998 Almanac of Business and Industrial Financial Ratios* SIC 8980 "Miscellaneous Services" and SIC 2096 "Other Food and Kindred Products" for businesses with less than $500,000 in assets.

4.5 Risk Assessment

- *Loan Risk* – AHC has been profitable for 2001 and 2002. Despite conservative sales projections for 2003, AHC is projected to have a positive cash balance in all months. Even if AHC meets 0% of its 2003 Nutriva sales projections, sufficient funds are available to make loan payments through to 2005. AHC also has sufficient equity in its location to take out a second mortgage. A $10,000 credit line has also been secured.

- *Runaway Overhead* – AHC has the following strategies to keep costs down to pay off loan and reinvest profits for expansion: (1) AHC leases its second level to Fabian's Hair. This lease expires 12/31/2003 leaving room for growth if needed. (2) For 2002, Bob has given up his apartment and replaced it with humbler living quarters. Personal living costs have been reduced $580 per month. (3) With Bob's high school, college, and fitness firm connections, it is quite easy for him to recruit qualified part-time workers eager to gain experience in the fitness industry. Although turnover is high, energy level is also high.

- *Product Liability* – AHC has obtained quotes from three sources for a commercial general liability policy with $1 million coverage. Quotes range from $3,100 to $3,400 per year.

- *Slow Product Sales* – AHC is able to produce Nutriva in quantities as low as 4,800. If the market is slow to accept Nutriva, inventory investment can easily be adjusted.

- *Competitor Reaction* – Nutriva's impact on the nutrition industry will be negligible in its first year and will likely draw little competitor attention. FY 2003 is a positioning year.

- *Service and Product Development Time Conflicts* – Bob will be hiring an assistant January 1, 2002 to assist in training, website updates, and sales (20 hours/week).

Supporting Documents

5.1 Assumptions Made for Nutriva Business Plan

Seeking Loan or Partnership

- **Purpose:** To manufacture, test market, and distribute Nutriva Sports Shake.
- **Projected Terms:** $50,000 for three years @10%; funding required by January 1, 2003. Loan secured by real estate assessed at $410,000 with $137,000 in equity.

Financial Assumptions

- *Nutriva Sales Breakdown* – For 2003, our market research estimates AHC will sell 10% of its Nutriva stock as singles at $3.95, 40% in 4-packs at $14.95 ($3.74), and 50% by the case, at 24 for $79.95 ($3.33). Average revenue per stock item factoring in quantity discounts would be $[(10\% \times 3.95) + (40\% \times 3.74) + (50\% \times \$3.33)] = \$3.56$. With market segment projections for 2003 at 15% for AHC location, 35% for website at 10% discount, and 50% for NHF retailers at 40% discount, our average revenue per stock item for 2003 is projected at $(15\% \times \$3.56) + (35\% \times \$3.00) + (50\% \times 2.00) = \$2.58$.
- *A/R Discount, Bad Debts, Credit Sales, Returns, and Shrinkage Cost* – AHC has estimated these "selling costs" to be 5% of production cost. Credit card sales at 2.4% processing charge are estimated to be 40% of sales for 2003. Sales on trade credit to MM and NHF segments are estimated at 50% of sales for 2003.
- *A/R Value* – For 2003, A/R's estimated at $14,386 – $12,768 = $1,618. ACP is projected at 41 days ($1,618 divided by $14,386/365days).
- *Depreciation* – Assets have been depreciated using the straight-line method.
- *Direct Cost of Goods Sold* – For 2004, total production costs ($1.09 per unit) PLUS 5% selling cost, 30% fulfillment, and 5% inflation ($0.44 per unit). For 2005, $0.46.
- *Inflation* – General AHC fixed and variable operating costs will increase at 5% per year.
- *Loans and Mortgage* – $50,000 in working capital @10% over three years will be secured by 10/31/2002 and be liquid by 01/01/2003. Monthly payment $1,613. Current mortgage rate of $280,000 @6% over 30 years until 2006. Monthly payment $1,679.
- *Property and Inventory Value* – For property taxes, land assessed at $260,000, building $150,000. Land "balance sheet" value, $160,000 (according to purchase price). Using the FIFO and "identified cost" methods, Nutriva end-of-year inventory was valued at $1.54, $1.26, and $1.09 per unit for 2003, and $1.09 for 2004 onwards.
- *Salaries* – Owner @$20,000 per year. For 2003, staff size will stay constant at one FT owner/manager and one PT support @$10 per hour (20 hrs/wk). For 2004, one FT marketing specialist will be hired @$20,000 plus 3% of sales, one FT support (40 hrs/wk).
- *Savings Interest* – @2.5%. For 2001, average balance of $36,040 earned $901 in interest.
- *Taxes* – Federal income tax, self-employment tax, state tax, and property tax projected at 32% to 44% depending on taxable income for year. San Diego property tax rate @$4,510 (1.1% of assessed valued). Annual IRA contribution of $2,000.
- *Utilities, Insurance* – Heat and electricity at $0.12 per sq. ft. × 1000 sq. ft. = $120 per month. Fire, property, general liability insurance policy at $3,100 per year.
- *Other Assumptions Made* – Boosters juice bars along with Natural Health Foods Inc. will retail Nutriva. All Company Inc. will purchase 1,000 Nutriva samples for April 17, 2003. Website visitors will be interested in purchasing Nutriva. Cost per book $8.50 ($4.00 printing, $4.50 fulfillment). Revenue per book $13.50 (55% × $29.95 list price). Payroll taxes, insurance, and benefits @40% wages.

2001 Operating Costs (000's)	
Fixed (Admin)	$13.1
Depreciation	6.7
Dues, Subscriptions	0.4
Insurance	0.8
Phone, Utilities	1.9
Other (Misc., Cleaning)	3.3
Variable (Selling)	24.7
Accounting, Legal	1.7
Advertising, Marketing	0.8
Motor Vehicle	3.2
Repairs, Maintenance	1.4
Supplies	1.1
Wages (Part-time Help)	4.1
Website, Phase I Design	2.9
Other (Misc. + Nutriva)	9.5
$Total	37.8

-15-

Feedback – Your *Assumptions Made Sheet* is the best place to add details about expenses, projections, research sources, calculations, and any other assumptions made in the preparation of your financial statements.

Cover Letter – After crunching the numbers, Bob has realized that it would be financially possible for him to launch Nutriva without any loan injection. Nevertheless, he is quite keen on getting María to join his team as a full partner. He believes her proven marketing and distribution skills will complement his leadership and people skills. Her involvement could help build Nutriva sales to a level much higher than what he could do alone or with a less qualified marketing manager (she has already gained world-wide shelf-space for prior clients of un-branded nutritional supplements).

In his cover letter, Bob plans to offer María Covas the option of becoming a full partner.

TIP – While bank lenders generally do not like creative financing solutions, investors are usually more willing to look at options. Since Bob feels María Covas would make an excellent member of the Nutriva Team, he might elaborate on investment options in his cover letter, with details open to negotiation.

Feedback – Bob has the experience and qualifications to offer fitness and nutrition services, but lacks business operating experience. Even though he is currently operating a successful service business, bankers and investors would be hesitant to give him funds for a new manufacturing division. Bob needs to make it clear in his plan and cover letter that he has professional help. One way he might do this is to provide more examples on how his advisors have helped him grow.

Final Thoughts – They say that property value depends on three things and three things only: location, location … location!

A business plan also depends on three things with one very important qualification: ideas, ideas, ideas …

SUPPORTED by FACTS!

If your business plan is full of ideas along with credible facts and numbers, then you have accomplished your business plan writing mission.

Although Bob's product costs are rather high and his sales forecasts seem to be based more on profit goals than actual market conditions, Bob has some good ideas. He also understands his customers, has marketable skills, and is dedicated to producing quality products and services. This combination should eventually gain Nutriva a market share.

5.2 Robert Jackson's Résumé

Summary:

Robert Jackson likes to take action, works with passion, knows how to get others to achieve, and isn't afraid of crunching the numbers. He has seven years experience as a physical trainer, is skilled in massage and conditioning, and has managed over 100 private clients including three celebrities. The *San Diego Times* describes him as: "Without a doubt, one of the city's most sought after trainers!"

Training Experience:

- three years as a chiropractic assistant
- two years as a massage therapist
- five years at California Fitness Centers as a personal trainer
- four years as a personal trainer for over 100 clients including Bill Carey of Microsoft, actor Jim Gates, and singers Tom Spears and Britney Jones
- 50 hours as a guest speaker for over 30 local High Schools
- articles published in *Flex*, *Black Belt*, *Ironman Magazine*, and *Health Magazine*
- six years Web design, html, cgi, php, Flash, and JavaScript coding

Areas of Expertise:

- Therapeutic Massage
- Hatha Yoga
- Pilates Mat Work
- Stress Management
- Heart Rate Monitor Training
- Holistic Nutrition

Education and Training:

- Bachelor Degree Program in Advanced Amma Therapeutic Massage from the New York College of Health Professionals
- Currently working on a Master of Arts in Holistic Health from Greenwich University, Norfolk Island, Australia, by way of long-distance education

Certifications and Association Memberships:

- Certified Massage Therapist – California College of Physical Arts
- Certified Personal Trainer – American Council on Exercise
- Certified Hatha Yoga Instructor
- Member of IDEA – Association of Fitness Professionals
- Member of Professional Coaches & Mentors Association

Athletic Highlights:

- 1st Place U.S. National Biathlon Championship
- 6th Place Ironman Triathlon (2.4–mile swim, 112–mile bike, 26.2–mile run)
- 3rd Degree Black Belt – Tae Kwon Do

5.3 Action Plan

To achieve the projected results of my three-year plan, I will take the following steps within the first six months of loan injection:

- Produce 600 cases of Nutriva (14,400 samples) in two production runs.
- Launch Nutriva January 15 with VIP guest list at AHC location.
- Complete Phase II of AHC's Internet plan. Conceptualize Phase III.
- Participate in 23rd Annual Natural Products Expo West 2003, Anaheim, CA.
- Begin recruitment of a marketing and distribution coordinator for Jan 1, 2004.

Page or Day #		Key Area		Page or Day #		Key Area	

Ideas

Contact/Company	Address	Phone/Fax	Email/URL

Table: Table:

Graph/Sketch:

DAILY PLANNER

Week

MONDAY
Date:

ABC	WEEKLY PLANNER	ABC	Tasks & Appointments	🕐

TUESDAY
Date:

ABC	Tasks & Appointments	🕐

WEDNESDAY
Date:

ABC	Tasks & Appointments	🕐

THURSDAY
Date:

ABC	Tasks & Appointments	🕐

FRIDAY
Date:

ABC	Tasks & Appointments	🕐

SATURDAY
Date:

ABC	Tasks & Appointments	🕐

SUNDAY
Date:

ABC	Tasks & Appointments	🕐

Quarterly Cash Flow Budget Analysis

For three months from: _____ to _____	THIS QUARTER			YEAR-TO-DATE		
Expected Cash Receipts	Estimate	Actual	Variation*	Estimate	Actual	Variation*
1. Cash Sales						
2. Accounts Receivable Collections						
3. _____						
4. Other Income (*interest income, dividends, asset sale*)						
5. TOTAL Cash Revenue						
Expected Cash Payments						
6. Inventory/Raw Materials						
7. Payroll (*wages, salaries, commissions, benefits, taxes*)						
8. Rent or Lease Payments						
9. Loan Principal Payments						
10. Advertising and Marketing						
11. Repairs and Maintenance						
12. Asset Purchases (*equipment, fixtures, computer*)						
13. Telephone and Utilities						
14. General Supplies						
15. _____						
16. _____						
17. _____						
18. Other Payments** (*auto, estimated income tax, interest*)						
19. TOTAL cash payments						
Cash Balances and Short-term Loans Needed						
20. Expected Cash Balance at Beginning of Quarter						
21. Cash Increase or Decrease (5 – 19)						
22. Expected Cash Balance at End of Quarter (20 + 21)						
23. Desired Working Cash Balance						
24. Short-term Loans Needed (23 – 22, if 23 is larger)						
25. Cash Available*** (22 – 23, if 22 is larger)						
Capital Cash:						
26. Cash Available (item 25 after deducting dividends, etc.)						
27. Desired Capital Cash (item 12, e.g., *for plant equipment*)						
28. Long-term Loans Needed (27 – 26, if 27 is larger).						

*Put a (+) or a (–) for variations or use parentheses for negative variations.

Income Statement Items						
1. Sales Revenues						
2. Cost of Goods Sold						
3. Operating Expenses						
4. Net Profit						
5. Taxes						
6. _____						

Balance Sheet Items						
1. Accounts Receivable						
2. Long-term Asset Repayments						
3. Loan Repayments						
4. Inventory on Hand						
5. Owner Withdrawals						
6. _____						

Budget Deviations	This Quarter			Year-to-Date		
1. Cash Flow Items						
2. Income Statement Items						
3. Balance Sheet Items						
4. Total Deviation						

Notes: A *Cash Flow Statement*—your *Yearly Budget*—becomes more useful to you as a business owner if you use it to evaluate actual figures compared with projections. A *Quarterly Budget Analysis* helps you gain more control over your business operations.

**18. *Other Payments* (auto, income tax, interest charges, licenses, permits, insurance, legal and accounting fees, outside labor, shipping, delivery, fulfillment, travel, packaging).

***25. *Cash Available* for dividends, cash expenditures, owner's draw, investments.

Index